The Holy Quran

Clear and Easy to Read

(English Language)

Copyright
TX0008897488

All rights reserved. King Fahd Glorious Quran Printing and the Prophet's Sunnah, peace and blessings be upon him. No part of this book may be reproduced or transmitted in any form or by any means, electronic or mechanical, including photocopying, recording, or by any information storage and retrieval system, without written permission from the Publisher.

International Islamic Books Publishing House

www.al-Qarni.com

"Allah, there is no god but He, the Living, the Eternal. He sent down to you the Book with the Truth, confirming what came before it; and He sent down the Torah and the Gospel."

Verses 3:2-3

CHAPTERS - SURAS

1. THE OPENING .... al-Fatihah 1
2. THE HEIFER .... al-Baqarah 1
3. FAMILY OF IMRAN .... Ali 'Imran 17
4. WOMEN .... an-Nisa' 27
5. THE TABLE .... al-Ma'idah 37
6. LIVESTOCK .... al-An'am 44
7. THE ELEVATIONS .... al-A'raf 53
8. THE SPOILS .... al-Anfal 63
9. REPENTANCE .... at-Tawbah 66
10. JONAH .... Yunus 73
11. HUD .... Hud 78
12. JOSEPH .... Yusuf 84
13. THUNDER .... ar-Ra'd 89
14. ABRAHAM .... Ibrahim 91
15. THE ROCK .... al-Hijr 94
16. THE BEE .... an-Nahl 96
17. THE NIGHT JOURNEY ...... al-Isra' 102
18. THE CAVE .... al-Kahf 106
19. MARY .... Maryam 111
20. TA-HA .... Ta-Ha 114
21. THE PROPHETS .... al-Anbiya 119
22. THE PILGRIMAGE .... al-Hajj 123
23. THE BELIEVERS .... al-Mu'minun 126
24. THE LIGHT .... an-Nur 130
25. THE CRITERION .... al-Furqan 133
26. THE POETS .... ash-Shu'ara' 136
27. THE ANT .... an-Naml 141
28. HISTORY .... al-Qasas 145
29. THE SPIDER .... al-'Ankabut 149

30. THE ROMANS	ar-Rum	152
31. LUQMAN	Luqman	154
32. PROSTRATION	as-Sajdah	156
33. THE CONFEDERATES	al-Ahzab	157
34. SHEBA	Saba'	161
35. ORIGINATOR	Fatir	163
36. YA-SEEN	Ya-Seen	165
37. THE ALIGNERS	as-Saffat	168
38. SAAD	Saad	172
39. THRONGS	az-Zumar	174
40. FORGIVER	Ghafir	178
41. DETAILED	Fussilat	181
42. CONSULTATION	ash-Shura	184
43. DECORATIONS	az-Zukhruf	186
44. SMOKE	ad-Dukhan	189
45. KNEELING	al-Jathiyah	190
46. THE DUNES	al-Ahqaf	192
47. MUHAMMAD	Muhammad	194
48. VICTORY	al-Fath	196
49. THE CHAMBERS	al-Hujurat	197
50. QAF	Qaf	198
51. THE SPREADERS	adh-Dhariyat	200
52. THE MOUNT	at-Tur	201
53. THE STAR	an-Najm	202
54. THE MOON	al-Qamar	204
55. THE COMPASSIONATE	ar-Rahman	205
56. THE INEVITABLE	al-Waqi'ah	207
57. IRON	al-Hadid`	209
58. THE ARGUMENT	al-Mujadilah	210
59. THE MOBILIZATION	al-Hashr	212
60. THE WOMAN TESTED	al-Mumtahina	213
61. COLUMN	as-Saff	214

62. FRIDAY	al-Jumu'ah		215
63. THE HYPOCRITES	al-Munafiqun		215
64. GATHERING	at-Taghabun		216
65. DIVORCE	at-Talaq		217
66. PROHIBITION	at-Tahrim		217
67. SOVEREIGNTY	al-Mulk		218
68. THE PEN	al-Qalam		219
69. THE REALITY	al-Haqqah		221
70. WAYS OF ASCENT	al-Ma'arij		222
71. NOAH	Nuh		223
72. THE JINN	al-Jinn		223
73. THE ENWRAPPED	al-Muzzammil		224
74. THE ENROBED	al-Muddathir		225
75. RESURRECTION	al-Qiyamah		226
76. MAN	al-Insan		227
77. THE UNLEASHED	al-Mursalat		228
78. THE EVENT	an-Naba'		229
79. THE SNATCHERS	an-Nazi'at		230
80. HE FROWNED	'Abasa		230
81. THE ROLLING	at-Takwir		231
82. THE SHATTERING	al-Infitar		232
83. THE DEFRAUDERS	al-Mutaffifin		232
84. THE RUPTURE	al-Inshiqaq		233
85. THE CONSTELLATIONS	al-Buruj		233
86. THE NIGHTLY VISITOR	at-Tariq		234
87. THE MOST HIGH	al-A'la		234
88. THE OVERWHELMING	al-Ghashiyah		235
89. THE DAWN	al-Fajr		235
90. THE LAND	al-Balad		236
91. THE SUN	ash-Shams		236
92. THE NIGHT	al-Layl		236
93. MORNING LIGHT	adh-Duha		237

94. THE SOOTHING	ash-Sharh	237
95. THE FIG	at-Tin	237
96. CLOT	al-'Alaq	238
97. DECREE	al-Qadr	238
98. CLEAR EVIDENCE	al-Bayyinah	238
99. THE QUAKE	az-Zalzalah	238
100. THE RACERS	al-'Adiyat	239
101. THE SHOCKER	al-Qari'ah	239
102. ABUNDANCE	at-Takathur	239
103. TIME	al-'Asr	239
104. THE BACKBITER	al-Humazah	239
105. THE ELEPHANT	al-Fil	240
106. QURAISH	Quraysh	240
107. ASSISTANCE	al-Ma'un	240
108. PLENTY	al-Kawthar	240
109. THE DISBELIEVERS	al-Kafirun	240
110. VICTORY	an-Nasr	240
111. THORNS	al-Masad	241
112. MONOTHEISM	al-Ikhlas	241
113. DAYBREAK	al-Falaq	241
114. MANKIND	an-Nas	241

1. THE OPENING (al-Fatihah)

**1. THE OPENING
(al-Fatihah)**

1. In the name of Allah, the Gracious, the Merciful.

2. Praise be to Allah, Lord of the Worlds.

3. The Most Gracious, the Most Merciful.

4. Master of the Day of Judgment.

5. It is You we worship, and upon You we call for help.

6. Guide us to the straight path.

7. The path of those You have blessed, not of those against whom there is anger, nor of those who are misguided.

**2. THE HEIFER
(al-Baqarah)**

*In the name of Allah,
the Gracious, the Merciful*

1. Alif, Lam, Meem.

2. This is the Book in which there is no doubt, a guide for the righteous.

3. Those who believe in the unseen, and perform the prayers, and give from what We have provided for them.

4. And those who believe in what was revealed to you, and in what was revealed before you, and are certain of the Hereafter.

5. These are upon guidance from their Lord. These are the successful.

6. As for those who disbelieve—it is the same for them, whether you have warned them, or have not warned them—they do not believe.

7. Allah has set a seal on their hearts and on their hearing, and over their vision is a veil. They will have a severe torment.

8. Among the people are those who say, "We believe in Allah and in the Last Day," but they are not believers.

9. They seek to deceive Allah and those who believe, but they deceive none but themselves, though they are not aware.

10. In their hearts is sickness, and Allah has increased their sickness. They will have a painful punishment because of their denial.

11. And when it is said to them, "Do not make trouble on earth," they say, "We are only reformers."

12. In fact, they are the troublemakers, but they are not aware.

13. And when it is said to them, "Believe as the people have believed," they say, "Shall we believe as the fools have believed?" In fact, it is they who are the fools, but they do not know.

14. And when they come across those who believe, they say, "We believe"; but when they are alone with their devils, they say, "We are with you; we were only ridiculing."

15. It is Allah who ridicules them, and leaves them bewildered in their transgression.

16. Those are they who have bartered error for guidance; but their trade does not profit them, and they are not guided.

17. Their likeness is that of a person who kindled a fire; when it illuminated all around him, Allah took away their light, and left them in darkness, unable to see.

18. Deaf, dumb, blind. They will not return.

19. Or like a cloudburst from the sky, in which is darkness, and thunder, and lightning. They press their fingers into their ears from the thunderbolts, in fear of death. But Allah surrounds the disbelievers.

20. The lightning almost snatches their sight away. Whenever it illuminates for them, they walk in it; but when it grows dark over them, they stand still. Had Allah willed, He could have taken away their hearing and their sight. Allah is capable of everything.

21. O people! Worship your Lord who created you and those before you, that you may attain piety.

2. THE HEIFER (al-Baqarah)

22. He who made the earth a habitat for you, and the sky a structure, and sends water down from the sky, and brings out fruits thereby, as a sustenance for you. Therefore, do not assign rivals to Allah while you know.

23. And if you are in doubt about what We have revealed to Our servant, then produce a chapter like these, and call your witnesses apart from Allah, if you are truthful.

24. But if you do not—and you will not—then beware the Fire whose fuel is people and stones, prepared for the disbelievers.

25. And give good news to those who believe and do righteous deeds; that they will have gardens beneath which rivers flow. Whenever they are provided with fruit therefrom as sustenance, they will say, "This is what we were provided with before," and they will be given the like of it. And they will have pure spouses therein, and they will abide therein forever.

26. Allah does not shy away from making an example of a gnat, or something above it. As for those who believe, they know that it is the Truth from their Lord. But as for those who disbelieve, they say, "What did Allah intend by this example?" He leads astray many thereby, and He guides many thereby; but He misleads thereby only the evildoers.

27. Those who violate Allah's covenant after its confirmation, and sever what Allah has commanded to be joined, and commit evil on earth. These are the losers.

28. How can you deny Allah, when you were dead and He gave you life, then He will put you to death, then He will bring you to life, then to Him you will be returned?

29. It is He who created for you everything on earth, then turned to the heaven, and made them seven heavens. And He is aware of all things.

30. When your Lord said to the angels, "I am placing a successor on earth." They said, "Will You place in it someone who will cause corruption in it and shed blood, while we declare Your praises and sanctify You?" He said, "I know what you do not know."

31. And He taught Adam the names, all of them; then he presented them to the angels, and said, "Tell Me the names of these, if you are sincere."

32. They said, "Glory be to You! We have no knowledge except what You have taught us. It is you who are the Knowledgeable, the Wise."

33. He said, "O Adam, tell them their names." And when he told them their names, He said, "Did I not tell you that I know the secrets of the heavens and the earth, and that I know what you reveal and what you conceal?"

34. And We said to the angels, "Bow down to Adam." They bowed down, except for Satan. He refused, was arrogant, and was one of the disbelievers.

35. We said, "O Adam, inhabit the Garden, you and your spouse, and eat from it freely as you please, but do not approach this tree, lest you become wrongdoers."

36. But Satan caused them to slip from it, and caused them to depart the state they were in. We said, "Go down, some of you enemies of one another. And you will have residence on earth, and enjoyment for a while."

37. Then Adam received words from his Lord, so He relented towards him. He is the Relenting, the Merciful.

38. We said, "Go down from it, all of you. Yet whenever guidance comes to you from Me, then whoever follows My guidance—they have nothing to fear, nor shall they grieve.

39. But as for those who disbelieve and reject Our signs—these are the inmates of the Fire—wherein they will remain forever."

40. O Children of Israel! Remember My blessings which I bestowed upon you, and fulfill your pledge to Me, and I will fulfill My pledge to you, and fear Me.

41. And believe in what I revealed, confirming what is with you; and do not be the first to

2. THE HEIFER (al-Baqarah)

deny it; and do not exchange My revelations for a small price; and be conscious of Me.

⁴². And do not mix truth with falsehood, and do not conceal the truth while you know.

⁴³. And attend to your prayers, and practice regular charity, and kneel with those who kneel.

⁴⁴. Do you command people to virtuous conduct, and forget yourselves, even though you read the Scripture? Do you not understand?

⁴⁵. And seek help through patience and prayer. But it is difficult, except for the devout.

⁴⁶. Those who know that they will meet their Lord, and that to Him they will return.

⁴⁷. O Children of Israel! Remember My favor which I bestowed upon you, and I that favored you over all nations.

⁴⁸. And beware of a Day when no soul will avail another in the least, nor will any intercession be accepted on its behalf, nor will any ransom be taken from it, nor will they be helped.

⁴⁹. And recall that We delivered you from the people of Pharaoh. They inflicted on you terrible persecution, killing your sons and sparing your women. Therein was a tremendous trial from your Lord.

⁵⁰. And recall that We parted the sea for you, so We saved you, and We drowned the people of Pharaoh as you looked on.

⁵¹. And recall that We appointed for Moses forty nights. Then you took to worshiping the calf after him, and you turned wicked.

⁵². Then We pardoned you after that, so that you might be grateful.

⁵³. And recall that We gave Moses the Scripture and the Criterion, so that you may be guided.

⁵⁴. And recall that Moses said to his people, "O my people, you have done wrong to yourselves by worshiping the calf. So repent to your Maker, and kill your egos. That would be better for you with your Maker." So He turned to you in repentance. He is the Accepter of Repentance, the Merciful.

⁵⁵. And recall that you said, "O Moses, we will not believe in you unless we see Allah plainly." Thereupon the thunderbolt struck you, as you looked on.

⁵⁶. Then We revived you after your death, so that you may be appreciative.

⁵⁷. And We shaded you with clouds, and We sent down to you manna and quails: "Eat of the good things We have provided for you." They did not wrong Us, but they used to wrong their own souls.

⁵⁸. And recall that We said, "Enter this town, and eat plentifully from it whatever you wish; but enter the gate humbly, and say, 'Pardon.' We will forgive your sins, and give increase to the virtuous."

⁵⁹. But the wrongdoers among them substituted words other than those given to them, so We sent down on the wrongdoers a plague from heaven, because of their wicked behavior.

⁶⁰. And recall when Moses prayed for water for his people. We said, "Strike the rock with your staff." Thereupon twelve springs gushed out from it, and each tribe recognized its drinking-place. "Eat and drink from Allah's provision, and do not corrupt the earth with disobedience."

⁶¹. And recall when you said, "O Moses, we cannot endure one kind of food, so call to your Lord to produce for us of what the earth grows: of its herbs, and its cucumbers, and its garlic, and its lentils, and its onions." He said, "Would you substitute worse for better? Go down to Egypt, where you will have what you asked for." They were struck with humiliation and poverty, and incurred wrath from Allah. That was because they rejected Allah's revelations and wrongfully killed the prophets. That was because they disobeyed and transgressed.

⁶². Those who believe, and those who are Jewish, and the Christians, and the Sabeans—any who believe in Allah and the Last Day, and

2. THE HEIFER (al-Baqarah)

act righteously—will have their reward with their Lord; they have nothing to fear, nor will they grieve.

63. And recall when We received a pledge from you, and raised the Mount above you: "Take what We have given you earnestly, and remember what is in it, that you may attain righteousness."

64. But after that you turned away. Were it not for Allah's grace and mercy towards you, you would have been among the losers.

65. And you surely knew those of you who violated the Sabbath. We said to them, "Be despicable apes!"

66. Thus We made it a deterrent for their generation, and for subsequent generations, and a lesson for the righteous.

67. And recall when Moses said to his people, "Allah commands you to sacrifice a heifer." They said, "Do you make a mockery of us?" He said, "Allah forbid that I should be so ignorant."

68. They said, "Call upon your Lord to show us which one." He said, "He says she is a heifer, neither too old, nor too young, but in between. So do what you are commanded."

69. They said, "Call upon your Lord to show us what her color is." He said, "He says she is a yellow heifer, bright in color, pleasing to the beholders."

70. They said, "Call upon your Lord to show us which one; the heifers look alike to us; and Allah willing, we will be guided."

71. He said, "He says she is a heifer, neither yoked to plow the earth, nor to irrigate the field; sound without blemish." They said, "Now you have brought the truth." So they slew her; though they almost did not.

72. And recall when you killed a person, and disputed in the matter; but Allah was to expose what you were hiding.

73. We said, "Strike him with part of it." Thus Allah brings the dead to life; and He shows you His signs, that you may understand.

74. Then after that your hearts hardened. They were as rocks, or even harder. For there are some rocks from which rivers gush out, and others that splinter and water comes out from them, and others that sink in awe of Allah. Allah is not unaware of what you do.

75. Do you hope that they will believe in you, when some of them used to hear the Word of Allah, and then deliberately distort it, even after understanding it?

76. And when they come across those who believe, they say, "We believe," but when they come together privately, they say, "Will you inform them of what Allah has disclosed to you, so that they might dispute with you concerning it before your Lord?" Do you not understand?

77. Do they not know that Allah knows what they conceal and what they reveal?

78. And among them are uneducated who know the Scripture only through hearsay, and they only speculate.

79. So woe to those who write the Scripture with their own hands, and then say, "This is from Allah," that they may exchange it for a little price. Woe to them for what their hands have written, and woe to them for what they earn.

80. And they say, "The Fire will not touch us except for a number of days." Say, "Have you received a promise from Allah—Allah never breaks His promise—or are you saying about Allah what you do not know?"

81. Indeed, whoever commits misdeeds, and becomes besieged by his iniquities—these are the inmates of the Fire, wherein they will dwell forever.

82. As for those who believe and do righteous deeds—these are the inhabitants of Paradise, wherein they will dwell forever.

83. We made a covenant with the Children of Israel: "Worship none but Allah; and be good to parents, and relatives, and orphans, and the needy; and speak nicely to people; and pray regularly, and give alms." Then you

2. THE HEIFER (al-Baqarah)

turned away, except for a few of you, recanting.

84. And We made a covenant with you: "You shall not shed the blood of your own, nor shall you evict your own from your homes." You agreed, and were all witnesses.

85. But here you are, killing your own, and expelling a group of your own from their homes—conspiring against them in wrongdoing and hostility. And if they come to you as captives, you ransom them, although it was forbidden to you. Is it that you believe in part of the Scripture, and disbelieve in part? What is the reward for those among you who do that but humiliation in this life? And on the Day of Resurrection, they will be assigned to the most severe torment. Allah is not unaware of what you do.

86. Those are they who bought the present life for the Hereafter, so the punishment will not be lightened for them, nor will they be helped.

87. We gave Moses the Scripture, and sent a succession of messengers after him. And We gave Jesus son of Mary the clear proofs, and We supported him with the Holy Spirit. Is it that whenever a messenger comes to you with anything your souls do not desire, you grew arrogant, calling some impostors, and killing others?

88. And they said, "Our hearts are sealed." Rather, Allah has cursed them for their ingratitude. They have little faith.

89. And when a scripture came to them from Allah, confirming what they have—although previously they were seeking victory against those who disbelieved—but when there came to them what they recognized, they disbelieved in it. So Allah's curse is upon the disbelievers.

90. Miserable is what they sold their souls for—rejecting what Allah has revealed, out of resentment that Allah would send down His grace upon whomever He chooses from among His servants. Thus they incurred wrath upon wrath. And there is a demeaning punishment for the disbelievers.

91. And when it is said to them, "Believe in what Allah has revealed," they say, "We believe in what was revealed to us," and they reject anything beyond that, although it is the truth which confirms what they have. Say, "Why did you kill Allah's prophets before, if you were believers?"

92. Moses came to you with clear proofs, yet you adopted the calf in his absence, and you were in the wrong.

93. And We made a covenant with you, and raised the Mount above you: "Take what We have given you firmly, and listen." They said, "We hear and disobey." And their hearts became filled with the love of the calf because of their disbelief. Say, "Wretched is what your faith commands you to do, if you are believers."

94. Say, "If the Final Home with Allah is yours alone, to the exclusion of all other people, then wish for death if you are sincere."

95. But they will never wish for it, because of what their hands have forwarded. Allah is aware of the evildoers.

96. You will find them, of all mankind, the most eager for life, even more than the polytheists. Every one of them wishes he could live a thousand years; but to be granted a long life will not nudge him from the punishment. Allah is Seeing of what they do.

97. Say, "Whoever is hostile to Gabriel—it is he who revealed it to your heart by Allah's leave, confirming what preceded it, and guidance and good news for the believers."

98. Whoever is hostile to Allah, and His angels, and His messengers, and Gabriel, and Michael—Allah is hostile to the faithless.

99. We have revealed to you clear signs, and none rejects them except the sinners.

100. Is it not that whenever they make a covenant, some of them toss it aside? In fact, most of them do not believe.

101. And when there came to them a messenger from Allah, confirming what they had, a faction of those who were given the Book

2. THE HEIFER (al-Baqarah)

threw the Book of Allah behind their backs, as if they do not know.

102. And they followed what the devils taught during the reign of Solomon. It was not Solomon who disbelieved, but it was the devils who disbelieved. They taught the people witchcraft and what was revealed in Babylon to the two angels Harut and Marut. They did not teach anybody until they had said, "We are a test, so do not lose faith." But they learned from them the means to cause separation between man and his wife. But they cannot harm anyone except with Allah's permission. And they learned what would harm them and not benefit them. Yet they knew that whoever deals in it will have no share in the Hereafter. Miserable is what they sold their souls for, if they only knew.

103. Had they believed and been righteous, the reward from Allah would have been better, if they only knew.

104. O you who believe! Do not say ambiguous words, but say words of respect, and listen. The disbelievers will have a painful torment.

105. It is never the wish of the disbelievers from among the People of the Book, nor of the polytheists, that any good should be sent down to you from your Lord. But Allah chooses for His mercy whomever He wills. Allah is Possessor of Sublime Grace.

106. We never nullify a verse, nor cause it to be forgotten, unless We bring one better than it, or similar to it. Do you not know that Allah is capable of all things?

107. Do you not know that to Allah belongs the sovereignty of the heavens and the earth, and that apart from Allah you have no guardian or helper?

108. Or do you want to question your Messenger as Moses was questioned before? Whoever exchanges faith for disbelief has strayed from the right path.

109. Many of the People of the Book wish to turn you back into unbelievers after you have believed, out of envy on their part, after the Truth has become clear to them. But pardon and overlook, until Allah brings His command. Allah has power over all things.

110. And perform the prayer, and give alms. Whatever good you forward for yourselves, you will find it with Allah. Allah is Seeing of everything you do.

111. And they say, "None will enter Heaven unless he is a Jew or a Christian." These are their wishes. Say, "Produce your proof, if you are truthful."

112. In fact, whoever submits himself to Allah, and is a doer of good, will have his reward with his Lord—they have nothing to fear, nor shall they grieve.

113. The Jews say, "The Christians are not based on anything;" and the Christians say, "The Jews are not based on anything." Yet they both read the Scripture. Similarly, the ignorant said the same thing. Allah will judge between them on the Day of Resurrection regarding their differences.

114. Who is more unjust than him who forbids the remembrance of Allah's name in places of worship, and contributes to their ruin? These ought not to enter them except in fear. For them is disgrace in this world, and for them is a terrible punishment in the Hereafter.

115. To Allah belong the East and the West. Whichever way you turn, there is Allah's presence. Allah is Omnipresent and Omniscient.

116. And they say, "Allah has begotten a son." Be He glorified. Rather, His is everything in the heavens and the earth; all are obedient to Him.

117. Originator of the heavens and the earth. Whenever He decrees a thing, He says to it, "Be," and it becomes.

118. Those who do not know say, "If only Allah would speak to us, or a sign would come to us." Thus said those who were before them. Their hearts are alike. We have made the signs clear for people who are certain.

2. THE HEIFER (al-Baqarah)

119. We have sent you with the truth—bringing good news, and giving warnings. You will not be questioned about the inmates of Hell.

120. The Jews and the Christians will not approve of you, unless you follow their creed. Say, "Allah's guidance is the guidance." Should you follow their desires, after the knowledge that has come to you, you will have in Allah neither guardian nor helper.

121. Those to whom We have given the Scripture follow it, as it ought to be followed—these believe in it. But as for those who reject it—these are the losers.

122. O Children of Israel! Remember My blessing which I bestowed upon you, and that I have favored you over all people.

123. And beware of a Day when no soul will avail another soul in any way, and no ransom will be accepted from it, and no intercession will benefit it, and they will not be helped.

124. And when his Lord tested Abraham with certain words, and he fulfilled them. He said, "I am making you a leader of humanity." He said, "And my descendants?" He said, "My pledge does not include the wrongdoers."

125. And We made the House a focal point for the people, and a sanctuary. Use the shrine of Abraham as a place of prayer. And We commissioned Abraham and Ishmael, "Sanctify My House for those who circle around it, and those who seclude themselves in it, and those who kneel and prostrate."

126. When Abraham said, "O My Lord, make this a peaceful land, and provide its people with fruits—whoever of them believes in Allah and the Last Day." He said, "And whoever disbelieves, I will give him a little enjoyment, then I will consign him to the punishment of the Fire; how miserable the destiny!"

127. As Abraham raises the foundations of the House, together with Ishmael, "Our Lord, accept it from us, You are the Hearer, the Knower.

128. Our Lord, and make us submissive to You, and from our descendants a community submissive to You. And show us our rites, and accept our repentance. You are the Acceptor of Repentance, the Merciful.

129. Our Lord, and raise up among them a messenger, of themselves, who will recite to them Your revelations, and teach them the Book and wisdom, and purify them. You are the Almighty, the Wise."

130. Who would forsake the religion of Abraham, except he who fools himself? We chose him in this world, and in the Hereafter he will be among the righteous.

131. When his Lord said to him, "Submit!" He said, "I have submitted to the Lord of the Worlds."

132. And Abraham exhorted his sons, and Jacob, "O my sons, Allah has chosen this religion for you, so do not die unless you have submitted."

133. Or were you witnesses when death approached Jacob, and he said to his sons, "What will you worship after Me?" They said, "We will worship your God, and the God of your fathers, Abraham, Ishmael, and Isaac; One God; and to Him we submit."

134. That was a community that has passed; for them is what they have earned, and for you is what you have earned; and you will not be questioned about what they used to do.

135. And they say, "Be Jews or Christians, and you will be guided." Say, "Rather, the religion of Abraham, the Monotheist; he was not an idolater."

136. Say, "We believe in Allah; and in what was revealed to us; and in what was revealed to Abraham, and Ishmael, and Isaac, and Jacob, and the Patriarchs; and in what was given to Moses and Jesus; and in what was given to the prophets—from their Lord. We make no distinction between any of them, and to Him we surrender."

137. If they believe in the same as you have believed in, then they have been guided. But if they turn away, then they are in schism. Allah will protect you against them; for He is the Hearer, the Knower.

2. THE HEIFER (al-Baqarah)

138. Allah's coloring. And who gives better coloring than Allah? "And we are devoted to Him."

139. Say, "Do you argue with us about Allah, when He is our Lord and your Lord, and We have our works, and you have your works, and we are sincere to Him?"

140. Or do you say that Abraham, Ishmael, Isaac, Jacob, and the Patriarchs were Jews or Christians? Say, "Do you know better, or Allah?" And who does greater wrong than he who conceals a testimony he has from Allah? Allah is not unaware of what you do.

141. That was a community that has passed. To them is what they have earned, and to you is what you have earned. And you will not be questioned about what they used to do.

142. The ignorant among the people will say, "What has turned them away from the direction of prayer they once followed?" Say, "To Allah belong the East and the West. He guides whom He wills to a straight path."

143. Thus We made you a moderate community, that you may be witnesses to humanity, and that the Messenger may be a witness to you. We only established the direction of prayer, which you once followed, that We may distinguish those who follow the Messenger from those who turn on their heels. It is indeed difficult, except for those whom Allah has guided. But Allah would never let your faith go to waste. Allah is Kind towards the people, Merciful.

144. We have seen your face turned towards the heaven. So We will turn you towards a direction that will satisfy you. So turn your face towards the Sacred Mosque. And wherever you may be, turn your faces towards it. Those who were given the Book know that it is the Truth from their Lord; and Allah is not unaware of what they do.

145. Even if you were to bring to those who were given the Book every proof, they would not follow your direction, nor are you to follow their direction, nor do they follow the direction of one another. And if you were to follow their desires, after the knowledge that has come to you, you would be in that case one of the wrongdoers.

146. Those to whom We have given the Book recognize it as they recognize their own children. But some of them conceal the truth while they know.

147. The truth is from your Lord, so do not be a skeptic.

148. To every community is a direction towards which it turns. Therefore, race towards goodness. Wherever you may be, Allah will bring you all together. Allah is capable of everything.

149. And wherever you come from, turn your face towards the Sacred Mosque. This is the truth from your Lord, and Allah is not heedless of what you do.

150. And wherever you come from, turn your face towards the Sacred Mosque. And wherever you may be, turn your faces towards it. So that the people may not have any argument against you—except those who do wrong among them. So do not fear them, but fear Me, that I may complete My blessings upon you, and that you may be guided.

151. Just as We sent to you a messenger from among you, who recites Our revelations to you, and purifies you, and teaches you the Book and wisdom, and teaches you what you did not know.

152. So remember Me, and I will remember you. And thank Me, and do not be ungrateful.

153. O you who believe! Seek help through patience and prayers. Allah is with the steadfast.

154. And do not say of those who are killed in the cause of Allah, "Dead." Rather, they are alive, but you do not perceive.

155. We will certainly test you with some fear and hunger, and some loss of possessions and lives and crops. But give good news to the steadfast.

156. Those who, when a calamity afflicts them, say, "To Allah we belong, and to Him we will return."

2. THE HEIFER (al-Baqarah)

157. Upon these are blessings and mercy from their Lord. These are the guided ones.

158. Safa and Marwa are among the rites of Allah. Whoever makes the Pilgrimage to the House, or performs the Umrah, commits no error by circulating between them. Whoever volunteers good—Allah is Appreciative and Cognizant.

159. Those who suppress the proofs and the guidance We have revealed, after We have clarified them to humanity in the Scripture—those—Allah curses them, and the cursers curse them.

160. Except those who repent, and reform, and proclaim. Those—I will accept their repentance. I am the Acceptor of Repentance, the Merciful.

161. But as for those who reject faith, and die rejecting—those—upon them is the curse of Allah, and of the angels, and of all humanity.

162. They will remain under it forever, and the torment will not be lightened for them, and they will not be reprieved.

163. Your God is one God. There is no god but He, the Benevolent, the Compassionate.

164. In the creation of the heavens and the earth; in the alternation of night and day; in the ships that sail the oceans for the benefit of mankind; in the water that Allah sends down from the sky, and revives the earth with it after it had died, and scatters in it all kinds of creatures; in the changing of the winds, and the clouds disposed between the sky and the earth; are signs for people who understand.

165. Yet among the people are those who take other than Allah as equals to Him. They love them as the love of Allah. But those who believe have greater love for Allah. If only the wrongdoers would realize, when they see the torment; that all power is Allah's, and that Allah is severe in punishment.

166. Those who were followed will then disown those who followed them, and they will see the retribution, and ties between them will be severed.

167. Those who followed will say, "If only we can have another chance, we will disown them, as they disowned us." Thus Allah will show them their deeds, as regrets to them, and they will not come out of the Fire.

168. O people! Eat of what is lawful and good on earth, and do not follow the footsteps of Satan. He is to you an open enemy.

169. He commands you to do evil and vice, and to say about Allah what you do not know.

170. And when it is said to them, "Follow what Allah has revealed," they say, "We will follow what we found our ancestors following." Even if their ancestors understood nothing, and were not guided?

171. The parable of those who disbelieve is that of someone who calls upon someone who hears nothing except screaming and yelling. Deaf, dumb, and blind—they do not understand.

172. O you who believe! Eat of the good things We have provided for you, and give thanks to Allah, if it is Him that you serve.

173. He has forbidden you carrion, and blood, and the flesh of swine, and what was dedicated to other than Allah. But if anyone is compelled, without desiring or exceeding, he commits no sin. Allah is Forgiving and Merciful.

174. Those who conceal what Allah revealed in the Book, and exchange it for a small price—those swallow nothing but fire into their bellies. And Allah will not speak to them on the Day of Resurrection, nor will He purify them, and they will have a painful punishment.

175. It is they who exchange guidance for error, and forgiveness for punishment. But why do they insist on the Fire?

176. That is because Allah has revealed the Book in truth; and those who differ about the Book are in deep discord.

177. Righteousness does not consist of turning your faces towards the East and the West. But righteous is he who believes in Allah, and the Last Day, and the angels, and the Scripture,

2. THE HEIFER (al-Baqarah)

and the prophets. Who gives money, though dear, to near relatives, and orphans, and the needy, and the homeless, and the beggars, and for the freeing of slaves; those who perform the prayers, and pay the obligatory charity, and fulfill their promise when they promise, and patiently persevere in the face of persecution, hardship, and in the time of conflict. These are the sincere; these are the pious.

178. O you who believe! Retaliation for the murdered is ordained upon you: the free for the free, the slave for the slave, the female for the female. But if he is forgiven by his kin, then grant any reasonable demand, and pay with good will. This is a concession from your Lord, and a mercy. But whoever commits aggression after that, a painful torment awaits him.

179. There is life for you in retaliation, O people of understanding, so that you may refrain.

180. It is decreed for you: when death approaches one of you, and he leaves wealth, to make a testament in favor of the parents and the relatives, fairly and correctly—a duty upon the righteous.

181. But whoever changes it after he has heard it, the guilt is upon those who change it. Allah is All-Hearing, All-Knowing.

182. Should someone suspect bias or injustice on the part of a testator, and then reconciles between them, he commits no sin. Allah is Forgiving and Merciful.

183. O you who believe! Fasting is prescribed for you, as it was prescribed for those before you, that you may become righteous.

184. For a specified number of days. But whoever among you is sick, or on a journey, then a number of other days. For those who are able: a ransom of feeding a needy person. But whoever volunteers goodness, it is better for him. But to fast is best for you, if you only knew.

185. Ramadan is the month in which the Quran was revealed. Guidance for humanity, and clear portents of guidance, and the Criterion. Whoever of you witnesses the month, shall fast it. But whoever is sick, or on a journey, then a number of other days. Allah desires ease for you, and does not desire hardship for you, that you may complete the number, and celebrate Allah for having guided you, so that you may be thankful.

186. And when My servants ask you about Me, I Am near; I answer the call of the caller when he calls on Me. So let them answer Me, and have faith in Me, that they may be rightly guided.

187. Permitted for you is intercourse with your wives on the night of the fast. They are a garment for you, and you are a garment for them. Allah knows that you used to betray yourselves, but He turned to you and pardoned you. So approach them now, and seek what Allah has ordained for you, and eat and drink until the white streak of dawn can be distinguished from the black streak. Then complete the fast until nightfall. But do not approach them while you are in retreat at the mosques. These are the limits of Allah, so do not come near them. Allah thus clarifies His revelations to the people, that they may attain piety.

188. And do not consume one another's wealth by unjust means, nor offer it as bribes to the officials in order to consume part of other people's wealth illicitly, while you know.

189. They ask you about the crescents. Say, "They are timetables for people, and for the Hajj." It is not virtuous that you approach homes from their backs, but virtue is to be pious. So approach homes from their doors, and observe Allah, that you may succeed.

190. And fight in the cause of Allah those who fight you, but do not commit aggression; Allah does not love the aggressors.

191. And kill them wherever you overtake them, and expel them from where they had expelled you. Oppression is more serious than murder. But do not fight them at the Sacred Mosque, unless they fight you there. If they fight you, then kill them. Such is the retribution of the disbelievers.

2. THE HEIFER (al-Baqarah)

192. But if they cease, then Allah is Forgiving and Merciful.

193. And fight them until there is no oppression, and worship becomes devoted to Allah alone. But if they cease, then let there be no hostility except against the oppressors.

194. The sacred month for the sacred month; and sacrilege calls for retaliation. Whoever commits aggression against you, retaliate against him in the same measure as he has committed against you. And be conscious of Allah, and know that Allah is with the righteous.

195. And spend in the cause of Allah, and do not throw yourselves with your own hands into ruin, and be charitable. Allah loves the charitable.

196. And carry out the Hajj and the Umrah for Allah. But if you are prevented, then whatever is feasible of offerings. And do not shave your heads until the offering has reached its destination. Whoever of you is sick, or has an injury of the head, then redemption of fasting, or charity, or worship. When you are secure: whoever continues the Umrah until the Hajj, then whatever is feasible of offering. But if he lacks the means, then fasting for three days during the Hajj and seven when you have returned, making ten in all. This is for he whose household is not present at the Sacred Mosque. And remain conscious of Allah, and know that Allah is stern in retribution.

197. The Hajj is during specific months. Whoever decides to perform the Hajj—there shall be no sexual relations, nor misconduct, nor quarrelling during the Hajj. And whatever good you do, Allah knows it. And take provisions, but the best provision is righteousness. And be mindful of Me, O people of understanding.

198. You commit no error by seeking bounty from your Lord. When you disperse from Arafat, remember Allah at the Sacred Landmark. And remember Him as He has guided you. Although, before that, you were of those astray.

199. Then disperse from where the people disperse, and ask Allah for forgiveness. Allah is Most Forgiving, Most Merciful.

200. When you have completed your rites, remember Allah as you remember your parents, or even more. Among the people is he who says, "Our Lord, give us in this world," yet he has no share in the Hereafter.

201. And among them is he who says, "Our Lord, give us goodness in this world, and goodness in the Hereafter, and protect us from the torment of the Fire."

202. These will have a share of what they have earned. Allah is swift in reckoning.

203. And remember Allah during the designated days. But whoever hurries on in two days commits no wrong, and whoever stays on commits no wrong—provided he maintains righteousness. And obey Allah, and know that to Him you will be gathered.

204. Among the people is he whose speech about the worldly life impresses you, and he calls Allah to witness what is in his heart, while he is the most hostile of adversaries.

205. When he gains power, he strives to spread corruption on earth, destroying properties and lives. Allah does not like corruption.

206. And when he is told, "Beware of Allah," his pride leads him to more sin. Hell is enough for him—a dreadful abode.

207. And among the people is he who sells himself seeking Allah's approval. Allah is kind towards the servants.

208. O you who believe! Enter into submission, wholeheartedly, and do not follow the footsteps of Satan; he is to you an outright enemy.

209. But if you slip after the proofs have come to you, know that Allah is Powerful and Wise.

210. Are they waiting for Allah Himself to come to them in the shadows of the clouds, together with the angels, and thus the matter is settled? All things are returned to Allah.

211. Ask the Children of Israel how many clear signs We have given them. Whoever alters

2. THE HEIFER (al-Baqarah)

the blessing of Allah after it has come to him—Allah is severe in retribution.

212. Beautified is the life of this world for those who disbelieve, and they ridicule those who believe. But the righteous will be above them on the Day of Resurrection. Allah provides to whomever He wills without measure.

213. Humanity used to be one community; then Allah sent the prophets, bringing good news and giving warnings. And He sent down with them the Scripture, with the truth, to judge between people regarding their differences. But none differed over it except those who were given it—after the proofs had come to them—out of mutual envy between them. Then Allah guided those who believed to the truth they had disputed, in accordance with His will. Allah guides whom He wills to a straight path.

214. Or do you expect to enter Paradise before the example of those who came before you had reached you? Adversity and hardship had afflicted them, and they were so shaken up, that the Messenger and those who believed with him said, "When is Allah's victory?" Indeed, Allah's victory is near.

215. They ask you what they should give. Say, "Whatever charity you give is for the parents, and the relatives, and the orphans, and the poor, and the wayfarer. Whatever good you do, Allah is aware of it.

216. Fighting is ordained for you, even though you dislike it. But it may be that you dislike something while it is good for you, and it may be that you like something while it is bad for you. Allah knows, and you do not know.

217. They ask you about fighting during the Holy Month. Say, "Fighting during it is deplorable; but to bar others from Allah's path, and to disbelieve in Him, and to prevent access to the Holy Mosque, and to expel its people from it, are more deplorable with Allah. And persecution is more serious than killing. They will not cease to fight you until they turn you back from your religion, if they can. Whoever among you turns back from his religion, and dies a disbeliever—those are they whose works will come to nothing, in this life, and in the Hereafter. Those are the inmates of the Fire, abiding in it forever.

218. Those who believed, and those who migrated and fought for the sake of Allah—those look forward to Allah's mercy. Allah is Forgiving and Merciful.

219. They ask you about intoxicants and gambling. Say, "There is gross sin in them, and some benefits for people, but their sinfulness outweighs their benefit." And they ask you about what they should give: say, "The surplus." Thus Allah explains the revelations to you, so that you may think.

220. About this world and the next. And they ask you about orphans. Say, "Improvement for them is best. And if you intermix with them, then they are your brethren." Allah knows the dishonest from the honest. Had Allah willed, He could have overburdened you. Allah is Mighty and Wise.

221. Do not marry idolatresses, unless they have believed. A believing maid is better than an idolatress, even if you like her. And do not marry idolaters, unless they have believed. A believing servant is better than an idolater, even if you like him. These call to the Fire, but Allah calls to the Garden and to forgiveness, by His leave. He makes clear His communications to the people, that they may be mindful.

222. And they ask you about menstruation: say, "It is harmful, so keep away from women during menstruation. And do not approach them until they have become pure. Once they have become pure, approach them in the way Allah has directed you." Allah loves the repentant, and He loves those who keep clean."

223. Your women are cultivation for you; so approach your cultivation whenever you like, and send ahead for yourselves. And fear Allah, and know that you will meet Him. And give good news to the believers.

224. And do not allow your oaths in Allah's name to hinder you from virtue, and righteousness, and making peace between people. Allah is Listener and Knower.

2. THE HEIFER (al-Baqarah)

225. Allah does not hold you responsible for your unintentional oaths, but He holds you responsible for your intentions. Allah is Forgiving and Forbearing.

226. Those who vow abstinence from their wives must wait for four months. But if they reconcile—Allah is Forgiving and Merciful.

227. And if they resolve to divorce—Allah is Hearing and Knowing.

228. Divorced women shall wait by themselves for three periods. And it is not lawful for them to conceal what Allah has created in their wombs, if they believe in Allah and the Last Day. Meanwhile, their husbands have the better right to take them back, if they desire reconciliation. And women have rights similar to their obligations, according to what is fair. But men have a degree over them. Allah is Mighty and Wise.

229. Divorce is allowed twice. Then, either honorable retention, or setting free kindly. It is not lawful for you to take back anything you have given them, unless they fear that they cannot maintain Allah's limits. If you fear that they cannot maintain Allah's limits, then there is no blame on them if she sacrifices something for her release. These are Allah's limits, so do not transgress them. Those who transgress Allah's limits are the unjust.

230. If he divorces her, she shall not be lawful for him again until she has married another husband. If the latter divorces her, then there is no blame on them for reuniting, provided they think they can maintain Allah's limits. These are Allah's limits; He makes them clear to people who know.

231. When you divorce women, and they have reached their term, either retain them amicably, or release them amicably. But do not retain them to hurt them and commit aggression. Whoever does that has wronged himself. And do not take Allah's revelations for a joke. And remember Allah's favor to you, and that He revealed to you the Scripture and Wisdom to teach you. And fear Allah, and know that Allah is aware of everything.

232. When you divorce women, and they have reached their term, do not prevent them from marrying their husbands, provided they agree on fair terms. Thereby is advised whoever among you believes in Allah and the Last Day. That is better and more decent for you. Allah knows, and you do not know.

233. Mothers may nurse their infants for two whole years, for those who desire to complete the nursing-period. It is the duty of the father to provide for them and clothe them in a proper manner. No soul shall be burdened beyond its capacity. No mother shall be harmed on account of her child, and no father shall be harmed on account of his child. The same duty rests upon the heir. If the couple desire weaning, by mutual consent and consultation, they commit no error by doing so. You commit no error by hiring nursing-mothers, as long as you pay them fairly. And be wary of Allah, and know that Allah is Seeing of what you do.

234. As for those among you who die and leave widows behind, their widows shall wait by themselves for four months and ten days. When they have reached their term, there is no blame on you regarding what they might honorably do with themselves. Allah is fully acquainted with what you do.

235. You commit no error by announcing your engagement to women, or by keeping it to yourselves. Allah knows that you will be thinking about them. But do not meet them secretly, unless you have something proper to say. And do not confirm the marriage tie until the writing is fulfilled. And know that Allah knows what is in your souls, so beware of Him. And know that Allah is Forgiving and Forbearing.

236. You commit no error by divorcing women before having touched them, or before having set the dowry for them. And compensate them—the wealthy according to his means, and the poor according to his means—with a fair compensation, a duty upon the doers of good.

2. THE HEIFER (al-Baqarah)

237. If you divorce them before you have touched them, but after you had set the dowry for them, give them half of what you specified—unless they forego the right, or the one in whose hand is the marriage contract foregoes it. But to forego is nearer to piety. And do not forget generosity between one another. Allah is seeing of everything you do.

238. Guard your prayers, and the middle prayer, and stand before Allah in devotion.

239. But if you are in fear, then on foot, or riding. And when you are safe, remember Allah, as He taught you what you did not know.

240. Those of you who die and leave wives behind—a will shall provide their wives with support for a year, provided they do not leave. If they leave, you are not to blame for what they do with themselves, provided it is reasonable. Allah is Mighty and Wise.

241. And divorced women shall be provided for, equitably—a duty upon the righteous.

242. Allah thus explains His revelations to you, so that you may understand.

243. Have you not considered those who fled their homes, by the thousands, fearful of death? Allah said to them, "Die." Then He revived them. Allah is Gracious towards the people, but most people are not appreciative.

244. Fight in the cause of Allah, and know that Allah is Hearing and Knowing.

245. Who is he who will offer Allah a generous loan, so He will multiply it for him manifold? Allah receives and amplifies, and to Him you will be returned.

246. Have you not considered the notables of the Children of Israel after Moses? When they said to a prophet of theirs, "Appoint a king for us, and we will fight in the cause of Allah." He said, "Is it possible that, if fighting was ordained for you, you would not fight?" They said, "Why would we not fight in the cause of Allah, when we were driven out of our homes, along with our children?" But when fighting was ordained for them, they turned away, except for a few of them. But Allah is aware of the wrongdoers.

247. Their prophet said to them, "Allah has appointed Saul to be your king." They said, "How can he have authority over us, when we are more worthy of authority than he, and he was not given plenty of wealth?" He said, "Allah has chosen him over you, and has increased him in knowledge and stature." Allah bestows His sovereignty upon whomever He wills. Allah is Embracing and Knowing.

248. And their prophet said to them, "The proof of his kingship is that the Ark will be restored to you, bringing tranquility from your Lord, and relics left by the family of Moses and the family of Aaron. It will be carried by the angels. In that is a sign for you, if you are believers."

249. When Saul set out with the troops, he said, "Allah will be testing you with a river. Whoever drinks from it does not belong with me. But whoever does not drink from it, does belong with me, except for whoever scoops up a little with his hand." But they drank from it, except for a few of them. Then, when he crossed it, he and those who believed with him, they said, "We have no strength to face Goliath and his troops today." But those who knew that they would meet Allah said, "How many a small group has defeated a large group by Allah's will. Allah is with the steadfast."

250. And when they confronted Goliath and his troops, they said, "Our Lord, pour down patience on us, and strengthen our foothold, and support us against the faithless people."

251. And they defeated them by Allah's leave, and David killed Goliath, and Allah gave him sovereignty and wisdom, and taught him as He willed. Were it not for Allah restraining the people, some by means of others, the earth would have gone to ruin. But Allah is gracious towards mankind.

252. These are Allah's revelations, which We recite to you in truth. You are one of the messengers.

253. These messengers: We gave some advantage over others. To some of them Allah spoke directly, and some He raised in rank.

2. THE HEIFER (al-Baqarah)

We gave Jesus son of Mary the clear miracles, and We strengthened him with the Holy Spirit. Had Allah willed, those who succeeded them would not have fought one another, after the clear signs had come to them; but they disputed; some of them believed, and some of them disbelieved. Had Allah willed, they would not have fought one another; but Allah does whatever He desires.

254. O you who believe! Spend from what We have given you, before a Day comes in which there is neither trading, nor friendship, nor intercession. The disbelievers are the wrongdoers.

255. Allah! There is no god except He, the Living, the Everlasting. Neither slumber overtakes Him, nor sleep. To Him belongs everything in the heavens and everything on earth. Who is he that can intercede with Him except with His permission? He knows what is before them, and what is behind them; and they cannot grasp any of His knowledge, except as He wills. His Throne extends over the heavens and the earth, and their preservation does not burden Him. He is the Most High, the Great.

256. There shall be no compulsion in religion; the right way has become distinct from the wrong way. Whoever renounces evil and believes in Allah has grasped the most trustworthy handle; which does not break. Allah is Hearing and Knowing.

257. Allah is the Lord of those who believe; He brings them out of darkness and into light. As for those who disbelieve, their lords are the evil ones; they bring them out of light and into darkness—these are the inmates of the Fire, in which they will abide forever.

258. Have you not considered him who argued with Abraham about his Lord, because Allah had given him sovereignty? Abraham said, "My Lord is He who gives life and causes death." He said, "I give life and cause death." Abraham said, "Allah brings the sun from the East, so bring it from the West," so the blasphemer was confounded. Allah does not guide the wrongdoing people.

259. Or like him who passed by a town collapsed on its foundations. He said, "How can Allah revive this after its demise?" Thereupon Allah caused him to die for a hundred years, and then resurrected him. He said, "For how long have you tarried?" He said, "I have tarried for a day, or part of a day." He said, "No. You have tarried for a hundred years. Now look at your food and your drink—it has not spoiled—and look at your donkey. We will make you a wonder for mankind. And look at the bones, how We arrange them, and then clothe them with flesh." So when it became clear to him, he said, "I know that Allah has power over all things."

260. And when Abraham said, "My Lord, show me how You give life to the dead." He said, "Have you not believed?" He said, "Yes, but to put my heart at ease." He said, "Take four birds, and incline them to yourself, then place a part on each hill, then call to them; and they will come rushing to you. And know that Allah is Powerful and Wise."

261. The parable of those who spend their wealth in Allah's way is that of a grain that produces seven spikes; in each spike is a hundred grains. Allah multiplies for whom He wills. Allah is Bounteous and Knowing.

262. Those who spend their wealth in the way of Allah, and then do not follow up what they spent with reminders of their generosity or with insults, will have their reward with their Lord—they have nothing to fear, nor shall they grieve.

263. Kind words and forgiveness are better than charity followed by insults. Allah is Rich and Clement.

264. O you who believe! Do not nullify your charitable deeds with reminders and hurtful words, like him who spends his wealth to be seen by the people, and does not believe in Allah and the Last Day. His likeness is that of a smooth rock covered with soil: a downpour strikes it, and leaves it bare—they gain nothing from their efforts. Allah does not guide the disbelieving people.

2. THE HEIFER (al-Baqarah)

265. And the parable of those who spend their wealth seeking Allah's approval, and to strengthen their souls, is that of a garden on a hillside. If heavy rain falls on it, its produce is doubled; and if no heavy rain falls, then dew is enough. Allah is seeing of everything you do.

266. Would anyone of you like to have a garden of palms and vines, under which rivers flow—with all kinds of fruit in it for him, and old age has stricken him, and he has weak children—then a tornado with fire batters it, and it burns down? Thus Allah makes clear the signs for you, so that you may reflect.

267. O you who believe! Give of the good things you have earned, and from what We have produced for you from the earth. And do not pick the inferior things to give away, when you yourselves would not accept it except with eyes closed. And know that Allah is Sufficient and Praiseworthy.

268. Satan promises you poverty, and urges you to immorality; but Allah promises you forgiveness from Himself, and grace. Allah is Embracing and Knowing.

269. He gives wisdom to whomever He wills. Whoever is given wisdom has been given much good. But none pays heed except those with insight.

270. Whatever charity you give, or a pledge you fulfill, Allah knows it. The wrongdoers have no helpers.

271. If you give charity openly, that is good. But if you keep it secret, and give it to the needy in private, that is better for you. It will atone for some of your misdeeds. Allah is cognizant of what you do.

272. Their guidance is not your responsibility, but Allah guides whom He wills. Any charity you give is for your own good. Any charity you give shall be for the sake of Allah. Any charity you give will be repaid to you in full, and you will not be wronged.

273. It is for the poor; those who are restrained in the way of Allah, and unable to travel in the land. The unaware would think them rich, due to their dignity. You will recognize them by their features. They do not ask from people insistently. Whatever charity you give, Allah is aware of it.

274. Those who spend their wealth by night and day, privately and publicly, will receive their reward from their Lord. They have nothing to fear, nor shall they grieve.

275. Those who swallow usury will not rise, except as someone driven mad by Satan's touch. That is because they say, "Commerce is like usury." But Allah has permitted commerce, and has forbidden usury. Whoever, on receiving advice from his Lord, refrains, may keep his past earnings, and his case rests with Allah. But whoever resumes—these are the dwellers of the Fire, wherein they will abide forever.

276. Allah condemns usury, and He blesses charities. Allah does not love any sinful ingrate.

277. Those who believe, and do good deeds, and pray regularly, and give charity—they will have their reward with their Lord; they will have no fear, nor shall they grieve.

278. O you who believe! Fear Allah, and forgo what remains of usury, if you are believers.

279. If you do not, then take notice of a war by Allah and His Messenger. But if you repent, you may keep your capital, neither wronging, nor being wronged.

280. But if he is in hardship, then deferment until a time of ease. But to remit it as charity is better for you, if you only knew.

281. And guard yourselves against a Day when you will be returned to Allah; then each soul will be rewarded fully for what it has earned, and they will not be wronged.

282. O you who believe! When you incur debt among yourselves for a certain period of time, write it down. And have a scribe write in your presence, in all fairness. And let no scribe refuse to write, as Allah has taught him. So let him write, and let the debtor dictate. And let him fear Allah, his Lord, and diminish nothing from it. But if the debtor is

mentally deficient, or weak, or unable to dictate, then let his guardian dictate with honesty. And call to witness two men from among you. If two men are not available, then one man and two women whose testimony is acceptable to all—if one of them fails to remember, the other would remind her. Witnesses must not refuse when called upon. And do not think it too trivial to write down, whether small or large, including the time of repayment. That is more equitable with Allah, and stronger as evidence, and more likely to prevent doubt—except in the case of a spot transaction between you—then there is no blame on you if you do not write it down. And let there be witnesses whenever you conclude a contract, and let no harm be done to either scribe or witness. If you do that, it is corruption on your part. And fear Allah. Allah teaches you. Allah is aware of everything.

283. If you are on a journey, and cannot find a scribe, then a security deposit should be handed over. But if you trust one another, let the trustee fulfill his trust, and let him fear Allah, his Lord. And do not conceal testimony. Whoever conceals it is sinner at heart. Allah is aware of what you do.

284. To Allah belongs everything in the heavens and the earth. Whether you reveal what is within your selves, or conceal it, Allah will call you to account for it. He forgives whom He wills, and He punishes whom He wills. Allah is Able to do all things.

285. The Messenger has believed in what was revealed to him from his Lord, as did the believers. They all have believed in Allah, and His angels, and His scriptures, and His messengers: "We make no distinction between any of His messengers." And they say, "We hear and we obey. Your forgiveness, our Lord. To you is the destiny."

286. Allah does not burden any soul beyond its capacity. To its credit is what it earns, and against it is what it commits. "Our Lord, do not condemn us if we forget or make a mistake. Our Lord, do not burden us as You have burdened those before us. Our Lord, do not burden us with more than we have strength to bear; and pardon us, and forgive us, and have mercy on us. You are our Lord and Master, so help us against the disbelieving people."

3. FAMILY OF IMRAN
(Ali 'Imran)

*In the name of Allah,
the Gracious, the Merciful*

1. Alif, Lam, Meem.

2. Allah, there is no god but He, the Living, the Eternal.

3. He sent down to you the Book with the Truth, confirming what came before it; and He sent down the Torah and the Gospel.

4. Aforetime, as guidance for mankind; and He sent down the Criterion. Those who have rejected Allah's signs will have a severe punishment. Allah is Mighty, Able to take revenge.

5. Nothing is hidden from Allah, on earth or in the heaven.

6. It is He who forms you in the wombs as He wills. There is no god except He, the Almighty, the Wise.

7. It is He who revealed to you the Book. Some of its verses are definitive; they are the foundation of the Book, and others are unspecific. As for those in whose hearts is deviation, they follow the unspecific part, seeking descent, and seeking to derive an interpretation. But none knows its interpretation except Allah and those firmly rooted in knowledge say, "We believe in it; all is from our Lord." But none recollects except those with understanding.

8. "Our Lord, do not cause our hearts to swerve after You have guided us, and bestow on us mercy from Your presence; You are the Giver."

9. "Our Lord, You will gather the people for a Day in which there is no doubt." Allah will never break His promise.

3. FAMILY OF IMRAN (Ali 'Imran)

10. As for those who disbelieve, neither their wealth nor their children will avail them anything against Allah. These will be fuel for the Fire.

11. Like the behavior of Pharaoh's people and those before them. They rejected Our signs, so Allah seized them for their sins. Allah is Strict in retribution.

12. Say to those who disbelieve, "You will be defeated, and rounded up into Hell—an awful resting-place."

13. There was a sign for you in the two parties that met. One party fighting in the way of Allah, and the other was disbelieving. They saw them with their own eyes twice their number. But Allah supports with His help whomever He wills. In that is a lesson for those with insight.

14. Adorned for the people is the love of desires, such as women, and children, and piles upon piles of gold and silver, and branded horses, and livestock, and fields. These are the conveniences of the worldly life, but with Allah lies the finest resort.

15. Say, "Shall I inform you of something better than that? For those who are righteous, with their Lord are Gardens beneath which rivers flow, where they will remain forever, and purified spouses, and acceptance from Allah." Allah is Observant of the servants.

16. Those who say, "Our Lord, we have believed, so forgive us our sins, and save us from the suffering of the Fire."

17. The patient, and the truthful, and the reverent, and the charitable, and the seekers of forgiveness at dawn.

18. Allah bears witness that there is no god but He, as do the angels, and those endowed with knowledge—upholding justice. There is no god but He, the Mighty, the Wise.

19. Religion with Allah is Islam. Those to whom the Scripture was given differed only after knowledge came to them, out of envy among themselves. Whoever rejects the signs of Allah—Allah is quick to take account.

20. If they argue with you, say, "I have surrendered myself to Allah, and those who follow me." And say to those who were given the Scripture, and to the unlearned, "Have you surrendered?" If they have surrendered, then they are guided; but if they turn away, then your duty is to convey. Allah is Seeing of the servants.

21. As for those who defy Allah's revelations, and kill the prophets unjustly, and kill those who advocate justice among the people—promise them a painful retribution.

22. They are those whose deeds will come to nothing, in this world and in the Hereafter; and they will have no saviors.

23. Have you not considered those who were given a share of the Scripture, as they were called to the Scripture of Allah to arbitrate between them; then some of them turned back, and declined?

24. That is because they said, "The Fire will not touch us except for a limited number of days." They have been misled in their religion by the lies they fabricated.

25. How about when We gather them for a Day in which there is no doubt, and each soul will be paid in full for what it has earned, and they will not be wronged?

26. Say, "O Allah, Owner of Sovereignty. You grant sovereignty to whom You will, and You strip sovereignty from whom you will. You honor whom you will, and You humiliate whom you will. In Your hand is all goodness. You are Capable of all things."

27. "You merge the night into the day, and You merge the day into the night; and you bring the living out of the dead, and You bring the dead out of the living; and You provide for whom you will without measure."

28. Believers are not to take disbelievers for friends instead of believers. Whoever does that has nothing to do with Allah, unless it is to protect your own selves against them. Allah warns you to beware of Him. To Allah is the destiny.

3. FAMILY OF IMRAN (Ali 'Imran)

29. Say, "Whether you conceal what is in your hearts, or disclose it, Allah knows it." He knows everything in the heavens and the earth. Allah is Powerful over everything.

30. On the Day when every soul finds all the good it has done presented. And as for the evil it has done, it will wish there were a great distance between them. Allah cautions you of Himself. Allah is Kind towards the servants.

31. Say, "If you love Allah, then follow me, and Allah will love you, and will forgive you your sins." Allah is Forgiving and Merciful.

32. Say, "Obey Allah and the Messenger." But if they turn away—Allah does not love the faithless.

33. Allah chose Adam, and Noah, and the family of Abraham, and the family of Imran, over all mankind.

34. Offspring one of the other. Allah is Hearer and Knower.

35. The wife of Imran said, "My Lord, I have vowed to You what is in my womb, dedicated, so accept from me; You are the Hearer and Knower."

36. And when she delivered her, she said, "My Lord, I have delivered a female," and Allah was well aware of what she has delivered, "and the male is not like the female, and I have named her Mary, and have commended her and her descendants to Your protection, from Satan the outcast."

37. Her Lord accepted her with a gracious reception, and brought her a beautiful upbringing, and entrusted her to the care of Zechariah. Whenever Zechariah entered upon her in the sanctuary, he found her with provision. He said, "O Mary, where did you get this from?" She said, "It is from Allah; Allah provides to whom He wills without reckoning."

38. Thereupon Zechariah prayed to his Lord; he said, "My Lord, bestow on me good offspring from Your presence; You are the Hearer of Prayers."

39. Then the angels called out to him, as he stood praying in the sanctuary: "Allah gives you good news of John; confirming a Word from Allah, and honorable, and moral, and a prophet; one of the upright."

40. He said, "My Lord, how will I have a son, when old age has overtaken me, and my wife is barren?" He said, "Even so, Allah does whatever He wills."

41. He said, "My Lord, give me a sign." He said, "Your sign is that you shall not speak to the people for three days, except by gestures. And remember your Lord much, and praise in the evening and the morning."

42. The angels said, "O Mary, Allah has chosen you, and has purified you. He has chosen you over all the women of the world.

43. "O Mary, be devoted to your Lord, and bow down, and kneel with those who kneel."

44. These are accounts from the Unseen, which We reveal to you. You were not with them when they cast their lots as to which of them would take charge of Mary; nor were you with them as they quarreled.

45. The Angels said, "O Mary, Allah gives you good news of a Word from Him. His name is the Messiah, Jesus, son of Mary, well-esteemed in this world and the next, and one of the nearest.

46. He will speak to the people from the crib, and in adulthood, and will be one of the righteous."

47. She said, "My Lord, how can I have a child, when no man has touched me?" He said, "It will be so. Allah creates whatever He wills. To have anything done, He only says to it, 'Be,' and it is."

48. And He will teach him the Scripture and wisdom, and the Torah and the Gospel.

49. A messenger to the Children of Israel: "I have come to you with a sign from your Lord. I make for you out of clay the figure of a bird; then I breathe into it, and it becomes a bird by Allah's leave. And I heal the blind and the leprous, and I revive the dead, by Allah's leave. And I inform you concerning what you

eat, and what you store in your homes. In that is a sign for you, if you are believers."

50. "And verifying what lies before me of the Torah, and to make lawful for you some of what was forbidden to you. I have come to you with a sign from your Lord; so fear Allah, and obey me."

51. "Allah is my Lord and your Lord, so worship Him. That is a straight path."

52. When Jesus sensed disbelief on their part, he said, "Who are my allies towards Allah?" The disciples said, "We are Allah's allies; we have believed in Allah, and bear witness that we submit."

53. "Our Lord, we have believed in what You have revealed, and we have followed the Messenger, so count us among the witnesses."

54. They planned, and Allah planned; but Allah is the Best of planners.

55. Allah said, "O Jesus, I am terminating your life, and raising you to Me, and clearing you of those who disbelieve. And I will make those who follow you superior to those who disbelieve, until the Day of Resurrection. Then to Me is your return; then I will judge between you regarding what you were disputing.

56. As for those who disbelieve, I will punish them with a severe punishment, in this world and the next, and they will have no helpers.

57. And as for those who believe and do good works, He will give them their rewards in full. Allah does not love the unjust."

58. This is what We recite to you of the Verses and the Wise Reminder.

59. The likeness of Jesus in Allah's sight is that of Adam: He created him from dust, then said to him, "Be," and he was.

60. The truth is from your Lord, so do not be of those who doubt.

61. And if anyone disputes with you about him, after the knowledge that has come to you, say, "Come, let us call our children and your children, and our women and your women, and ourselves and yourselves, and let us invoke Allah's curse on the liars."

62. This is the narrative of truth: there is no god but Allah. Allah is the Mighty, the Wise.

63. But if they turn away—Allah knows the corrupt.

64. Say, "O People of the Book, come to terms common between us and you: that we worship none but Allah, and that we associate nothing with Him, and that none of us takes others as lords besides Allah." And if they turn away, say, "Bear witness that we have submitted."

65. O People of the Book! Why do you argue about Abraham, when the Torah and the Gospel were not revealed until after him? Will you not reason?

66. Here you are—you argue about things you know, but why do you argue about things you do not know? Allah knows, and you do not know.

67. Abraham was neither a Jew nor a Christian, but he was a Monotheist, a Muslim. And he was not of the Polytheists.

68. The people most deserving of Abraham are those who followed him, and this prophet, and those who believe. Allah is the Guardian of the believers.

69. A party of the People of the Book would love to lead you astray, but they only lead themselves astray, and they do not realize it.

70. O People of the Book! Why do you reject the revelations of Allah, even as you witness?

71. O People of the Book! Why do you confound the truth with falsehood, and knowingly conceal the truth?

72. Some of the People of the Book say, "Believe in what was revealed to the believers at the beginning of the day, and reject it at its end, so that they may return."

73. And trust none except those who follow your religion." Say, "Guidance is Allah's guidance. If someone is given the like of what you were given, or they argue with you before your Lord, say, "All grace is in Allah's hand;

3. FAMILY OF IMRAN (Ali 'Imran)

He gives it to whomever He wills." Allah is Bounteous and Knowing.

74. He specifies His mercy for whomever He wills. Allah is Possessor of Sublime Grace.

75. Among the People of the Book is he, who, if you entrust him with a heap of gold, he will give it back to you. And among them is he, who, if you entrust him with a single coin, he will not give it back to you, unless you keep after him. That is because they say, "We are under no obligation towards the gentiles." They tell lies about Allah, and they know it.

76. Indeed, whoever fulfills his commitments and maintains piety—Allah loves the pious.

77. Those who exchange the covenant of Allah, and their vows, for a small price, will have no share in the Hereafter, and Allah will not speak to them, nor will He look at them on the Day of Resurrection, nor will He purify them. They will have a painful punishment.

78. And among them are those who twist the Scripture with their tongues, that you may think it from the Scripture, when it is not from the Scripture. And they say, "It is from Allah," when it is not from Allah. They tell lies and attribute them to Allah, knowingly.

79. No person to whom Allah has given the Scripture, and wisdom, and prophethood would ever say to the people, "Be my worshipers rather than Allah's." Rather, "Be people of the Lord, according to the Scripture you teach, and the teachings you learn."

80. Nor would he command you to take the angels and the prophets as lords. Would he command you to infidelity after you have submitted?

81. Allah received the covenant of the prophets, "Inasmuch as I have given you of scripture and wisdom; should a messenger come to you verifying what you have, you shall believe in him, and support him." He said, "Do you affirm My covenant and take it upon yourselves?" They said, "We affirm it." He said, "Then bear witness, and I am with you among the witnesses."

82. Whoever turns away after that—these are the deceitful.

83. Do they desire other than the religion of Allah, when to Him has submitted everything in the heavens and the earth, willingly or unwillingly, and to Him they will be returned?

84. Say, "We believe in Allah, and in what was revealed to us; and in what was revealed to Abraham, and Ishmael, and Isaac, and Jacob, and the Patriarchs; and in what was given to Moses, and Jesus, and the prophets from their Lord. We make no distinction between any of them, and to Him we submit."

85. Whoever seeks other than Islam as a religion, it will not be accepted from him, and in the Hereafter he will be among the losers.

86. How will Allah guide a people who disbelieved after having believed, and had witnessed that the Messenger is true, and the clear proofs had come to them? Allah does not guide the unjust people.

87. Those—their penalty is that upon them falls the curse of Allah, and of the angels, and of all mankind.

88. Remaining in it eternally, without their punishment being eased from them, and without being reprieved.

89. Except those who repent afterwards, and reform; for Allah is Forgiving and Merciful.

90. As for those who disbelieve after having believed, then plunge deeper into disbelief, their repentance will not be accepted; these are the lost.

91. As for those who disbelieve and die disbelievers, even the earth full of gold would not be accepted from any of them, were he to offer it for ransom. These will have a painful torment, and will have no saviors.

92. You will not attain virtuous conduct until you give of what you cherish. Whatever you give away, Allah is aware of it.

93. All food was permissible to the Children of Israel, except what Israel forbade for itself before the Torah was revealed. Say, "Bring the Torah, and read it, if you are truthful."

3. FAMILY OF IMRAN (Ali 'Imran)

94. Whoever forges lies about Allah after that—these are the unjust.

95. Say, "Allah has spoken the truth, so follow the religion of Abraham the Monotheist; he was not a Pagan."

96. The first house established for mankind is the one at Bekka; blessed, and guidance for all people.

97. In it are evident signs; the Station of Abraham. Whoever enters it attains security. Pilgrimage to the House is a duty to Allah for all who can make the journey. But as for those who refuse—Allah is Independent of the worlds.

98. Say, "O People of the Scripture, why do you reject the Revelations of Allah, when Allah witnesses what you do?"

99. Say, "O People of the Scripture, why do you hinder from Allah's path those who believe, seeking to distort it, even though you are witnesses? Allah is not unaware of what you do."

100. O you who believe! If you obey a party of those who were given the Scripture, they will turn you, after your belief, into disbelievers.

101. And how could you disbelieve, when Allah's revelations are being recited to you, and among you is His Messenger? Whoever cleaves to Allah has been guided to a straight path.

102. O you who believe! Revere Allah with due reverence, and do not die except as Muslims.

103. And hold fast to the rope of Allah, altogether, and do not become divided. And remember Allah's blessings upon you; how you were enemies, and He reconciled your hearts, and by His grace you became brethren. And you were on the brink of a pit of fire, and He saved you from it. Allah thus clarifies His revelations for you, so that you may be guided.

104. And let there be among you a community calling to virtue, and advocating righteousness, and deterring from evil. These are the successful.

105. And do not be like those who separated and disputed after the clear proofs came to them; for them is a great punishment.

106. On the Day when some faces will be whitened, and some faces will be blackened. As for those whose faces are blackened: "Did you disbelieve after your belief?" Then taste the punishment for having disbelieved.

107. But as for those whose faces are whitened: they are in Allah's mercy, remaining in it forever.

108. These are the revelations of Allah. We recite them to you in truth. Allah desires no injustice for mankind.

109. To Allah belongs everything in the heavens and everything on earth, and to Allah all events are referred.

110. You are the best community that ever emerged for humanity: you advocate what is moral, and forbid what is immoral, and believe in Allah. Had the People of the Scripture believed, it would have been better for them. Among them are the believers, but most of them are sinners.

111. They will do you no harm, beyond insulting you. And if they fight you, they will turn around and flee, then they will not be helped.

112. They shall be humiliated wherever they are encountered, except through a rope from Allah, and a rope from the people; and they incurred wrath from Allah, and were stricken with misery. That is because they rejected Allah's revelations, and killed the prophets unjustly. That is because they rebelled and committed aggression.

113. They are not alike. Among the People of the Scripture is a community that is upright; they recite Allah's revelations throughout the night, and they prostrate themselves.

114. They believe in Allah and the Last Day, and advocate righteousness and forbid evil, and are quick to do good deeds. These are among the righteous.

115. Whatever good they do, they will not be denied it. Allah knows the righteous.

3. FAMILY OF IMRAN (Ali 'Imran)

116. As for those who disbelieve, neither their possessions nor their children will avail them anything against Allah. These are the inhabitants of the Fire, abiding therein forever.

117. The parable of what they spend in this worldly life is that of a frosty wind that strikes the harvest of a people who have wronged their souls, and destroys it. Allah did not wrong them, but they wronged their own selves.

118. O you who believe! Do not befriend outsiders who never cease to wish you harm. They love to see you suffer. Hatred has already appeared from their mouths, but what their hearts conceal is worse. We have made the messages clear for you, if you understand.

119. There you are, you love them, but they do not love you, and you believe in the entire scripture. And when they meet you, they say, "We believe;" but when they are alone, they bite their fingers in rage at you. Say, "Die in your rage; Allah knows what is within the hearts."

120. If something good happens to you, it upsets them; but if something bad befalls you, they rejoice at it. But if you persevere and maintain righteousness, their schemes will not harm you at all. Allah comprehends what they do.

121. Remember when you left your home in the morning, to assign battle-positions for the believers. Allah is Hearing and Knowing.

122. When two groups among you almost faltered, but Allah was their Protector. So in Allah let the believers put their trust.

123. Allah had given you victory at Badr, when you were weak. So fear Allah, that you may be thankful.

124. When you said to the believers, "Is it not enough for you that your Lord has reinforced you with three thousand angels, sent down?"

125. It is; but if you persevere and remain cautious, and they attack you suddenly, your Lord will reinforce you with five thousand angels, well trained.

126. Allah made it but a message of hope for you, and to reassure your hearts thereby. Victory comes only from Allah the Almighty, the Wise.

127. He thus cuts off a section of those who disbelieved, or subdues them, so they retreat disappointed.

128. It is no concern of yours whether He redeems them or punishes them. They are wrongdoers.

129. To Allah belongs everything in the heavens and the earth. He forgives whom He wills, and He punishes whom He wills. Allah is Most Forgiving, Most Merciful.

130. O you who believe! Do not feed on usury, compounded over and over, and fear Allah, so that you may prosper.

131. And guard yourselves against the Fire that is prepared for the disbelievers.

132. And obey Allah and the Messenger, that you may obtain mercy.

133. And race towards forgiveness from your Lord, and a Garden as wide as the heavens and the earth, prepared for the righteous.

134. Those who give in prosperity and adversity, and those who restrain anger, and those who forgive people. Allah loves the doers of good.

135. And those who, when they commit an indecency or wrong themselves, remember Allah and ask forgiveness for their sins—and who forgives sins except Allah? And they do not persist in their wrongdoing while they know.

136. Those—their reward is forgiveness from their Lord, and gardens beneath which rivers flow, abiding therein forever. How excellent is the reward of the workers.

137. Many societies have passed away before you. So travel the earth and note the fate of the deniers.

138. This is a proclamation to humanity, and guidance, and advice for the righteous.

3. FAMILY OF IMRAN (Ali 'Imran)

139. And do not waver, nor feel remorse. You are the superior ones, if you are believers.

140. If a wound afflicts you, a similar wound has afflicted the others. Such days We alternate between the people, that Allah may know those who believe, and take martyrs from among you. Allah does not love the evildoers.

141. So that Allah may prove those who believe, and eliminate the disbelievers.

142. Or do you expect to enter Paradise, before Allah has distinguished those among you who strive, and before He has distinguished the steadfast?

143. You used to wish for death before you have faced it. Now you have seen it before your own eyes.

144. Muhammad is no more than a messenger. Messengers have passed on before him. If he dies or gets killed, will you turn on your heels? He who turns on his heels will not harm Allah in any way. And Allah will reward the appreciative.

145. No soul can die except by Allah's leave, at a predetermined time. Whoever desires the reward of the world, We will give him some of it; and whoever desires the reward of the Hereafter, We will give him some of it; and We will reward the appreciative.

146. How many a prophet fought alongside him numerous godly people? They did not waver for what afflicted them in the cause of Allah, nor did they weaken, nor did they give in. Allah loves those who endure.

147. Their only words were, "Our Lord, forgive us our offences, and our excesses in our conduct, and strengthen our foothold, and help us against the disbelieving people."

148. So Allah gave them the reward of this world, and the excellent reward of the Hereafter. Allah loves the doers of good.

149. O you who believe! If you obey those who disbelieve, they will turn you back on your heels, and you end up losers.

150. Allah is your Master, and He is the Best of Helpers.

151. We will throw terror into the hearts of those who disbelieve, because they attribute to Allah partners for which He revealed no sanction. Their lodging is the Fire. Miserable is the lodging of the evildoers.

152. Allah has fulfilled His promise to you, and you defeated them by His leave; until when you faltered, and disputed the command, and disobeyed after He had shown you what you like. Some of you want this world, and some of you want the next. Then He turned you away from them, to test you; but He pardoned you. Allah is Gracious towards the believers.

153. Remember when you fled, not caring for anyone, even though the Messenger was calling you from your rear. Then He repaid you with sorrow upon sorrow, so that you would not grieve over what you missed, or for what afflicted you. Allah is Informed of what you do.

154. Then after the setback, He sent down security upon you. Slumber overcame some of you, while others cared only for themselves, thinking of Allah thoughts that were untrue—thoughts of ignorance—saying, "Is anything up to us?" Say, "Everything is up to Allah." They conceal within themselves what they do not reveal to you. And they say, "If it was up to us, none of us would have been killed here." Say, "Even if you Had stayed in your homes, those destined to be killed would have marched into their death beds." Allah thus tests what is in your minds, and purifies what is in your hearts. Allah knows what the hearts contain.

155. Those of you who turned back on the day when the two armies clashed—it was Satan who caused them to backslide, on account of some of what they have earned. But Allah has forgiven them. Allah is Forgiving and Prudent.

156. O you who believe! Do not be like those who disbelieved, and said of their brethren

3. FAMILY OF IMRAN (Ali 'Imran)

who marched in the land, or went on the offensive, "Had they stayed with us, they would not have died or been killed." So that Allah may make it a cause of regret in their hearts. Allah gives life and causes death. Allah is Seeing of what you do.

157. If you are killed in the cause of Allah, or die—forgiveness and mercy from Allah are better than what they hoard.

158. If you die, or are killed—to Allah you will be gathered up.

159. It is by of grace from Allah that you were gentle with them. Had you been harsh, hardhearted, they would have dispersed from around you. So pardon them, and ask forgiveness for them, and consult them in the conduct of affairs. And when you make a decision, put your trust in Allah; Allah loves the trusting.

160. If Allah supports you, there is none who can overcome you. But if He fails you, who is there to help you after Him? So in Allah let the believers put their trust.

161. It is not for a prophet to act dishonestly. Whoever acts dishonestly will bring his dishonesty on the Day of Resurrection. Then every soul will be paid in full for what it has earned, and they will not be wronged.

162. Is someone who pursues Allah's approval the same as someone who incurs Allah's wrath and his refuge is Hell—the miserable destination?

163. They have different ranks with Allah, and Allah is Seeing of what they do.

164. Allah has blessed the believers, as He raised up among them a messenger from among themselves, who recites to them His revelations, and purifies them, and teaches them the Scripture and wisdom; although before that they were in evident error.

165. And when a calamity befell you, even after you had inflicted twice as much, you said, "How is this?" Say, "It is from your own selves." Allah is Able to do all things.

166. What befell you on the day the two armies clashed was with Allah's permission; that He may know the believers.

167. And that He may know the hypocrites. And it was said to them, "Come, fight in the cause of Allah, or contribute." They said, "If we knew how to fight, we would have followed you." On that day they were closer to infidelity than they were to faith. They say with their mouths what is not in their hearts; but Allah knows what they hide.

168. Those who said of their brethren, as they stayed behind, "Had they obeyed us, they would not have been killed." Say, "Then avert death from yourselves, if you are truthful."

169. Do not consider those killed in the cause of Allah as dead. In fact, they are alive, at their Lord, well provided for.

170. Delighting in what Allah has given them out of His grace, and happy for those who have not yet joined them; that they have nothing to fear, nor will they grieve.

171. They rejoice in grace from Allah, and bounty, and that Allah will not waste the reward of the faithful.

172. Those who responded to Allah and the Messenger, despite the persecution they had suffered. For the virtuous and the pious among them is a great reward.

173. Those to whom the people have said, "The people have mobilized against you, so fear them." But this only increased them in faith, and they said, "Allah is enough for us; He is the Excellent Protector."

174. So they came back with grace from Allah, and bounty, and no harm having touched them. They pursued what pleases Allah. Allah possesses immense grace.

175. That is only Satan frightening his partisans; so do not fear them, but fear Me, if you are believers.

176. And do not be saddened by those who rush into disbelief. They will not harm Allah in the least. Allah desires to give them no

3. FAMILY OF IMRAN (Ali 'Imran)

share in the Hereafter. A terrible torment awaits them.

177. Those who exchange blasphemy for faith will not harm Allah in the least. A painful torment awaits them.

178. Those who disbelieve should not assume that We respite them for their own good. In fact, We only respite them so that they may increase in sinfulness. A humiliating torment awaits them.

179. Allah will not leave the believers as you are, without distinguishing the wicked from the sincere. Nor will Allah inform you of the future, but Allah elects from among His messengers whom He wills. So believe in Allah and His messengers. If you believe and practice piety, you will have a splendid reward.

180. Those who withhold what Allah has given them of his bounty should not assume that is good for them. In fact, it is bad for them. They will be encircled by their hoardings on the Day of Resurrection. To Allah belongs the inheritance of the heavens and the earth, and Allah is well acquainted with what you do.

181. Allah has heard the statement of those who said, "Allah is poor, and we are rich." We will write down what they said, and their wrongful killing of the prophets; and We will say, "Taste the torment of the burning."

182. "This is on account of what your hands have forwarded, and because Allah is not unjust towards the creatures."

183. Those who said, "Allah has made a covenant with us, that we shall not believe in any messenger unless he brings us an offering to be consumed by fire." Say, "Messengers have come to you before me with proofs, and with what you asked for; so why did you assassinate them, if you are truthful?"

184. If they accuse you of lying, messengers before you were accused of lying. They came with the proofs, and the Psalms, and the Illuminating Scripture.

185. Every soul will have a taste of death, and you will receive your recompense on the Day of Resurrection. Whoever is swayed from the Fire, and admitted to Paradise, has won. The life of this world is merely enjoyment of delusion.

186. You will be tested through your possessions and your persons; and you will hear from those who received the Scripture before you, and from the idol worshipers, much abuse. But if you persevere and lead a righteous life—that indeed is a mark of great determination.

187. Allah received a pledge from those who were given the Scripture: "You shall proclaim it to the people, and not conceal it." But they disregarded it behind their backs, and exchanged it for a small price. What a miserable exchange they made.

188. Do not think that those who rejoice in what they have done, and love to be praised for what they have not done—do not think they can evade the punishment. They will have a painful punishment.

189. To Allah belongs the sovereignty of the heavens and the earth. Allah has power over all things.

190. In the creation of the heavens and the earth, and in the alternation of night and day, are signs for people of understanding.

191. Those who remember Allah while standing, and sitting, and on their sides; and they reflect upon the creation of the heavens and the earth: "Our Lord, You did not create this in vain, glory to You, so protect us from the punishment of the Fire."

192. "Our Lord, whomever You commit to the Fire, You have disgraced. The wrongdoers will have no helpers."

193. "Our Lord, we have heard a caller calling to the faith: 'Believe in your Lord,' and we have believed. Our Lord! Forgive us our sins, and remit our misdeeds, and make us die in the company of the virtuous."

194. "Our Lord, and give us what You have promised us through Your messengers, and do not disgrace us on the Day of Resurrection. Surely You never break a promise."

195. And so their Lord answered them: "I will not waste the work of any worker among you, whether male or female. You are one of another. For those who emigrated, and were expelled from their homes, and were persecuted because of Me, and fought and were killed—I will remit for them their sins, and will admit them into gardens beneath which rivers flow—a reward from Allah. With Allah is the ultimate reward."

196. Do not be impressed by the disbelievers' movements in the land.

197. A brief enjoyment, then their abode is Hell. What a miserable resort.

198. As for those who feared their Lord: for them will be gardens beneath which rivers flow, wherein they will abide forever—hospitality from Allah. What Allah possesses is best for the just.

199. Among the People of the Scripture are those who believe in Allah, and in what was revealed to you, and in what was revealed to them. They are humble before Allah, and they do not sell Allah's revelations for a cheap price. These will have their reward with their Lord. Allah is swift in reckoning.

200. O you who believe! Be patient, and advocate patience, and be united, and revere Allah, so that you may thrive.

4. WOMEN
(an-Nisa')

In the name of Allah,
the Gracious, the Merciful

1. O people! Fear your Lord, who created you from a single soul, and created from it its mate, and propagated from them many men and women. And revere Allah whom you ask about, and the parents. Surely, Allah is Watchful over you.

2. And give orphans their properties, and do not substitute the bad for the good. And do not consume their properties by combining them with yours, for that would be a serious sin.

3. If you fear you cannot act fairly towards the orphans—then marry the women you like—two, or three, or four. But if you fear you will not be fair, then one, or what you already have. That makes it more likely that you avoid bias.

4. Give women their dowries graciously. But if they willingly forego some of it, then consume it with enjoyment and pleasure.

5. Do not give the immature your money which Allah has assigned to you for support. But provide for them from it, and clothe them, and speak to them with kind words.

6. Test the orphans until they reach the age of marriage. If you find them to be mature enough, hand over their properties to them. And do not consume it extravagantly or hastily before they grow up. The rich shall not charge any wage, but the poor may charge fairly. When you hand over their properties to them, have it witnessed for them. Allah suffices as a Reckoner.

7. Men receive a share of what their parents and relatives leave, and women receive a share of what their parents and relatives leave; be it little or much—a legal share.

8. If the distribution is attended by the relatives, and the orphans, and the needy, give them something out of it, and speak to them kindly.

9. Those who are concerned about the fate of their weak children, in case they leave them behind, should fear Allah, and speak appropriate words.

10. Those who consume the wealth of orphans illicitly consume only fire into their bellies; and they will roast in a Blaze.

11. Allah instructs you regarding your children: The male receives the equivalent of the share of two females. If they are daughters, more than two, they get two-thirds of what he leaves. If there is only one, she gets one-half. As for the parents, each gets one-sixth of what he leaves, if he had children. If he had no children, and his parents inherit from

4. WOMEN (an-Nisa')

him, his mother gets one-third. If he has siblings, his mother gets one-sixth. After fulfilling any bequest and paying off debts. Your parents and your children—you do not know which are closer to you in welfare. This is Allah's Law. Allah is Knowing and Judicious.

12. You get one-half of what your wives leave behind, if they had no children. If they had children, you get one-fourth of what they leave. After fulfilling any bequest and paying off debts. They get one-fourth of what you leave behind, if you have no children. If you have children, they get one-eighth of what you leave. After fulfilling any bequest and paying off debts. If a man or woman leaves neither parents nor children, but has a brother or sister, each of them gets one-sixth. If there are more siblings, they share one-third. After fulfilling any bequest and paying off debts, without any prejudice. This is a will from Allah. Allah is Knowing and Clement.

13. These are the bounds set by Allah. Whoever obeys Allah and His Messenger, He will admit him into Gardens beneath which rivers flow, to abide therein forever. That is the great attainment.

14. But whoever disobeys Allah and His Messenger, and oversteps His bounds, He will admit him into a Fire, wherein he abides forever, and he will have a shameful punishment.

15. Those of your women who commit lewdness, you must have four witnesses against them, from among you. If they testify, confine them to the homes until death claims them, or Allah makes a way for them.

16. If two men among you commit it, punish them both. But if they repent and reform, leave them alone. Allah is Redeemer, Full of Mercy.

17. Repentance is available from Allah for those who commit evil out of ignorance, and then repent soon after. These—Allah will relent towards them. Allah is Knowing and Wise.

18. But repentance is not available for those who commit evils, until when death approaches one of them, he says, "Now I repent," nor for those who die as disbelievers. These—We have prepared for them a painful torment.

19. O you who believe! It is not permitted for you to inherit women against their will. And do not coerce them in order to take away some of what you had given them, unless they commit a proven adultery. And live with them in kindness. If you dislike them, it may be that you dislike something in which Allah has placed much good.

20. If you wish to replace one wife with another, and you have given one of them a fortune, take nothing back from it. Would you take it back fraudulently and sinfully?

21. And how can you take it back, when you have been intimate with one another, and they have received from you a solid commitment?

22. Do not marry women whom your fathers married, except what is already past. That is improper, indecent, and a bad custom.

23. Forbidden for you are your mothers, your daughters, your sisters, your paternal aunts, your maternal aunts, your brother's daughters, your sister's daughters, your foster-mothers who nursed you, your sisters through nursing, your wives' mothers, and your stepdaughters in your guardianship—born of wives you have gone into—but if you have not gone into them, there is no blame on you. And the wives of your genetic sons, and marrying two sisters simultaneously. Except what is past. Allah is Oft-Forgiving, Most Merciful.

24. And all married women, except those you rightfully possess. This is Allah's decree, binding upon you. Permitted for you are those that lie outside these limits, provided you seek them in legal marriage, with gifts from your property, seeking wedlock, not prostitution. If you wish to enjoy them, then give them their dowry—a legal obligation. You commit no error by agreeing to any

4. WOMEN (an-Nisa')

change to the dowry. Allah is All-Knowing, Most Wise.

25. If any of you lack the means to marry free believing women, he may marry one of the believing maids under your control. Allah is well aware of your faith. You are from one another. Marry them with the permission of their guardians, and give them their recompense fairly—to be protected—neither committing adultery, nor taking secret lovers. When they are married, if they commit adultery, their punishment shall be half that of free women. That is for those among you who fear falling into decadence. But to practice self-restraint is better for you. Allah is Most Forgiving, Most Merciful.

26. Allah intends to make things clear to you, and to guide you in the ways of those before you, and to redeem you. Allah is Most Knowing, Most Wise.

27. Allah intends to redeem you, but those who follow their desires want you to turn away utterly.

28. Allah intends to lighten your burden, for the human being was created weak.

29. O you who believe! Do not consume each other's wealth illicitly, but trade by mutual consent. And do not kill yourselves, for Allah is Merciful towards you.

30. Whoever does that, out of hostility and wrongdoing, We will cast him into a Fire. And that would be easy for Allah.

31. If you avoid the worst of what you are forbidden, We will remit your sins, and admit you by a Gate of Honor.

32. Do not covet what Allah has given to some of you in preference to others. For men is a share of what they have earned, and for women is a share of what they have earned. And ask Allah of his bounty. Allah has knowledge of everything.

33. To everyone We have assigned beneficiaries in what is left by parents and relatives. Those with whom you have made an agreement, give them their share. Allah is Witness over all things.

34. Men are the protectors and maintainers of women, as Allah has given some of them an advantage over others, and because they spend out of their wealth. The good women are obedient, guarding what Allah would have them guard. As for those from whom you fear disloyalty, admonish them, and abandon them in their beds, then strike them. But if they obey you, seek no way against them. Allah is Sublime, Great.

35. If you fear a breach between the two, appoint an arbiter from his family and an arbiter from her family. If they wish to reconcile, Allah will bring them together. Allah is Knowledgeable, Expert.

36. Worship Allah, and ascribe no partners to Him, and be good to the parents, and the relatives, and the orphans, and the poor, and the neighbor next door, and the distant neighbor, and the close associate, and the traveler, and your servants. Allah does not love the arrogant showoff.

37. Those who are stingy, and exhort people to stinginess, and conceal what Allah has given them from His bounty. We have prepared for the disbelievers a disgraceful punishment.

38. And those who spend their money to be seen by people, and believe neither in Allah nor in the Last Day. Whoever has Satan as a companion—what an evil companion.

39. What would they have lost, had they believed in Allah and the Last Day, and gave out of what Allah has provided for them? Allah knows them very well.

40. Allah does not commit an atom's weight of injustice; and if there is a good deed, He doubles it, and gives from His Presence a sublime compensation.

41. Then how will it be, when We bring a witness from every community, and We bring you as a witness against these?

42. On that Day, those who disbelieved and disobeyed the Messenger will wish that the earth were leveled over them. They will conceal nothing from Allah.

4. WOMEN (an-Nisa')

43. O you who believe! Do not approach the prayer while you are drunk, so that you know what you say; nor after sexual orgasm—unless you are travelling—until you have bathed. If you are sick, or traveling, or one of you comes from the toilet, or you have had intercourse with women, and cannot find water, find clean sand and wipe your faces and your hands with it. Allah is Pardoning and Forgiving.

44. Have you not considered those who were given a share of the Book? They buy error, and wish you would lose the way.

45. But Allah knows your enemies best. Allah is sufficient as a Protector, and Allah is sufficient as a Supporter.

46. Among the Jews are some who take words out of context, and say, "We hear and we disobey", and "Hear without listening", and "Observe us," twisting with their tongues and slandering the religion. Had they said, "We hear and we obey", and "Listen," and "Give us your attention," it would have been better for them, and more upright. But Allah has cursed them for their disbelief; they do not believe except a little.

47. O you who were given the Book! Believe in what We sent down, confirming what you have, before We obliterate faces and turn them inside out, or curse them as We cursed the Sabbath-breakers. The command of Allah is always done.

48. Allah does not forgive association with Him, but He forgives anything less than that to whomever He wills. Whoever associates anything with Allah has devised a monstrous sin.

49. Have you not considered those who claim purity for themselves? Rather, Allah purifies whom He wills, and they will not be wronged a whit.

50. See how they devise lies against Allah. That alone is an outright sin.

51. Have you not considered those who were given a share of the Book? They believe in superstition and evil powers, and say of those who disbelieve, "These are better guided on the way than the believers."

52. Those are they whom Allah has cursed. Whomever Allah curses, you will find no savior for him.

53. Or do they own a share of the kingdom? Then they would not give people a speck.

54. Or do they envy the people for what Allah has given them of His grace? We have given the family of Abraham the Book and wisdom, and We have given them a great kingdom.

55. Among them are those who believed in it, and among them are those who held back from it. Hell is a sufficient Inferno.

56. Those who reject Our revelations—We will scorch them in a Fire. Every time their skins are cooked, We will replace them with other skins, so they will experience the suffering. Allah is Most Powerful, Most Wise.

57. As for those who believe and do good deeds, We will admit them into Gardens beneath which rivers flow, abiding therein forever. They will have purified spouses therein, and We will admit them into a shady shade.

58. Allah instructs you to give back things entrusted to you to their owners. And when you judge between people, judge with justice. Allah's instructions to you are excellent. Allah is All-Hearing, All-Seeing.

59. O you who believe! Obey Allah and obey the Messenger and those in authority among you. And if you dispute over anything, refer it to Allah and the Messenger, if you believe in Allah and the Last Day. That is best, and a most excellent determination.

60. Have you not observed those who claim that they believe in what was revealed to you, and in what was revealed before you, yet they seek Satanic sources for legislation, in spite of being commanded to reject them? Satan means to mislead them far away.

61. And when it is said to them, "Come to what Allah has revealed, and to the Messenger," you see the hypocrites shunning you completely.

4. WOMEN (an-Nisa')

62. How about when a disaster strikes them because what their hands have put forward, and then they come to you swearing by Allah: "We only intended goodwill and reconciliation"?

63. They are those whom Allah knows what is in their hearts. So ignore them, and admonish them, and say to them concerning themselves penetrating words.

64. We did not send any messenger except to be obeyed by Allah's leave. Had they, when they wronged themselves, come to you, and prayed for Allah's forgiveness, and the Messenger had prayed for their forgiveness, they would have found Allah Relenting and Merciful.

65. But no, by your Lord, they will not believe until they call you to arbitrate in their disputes, and then find within themselves no resentment regarding your decisions, and submit themselves completely.

66. Had We decreed for them: "Kill yourselves," or "Leave your homes," they would not have done it, except for a few of them. But had they done what they were instructed to do, it would have been better for them, and a firmer confirmation.

67. And We would have given them from Our presence a rich compensation.

68. And We would have guided them on a straight path.

69. Whoever obeys Allah and the Messenger—these are with those whom Allah has blessed—among the prophets, and the sincere, and the martyrs, and the upright. Excellent are those as companions.

70. That is the grace from Allah. Allah suffices as Knower.

71. O you who believe! Take your precautions, and mobilize in groups, or mobilize altogether.

72. Among you is he who lags behind. Then, when a calamity befalls you, he says, "Allah has favored me, that I was not martyred with them."

73. But when some bounty from Allah comes to you, he says—as if no affection existed between you and him—"If only I had been with them, I would have achieved a great victory."

74. Let those who sell the life of this world for the Hereafter fight in the cause of Allah. Whoever fights in the cause of Allah, and then is killed, or achieves victory, We will grant him a great compensation.

75. And why would you not fight in the cause of Allah, and the helpless men, and women, and children, cry out, "Our Lord, deliver us from this town whose people are oppressive, and appoint for us from Your Presence a Protector, and appoint for us from Your Presence a Victor."

76. Those who believe fight in the cause of Allah, while those who disbelieve fight in the cause of Evil. So fight the allies of the Devil. Surely the strategy of the Devil is weak.

77. Have you not considered those who were told, "Restrain your hands, and perform your prayers, and spend in regular charity"? But when fighting was ordained for them, a faction of them feared the people as Allah is ought to be feared, or even more. And they said, "Our Lord, why did You ordain fighting for us? If only You would postpone it for us for a short while." Say, "The enjoyments of this life are brief, but the Hereafter is better for the righteous, and you will not be wronged one bit."

78. Wherever you may be, death will catch up with you, even if you were in fortified towers. When a good fortune comes their way, they say, "This is from Allah." But when a misfortune befalls them, they say, "This is from you." Say, "All is from Allah." So what is the matter with these people, that they hardly understand a thing?

79. Whatever good happens to you is from Allah, and whatever bad happens to you is from your own self. We sent you to humanity as a messenger, and Allah is Witness enough.

80. Whoever obeys the Messenger is obeying Allah. And whoever turns away—We did not send you as a watcher over them.

4. WOMEN (an-Nisa')

81. They profess obedience, but when they leave your presence, some of them conspire something contrary to what you said. But Allah writes down what they conspire. So avoid them, and put your trust in Allah. Allah is Guardian enough.

82. Do they not ponder the Quran? Had it been from any other than Allah, they would have found in it much discrepancy.

83. When some news of security or alarm comes their way, they broadcast it. But had they referred it to the Messenger, and to those in authority among them, those who can draw conclusions from it would have comprehended it. Were it not for Allah's blessing and mercy upon you, you would have followed the Devil, except for a few.

84. So fight in the cause of Allah; you are responsible only for yourself. And rouse the believers. Perhaps Allah will restrain the might of those who disbelieve. Allah is Stronger in Might, and More Punishing.

85. Whoever intercedes for a good cause has a share in it, and whoever intercedes for an evil cause shares in its burdens. Allah keeps watch over everything.

86. When you are greeted with a greeting, respond with a better greeting, or return it. Allah keeps count of everything.

87. Allah—there is no god except He. He will gather you to the Day of Resurrection, in which there is no doubt. And who speaks more truly than Allah?

88. What is the matter with you, divided into two factions regarding the hypocrites, when Allah Himself has overwhelmed them on account of what they did? Do you want to guide those whom Allah has led astray? Whomever Allah leads astray—you will never find for him a way.

89. They would love to see you disbelieve, just as they disbelieve, so you would become equal. So do not befriend any of them, unless they emigrate in the way of Allah. If they turn away, seize them and execute them wherever you may find them; and do not take from among them allies or supporters.

90. Except those who join people with whom you have a treaty, or those who come to you reluctant to fight you or fight their own people. Had Allah willed, He would have given them power over you, and they would have fought you. If they withdraw from you, and do not fight you, and offer you peace, then Allah assigns no excuse for you against them.

91. You will find others who want security from you, and security from their own people. But whenever they are tempted into civil discord, they plunge into it. So if they do not withdraw from you, nor offer you peace, nor restrain their hands, seize them and execute them wherever you find them. Against these, We have given you clear authorization.

92. Never should a believer kill another believer, unless by error. Anyone who kills a believer by error must set free a believing slave, and pay compensation to the victim's family, unless they remit it as charity. If the victim belonged to a people who are hostile to you, but is a believer, then the compensation is to free a believing slave. If he belonged to a people with whom you have a treaty, then compensation should be handed over to his family, and a believing slave set free. Anyone who lacks the means must fast for two consecutive months, by way of repentance to Allah. Allah is All-Knowing, Most Wise.

93. Whoever kills a believer deliberately, the penalty for him is Hell, where he will remain forever. And Allah will be angry with him, and will curse him, and will prepare for him a terrible punishment.

94. O you who believe! When you journey in the way of Allah, investigate, and do not say to him who offers you peace, "You are not a believer," aspiring for the goods of this world. With Allah are abundant riches. You yourselves were like this before, and Allah bestowed favor on you; so investigate. Allah is well aware of what you do.

4. WOMEN (an-Nisa')

95. Not equal are the inactive among the believers—except the disabled—and the strivers in the cause of Allah with their possessions and their persons. Allah prefers the strivers with their possessions and their persons above the inactive, by a degree. But Allah has promised goodness to both. Yet Allah favors the strivers, over the inactive, with a great reward.

96. Degrees from Him, and forgiveness, and mercy. Allah is Forgiving and Merciful.

97. While the angels are removing the souls of those who have wronged themselves, they will say, "What was the matter with you?" They will say, "We were oppressed in the land." They will say, "Was Allah's earth not vast enough for you to emigrate in it?" These—their refuge is Hell. What a wretched retreat!

98. Except for the weak among men, and women, and children who have no means to act, and no means to find a way out.

99. These—Allah may well pardon them. Allah is Pardoning and Forgiving.

100. Anyone who emigrates for the sake of Allah will find on earth many places of refuge, and plentitude. Anyone who leaves his home, emigrating to Allah and His Messenger, and then is overtaken by death, his compensation falls on Allah. Allah is Forgiver, Most Merciful.

101. When you travel in the land, there is no blame on you for shortening the prayers, if you fear that the disbelievers may harm you. The disbelievers are your manifest enemies.

102. When you are among them, and you stand to lead them in prayer, let a group of them stand with you, and let them hold their weapons. Then, when they have done their prostrations, let them withdraw to the rear, and let another group, that have not prayed yet, come forward and pray with you; and let them take their precautions and their weapons. Those who disbelieve would like you to neglect your weapons and your equipment, so they can attack you in a single assault. You commit no error, if you are hampered by rain or are sick, by putting down your weapons; but take precautions. Indeed, Allah has prepared for the disbelievers a demeaning punishment.

103. When you have completed the prayer, remember Allah, standing, or sitting, or on your sides. And when you feel secure, perform the prayer. The prayer is obligatory for believers at specific times.

104. And do not falter in the pursuit of the enemy. If you are aching, they are aching as you are aching, but you expect from Allah what they cannot expect. Allah is Knowledgeable and Wise.

105. We have revealed to you the Scripture, with the truth, so that you judge between people in accordance with what Allah has shown you. And do not be an advocate for the traitors.

106. And ask Allah for forgiveness. Allah is Forgiver and Merciful.

107. And do not argue on behalf of those who deceive themselves. Allah does not love the deceitful sinner.

108. They hide from the people, but they cannot hide from Allah. He is with them, as they plot by night with words He does not approve. Allah comprehends what they do.

109. There you are, arguing on their behalf in the present life, but who will argue with Allah on their behalf on the Day of Resurrection? Or who will be their representative?

110. Whoever commits evil, or wrongs his soul, then implores Allah for forgiveness, will find Allah Forgiving and Merciful.

111. And Whoever earns a sin, earns it against himself. Allah is Aware and Wise.

112. And whoever commits a mistake, or a sin, and then blames it on an innocent person, has taken a slander and a clear sin.

113. Were it not for Allah's grace towards you, and His mercy, a faction of them would have managed to mislead you. But they only mislead themselves, and they cannot harm you in

4. WOMEN (an-Nisa')

any way. Allah has revealed to you the Scripture and wisdom, and has taught you what you did not know. Allah's goodness towards you is great.

114. There is no good in much of their private counsels, except for him who advocates charity, or kindness, or reconciliation between people. Whoever does that, seeking Allah's approval, We will give him a great compensation.

115. Whoever makes a breach with the Messenger, after the guidance has become clear to him, and follows other than the path of the believers, We will direct him in the direction he has chosen, and commit him to Hell—what a terrible destination!

116. Allah will not forgive that partners be associated with Him; but will forgive anything less than that, to whomever He wills. Anyone who ascribes partners to Allah has strayed into far error.

117. They invoke in His stead only females. In fact, they invoke none but a rebellious devil.

118. Allah has cursed him. And he said, "I will take to myself my due share of Your servants."

119. "And I will mislead them, and I will entice them, and I will prompt them to slit the ears of cattle, and I will prompt them to alter the creation of Allah." Whoever takes Satan as a lord, instead of Allah, has surely suffered a profound loss.

120. He promises them, and he raises their expectations, but Satan promises them nothing but delusions.

121. These—their place is Hell, and they will find no escape from it.

122. But as for those who believe and do righteous deeds, We will admit them into gardens beneath which rivers flow, where they will abide forever. The promise of Allah is true—and who is more truthful in speech than Allah?

123. It is not in accordance with your wishes, nor in accordance with the wishes of the People of the Scripture. Whoever works evil will pay for it, and will not find for himself, besides Allah, any protector or savior.

124. But whoever works righteousness, whether male or female, and is a believer—those will enter Paradise, and will not be wronged a whit.

125. And who is better in religion than he who submits himself wholly to Allah, and is a doer of good, and follows the faith of Abraham the Monotheist? Allah has chosen Abraham for a friend.

126. To Allah belongs what is in the heavens and what is on earth, and Allah encompasses everything.

127. They ask you for a ruling about women. Say, "Allah gives you a ruling about them, and so does what is stated to you in the Book about widowed women from whom you withhold what is decreed for them, yet you desire to marry them, and about helpless children: that you should treat the orphans fairly." Whatever good you do, Allah knows it.

128. If a woman fears maltreatment or desertion from her husband, there is no fault in them if they reconcile their differences, for reconciliation is best. Souls are prone to avarice; yet if you do what is good, and practice piety—Allah is Cognizant of what you do.

129. You will not be able to treat women with equal fairness, no matter how much you desire it. But do not be so biased as to leave another suspended. If you make amends, and act righteously—Allah is Forgiving and Merciful.

130. And if they separate, Allah will enrich each from His abundance. Allah is Bounteous and Wise.

131. To Allah belongs everything in the heavens and everything on earth. We have instructed those who were given the Book before you, and you, to be conscious of Allah.

4. WOMEN (an-Nisa')

But if you refuse—to Allah belongs everything in the heavens and everything on earth. Allah is in no need, Praiseworthy.

132. To Allah belongs everything in the heavens and everything on earth. Allah suffices as Manager.

133. If He wills, He can do away with you, O people, and bring others. Allah is Able to do that.

134. Whoever desires the reward of this world—with Allah is the reward of this world and the next. Allah is All-Hearing, All-Seeing.

135. O you who believe! Stand firmly for justice, as witnesses to Allah, even if against yourselves, or your parents, or your relatives. Whether one is rich or poor, Allah takes care of both. So do not follow your desires, lest you swerve. If you deviate, or turn away—then Allah is Aware of what you do.

136. O you who believe! Believe in Allah and His messenger, and the Book He sent down to His messenger, and the Book He sent down before. Whoever rejects Allah, His angels, His Books, His messengers, and the Last Day, has strayed far in error.

137. Those who believe, then disbelieve, then believe, then disbelieve, then increase in disbelief, Allah will not forgive them, nor will He guide them to a way.

138. Inform the hypocrites that they will have a painful punishment.

139. Those who ally themselves with the disbelievers instead of the believers. Do they seek glory in them? All glory belongs to Allah.

140. He has revealed to you in the Book that when you hear Allah's revelations being rejected, or ridiculed, do not sit with them until they engage in some other subject. Otherwise, you would be like them. Allah will gather the hypocrites and the disbelievers, into Hell, altogether.

141. Those who lie in wait for you: if you attain victory from Allah, they say, "Were we not with you?" But if the disbelievers get a turn, they say, "Did we not side with you, and defend you from the believers?" Allah will judge between you on the Day of Resurrection; and Allah will give the disbelievers no means of overcoming the believers.

142. The hypocrites try to deceive Allah, but He is deceiving them. And when they stand for prayer, they stand lazily, showing off in front of people, and remembering Allah only a little.

143. Wavering in between, neither with these, nor with those. Whomever Allah sends astray, you will never find for him a way.

144. O you who believe! Do not befriend disbelievers rather than believers. Do you want to give Allah a clear case against you?

145. The hypocrites will be in the lowest level of the Fire, and you will find no helper for them.

146. Except those who repent, and reform, and hold fast to Allah, and dedicate their religion to Allah alone. These are with the believers; and Allah will give the believers a great reward.

147. What would Allah accomplish by your punishment, if you have given thanks, and have believed? Allah is Appreciative and Cognizant.

148. Allah does not like the public uttering of bad language, unless someone was wronged. Allah is Hearing and Knowing.

149. If you let a good deed be shown, or conceal it, or pardon an offense—Allah is Pardoning and Capable.

150. Those who disbelieve in Allah and His messengers, and want to separate between Allah and His messengers, and say, "We believe in some, and reject some," and wish to take a path in between.

151. These are the unbelievers, truly. We have prepared for the unbelievers a shameful punishment.

4. WOMEN (an-Nisa')

¹⁵². As for those who believe in Allah and His messengers, and make no distinction between any of them—He will give them their rewards. Allah is Forgiver and Merciful.

¹⁵³. The People of the Scripture challenge you to bring down to them a book from the sky. They had asked Moses for something even greater. They said, "Show us Allah plainly." The thunderbolt struck them for their wickedness. Then they took the calf for worship, even after the clear proofs had come to them. Yet We pardoned that, and We gave Moses a clear authority.

¹⁵⁴. And We raised the Mount above them in accordance with their covenant, and We said to them, "Enter the gate humbly", and We said to them, "Do not violate the Sabbath", and We received from them a solemn pledge.

¹⁵⁵. But for their violation of their covenant, and their denial of Allah's revelations, and their killing of the prophets unjustly, and their saying, "Our minds are closed." In fact, Allah has sealed them for their disbelief, so they do not believe, except for a few.

¹⁵⁶. And for their faithlessness, and their saying against Mary a monstrous slander.

¹⁵⁷. And for their saying, "We have killed the Messiah, Jesus, the son of Mary, the Messenger of Allah." In fact, they did not kill him, nor did they crucify him, but it appeared to them as if they did. Indeed, those who differ about him are in doubt about it. They have no knowledge of it, except the following of assumptions. Certainly, they did not kill him.

¹⁵⁸. Rather, Allah raised him up to Himself. Allah is Mighty and Wise.

¹⁵⁹. There is none from the People of the Scripture but will believe in him before his death, and on the Day of Resurrection he will be a witness against them.

¹⁶⁰. Due to wrongdoing on the part of the Jews, We forbade them good things that used to be lawful for them; and for deterring many from Allah's path.

¹⁶¹. And for their taking usury, although they were forbidden it; and for their consuming people's wealth dishonestly. We have prepared for the faithless among them a painful torment.

¹⁶². But those among them firmly rooted in knowledge, and the believers, believe in what was revealed to you, and in what was revealed before you; and the observers of prayers, and the givers of charity, and the believers in Allah and the Last Day—upon these We will bestow an immense reward.

¹⁶³. We have inspired you, as We had inspired Noah and the prophets after him. And We inspired Abraham, and Ishmael, and Isaac, and Jacob, and the Patriarchs, and Jesus, and Job, and Jonah, and Aaron, and Solomon. And We gave David the Psalms.

¹⁶⁴. Some messengers We have already told you about, while some messengers We have not told you about. And Allah spoke to Moses directly.

¹⁶⁵. Messengers delivering good news, and bringing warnings; so that people may have no excuse before Allah after the coming of the messengers. Allah is Powerful and Wise.

¹⁶⁶. But Allah bears witness to what He revealed to you. He revealed it with His knowledge. And the angels bear witness. Though Allah is a sufficient witness.

¹⁶⁷. Those who disbelieve and repel from Allah's path have gone far astray.

¹⁶⁸. Those who disbelieve and transgress; Allah is not about to forgive them, nor will He guide them to any path.

¹⁶⁹. Except to the path of Hell, where they will dwell forever. And that is easy for Allah.

¹⁷⁰. O people! The Messenger has come to you with the truth from your Lord, so believe—that is best for you. But if you disbelieve, to Allah belongs everything in the heavens and the earth. Allah is Omniscient and Wise.

¹⁷¹. O People of the Scripture! Do not exaggerate in your religion, and do not say about Allah except the truth. The Messiah, Jesus, the son of Mary, is the Messenger of Allah, and His Word that He conveyed to Mary, and a

5. THE TABLE (al-Ma'idah)

Spirit from Him. So believe in Allah and His messengers, and do not say, "Three." Refrain—it is better for you. Allah is only one God. Glory be to Him—that He should have a son. To Him belongs everything in the heavens and the earth, and Allah is a sufficient Protector.

172. The Messiah does not disdain to be a servant of Allah, nor do the favored angels. Whoever disdains His worship, and is too arrogant—He will round them up to Himself altogether.

173. But as for those who believe and do good works, He will pay them their wages in full, and will increase His grace for them. But as for those who disdain and are too proud, He will punish them with an agonizing punishment. And they will find for themselves, apart from Allah, no lord and no savior.

174. O people! A proof has come to you from your Lord, and We sent down to you a clear light.

175. As for those who believe in Allah, and hold fast to Him, He will admit them into mercy and grace from Him, and will guide them to Himself in a straight path.

176. They ask you for a ruling. Say, "Allah gives you a ruling concerning the person who has neither parents nor children." If a man dies, and leaves no children, and he had a sister, she receives one-half of what he leaves. And he inherits from her if she leaves no children. But if there are two sisters, they receive two-thirds of what he leaves. If the siblings are men and women, the male receives the share of two females." Allah makes things clear for you, lest you err. Allah is Aware of everything.

5. THE TABLE
(al-Ma'idah)

*In the name of Allah,
the Gracious, the Merciful*

1. O you who believe! Fulfill your commitments. Livestock animals are permitted for you, except those specified to you; but not wild game while you are in pilgrim sanctity. Allah decrees whatever He wills.

2. O you who believe! Do not violate Allah's sacraments, nor the Sacred Month, nor the offerings, nor the garlanded, nor those heading for the Sacred House seeking blessings from their Lord and approval. When you have left the pilgrim sanctity, you may hunt. And let not the hatred of people who barred you from the Sacred Mosque incite you to aggression. And cooperate with one another in virtuous conduct and conscience, and do not cooperate with one another in sin and hostility. And fear Allah. Allah is severe in punishment.

3. Prohibited for you are carrion, blood, the flesh of swine, and animals dedicated to other than Allah; also the flesh of animals strangled, killed violently, killed by a fall, gored to death, mangled by wild animals—except what you rescue, and animals sacrificed on altars; and the practice of drawing lots. For it is immoral. Today, those who disbelieve have despaired of your religion, so do not fear them, but fear Me. Today I have perfected your religion for you, and have completed My favor upon you, and have approved Islam as a religion for you. But whoever is compelled by hunger, with no intent of wrongdoing—Allah is Forgiving and Merciful.

4. They ask you what is permitted for them. Say, "Permitted for you are all good things, including what trained dogs and falcons catch for you." You train them according to what Allah has taught you. So eat from what they catch for you, and pronounce Allah's name over it. And fear Allah. Allah is Swift in reckoning.

5. Today all good things are made lawful for you. And the food of those given the Scripture is lawful for you, and your food is lawful for them. So are chaste believing women, and chaste women from the people who were given the Scripture before you, provided you give them their dowries, and take them in marriage, not in adultery, nor as mistresses. But whoever rejects faith, his work will be in

5. THE TABLE (al-Ma'idah)

vain, and in the Hereafter he will be among the losers.

6. O you who believe! When you rise to pray, wash your faces and your hands and arms to the elbows, and wipe your heads, and your feet to the ankles. If you had intercourse, then purify yourselves. If you are ill, or travelling, or one of you returns from the toilet, or you had contact with women, and could not find water, then use some clean sand and wipe your faces and hands with it. Allah does not intend to burden you, but He intends to purify you, and to complete His blessing upon you, that you may be thankful.

7. And Remember Allah's blessings upon you, and His covenant which He covenanted with you; when you said, "We hear and we obey." And remain conscious of Allah, for Allah knows what the hearts contain.

8. O you who believe! Be upright to Allah, witnessing with justice; and let not the hatred of a certain people prevent you from acting justly. Adhere to justice, for that is nearer to piety; and fear Allah. Allah is informed of what you do.

9. Allah has promised those who believe and work righteousness: they will have forgiveness and a great reward.

10. As for those who disbelieve and reject Our revelations—these are the inmates of Hell.

11. O you who believe! Remember Allah's blessings upon you; when certain people intended to extend their hands against you, and He restrained their hands from you. So reverence Allah, and in Allah let the believers put their trust.

12. Allah received a pledge from the Children of Israel, and We raised among them twelve chiefs. Allah said, "I am with you; if you perform the prayer, and pay the alms, and believe in My messengers and support them, and lend Allah a loan of righteousness; I will remit your sins, and admit you into Gardens beneath which rivers flow. But whoever among you disbelieves afterwards has strayed from the right way."

13. Because of their breaking their pledge, We cursed them, and made their hearts hard. They twist the words out of their context, and they disregarded some of what they were reminded of. You will always witness deceit from them, except for a few of them. But pardon them, and overlook. Allah loves the doers of good.

14. And from those who say, "We are Christians," We received their pledge, but they neglected some of what they were reminded of. So We provoked enmity and hatred among them until the Day of Resurrection; Allah will then inform them of what they used to craft.

15. O People of the Book! Our Messenger has come to you, clarifying for you much of what you kept hidden of the Book, and overlooking much. A light from Allah has come to you, and a clear Book.

16. Allah guides with it whoever follows His approval to the ways of peace, and He brings them out of darkness into light, by His permission, and He guides them in a straight path.

17. They disbelieve those who say, "Allah is the Christ, the son of Mary." Say, "Who can prevent Allah, if He willed, from annihilating the Christ son of Mary, and his mother, and everyone on earth?" To Allah belongs the sovereignty of the heavens and the earth and what is between them. He creates whatever He wills, and Allah has power over everything.

18. The Jews and the Christians say, "We are the children of Allah, and His beloved." Say, "Why then does He punish you for your sins?" In fact, you are humans from among those He created. He forgives whom He wills, and He punishes whom He wills. To Allah belongs the dominion of the heavens and the earth and what lies between them, and to Him is the return.

19. O People of the Book! Our Messenger has come to you, making things clear to you—after a cessation of messengers—so that you cannot say, "No preacher has come to us, and no warner." In fact, a preacher has come to

5. THE TABLE (al-Ma'idah)

you, and a warner; and Allah is Capable of everything.

20. When Moses said to his people, "O my people, remember Allah's blessings upon you, when He placed prophets among you, and made you kings, and gave you what He never gave any other people."

21. "O my people, enter the Holy Land which Allah has assigned for you, and do not turn back, lest you return as losers."

22. They said, "O Moses, there are tyrannical people in it; we will not enter it until they leave it. If they leave it, we will be entering."

23. Two men of those who feared, but whom Allah had blessed, said, "Go at them by the gate; and when you have entered it, you will prevail. And put your trust in Allah, if you are believers."

24. They said, "O Moses, we will not enter it, ever, as long as they are in it. So go ahead, you and your Lord, and fight. We are staying right here."

25. He said, "My Lord! I have control only over myself and my brother, so separate between us and between the wicked people."

26. He said, "It is forbidden for them for forty years. They will wander aimlessly in the land. So do not grieve over the defiant people."

27. And relate to them the true story of Adam's two sons: when they offered an offering, and it was accepted from one of them, but it was not accepted from the other. He Said, "I will kill you." He Said, "Allah accepts only from the righteous."

28. "If you extend your hand to kill me, I will not extend my hand to kill you; for I fear Allah, Lord of the Worlds."

29. "I would rather you bear my sin and your sin, and you become among the inmates of the Fire. Such is the reward for the evildoers."

30. Then His soul prompted him to kill his brother, so he killed him, and became one of the losers.

31. Then Allah sent a raven digging the ground, to show him how to cover his brother's corpse. He said, "Woe to me! I was unable to be like this raven, and bury my brother's corpse." So he became full of regrets.

32. Because of that We ordained for the Children of Israel: that whoever kills a person—unless it is for murder or corruption on earth—it is as if he killed the whole of mankind; and whoever saves it, it is as if he saved the whole of mankind. Our messengers came to them with clarifications, but even after that, many of them continue to commit excesses in the land.

33. The punishment for those who fight Allah and His Messenger, and strive to spread corruption on earth, is that they be killed, or crucified, or have their hands and feet cut off on opposite sides, or be banished from the land. That is to disgrace them in this life; and in the Hereafter they will have a terrible punishment.

34. Except for those who repent before you apprehend them. So know that Allah is Forgiving and Merciful.

35. O you who believe! Be conscious of Allah, and seek the means of approach to Him, and strive in His cause, so that you may succeed.

36. As for those who disbelieve, even if they owned everything on earth, and the like of it with it, and they offered it to ransom themselves from the torment of the Day of Resurrection, it will not be accepted from them. For them is a painful punishment.

37. They will want to leave the Fire, but they will not leave it. For them is a lasting punishment.

38. As for the thief, whether male or female, cut their hands as a penalty for what they have reaped—a deterrent from Allah. Allah is Mighty and Wise.

39. But whoever repents after his crime, and reforms, Allah will accept his repentance. Allah is Forgiving and Merciful.

40. Do you not know that to Allah belongs the kingdom of the heavens and the earth? He

5. THE TABLE (al-Ma'idah)

punishes whom He wills, and He forgives whom He wills. And Allah is Capable of everything.

41. O Messenger! Do not let those who are quick to disbelief grieve you—from among those who say with their mouths, "We believe," but their hearts do not believe; and from among the Jews—listeners to lies, listeners to other people who did not come to you. They distort words from their places, and they say, "If you are given this, accept it; but if you are not given it, beware." Whomever Allah has willed to divert, you have nothing for him from Allah. Those are they whose hearts Allah does not intend to purify. For them is disgrace in this world, and for them is a great punishment in the Hereafter.

42. Listeners to falsehoods, eaters of illicit earnings. If they come to you, judge between them, or turn away from them. If you turn away from them, they will not harm you in the least. But if you judge, judge between them equitably. Allah loves the equitable.

43. But why do they come to you for judgment, when they have the Torah, in which is Allah's Law? Yet they turn away after that. These are not believers.

44. We have revealed the Torah, wherein is guidance and light. The submissive prophets ruled the Jews according to it, so did the rabbis and the scholars, as they were required to protect Allah's Book, and were witnesses to it. So do not fear people, but fear Me. And do not sell My revelations for a cheap price. Those who do not rule according to what Allah revealed are the unbelievers.

45. And We wrote for them in it: a life for a life, an eye for an eye, a nose for a nose, an ear for an ear, a tooth for a tooth, and an equal wound for a wound; but whoever forgoes it in charity, it will serve as atonement for him. Those who do not rule according to what Allah revealed are the evildoers.

46. In their footsteps, We sent Jesus son of Mary, fulfilling the Torah that preceded him; and We gave him the Gospel, wherein is guidance and light, and confirming the Torah that preceded him, and guidance and counsel for the righteous.

47. So let the people of the Gospel rule according to what Allah revealed in it. Those who do not rule according to what Allah revealed are the sinners.

48. And We revealed to you the Book, with truth, confirming the Scripture that preceded it, and superseding it. So judge between them according to what Allah revealed, and do not follow their desires if they differ from the truth that has come to you. For each of you We have assigned a law and a method. Had Allah willed, He could have made you a single nation, but He tests you through what He has given you. So compete in righteousness. To Allah is your return, all of you; then He will inform you of what you had disputed.

49. And judge between them according to what Allah revealed, and do not follow their desires. And beware of them, lest they lure you away from some of what Allah has revealed to you. But if they turn away, know that Allah intends to strike them with some of their sins. In fact, a great many people are corrupt.

50. Is it the laws of the time of ignorance that they desire? Who is better than Allah in judgment for people who are certain?

51. O you who believe! Do not take the Jews and the Christians as allies; some of them are allies of one another. Whoever of you allies himself with them is one of them. Allah does not guide the wrongdoing people.

52. You will see those in whose hearts is sickness racing towards them. They say, "We fear the wheel of fate may turn against us." But perhaps Allah will bring about victory, or some event of His making; thereupon they will regret what they concealed within themselves.

53. Those who believe will say, "Are these the ones who swore by Allah with their strongest oaths that they are with you?" Their works have failed, so they became losers.

5. THE TABLE (al-Ma'idah)

54. O you who believe! Whoever of you goes back on his religion—Allah will bring a people whom He loves and who love Him, kind towards the believers, stern with the disbelievers. They strive in the way of Allah, and do not fear the blame of the critic. That is the grace of Allah; He bestows it upon whomever He wills. Allah is Embracing and Knowing.

55. Your allies are Allah, and His Messenger, and those who believe—those who pray regularly, and give charity, and bow down.

56. Whoever allies himself with Allah, and His Messenger, and those who believe—surely the Party of Allah is the victorious.

57. O you who believe! Do not befriend those who take your religion in mockery and as a sport, be they from among those who were given the Scripture before you, or the disbelievers. And obey Allah, if you are believers.

58. When you call to the prayer, they take it as a joke and a trifle. That is because they are people who do not reason.

59. Say, "O People of the Scripture! Do you resent us only because we believe in Allah, and in what was revealed to us, and in what was revealed previously; and most of you are sinners?"

60. Say, "Shall I inform you of worse than that for retribution from Allah? He whom Allah has cursed, and with whom He became angry; and He turned some of them into apes, and swine, and idol worshipers. These are in a worse position, and further away from the right way."

61. When they come to you, they say, "We believe," though they have entered with disbelief, and they have departed with it. But Allah is well aware of what they hide.

62. You see many of them competing with one another in sin and hostility, and their consuming of what is illicit. What they have been doing is truly evil.

63. Why do the rabbis and the priests not prevent them from speaking sinfully and from consuming forbidden wealth? Evil is what they have been doing.

64. The Jews say, "Allah's hand is tied." It is their hands that are tied, and they are cursed for what they say. In fact, His hands are outstretched; He gives as He wills. Certainly, what was revealed to your from your Lord will increase many of them in defiance and blasphemy. And We placed between them enmity and hatred, until the Day of Resurrection. Whenever they kindle the fire of war, Allah extinguishes it. And they strive to spread corruption on earth. Allah does not love the corrupters.

65. Had the People of the Scripture believed and been righteous, We would have remitted their sins, and admitted them into the Gardens of Bliss.

66. Had they observed the Torah, and the Gospel, and what was revealed to them from their Lord, they would have consumed amply from above them, and from beneath their feet. Among them is a moderate community, but evil is what many of them are doing.

67. O Messenger, convey what was revealed to you from your Lord. But if you do not, then you would not have delivered His message. And Allah will protect you from the people. Allah does not guide the disbelieving people.

68. Say, "O People of the Scripture! You have no basis until you uphold the Torah, and the Gospel, and what is revealed to you from your Lord." But what is revealed to you from your Lord will increase many of them in rebellion and disbelief, so do not be sorry for the disbelieving people.

69. Those who believe, and the Jews, and the Sabians, and the Christians—whoever believes in Allah and the Last Day, and does what is right—they have nothing to fear, nor shall they grieve.

70. We made a covenant with the Children of Israel, and We sent to them messengers. Whenever a messenger came to them with what their souls did not desire, some of them they accused of lying, and others they put to death.

5. THE TABLE (al-Ma'idah)

71. They assumed there would be no punishment, so they turned blind and deaf. Then Allah redeemed them, but then again many of them turned blind and deaf. But Allah is Seeing of what they do.

72. They disbelieve those who say, "Allah is the Messiah the son of Mary." But the Messiah himself said, "O Children of Israel, worship Allah, my Lord and your Lord. Whoever associates others with Allah, Allah has forbidden him Paradise, and his dwelling is the Fire. The wrongdoers have no saviors."

73. They disbelieve those who say, "Allah is the third of three." But there is no deity except the One God. If they do not refrain from what they say, a painful torment will befall those among them who disbelieve.

74. Will they not repent to Allah and ask His forgiveness? Allah is Forgiving and Merciful.

75. The Messiah son of Mary was only a messenger, before whom other Messengers had passed away, and his mother was a woman of truth. They both used to eat food. Note how We make clear the revelations to them; then note how deluded they are.

76. Say, "Do you worship, besides Allah, what has no power to harm or benefit you?" But Allah: He is the Hearer, the Knower.

77. Say, "O People of the Scripture! Do not exaggerate in your religion beyond the truth; and do not follow the opinions of people who went astray before, and misled many, and themselves strayed off the balanced way."

78. Cursed were those who disbelieved from among the Children of Israel by the tongue of David and Jesus son of Mary. That is because they rebelled and used to transgress.

79. They used not to prevent one another from the wrongs they used to commit. Evil is what they used to do.

80. You will see many of them befriending those who disbelieve. Terrible is what their souls prompts them to do. The wrath of Allah fell upon them, and in the torment they will remain.

81. Had they believed in Allah and the Prophet, and in what was revealed to him, they would not have befriended them. But many of them are immoral.

82. You will find that the people most hostile towards the believers are the Jews and the polytheists. And you will find that the nearest in affection towards the believers are those who say, "We are Christians." That is because among them are priests and monks, and they are not arrogant.

83. And when they hear what was revealed to the Messenger, you see their eyes overflowing with tears, as they recognize the truth in it. They say, "Our Lord, we have believed, so count us among the witnesses."

84. "And why should we not believe in Allah, and in the truth that has come to us, and hope that our Lord will include us among the righteous people?"

85. Allah will reward them for what they say—Gardens beneath which rivers flow, where they will stay forever. Such is the reward of the righteous.

86. But as for those who disbelieve and deny Our signs—these are the inmates of the Fire.

87. O you who believe! Do not prohibit the good things Allah has permitted for you, and do not commit aggression. Allah does not love the aggressors.

88. And eat of the lawful and good things Allah has provided for you; and be conscious of Allah, in whom you are believers.

89. Allah does not hold you accountable for your unintended oaths, but He holds you accountable for your binding oaths. The atonement for it is by feeding ten needy people from the average of what you feed your families, or by clothing them, or by freeing a slave. Anyone who lacks the means shall fast for three days. That is the atonement for breaking your oaths when you have sworn them. So keep your oaths. Thus Allah makes clear His Revelations to you, that you may be grateful.

5. THE TABLE (al-Ma'idah)

90. O you who believe! Intoxicants, gambling, idolatry, and divination are abominations of Satan's doing. Avoid them, so that you may prosper.

91. Satan wants to provoke strife and hatred among you through intoxicants and gambling, and to prevent you from the remembrance of Allah, and from prayer. Will you not desist?

92. Obey Allah and obey the Messenger, and be cautious. If you turn away—know that the duty of Our Messenger is clear communication.

93. Those who believe and do righteous deeds will not be blamed for what they may have eaten, provided they obey, and believe, and do good deeds, then maintain piety and faith, then remain righteous and charitable. Allah loves the charitable.

94. O you who believe! Allah will test you with something of the game your hands and spears obtain, that Allah may know who fears Him at heart. Whoever commits aggression after that will have a painful punishment.

95. O you who believe! do not kill game while you are in pilgrim sanctity. Whoever of you kills any intentionally, its penalty shall be a domestic animal comparable to what he killed, as determined by two honest persons among you—an offering delivered to the Kaabah. Or he may atone by feeding the needy, or its equivalent in fasting, so that he may taste the consequences of his conduct. Allah forgives what is past. But whoever repeats, Allah will take revenge on him. Allah is Almighty, Avenger.

96. Permitted for you is the catch of sea, and its food—as sustenance for you and for travelers. But forbidden for you is the game of land while you are in pilgrim sanctity. And fear Allah, to whom you will be gathered.

97. Allah has appointed the Kaabah, the Sacred House, a sanctuary for the people, and the Sacred Month, and the offerings, and the garlanded. That you may know that Allah knows everything in the heavens and the earth, and that Allah is Cognizant of all things.

98. Know that Allah is severe in retribution, and that Allah is Forgiving and Merciful.

99. The Messenger's sole duty is to convey. Allah knows what you reveal and what you conceal.

100. Say: "The bad and the good are not equal, even though the abundance of the bad may impress you. So be conscious of Allah, O you who possess intelligence, that you may succeed."

101. O you who believe! Do not ask about things that would trouble you if disclosed to you. But if you were to ask about them while the Quran is being revealed, they will become obvious to you. Allah forgives that. Allah is Forgiving and Clement.

102. A people before you asked about them, but then came to reject them.

103. Allah did not institute the superstitions of Bahirah, Saibah, Wasilah, or of Hami; but those who disbelieve fabricate lies about Allah—most of them do not understand.

104. And when it is said to them, "Come to what Allah has revealed, and to the Messenger," they say, "Sufficient for us is what we found our forefathers upon." Even if their forefathers knew nothing, and were not guided?

105. O you who believe! You are responsible for your own souls. He who has strayed cannot harm you if you are guided. To Allah is you return, all of you, and He will inform you of what you used to do.

106. O you who believe! When death approaches one of you, let two reliable persons from among you act as witnesses to the making of a bequest, or two persons from another people if you are travelling in the land and the event of death approaches you. Engage them after the prayer. If you have doubts, let them swear by Allah: "We will not sell our testimony for any price, even if he was a near relative, and we will not conceal Allah's testimony, for then we would be sinners."

107. If it is discovered that they are guilty of perjury: let two others take their place, two

from among those responsible for the claim, and have them swear by Allah, "Our testimony is more truthful than their testimony, and we will not be biased, for then we would be wrongdoers."

108. That makes it more likely that they will give true testimony, fearing that their oaths might be contradicted by subsequent oaths. So fear Allah, and listen. Allah does not guide the disobedient people.

109. On the Day when Allah will gather the messengers, then say, "What response were you given?" They will say, "We have no knowledge; it is you who are the Knower of the unseen."

110. When Allah will say, "O Jesus son of Mary, recall My favor upon you and upon your mother, how I supported you with the Holy Spirit. You spoke to the people from the crib, and in maturity. How I taught you the Scripture and wisdom, and the Torah and the Gospel. And recall that you molded from clay the shape of a bird, by My leave, and then you breathed into it, and it became a bird, by My leave. And you healed the blind and the leprous, by My leave; and you revived the dead, by My leave. And recall that I restrained the Children of Israel from you when you brought them the clear miracles. But those who disbelieved among them said, 'This is nothing but obvious sorcery.'"

111. "And when I inspired the disciples: 'Believe in Me and in My Messenger.' They said, 'We have believed, so bear witness that We have submitted.'"

112. "And when the disciples said, 'O Jesus son of Mary, is your Lord able to bring down for us a feast from heaven?' He said, 'Fear Allah, if you are believers.'"

113. They said, "We wish to eat from it, so that our hearts may be reassured, and know that you have told us the truth, and be among those who witness it."

114. Jesus son of Mary said, "O Allah, our Lord, send down for us a table from heaven, to be a festival for us, for the first of us and the last of us, and a sign from You; and provide for us; You are the Best of providers."

115. Allah said, "I will send it down to you. But whoever among you disbelieves thereafter, I will punish him with a punishment the like of which I never punish any other being."

116. And Allah will say, "O Jesus son of Mary, did you say to the people, 'Take me and my mother as gods rather than Allah?'" He will say, "Glory be to You! It is not for me to say what I have no right to. Had I said it, You would have known it. You know what is in my soul, and I do not know what is in your soul. You are the Knower of the hidden.

117. I only told them what You commanded me: that you shall worship Allah, my Lord and your Lord. And I was a witness over them while I was among them; but when You took me to Yourself, you became the Watcher over them—You are Witness over everything.

118. If You punish them, they are Your servants; but if You forgive them, You are the Mighty and Wise."

119. Allah will say, "This is a Day when the truthful will benefit from their truthfulness." They will have Gardens beneath which rivers flow, wherein they will remain forever. Allah is pleased with them, and they are pleased with Him. That is the great attainment.

120. To Allah belongs the sovereignty of the heavens and the earth and what lies in them, and He has power over everything.

6. LIVESTOCK
(al-An'am)

*In the name of Allah,
the Gracious, the Merciful*

1. Praise be to Allah, Who created the heavens and the earth, and made the darkness and the light. Yet those who disbelieve ascribe equals to their Lord.

2. It is He who created you from clay, then decided a term—a term determined by him. Yet you doubt.

6. LIVESTOCK (al-An'am)

3. He is Allah in the heavens and the earth. He knows what you keep secret and what you make public; and He knows what you earn.

4. Not one of their Lord's signs comes to them, but they turn away from it.

5. They denied the truth when it has come to them; but soon will reach them the news of what they used to ridicule.

6. Have they not considered how many generations We destroyed before them? We had established them on earth more firmly than We established you, and We sent the clouds pouring down abundant rain on them, and We made rivers flow beneath them. But We destroyed them for their sins, and established other civilizations after them.

7. Had We sent down upon you a book on paper, and they had touched it with their hands, those who disbelieve would have said, "This is nothing but plain magic."

8. And they say, "Why was an angel not sent down to him." Had We sent down an angel, the matter would have been settled, and they would not have been reprieved.

9. Had We made him an angel, We would have made him a man, and confused them when they are already confused.

10. Messengers before you were ridiculed, but those who mocked them became besieged by what they ridiculed.

11. Say, "Travel the earth and observe the final fate of the deniers."

12. Say, "To whom belongs what is in the heavens and the earth?" Say, "To Allah." He has inscribed for Himself mercy. He will gather you to the Day of Resurrection, in which there is no doubt. Those who lost their souls do not believe.

13. To Him belongs whatever rests in the night and the day. He is the Hearing, the Knowing.

14. Say, "Shall I take for myself a protector other than Allah, Originator of the heavens and the earth, and He feeds and is not fed?" Say, "I am instructed to be the first of those who submit." And do not be among the idolaters.

15. Say, "I fear, should I defy my Lord, the punishment of a tremendous Day."

16. Whoever is spared on that Day—He had mercy on him. That is the clear victory.

17. If Allah touches you with adversity, none can remove it except He. And if He touches you with good—He is Capable of everything.

18. He is the Supreme over His servants. He is the Wise, the Expert.

19. Say, "What thing is more solemn in testimony?" Say, "Allah is Witness between you and me. This Quran was revealed to me, that I may warn you with it, and whomever it may reach. Do you indeed testify that there are other gods with Allah?" Say, "I myself do not testify." Say, "He is but One God, and I am innocent of your idolatry."

20. Those to whom We have given the Book recognize it as they recognize their own children; but those who have lost their souls do not believe.

21. Who does greater wrong than someone who fabricates lies against Allah, or denies His revelations? The wrongdoers will not succeed.

22. On the Day when We gather them all together, then say to the idolaters, "Where are your idols, those you used to claim?"

23. Then their only argument will be to say, "By Allah, our Lord, we were not idolaters."

24. Look how they lied to themselves. And what they invented deserted them.

25. Among them are those who listen to you; but We place covers over their hearts, to prevent them from understanding it, and heaviness in their ears. Even if they see every sign, they will not believe in it. Until, when they come to you, to argue with you, those who disbelieve will say, "These are nothing but myths of the ancients."

26. They keep others from it, and avoid it themselves; but they ruin only their own souls, and they do not realize.

6. LIVESTOCK (al-An'am)

27. If only you could see, when they are made to stand before the Fire; they will say, "If only we could be sent back, and not reject the revelations of our Lord, and be among the faithful."

28. What they used to conceal before will become clear to them. And even if they were sent back, they would revert to what they were forbidden. They are liars.

29. And they say, "There is nothing but our life in this world, and we will not be resurrected."

30. If only you could see, when they are stationed before their Lord. He will say, "Is this not real?" They will say, "Yes indeed, by our Lord." He will say, "Then taste the torment for having disbelieved."

31. Losers are those who deny the encounter with Allah. Then, when the Hour comes upon them suddenly, they will say, "Alas for us, how we have neglected it." And they will carry their burdens on their backs—evil is what they carry.

32. The life of this world is nothing but game and distraction, but the Home of the Hereafter is better for those who are righteous. Do you not understand?

33. We know that what they say grieves you. It is not you they reject, but it is Allah's revelations that the wicked deny.

34. Other messengers before you were rejected, but they endured rejection and persecution until Our help came to them. There can be no change to Allah's words. News of the Messengers has already reached you.

35. If you find their rejection hard to bear, then if you can, seek a tunnel into the earth, or a stairway into the heaven, and bring them a sign. Had Allah willed, He could have gathered them to guidance. So do not be of the ignorant.

36. Only those who listen will respond. As for the dead, Allah will resurrect them; then to Him they will be returned.

37. And they say, "If only a sign could come down to him from his Lord." Say, "Allah is Able to send down a sign, but most of them do not know."

38. There is no animal on land, nor a bird flying with its wings, but are communities like you. We neglected nothing in the Scripture. Then to their Lord they will be gathered.

39. Those who reject Our revelations are deaf and dumb, in total darkness. Whomever Allah wills, He leaves astray; and whomever He wills, He sets on a straight path.

40. Say, "Have you considered? if Allah's punishment came upon you, or the Hour overtook you, would you call upon any other than Allah, if you are sincere?"

41. In fact, it is Him you will call upon; and if He wills, he will remove what you called Him for, and you will forget what you idolized.

42. We sent messengers to communities before you, and We afflicted them with suffering and hardship, that they may humble themselves.

43. If only, when Our calamity came upon them, they humbled themselves. But their hearts hardened, and Satan made their deeds appear good to them.

44. Then, when they disregarded what they were reminded of, We opened for them the gates of all things. Until, when they delighted in what they were given, We seized them suddenly; and at once, they were in despair.

45. Thus the last remnant of the people who did wrong was cut off. And praise be to Allah, Lord of the Worlds.

46. Say, "Have you considered? If Allah took away your hearing and your sight, and set a seal on your hearts, what god other than Allah would restore them to you?" Note how We explain the revelations in various ways, yet they still turn away.

47. Say, "Have you considered? if Allah's punishment descended on you suddenly or gradually, would any be destroyed except the wrongdoing people?"

48. We sent the messengers only as bearers of good news and as warners. Those who believe

and reform have nothing to fear, nor shall they grieve.

49. But as for those who reject Our revelations, torment will afflict them because of their defiance.

50. Say, "I do not say to you that I possess the treasuries of Allah, nor do I know the future, nor do I say to you that I am an angel. I only follow what is inspired to me." Say, "Are the blind and the seeing alike? Do you not think?"

51. And warn with it those who fear to be gathered before their Lord—they have no protector or intercessor apart from him—perhaps they will grow in piety.

52. And do not drive away those who call upon their Lord, morning and evening, seeking His attention. You are not accountable for them in any way, nor are they accountable for you in any way. If you drive them away, you would be one of the unjust.

53. Thus We try some of them by means of others, that they may say, "Are these the ones whom Allah has favored from among us?" Is Allah not aware of the appreciative?

54. When those who believe in Our revelations come to you, say, "Peace be upon you, your Lord has prescribed mercy for Himself. Whoever among you does wrong out of ignorance, and then repents afterwards and reforms—He is Forgiving and Merciful."

55. Thus We explain the revelations, and expose the path of the unrighteous.

56. Say, "I am forbidden from worshiping those you pray to besides Allah." Say, "I will not follow your desires; else I would be lost and not be of those guided."

57. Say, "I stand on clear evidence from my Lord, and you have rejected Him. I do not possess what you seek me to hasten; the decision belongs solely to Allah. He states the truth, and He is the Best of Judges."

58. Say, "If I possessed what you seek me to hasten, the matter between you and me would have been settled. Allah is well aware of the unjust."

59. With Him are the keys of the unseen; none knows them except He. And He knows everything on land and in the sea. Not a leaf falls but He knows it; and there is not a single grain in the darkness of earth, nor is there anything wet or dry, but is in a clear record.

60. It is He Who takes you by night, and He knows what you earn by day. Then He raises you up in it, until a fixed term is fulfilled. Then to Him is your return, then He will inform you of what you used to do.

61. He is the Conqueror over His servants, and He sends guardians over you, until, when death overtakes one of you, Our envoys take him away, and they never fail.

62. Then they are brought back to Allah, their True Master. Unquestionably, His is the judgment, and He is the Swiftest of reckoners.

63. Say, "Who delivers you from the darkness of land and sea?" You call upon Him humbly and inwardly: "If He delivers us from this, We will surely be among the thankful."

64. Say, "It is Allah who delivers you from it, and from every disaster. Yet then you associate others with Him."

65. Say, "He is Able to send upon you an affliction, from above you, or from under your feet. Or He can divide you into factions, and make you taste the violence of one another. Note how We explain the revelations, so that they may understand."

66. But your people rejected it, though it is the truth. Say, "I am not responsible for you."

67. For every happening is a finality, and you will surely know.

68. When you encounter those who gossip about Our revelations, turn away from them, until they engage in another topic. But should Satan make you forget, do not sit after the recollection with the wicked people.

6. LIVESTOCK (al-An'am)

69. The righteous are in no way accountable for them; it is only a reminder, that they may be careful.

70. So leave alone those who take their religion for play and pastime, and whom the worldly life has deceived. But remind with it, lest a soul becomes damned on account of what it has earned. It has no helper or intercessor besides Allah. Even if it offers every equivalent, none will be accepted from it. These are the ones who are delivered to perdition by their actions. They will have a drink of scalding water, and a painful punishment, because they used to disbelieve.

71. Say, "Shall we invoke besides Allah something that can neither benefit us nor harm us, and turn back on our heels after Allah has guided us; like someone seduced by the devils and confused on earth, who has friends calling him to guidance: 'Come to us'?" Say, "The guidance of Allah is the guidance, and we are commanded to surrender to the Lord of the Universe."

72. "And to perform the prayers, and to revere Him; it is to Him that you will be gathered."

73. It is He who created the heavens and the earth in truth. On the Day when He says: "Be," it will be. His saying is the truth, and His is the sovereignty on the Day when the trumpet is blown. The Knower of secrets and declarations. He is the Wise, the Expert.

74. Abraham said to his father Azar, "Do you take idols for gods? I see that you and your people are in evident error."

75. Thus We showed Abraham the empire of the heavens and the earth, that he might be one of those with certainty.

76. When the night fell over him, he saw a planet. He said, "This is my lord." But when it set, he said, "I do not love those that set."

77. Then, when he saw the moon rising, he said, "This is my lord." But when it set, he said, "If my Lord does not guide me, I will be one of the erring people."

78. Then, when he saw the sun rising, he said, "This is my lord, this is bigger." But when it set, he said, "O my people, I am innocent of your idolatry."

79. I have directed my attention towards Him Who created the heavens and the earth—a monotheist—and I am not of the idolaters."

80. And his people argued with him. He said, "Do you argue with me about Allah, when He has guided me? I do not fear what you associate with Him, unless my Lord wills it. My Lord comprehends all things in knowledge. Will you not reconsider?

81. And why should I fear those you associate with Him, and you do not fear associating others with Allah for which He sent down to you no authority? Which side is more entitled to security, if you are aware?"

82. Those who believe, and do not obscure their faith with wrongdoing—those will have security, and they are guided.

83. That was Our argument which We gave to Abraham against his people. We elevate by degrees whomever We will. Your Lord is Wise and Informed.

84. And We gave him Isaac and Jacob—each of them We guided. And We guided Noah previously; and from his descendants David, and Solomon, and Job, and Joseph, and Moses, and Aaron. Thus We reward the righteous.

85. And Zechariah, and John, and Jesus, and Elias—every one of them was of the upright.

86. And Ishmael, and Elijah, and Jonah, and Lot—We favored each one of them over all other people.

87. And of their ancestors, and their descendants, and their siblings—We chose them, and guided them to a straight path.

88. Such is Allah's guidance. He guides with it whomever He wills of His servants. Had they associated, their deeds would have gone in vain.

89. Those are they to whom We gave the Book, and wisdom, and prophethood. If these reject them, We have entrusted them to others who do not reject them.

6. LIVESTOCK (al-An'am)

90. Those are they whom Allah has guided, so follow their guidance. Say, "I ask of you no compensation for it; it is just a reminder for all mankind."

91. They do not value Allah as He should be valued, when they say, "Allah did not reveal anything to any human being." Say, "Who revealed the Scripture which Moses brought—a light and guidance for humanity? You put it on scrolls, displaying them, yet concealing much. And you were taught what you did not know—neither you, nor your ancestors. Say, "Allah;" then leave them toying away in their speculation.

92. This too is a Scripture that We revealed—blessed—verifying what preceded it, that you may warn the Mother of Cities and all around it. Those who believe in the Hereafter believe in it, and are dedicated to their prayers.

93. Who does greater wrong than someone who invents falsehood against Allah, or says, "It was revealed to me," when nothing was revealed to him, or says, "I will reveal the like of what Allah revealed"? If only you could see the wrongdoers in the floods of death, as the angels with arms outstretched: "Give up your souls. Today you are being repaid with the torment of shame for having said about Allah other than the truth, and for being too proud to accept His revelations."

94. "You have come to Us individually, just as We created you the first time, leaving behind you everything We gave you. We do not see with you your intercessors—those you claimed were your partners. The link between you is cut, and what you had asserted has failed you."

95. It is Allah Who splits the grain and the seed. He brings the living from the dead, and He brings the dead from the living. Such is Allah. So how could you deviate?

96. It is He Who breaks the dawn. And He made the night for rest, and the sun and the moon for calculation. Such is the disposition of the Almighty, the All-Knowing.

97. And it is He Who created the stars for you, that you may be guided by them in the darkness of land and sea. We thus explain the revelations for people who know.

98. And it is He who produced you from a single person, then a repository, then a depository. We have detailed the revelations for people who understand.

99. And it is He who sends down water from the sky. With it We produce vegetation of all kinds, from which We bring greenery, from which We produce grains in clusters. And palm-trees with hanging clusters, and vineyards, and olives, and pomegranates—similar and dissimilar. Watch their fruits as they grow and ripen. Surely in this are signs for people who believe.

100. Yet they attributed to Allah partners—the sprites—although He created them. And they invented for Him sons and daughters, without any knowledge. Glory be to Him. He is exalted, beyond what they describe.

101. Originator of the heavens and the earth—how can He have a son when He never had a companion? He created all things, and He has knowledge of all things.

102. Such is Allah, your Lord. There is no god except He, the Creator of all things; so worship Him. He is responsible for everything.

103. No vision can grasp Him, but His grasp is over all vision. He is the Subtle, the Expert.

104. "Insights have come to you from your Lord. Whoever sees, it is to the benefit of his soul; and whoever remains blind, it is to its detriment. I am not a guardian over you."

105. We thus diversify the revelations, lest they say, "You have studied," and to clarify them for people who know.

106. Follow what was revealed to you from your Lord. There is no god but He. And turn away from the polytheists.

107. Had Allah willed, they would not have practiced idolatry. We did not appoint you as a guardian over them, and you are not a manager over them.

6. LIVESTOCK (al-An'am)

108. Do not insult those they call upon besides Allah, lest they insult Allah out of hostility and ignorance. We made attractive to every community their deeds. Then to their Lord is their return, and He will inform them of what they used to do.

109. They swear by Allah, with their most solemn oaths, that if a miracle were to come to them, they would believe in it. Say, "The miracles are only with Allah." But how do you know? Even if it did come, they still would not believe.

110. And We turn away their hearts and their visions, as they refused to believe in it the first time, and We leave them blundering in their rebellion.

111. Even if We sent down the angels to them, and the dead spoke to them, and We gathered all things before them, they still would not believe, unless Allah wills; but most of them are ignorant.

112. Likewise, We have assigned for every prophet an enemy—human and jinn devils—inspiring one another with fancy words in order to deceive. But had your Lord willed, they would not have done it. So leave them to their fabrications.

113. So that the hearts of those who do not believe in the Hereafter may incline to it, and be content with it, and that they may perpetrate whatever they perpetrate.

114. "Shall I seek a judge other than Allah, when He is the One who revealed to you the Book, explained in detail?" Those to whom We gave the Book know that it is the truth revealed from your Lord. So do not be of those who doubt.

115. The Word of your Lord has been completed, in truth and justice. There is no changing to His words. He is the Hearer, the Knower.

116. If you were to obey most of those on earth, they would divert you from Allah's path. They follow nothing but assumptions, and they only conjecture.

117. Your Lord knows best who strays from His path, and He knows best the guided ones.

118. So eat of that over which the Name of Allah was pronounced, if you indeed believe in His revelations.

119. And why should you not eat of that over which the Name of Allah is pronounced, when He has detailed for you what is prohibited for you, unless you are compelled by necessity? Many lead astray with their opinions, through lack of knowledge. Your Lord knows best the transgressors.

120. So abandon sin, outward and inward. Those who commit sins will be repaid for what they used to perpetrate.

121. And do not eat from that over which the Name of Allah was not pronounced, for it is abomination. The devils inspire their followers to argue with you; but if you obey them, you would be polytheists.

122. Is he who was dead, then We gave him life, and made for him a light by which he walks among the people, like he who is in total darkness, and cannot get out of it? Thus the doings of disbelievers are made to appear good to them.

123. And thus We set up in every city its leading wicked sinners, to conspire in it, but they conspire only against themselves, and they do not realize it.

124. When a sign comes to them, they say, "We will not believe unless we are given the like of what was given to Allah's messengers." Allah knows best where to place His message. Humiliation from Allah and severe torment will afflict the criminals for their scheming.

125. Whomever Allah desires to guide, He spreads open his heart to Islam; and whomever He desires to misguide, He makes his heart narrow, constricted, as though he were climbing up the sky. Allah thus lays defilement upon those who do not believe.

126. This is the straight path of your Lord. We have explained the revelations in detail for people who recollect.

6. LIVESTOCK (al-An'am)

127. For them is the Home of Peace with their Lord, and He is their Master—because of what they used to do.

128. On the Day when He gathers them all together: "O assembly of jinn, you have exploited multitudes of humans." Their adherents among mankind will say, "Our Lord, we have profited from one another, but we have reached the term that you have assigned for us." He will say, "The Fire is your dwelling, wherein you will remain, except as Allah wills. Your Lord is Wise and Informed.

129. Thus We make some of the wrongdoers befriend one another, because of what they used to do.

130. "O assembly of jinn and humans, did there not come to you messengers from among you, relating to you My revelations, and warning you of the meeting of this Day of yours?" They will say, "We testify against ourselves." The life of the world seduced them. They will testify against themselves that they were disbelievers.

131. That is because your Lord would not destroy towns for injustice while their inhabitants are unaware.

132. They all have ranks according to what they did; and your Lord is not unaware of what they do.

133. Your Lord is the Rich Beyond Need, the Possessor of Mercy. If He wills, He can do away with you, and substitute whomever He wills in your place, just as He produced you from the descendants of another people.

134. What you are promised is coming, and you cannot thwart it.

135. Say, "O my people! Work according to your ability, and so will I." You will come to know to whom will belong the sequel of the abode." The wrongdoers will not prevail.

136. And they set aside for Allah a share of the crops and the livestock He created, and they say, "This is for Allah," according to their claim, "and this is for our idols." But the share of their idols does not reach Allah, yet the share of Allah reaches their idols. Evil is their judgment.

137. Likewise, their idols entice many idolaters to kill their children, in order to lead them to their ruin, and confuse them in their religion. Had Allah willed, they would not have done it; so leave them to their fraud.

138. And they say, "These animals and crops are restricted; none may eat them except those we permit," by their claims, and animals whose backs are forbidden, and animals over which they do not pronounce the name of Allah—fabricating lies against Him. He will repay them for what they used to invent.

139. And they say, "What lies in the wombs of these animals is exclusively for our males, and prohibited to our wives." But if it is stillborn, they can share in it. He will surely punish them for their allegations. He is Wise and Knowing.

140. Lost are those who kill their children foolishly, with no basis in knowledge, and forbid what Allah has provided for them—innovations about Allah. They have gone astray. They are not guided.

141. It is He who produces gardens, both cultivated and wild, and date-palms, and crops of diverse tastes, and olives and pomegranates, similar and dissimilar. Eat of its fruit when it yields, and give its due on the day of its harvest, and do not waste. He does not love the wasteful.

142. Among the livestock are some for transportation, and some for clothing. Eat of what Allah has provided for you, and do not follow the footsteps of Satan. He is to you an outright enemy.

143. Eight pairs: two of the sheep, and two of the goats. Say, "Did He forbid the two males, or the two females, or what the wombs of the two females contain? Inform me with knowledge, if you are truthful."

144. And two of the camels, and two of the cattle. Say, "Did He forbid the two males, or the two females, or what the wombs of the two

6. LIVESTOCK (al-An'am)

females contain? Were you present when Allah enjoined this upon you?" Who does greater wrong than he who invents lies and attributes them to Allah, in order to mislead people without knowledge? Allah does not guide the wicked people.

145. Say, "In what was revealed to me, I find nothing forbidden to a consumer who eats it, except carrion, or spilled blood, or the flesh of swine—because it is impure—or a sinful offering dedicated to other than Allah. But if someone is compelled by necessity, without being deliberate or malicious—your Lord is Forgiving and Merciful.

146. For the Jews We forbade everything with claws. As of cattle and sheep: We forbade them their fat, except what adheres to their backs, or the entrails, or what is mixed with bone. This is how We penalized them for their inequity. We are indeed truthful.

147. If they accuse you of lying, say, "Your Lord is Possessor of infinite mercy, but His wrath cannot be averted from the guilty people."

148. The polytheists will say, "Had Allah willed, we would not have practiced idolatry, nor would have our forefathers, nor would we have prohibited anything." Likewise those before them lied, until they tasted Our might. Say, "Do you have any knowledge that you can produce for us? You follow nothing but conjecture, and you only guess."

149. Say, "To Allah belongs the conclusive argument. Had He willed, He would have guided you all."

150. Say, "Produce your witnesses who would testify that Allah has prohibited this." If they testify, do not testify with them. And do not follow the whims of those who deny Our revelation, and those who do not believe in the Hereafter, and those who equate others with their Lord.

151. Say, "Come, let me tell you what your Lord has forbidden you: that you associate nothing with Him; that you honor your parents; that you do not kill your children because of poverty—We provide for you and for them; that you do not come near indecencies, whether outward or inward; and that you do not kill the soul which Allah has sanctified—except in the course of justice. All this He has enjoined upon you, so that you may understand."

152. And do not come near the property of the orphan, except with the best intentions, until he reaches maturity. And give full weight and full measure, equitably. We do not burden any soul beyond its capacity. And when you speak, be fair, even if it concerns a close relative. And fulfill your covenant with Allah. All this He has enjoined upon you, so that you may take heed.

153. This is My path, straight, so follow it. And do not follow the other paths, lest they divert you from His path. All this He has enjoined upon you, that you may refrain from wrongdoing.

154. Then We gave Moses the Scripture, perfect for the righteous, and explaining everything clearly, and a beacon, and mercy, that they may believe in the encounter with their Lord.

155. This too is a blessed Scripture that We revealed; so follow it, and be righteous, that you may receive mercy.

156. Lest you say, "The Scripture was revealed to two parties before us, and we were unaware of their teachings."

157. Or lest you say, "Had the Scripture been revealed to us, we would have been better guided than they." Clarification has come to you from your Lord, and guidance, and mercy. Who then does greater wrong than he who gives the lie to Allah's messages, and turns away from them? We will repay those who turn away from Our messages with the worst kind of punishment, because of their turning away.

158. Are they waiting for anything but for the angels to come to them, or for your Lord to arrive, or for some of your Lord's signs to come? On the Day when some of your Lord's signs come, no soul will benefit from its faith unless it had believed previously, or had

earned goodness through its faith. Say, "Wait, we too are waiting."

159. As for those who divided their religion and became sects—you have nothing to do with them. Their case rests with Allah; then He will inform them of what they used to do.

160. Whoever comes up with a good deed will have ten times its like; and whoever comes up with an evil deed will be repaid only with its equivalent—they will not be wronged.

161. Say, "My Lord has guided me to a straight path, an upright religion, the creed of Abraham the Monotheist, who was not a polytheist."

162. Say, "My prayer and my worship, and my life and my death, are devoted to Allah, the Lord of the Worlds.

163. No associate has He. Thus I am commanded, and I am the first of those who submit."

164. Say, "Am I to seek a Lord other than Allah, when He is the Lord of all things?" No soul gets except what it is due, and no soul bears the burdens of another. Then to your Lord is your return, then He will inform you regarding your disputes.

165. It is He who made you successors on the earth, and raised some of you in ranks over others, in order to test you through what He has given you. Your Lord is Quick in retribution, and He is Forgiving and Merciful.

7. THE ELEVATIONS (al-A'raf)

*In the name of Allah,
the Gracious, the Merciful*

1. Alif, Lam, Meem, Saad.

2. A Scripture was revealed to you, so let there be no anxiety in your heart because of it. You are to warn with it—and a reminder for the believers.

3. Follow what is revealed to you from your Lord, and do not follow other masters beside Him. Little you recollect.

4. How many a town have We destroyed? Our might came upon them by night, or while they were napping.

5. When Our might came upon them, their only cry was, "We were indeed wrongdoers."

6. We will question those to whom messengers were sent, and We will question the messengers.

7. We will narrate to them with knowledge, for We were never absent.

8. The scales on that Day will be just. Those whose weights are heavy—it is they who are the successful.

9. But as for those whose weights are light—it is they who have lost their souls, because they used to mistreat Our revelations.

10. We have established you firmly on earth, and made for you in it livelihood—but rarely do you give thanks.

11. We created you, then We shaped you, then We said to the angels, "Bow down before Adam;" so they bowed down, except for Satan; he was not of those who bowed down.

12. He said, "What prevented you from bowing down when I have commanded you?" He said, "I am better than he; You created me from fire, and You created him from mud."

13. He said, "Get down from it! It is not for you to act arrogantly in it. Get out! You are one of the lowly!"

14. He said, "Give me respite, until the Day they are resurrected."

15. He said, "You are of those given respite."

16. He said, "Because you have lured me, I will waylay them on Your straight path.

17. Then I will come at them from before them, and from behind them, and from their right, and from their left; and you will not find most of them appreciative."

18. He said, "Get out of it, despised and vanquished. Whoever among them follows you—I will fill up Hell with you all.

19. And you, Adam, inhabit the Garden, you and your wife, and eat whatever you wish; but

7. THE ELEVATIONS (al-A'raf)

do not approach this tree, lest you become sinners."

20. But Satan whispered to them, to reveal to them their nakedness, which was invisible to them. He said, "Your Lord has only forbidden you this tree, lest you become angels, or become immortals."

21. And he swore to them, "I am a sincere advisor to you."

22. So he lured them with deceit. And when they tasted the tree, their nakedness became evident to them, and they began covering themselves with the leaves of the Garden. And their Lord called out to them, "Did I not forbid you from this tree, and say to you that Satan is a sworn enemy to you?"

23. They said, "Our Lord, we have done wrong to ourselves. Unless You forgive us, and have mercy on us, we will be among the losers."

24. He said, "Fall, some of you enemies to one another. On earth you will have residence and livelihood for a while."

25. He said, "In it you will live, and in it you will die, and from it you will be brought out."

26. O children of Adam! We have provided you with clothing to cover your bodies, and for luxury. But the clothing of piety—that is best. These are some of Allah's revelations, so that they may take heed.

27. O Children of Adam! Do not let Satan seduce you, as he drove your parents out of the Garden, stripping them of their garments, to show them their nakedness. He sees you, him and his clan, from where you cannot see them. We have made the devils friends of those who do not believe.

28. And when they commit an indecency, they say, "We found our parents doing this, and Allah has commanded us to do it." Say, "Allah does not command indecencies. Are you attributing to Allah what you do not know?"

29. Say, "My Lord commands justice, and to stand devoted at every place of worship. So call upon Him, and dedicate your faith to Him alone. Just as He originated you, so you will return."

30. Some He has guided, and some have deserved misguidance. They have adopted the devils for patrons rather than Allah, and they assume that they are guided.

31. O Children of Adam! Dress properly at every place of worship, and eat and drink, but do not be excessive. He does not love the excessive.

32. Say, "Who forbade Allah's finery which He has produced for His servants, and the delights of livelihood?" Say, "They are for those who believe, in this present world, but exclusively theirs on the Day of Resurrection." We thus detail the revelations for people who know.

33. Say, "My Lord has forbidden immoralities—both open and secret—and sin, and unjustified aggression, and that you associate with Allah anything for which He revealed no sanction, and that you say about Allah what you do not know."

34. For every nation is an appointed time. When their time has come, they cannot delay it by one hour, nor can they advance it.

35. O Children of Adam! When messengers from among you come to you, relating to you My revelations—whoever practices piety and reforms—upon them shall be no fear, nor shall they grieve.

36. But as for those who reject Our revelations, and are too proud to accept them—these are the inmates of the Fire, where they will remain forever.

37. Who does greater wrong than he who invents lies about Allah, or denies His revelations? These—their share of the decree will reach them. Until, when Our envoys come to them, to take their souls away, they will say, "Where are they whom you used to pray to besides Allah?" They will say, "They have abandoned us," and they will testify against themselves that they were faithless.

38. He will say, "Join the crowds of jinn and humans who have gone into the Fire before

7. THE ELEVATIONS (al-A'raf)

you." Every time a crowd enters, it will curse its sister-crowd. Until, when they are all in it, the last of them will say to the first of them, "Our Lord, these are the ones who misled us, so inflict on them a double punishment in the Fire." He will say, "Each will have a double, but you do not know."

39. The first of them will say to the last of them, "You have no advantage over us, so taste the torment for what you used to earn."

40. Those who reject Our revelations and are too arrogant to uphold them—the doors of Heaven will not be opened for them, nor will they enter Paradise, until the camel passes through the eye of the needle. Thus We repay the guilty.

41. For them is a couch of hell, and above them are sheets of fire. Thus We repay the wrongdoers.

42. As for those who believe and do righteous works—We never burden any soul beyond its capacity—these are the inhabitants of the Garden; abiding therein eternally.

43. We will remove whatever rancor is in their hearts. Rivers will flow beneath them. And they will say, "Praise be to Allah, who has guided us to this. Had Allah not guided us, we would never be guided. The messengers of our Lord did come with the truth." And it will be proclaimed to them, "This is the Garden you are made to inherit, on account of what you used to do."

44. And the inhabitants of the Garden will call out to the inmates of the Fire, "We found what our Lord promised us to be true; did you find what your Lord promised you to be true?" They will say, "Yes." Thereupon a caller will announce in their midst, "The curse of Allah is upon the wrongdoers."

45. "Those who hinder from the path of Allah, and seek to distort it, and who deny the Hereafter."

46. And between them is a partition, and on the Elevations are men who recognize everyone by their features. They will call to the inhabitants of the Garden, "Peace be upon you." They have not entered it, but they are hoping.

47. And when their eyes are directed towards the inmates of the Fire, they will say, "Our Lord, do not place us among the wrongdoing people."

48. And the dwellers of the Elevations will call to men they recognize by their features, saying, "Your hoardings did not avail you, nor did your arrogance."

49. "Are these the ones you swore Allah will not touch with mercy?" "Enter the Garden; you have nothing to fear, and you will not grieve."

50. The inmates of the Fire will call on the inhabitants of the Garden, "Pour some water over us, or some of what Allah has provided for you." They will say, "Allah has forbidden them for the disbelievers."

51. Those who took their religion lightly, and in jest, and whom the worldly life deceived. Today We will ignore them, as they ignored the meeting on this Day of theirs, and they used to deny Our revelations.

52. We have given them a Scripture, which We detailed with knowledge—guidance and mercy for people who believe.

53. Are they waiting for anything but its fulfillment? The Day its fulfillment comes true, those who disregarded it before will say, "The messengers of our Lord did come with the truth. Have we any intercessors to intercede for us? Or, could we be sent back, to behave differently from the way we behaved before?" They ruined their souls, and what they used to invent has failed them.

54. Your Lord is Allah; He who created the heavens and the earth in six days, then established Himself on the Throne. The night overtakes the day, as it pursues it persistently; and the sun, and the moon, and the stars are subservient by His command. His is the creation, and His is the command. Blessed is Allah, Lord of all beings.

55. Call upon your Lord humbly and privately. He does not love the aggressors.

7. THE ELEVATIONS (al-A'raf)

56. And do not corrupt on earth after its reformation, and pray to Him with fear and hope. Allah's mercy is close to the doers of good.

57. It is He who sends the wind ahead of His mercy. Then, when they have gathered up heavy clouds, We drive them to a dead land, where We make water come down, and with it We bring out all kinds of fruits. Thus We bring out the dead—perhaps you will reflect.

58. As for the good land, it yields its produce by the leave of its Lord. But as for the bad, it produces nothing but hardship and misery. Thus We explain the revelations in various ways for people who are thankful.

59. We sent Noah to his people. He said, "O my people! Worship Allah; you have no god other than Him. I fear for you the punishment of a tremendous Day."

60. The dignitaries among his people said, "We see that you are in obvious error."

61. He said, "O my people, I am not in error, but I am a messenger from the Lord of the Worlds."

62. "I deliver to you the messages of my Lord, and I advise you, and I know from Allah what you do not know."

63. "Do you wonder that a reminder has come to you from your Lord, through a man from among you, to warn you, and to lead you to righteousness, so that you may attain mercy?"

64. But they called him a liar. So We saved him and those with him in the Ark, and We drowned those who rejected Our revelations. They were blind people.

65. And to Aad, their brother Hud. He said, "O my people! Worship Allah; you have no god other than Him. Will you not take heed?"

66. The elite of his people who disbelieved said, "We see foolishness in you, and we think that you are a liar."

67. He said, "O my people! There is no foolishness in me, but I am a messenger from the Lord of the Worlds.

68. "I convey to you the messages of my Lord, and I am a trustworthy adviser to you."

69. "Are you surprised that a reminder has come to you from your Lord, through a man from among you, to warn you? Remember how He made you successors after the people of Noah, and increased you greatly in stature. And remember Allah's blessings, so that you may prosper."

70. They said, "Did you come to us to make us worship Allah alone, and abandon what our ancestors used to worship? Then bring us what you threaten us with, if you are truthful."

71. He said, "Condemnation and wrath have befallen you from your Lord. Are you arguing with me over names, which you and your ancestors invented, for which Allah sent down no authority? Just wait; I am waiting with you."

72. So We saved him and those with him, by mercy from Us, and We cut off the roots of those who rejected Our revelations and were not believers.

73. And to Thamood, their brother Saleh. He said, "O my people! Worship Allah; you have no god other than Him. Clarification has come to you from your Lord. This she-camel of Allah is a sign for you. So leave her to graze on Allah's earth, and do her no harm, lest a painful penalty seizes you."

74. "And remember how He made you successors after Aad, and settled you in the land. You make for yourselves mansions on its plains, and carve out dwellings in the mountains. So remember Allah's benefits, and do not roam the earth corruptingly."

75. The elite of his people, who were arrogant, said to the common people who had believed, "Do you know that Saleh is sent from his Lord?" They said, "We are believers in what he was sent with."

76. Those who were arrogant said, "We reject what you believe in."

77. So they hamstrung the she-camel, and defied the command of their Lord, and said, "O

7. THE ELEVATIONS (al-A'raf)

Saleh, bring upon us what you threaten us with, if you are one of the messengers."

78. Whereupon the quake overtook them, and they became lifeless bodies in their homes.

79. Then he turned away from them, and said, "O my people, I have delivered to you the message of my Lord, and I have advised you, but you do not like those who give advice."

80. And Lot, when he said to his people, "Do you commit lewdness no people anywhere have ever committed before you?"

81. "You lust after men rather than women. You are an excessive people."

82. And his people's only answer was to say, "Expel them from your town; they are purist people."

83. But We saved him and his family, except for his wife; she was of those who lagged behind.

84. And We rained down on them a rain; note the consequences for the sinners.

85. And to Median, their brother Shuaib. He said, "O my people, worship Allah; you have no god other than Him. A clear proof has come to you from your Lord. Give full measure and weight, and do not cheat people out of their rights, and do not corrupt the land once it has been set right. This is better for you, if you are believers."

86. "And do not lurk on every path, making threats and turning away from the path of Allah those who believe in Him, seeking to distort it. And remember how you were few, and how He made you numerous. So note the consequences for the corrupters."

87. "Since some of you believed in what I was sent with, and some did not believe, be patient until Allah judges between us; for He is the Best of Judges."

88. The arrogant elite among his people said, "O Shuaib, We will evict you from our town, along with those who believe with you, unless you return to our religion." He said, "Even if we are unwilling?"

89. "We would be fabricating falsehood against Allah, if we were to return to your religion, after Allah has saved us from it. It is not for us to return to it, unless Allah, our Lord, wills. Our Lord embraces all things in knowledge. In Allah we place our trust. Our Lord, decide between us and our people in truth, for You are the Best of Deciders."

90. The elite of his people who disbelieved said, "If you follow Shuaib, you will be losers."

91. Thereupon, the quake struck them; and they became lifeless bodies in their homes.

92. Those who rejected Shuaib—as if they never prospered therein. Those who rejected Shuaib—it was they who were the losers.

93. So he turned away from them, and said, "O my people, I have delivered to you the messages of my Lord, and I have advised you, so why should I grieve over a disbelieving people?"

94. We did not send any prophet to any town but We afflicted its people with misery and adversity, so that they may humble themselves.

95. Then We substituted prosperity in place of hardship. Until they increased in number, and said, "Adversity and prosperity has touched our ancestors." Then We seized them suddenly, while they were unaware.

96. Had the people of the towns believed and turned righteous, We would have opened for them the blessings of the heaven and the earth; but they rejected the truth, so We seized them by what they were doing.

97. Do the people of the towns feel secure that Our might will not come upon them by night, while they sleep?

98. Do the people of the towns feel secure that Our might will not come upon them by day, while they play?

99. Do they feel safe from Allah's plan? None feel safe from Allah's plan except the losing people.

7. THE ELEVATIONS (al-A'raf)

100. Is it not guidance for those who inherit the land after its inhabitants, that if We willed, We could strike them for their sins? And seal up their hearts, so that they would not hear?

101. These towns—We narrate to you some of their tales. Their messengers came to them with the clear signs, but they would not believe in what they had rejected previously. Thus Allah seals the hearts of the disbelievers.

102. We found most of them untrue to their covenants; We found most of them corrupt.

103. Then, after them, We sent Moses with Our miracles to Pharaoh and his establishment, but they denounced them. So consider the end of the evildoers.

104. Moses said, "O Pharaoh, I am a messenger from the Lord of the Worlds."

105. "It is only proper that I should not say about Allah anything other than the truth. I have come to you with clear evidence from your Lord, so let the Children of Israel go with me."

106. He said, "If you brought a miracle, then present it, if you are truthful."

107. So he threw his staff, and it was an apparent serpent.

108. And He pulled out his hand, and it was white to the onlookers.

109. The notables among Pharaoh's people said, "This is really a skilled magician."

110. "He wants to evict you from your land, so what do you recommend?"

111. They said, "Put him off, and his brother, and send heralds to the cities."

112. "And let them bring you every skillful magician."

113. The magicians came to Pharaoh, and said, "Surely there is a reward for us, if we are the victors."

114. He said, "Yes, and you will be among my favorites."

115. They said, "O Moses! Either you throw, or we are the ones to throw."

116. He said, "You throw!" And when they threw, they beguiled the eyes of the people, and intimidated them, and produced a mighty magic.

117. And We inspired Moses: "Throw your staff." And at once, it swallowed what they were faking.

118. So the truth came to pass, and what they were producing came to nothing.

119. There they were defeated, and utterly reduced.

120. And the magicians fell to their knees.

121. They said, "We have believed in the Lord of the Worlds."

122. "The Lord of Moses and Aaron."

123. Pharaoh said, "Did you believe in Him before I have given you permission? This is surely a conspiracy you schemed in the city, in order to expel its people from it. You will surely know."

124. "I will cut off your hands and your feet on opposite sides; then I will crucify you all."

125. They said, "It is to our Lord that we will return."

126. "You are taking vengeance on us only because we have believed in the signs of our Lord when they have come to us." "Our Lord! Pour out patience upon us, and receive our souls in submission."

127. The chiefs of Pharaoh's people said, "Will you let Moses and his people cause trouble in the land, and forsake you and your gods?" He said, "We will kill their sons, and spare their women. We have absolute power over them."

128. Moses said to his people, "Seek help in Allah, and be patient. The earth belongs to Allah. He gives it in inheritance to whomever He wills of His servants, and the future belongs to the righteous."

129. They said, "We were persecuted before you came to us, and after you came to us." He said, "Perhaps your Lord will destroy your enemy, and make you successors in the land; then He will see how you behave."

7. THE ELEVATIONS (al-A'raf)

130. And We afflicted the people of Pharaoh with barren years, and with shortage of crops, that they may take heed.

131. When something good came their way, they said, "This is ours." And when something bad happened to them, they ascribed the evil omen to Moses and those with him. In fact, their omen is with Allah, but most of them do not know.

132. And they said, "No matter what sign you bring us, to bewitch us with, we will not believe in you."

133. So We let loose upon them the flood, and the locusts, and the lice, and the frogs, and blood—all explicit signs—but they were too arrogant. They were a sinful people.

134. Whenever a plague befell them, they would say, "O Moses, pray to your Lord for us, according to the covenant He made with you. If you lift the plague from us, we will believe in you, and let the Children of Israel go with you."

135. But when We lifted the plague from them, for a term they were to fulfill, they broke their promise.

136. So We took vengeance on them, and drowned them in the sea—because they rejected Our signs, and paid no heed to them.

137. And We made the oppressed people inherit the eastern and western parts of the land, which We had blessed. Thus the fair promise of your Lord to the Children of Israel was fulfilled, because of their endurance. And We destroyed what Pharaoh and his people had built, and what they had harvested.

138. And We delivered the Children of Israel across the sea. And when they came upon a people who were devoted to some statues of theirs, they said, "O Moses, make for us a god, as they have gods." He said, "You are truly an ignorant people."

139. "What these people are concerned with is perdition, and their deeds are based on falsehoods."

140. He said, "Shall I seek for you a god other than Allah, when He has favored you over all other people?"

141. Remember how We saved you from Pharaoh's people, who subjected you to the worst of sufferings—killing your sons and sparing your women. In that was a tremendous trial from your Lord.

142. And We appointed to Moses thirty nights, and completed them with ten; and thus the time appointed by his Lord was forty nights. And Moses said to his brother Aaron: "Take my place among my people, and be upright, and do not follow the way of the mischief-makers."

143. And when Moses came to Our appointment, and his Lord spoke to him, he said, "My Lord, allow me to look and see You." He said, "You will not see Me, but look at the mountain; if it stays in its place, you will see Me." But when his Lord manifested Himself to the mountain, He turned it into dust, and Moses fell down unconscious. Then, when he recovered, he said, "Glory be to you, I repent to you, and I am the first of the believers."

144. He said, "O Moses, I have chosen you over all people for My messages and for My Words. So take what I have given you, and be one of the thankful."

145. And We inscribed for him in the Tablets all kinds of enlightenments, and decisive explanation of all things. "Hold fast to them, and exhort your people to adopt the best of them. I will show you the fate of the sinners."

146. I will turn away from My revelations those who behave proudly on earth without justification. Even if they see every sign, they will not believe in it; and if they see the path of rectitude, they will not adopt it for a path; and if they see the path of error, they will adopt it for a path. That is because they denied Our revelations, and paid no attention to them.

147. Those who deny Our revelations and the meeting of the Hereafter—their deeds will come to nothing. Will they be repaid except according to what they used to do?

7. THE ELEVATIONS (al-A'raf)

148. In his absence, the people of Moses adopted a calf made from their ornaments—a body which lowed. Did they not see that it could not speak to them, nor guide them in any way? They took it for worship. They were in the wrong.

149. Then, when they regretted, and realized that they had erred, they said, "Unless our Lord extends His mercy to us, and forgives us, we will be among the losers."

150. And when Moses returned to his people, angry and disappointed, he said, "What an awful thing you did in my absence. Did you forsake the commandments of your Lord so hastily?" And he threw down the tablets; and he took hold of his brother's head, dragging him towards himself. He said, "Son of my mother, the people have overpowered me, and were about to kill me; so do not allow the enemies to gloat over me, and do not count me among the unjust people."

151. He said, "My Lord, forgive me and my brother, and admit us into Your mercy; for you are the Most Merciful of the merciful."

152. Those who idolized the calf have incurred wrath from their Lord, and humiliation in this life. We thus requite the innovators.

153. As for those who commit sins, and then repent afterwards and believe—your Lord, thereafter, is Forgiving and Merciful.

154. When the anger abated in Moses, he took up the tablets. In their transcript is guidance and mercy for those in awe of their Lord.

155. And Moses chose from his people seventy men for Our appointment. When the tremor shook them, he said, "My Lord, had You willed, You could have destroyed them before, and me too. Will you destroy us for what the fools among us have done? This is but Your test—with it You misguide whomever You will, and guide whomever You will. You are our Protector, so forgive us, and have mercy on us. You are the Best of Forgivers."

156. "And inscribe for us goodness in this world, and in the Hereafter. We have turned to You." He said, "My punishment—I inflict it upon whomever I will, but My mercy encompasses all things. I will specify it for those who act righteously and practice regular charity, and those who believe in Our signs."

157. Those who follow the Messenger, the Unlettered Prophet, whom they find mentioned in the Torah and the Gospel in their possession. He directs them to righteousness, and deters them from evil, and allows for them all good things, and prohibits for them wickedness, and unloads the burdens and the shackles that are upon them. Those who believe in him, and respect him, and support him, and follow the light that came down with him—these are the successful.

158. Say, "O people, I am the Messenger of Allah to you all—He to whom belongs the kingdom of the heavens and the earth. There is no god but He. He gives life and causes death." So believe in Allah and His Messenger, the Unlettered Prophet, who believes in Allah and His words. And follow him, that you may be guided.

159. Among the people of Moses is a community that guides by truth, and thereby does justice.

160. We divided them into twelve tribal communities. And We inspired Moses, when his people asked him for something to drink: "Strike the rock with your staff." Whereupon twelve springs gushed from it. Each group recognized its drinking-place. And We shaded them with clouds, and We sent down upon them manna and quails: "Eat of the good things We have provided for you." They did not wrong Us, but they used to wrong their own selves.

161. And it was said to them, "Settle this town, and eat therein whatever you wish, and speak modestly, and enter the gate in humility—We will forgive your sins, and will promote the righteous."

162. But the wicked among them substituted other words for the words given to them; so We sent down upon them a plague from the sky, because of their wrongdoing.

7. THE ELEVATIONS (al-A'raf)

163. Ask them about the town by the sea, when they violated the Sabbath. When they observed the Sabbath, their fish would come to them abundantly. But when they violated the Sabbath, their fish would not come to them. Thus We tried them because they disobeyed.

164. And when a group of them said, "Why do you counsel a people whom Allah will annihilate, or punish with a severe punishment?" They said, "As an excuse to your Lord, and so that they may become righteous."

165. Then, when they neglected what they were reminded of, We saved those who prohibited evil, and We seized those who did wrong with a terrible punishment, because of their sinfulness.

166. Then, when they rebelled against the commands to refrain, We said to them, "Be despicable apes."

167. Your Lord has announced that, He would send against them, until the Day of Resurrection, those who would inflict terrible suffering upon them. Your Lord is swift in retribution, yet He is Forgiving and Merciful.

168. And We scattered them into communities on earth. Some of them righteous, and some of them short of that. And We tested them with fortunes and misfortunes, so that they may return.

169. They were succeeded by generations who inherited the Scripture and chose the materials of this world, saying, "We will be forgiven." And should similar materials come their way, they would again seize them. Did they not make a covenant to uphold the Scripture, and to not say about Allah except the truth? Did they not study its contents? But the Home of the Hereafter is better for the cautious; will you not understand?

170. Those who adhere to the Scripture, and practice prayer—We will not waste the reward of the reformers.

171. And when We suspended the mountain over them, as if it was an umbrella, and they thought it would fall on them: "Hold fast to what We have given you, and remember what it contains, so that you may be saved."

172. And when Your Lord summoned the descendants of Adam, and made them testify about themselves. "Am I not your Lord?" They said, "Yes, we testify." Thus you cannot say on the Day of Resurrection, "We were unaware of this."

173. Nor can you Say, "Our ancestors practiced idolatry before; and we are their descendants who came after them; will you destroy us for what the falsifiers did?"

174. We thus elaborate the revelations, so that they may return.

175. And relate to them the story of him to whom We delivered Our signs, but he detached himself from them, so Satan went after him, and he became one of the perverts.

176. Had We willed, We could have elevated him through them; but he clung to the ground, and followed his desires. His metaphor is that of a dog: if you chase it, it pants; and if you leave it alone, it pants. Such is the metaphor of the people who deny Our signs. So tell the tale, so that they may ponder.

177. Evil is the metaphor of the people who reject Our signs and wrong themselves.

178. Whomever Allah guides is the guided one. And whomever He sends astray—these are the losers.

179. We have destined for Hell multitudes of jinn and humans. They have hearts with which they do not understand. They have eyes with which they do not see. They have ears with which they do not hear. These are like cattle. In fact, they are further astray. These are the heedless.

180. To Allah belong the Most Beautiful Names, so call Him by them, and disregard those who blaspheme His names. They will be repaid for what they used to do.

181. Among those We created is a community—they guide by truth, and do justice thereby.

7. THE ELEVATIONS (al-A'raf)

¹⁸². As for those who reject Our messages, We will gradually lead them from where they do not know.

¹⁸³. And I will encourage them. My plan is firm.

¹⁸⁴. Do they not think? There is no madness in their friend. He is but a plain warner.

¹⁸⁵. Have they not observed the government of the heavens and the earth, and all the things that Allah created, and that their time may have drawn near? Which message, besides this, will they believe in?

¹⁸⁶. Whomever Allah misguides has no guide. And He leaves them blundering in their transgression.

¹⁸⁷. They ask you about the Hour, "When will it come?" Say, "Knowledge of it rests with my Lord. None can reveal its coming except He. It weighs heavily on the heavens and the earth. It will not come upon you except suddenly." They ask you as if you are responsible for it. Say, "Knowledge of it rests with Allah," but most people do not know.

¹⁸⁸. Say, "I have no control over any benefit or harm to myself, except as Allah wills. Had I known the future, I would have acquired much good, and no harm would have touched me. I am only a warner, and a herald of good news to a people who believe."

¹⁸⁹. It is He who created you from a single person, and made from it its mate, that he may find comfort with her. Then, when he has covered her, she conceives a light load, and she carries it around. But when she has grown heavy, they pray to Allah their Lord, "if You give us a good child, we will be among the thankful."

¹⁹⁰. But when He has given them a good child, they attribute partners to Him in what He has given them. Allah is exalted above what they associate.

¹⁹¹. Do they idolize those who create nothing, and are themselves created?

¹⁹². And can neither help them, nor help their own selves?

¹⁹³. And if you invite them to guidance, they will not follow you. It is the same for you, whether you invite them, or remain silent.

¹⁹⁴. Those you call upon besides Allah are servants like you. So call upon them, and let them answer you, if you are truthful.

¹⁹⁵. Do they have feet with which they walk? Or do they have hands with which they strike? Or do they have eyes with which they see? Or do they have ears with which they hear? Say, "Call upon your partners, then plot against me, and do not wait."

¹⁹⁶. "My Master is Allah, He Who sent down the Book, and He takes care of the righteous."

¹⁹⁷. Those you call upon besides Him cannot help you, nor can they help themselves.

¹⁹⁸. And if you call them to guidance, they will not hear. And you see them looking at you, yet they do not see.

¹⁹⁹. Be tolerant, and command decency, and avoid the ignorant.

²⁰⁰. And when a suggestion from Satan assails you, take refuge with Allah. He is Hearing and Knowing.

²⁰¹. Those who are righteous—when an impulse from Satan strikes them, they remind themselves, and immediately see clearly.

²⁰². But their brethren lead them relentlessly into error, and they never stop short.

²⁰³. If you do not produce a miracle for them, they say, "Why don't you improvise one." Say, "I only follow what is inspired to me from my Lord." These are insights from your Lord, and guidance, and mercy, for a people who believe.

²⁰⁴. When the Quran is recited, listen to it, and pay attention, so that you may experience mercy.

²⁰⁵. And remember your Lord within yourself, humbly and fearfully, and quietly, in the morning and the evening, and do not be of the neglectful.

²⁰⁶. Those who are in the presence of your Lord are not too proud to worship Him. They

recite His praises, and to Him they bow down.

8. THE SPOILS
(al-Anfal)

In the name of Allah, the Gracious, the Merciful

1. They ask you about the bounties. Say, "The bounties are for Allah and the Messenger." So be mindful of Allah, and settle your differences, and obey Allah and His Messenger, if you are believers.

2. The believers are those whose hearts tremble when Allah is mentioned, and when His revelations are recited to them, they strengthen them in faith, and upon their Lord they rely.

3. Those who perform the prayer; and from Our provisions to them, they spend.

4. These are the true believers. They have high standing with their Lord, and forgiveness, and a generous provision.

5. Even as your Lord brought you out of your home with the truth, some believers were reluctant.

6. Arguing with you about the truth after it was made clear, as if they were being driven to death as they looked on.

7. Allah has promised you one of the two groups—that it would be yours—but you wanted the unarmed group to be yours. Allah intends to prove the truth with His words, and to uproot the disbelievers.

8. In order to confirm the truth and nullify falsehood, even though the guilty dislike it.

9. When you appealed to your Lord for help, He answered you, "I am reinforcing you with one thousand angels in succession."

10. Allah only made it a message of hope, and to set your hearts at rest. Victory comes only from Allah. Allah is Mighty and Wise.

11. He made drowsiness overcome you, as a security from Him. And He sent down upon you water from the sky, to cleanse you with it, and to rid you of Satan's pollution, and to fortify your hearts, and to strengthen your foothold.

12. Your Lord inspired the angels: "I am with you, so support those who believe. I will cast terror into the hearts of those who disbelieve. So strike above the necks, and strike off every fingertip of theirs."

13. That is because they opposed Allah and His Messenger. Whoever opposes Allah and His Messenger—Allah is severe in retribution.

14. "Here it is; so taste it." For the disbelievers there is the suffering of the Fire.

15. O you who believe! When you meet those who disbelieve on the march, never turn your backs on them.

16. Anyone who turns his back on them on that Day, except while maneuvering for battle, or to join another group, has incurred wrath from Allah, and his abode is Hell—what a miserable destination!

17. It was not you who killed them, but it was Allah who killed them. And it was not you who launched when you launched, but it was Allah who launched. That He may bestow upon the believers an excellent reward. Allah is Hearing and Knowing.

18. Such is the case. Allah will undermine the strategy of the disbelievers.

19. If you desire a verdict, the verdict has come to you. And if you desist, it would be best for you. And if you return, We will return; and your troops, however numerous, will not benefit you. Allah is with the believers.

20. O you who believe! Obey Allah and His Messenger, and do not turn away from him when you hear.

21. And be not like those who say, "We hear," when they do not hear.

22. The worst of animals to Allah are the deaf and dumb—those who do not reason.

23. Had Allah recognized any good in them, He would have made them hear; and had He

8. THE SPOILS (al-Anfal)

made them hear, they would have turned away defiantly.

24. O you who believe! Respond to Allah and to the Messenger when He calls you to what will revive you. And know that Allah stands between a man and his heart, and that to Him you will be gathered.

25. And beware of discord which does not afflict the wrongdoers among you exclusively; and know that Allah is severe in retribution.

26. And remember when you were few, oppressed in the land, fearing that people may capture you; but He sheltered you, and supported you with His victory, and provided you with good things—so that you may be thankful.

27. O you who believe! Do not betray Allah and the Messenger, nor betray your trusts, while you know.

28. And know that your possessions and your children are a test, and that Allah possesses an immense reward.

29. O you who believe! If you remain conscious of Allah, He will give you a criterion, and will remit from you your sins, and will forgive you. Allah is possessor of infinite grace.

30. When the disbelievers plotted against you, to imprison you, or kill you, or expel you. They planned, and Allah planned, but Allah is the Best of planners.

31. And when Our revelations are recited to them, they say, "We have heard. Had we wanted, we could have said the like of this; these are nothing but myths of the ancients."

32. And they said, "Our God, if this is the truth from You, then rain down on us stones from the sky, or visit us with a painful affliction."

33. But Allah would not punish them while you are amongst them. And Allah would not punish them as long as they seek forgiveness.

34. Yet why should Allah not punish them, when they are turning others away from the Sacred Mosque, although they are not its custodians? Its rightful custodians are the pious; but most of them do not know.

35. Their prayer at the House was nothing but whistling and clapping—so taste the punishment for your blasphemy.

36. Those who disbelieve spend their wealth to repel from Allah's path. They will spend it, then it will become a source of sorrow for them, and then they will be defeated. Those who disbelieve will be herded into Hell.

37. That Allah may distinguish the bad from the good, and heap the bad on top of one another, and pile them together, and throw them in Hell. These are the losers.

38. Say to those who disbelieve: if they desist, their past will be forgiven. But if they persist—the practice of the ancients has passed away.

39. Fight them until there is no more persecution, and religion becomes exclusively for Allah. But if they desist—Allah is Seeing of what they do.

40. And if they turn away, know that Allah is your Protector. The Best Protector, and the Best Supporter.

41. And know that whatever spoils you gain, to Allah belongs its fifth, and to the Messenger, and the relatives, and the orphans, and the poor, and to the wayfarer, provided you believe in Allah and in what We revealed to Our servant on the Day of Distinction, the day when the two armies met. Allah is Capable of everything.

42. Recall when you were on the nearer bank, and they were on the further bank, and the caravan was below you. Had you planned for this meeting, you would have disagreed on the timing, but Allah was to carry out a predetermined matter, so that those who perish would perish by clear evidence, and those who survive would survive by clear evidence. Allah is Hearing and Knowing.

43. Allah made them appear in your dream as few. Had He made them appear as many, you would have lost heart, and disputed in the

8. THE SPOILS (al-Anfal)

matter. But Allah saved the situation. He knows what the hearts contain.

44. When you met, He made them appear as few in your eyes, and made you appear fewer in their eyes, so that Allah may conclude a predetermined matter. To Allah all matters revert.

45. O you who believe! When you meet a force, stand firm, and remember Allah much, so that you may prevail.

46. And obey Allah and His Messenger, and do not dispute, lest you falter and lose your courage. And be steadfast. Allah is with the steadfast.

47. And do not be like those who left their homes boastfully, showing off before the people, and barring others from the path of Allah. Allah comprehends what they do.

48. Satan made their deeds appear good to them, and said, "You cannot be defeated by any people today, and I am at your side." But when the two armies came in sight of one another, he turned on his heels, and said, "I am innocent of you; I see what you do not see; I fear Allah; Allah is severe in punishment."

49. The hypocrites and those in whose hearts is sickness said, "Their religion has deluded these people." But whoever puts his trust in Allah—Allah is Mighty and Wise.

50. If only you could see, as the angels take away those who disbelieve, striking their faces and their backs: "Taste the agony of the Burning."

51. "That is because of what your hands have committed, and because Allah is not unjust to the servants."

52. Like the behavior of the people of Pharaoh, and those before them. They rejected the signs of Allah, so Allah seized them for their sins. Allah is Powerful, Severe in punishment.

53. That is because Allah would never change a blessing He has bestowed on a people unless they change what is within themselves, and because Allah is Hearing and Knowing.

54. Such was the case with the people of Pharaoh, and those before them. They denied the signs of their Lord, so We annihilated them for their wrongs, and We drowned the people of Pharaoh—they were all evildoers.

55. The worst of creatures in Allah's view are those who disbelieve. They have no faith.

56. Those of them with whom you made a treaty, but they violate their agreement every time. They are not righteous.

57. If you confront them in battle, make of them a fearsome example for those who follow them, that they may take heed.

58. If you fear treachery on the part of a people, break off with them in a like manner. Allah does not like the treacherous.

59. Let not the disbelievers assume that they are ahead. They will not escape.

60. And prepare against them all the power you can muster, and all the cavalry you can mobilize, to terrify thereby Allah's enemies and your enemies, and others besides them whom you do not know, but Allah knows them. Whatever you spend in Allah's way will be repaid to you in full, and you will not be wronged.

61. But if they incline towards peace, then incline towards it, and put your trust in Allah. He is the Hearer, the Knower.

62. If they intend to deceive you—Allah is sufficient for you. It is He who supported you with His aid, and with the believers.

63. And He united their hearts. Had you spent everything on earth, you would not have united their hearts, but Allah united them together. He is Mighty and Wise.

64. O prophet! Count on Allah, and on the believers who have followed you.

65. O prophet! Rouse the believers to battle. If there are twenty steadfast among you, they will defeat two hundred; and if there are a hundred of you, they will defeat a thousand of those who disbelieve; because they are a people who do not understand.

66. Allah has now lightened your burden, knowing that there is weakness in you. If there are a hundred steadfast among you, they will defeat two hundred; and if there are a thousand of you, they will defeat two thousand by Allah's leave. Allah is with the steadfast.

67. It is not for a prophet to take prisoners before he has subdued the land. You desire the materials of this world, but Allah desires the Hereafter. Allah is Strong and Wise.

68. Were it not for a predetermined decree from Allah, an awful punishment would have afflicted you for what you have taken.

69. So consume what you have gained, legitimate and wholesome; and remain conscious of Allah. Allah is Forgiving and Merciful.

70. O prophet! Say to those you hold prisoners, "If Allah finds any good in your hearts, He will give you better than what was taken from you, and He will forgive you. Allah is Forgiving and Merciful."

71. But if they intend to betray you, they have already betrayed Allah, and He has overpowered them. Allah is Knowing and Wise.

72. Those who believed, and emigrated, and struggled in Allah's cause with their possessions and their persons, and those who provided shelter and support—these are allies of one another. As for those who believed, but did not emigrate, you owe them no protection, until they have emigrated. But if they ask you for help in religion, you must come to their aid, except against a people with whom you have a treaty. Allah is Seeing of what you do.

73. As for those who disbelieve, they are allies of one another. Unless you do this, there will be turmoil in the land, and much corruption.

74. Those who believed, and emigrated, and struggled for Allah's cause, and those who gave shelter and support—these are the true believers. They will have forgiveness, and a bountiful provision.

75. As for those who believed afterwards, and emigrated and struggled with you—these belong with you. But family members are nearer to one another in the Book of Allah. Allah is Cognizant of everything.

9. REPENTANCE (at-Tawbah)

1. A declaration of immunity from Allah and His Messenger to the polytheists with whom you had made a treaty.

2. So travel the land for four months, and know that you cannot escape Allah, and that Allah will disgrace the disbelievers.

3. And a proclamation from Allah and His Messenger to the people on the day of the Greater Pilgrimage, that Allah has disowned the polytheists, and so did His Messenger. If you repent, it will be better for you. But if you turn away, know that you cannot escape Allah. And announce to those who disbelieve a painful punishment.

4. Except for those among the polytheists with whom you had made a treaty, and did not violate any of its terms, nor aided anyone against you. So fulfill the treaty with them to the end of its term. Allah loves the righteous.

5. When the Sacred Months have passed, kill the polytheists wherever you find them. And capture them, and besiege them, and lie in wait for them at every ambush. But if they repent, and perform the prayers, and pay the alms, then let them go their way. Allah is Most Forgiving, Most Merciful.

6. And if anyone of the polytheists asks you for protection, give him protection so that he may hear the Word of Allah; then escort him to his place of safety. That is because they are a people who do not know.

7. How can there be a treaty with the polytheists on the part of Allah and His Messenger, except for those with whom you made a treaty at the Sacred Mosque? As long as they are upright with you, be upright with them. Allah loves the pious.

9. REPENTANCE (at-Tawbah)

8. How? Whenever they overcome you, they respect neither kinship nor treaty with you. They satisfy you with lip service, but their hearts refuse, and most of them are immoral.

9. They traded away Allah's revelations for a cheap price, so they barred others from His path. How evil is what they did.

10. Towards a believer they respect neither kinship nor treaty. These are the transgressors.

11. But if they repent, and perform the prayers, and give the obligatory charity, then they are your brethren in faith. We detail the revelations for a people who know.

12. But if they violate their oaths after their pledge, and attack your religion, then fight the leaders of disbelief—they have no faith—so that they may desist.

13. Will you not fight a people who violated their oaths, and planned to exile the Messenger, and initiated hostilities against you? Do you fear them? It is Allah you should fear, if you are believers.

14. Fight them. Allah will punish them at your hands, and humiliate them, and help you against them, and heal the hearts of a believing people.

15. And He will remove the anger of their hearts. Allah redeems whomever He wills. Allah is Knowledgeable and Wise.

16. Or do you think that you will be left alone, without Allah identifying which of you will strive, and take no supporters apart from Allah, His Messenger, and the believers? Allah is well Aware of what you do.

17. It is not for the polytheists to attend Allah's places of worship while professing their disbelief. These—their works are in vain, and in the Fire they will abide.

18. The only people to attend Allah's places of worship are those who believe in Allah and the Last Day, and pray regularly, and practice regular charity, and fear none but Allah. These are most likely to be guided.

19. Do you consider giving water to pilgrims and maintaining the Sacred Mosque the same as believing in Allah and the Last Day and striving in Allah's path? They are not equal in Allah's sight. Allah does not guide the unjust people.

20. Those who believe, and emigrate, and strive in Allah's path with their possessions and their persons, are of a higher rank with Allah. These are the winners.

21. Their Lord announces to them good news of mercy from Him, and acceptance, and gardens wherein they will have lasting bliss.

22. Abiding therein forever. With Allah is a great reward.

23. O you who believe! Do not ally yourselves with your parents and your siblings if they prefer disbelief to belief. Whoever of you allies himself with them—these are the wrongdoers.

24. Say, "If your parents, and your children, and your siblings, and your spouses, and your relatives, and the wealth you have acquired, and a business you worry about, and homes you love, are more dear to you than Allah, and His Messenger, and the struggle in His cause, then wait until Allah executes His judgment." Allah does not guide the sinful people.

25. Allah has given you victory in numerous regions; but on the day of Hunayn, your great number impressed you, but it availed you nothing; and the land, as spacious as it was, narrowed for you; and you turned your backs in retreat.

26. Then Allah sent down His serenity upon His Messenger, and upon the believers; and He sent down troops you did not see; and He punished those who disbelieved. Such is the recompense of the disbelievers.

27. Then, after that, Allah will relent towards whomever He wills. Allah is Forgiving and Merciful.

28. O you who believe! The polytheists are polluted, so let them not approach the Sacred Mosque after this year of theirs. And if you

9. REPENTANCE (at-Tawbah)

fear poverty, Allah will enrich you from His grace, if He wills. Allah is Aware and Wise.

29. Fight those who do not believe in Allah, nor in the Last Day, nor forbid what Allah and His Messenger have forbidden, nor abide by the religion of truth—from among those who received the Scripture—until they pay the due tax, willingly or unwillingly.

30. The Jews said, "Ezra is the son of Allah," and the Christians said, "The Messiah is the son of Allah." These are their statements, out of their mouths. They emulate the statements of those who blasphemed before. May Allah assail them! How deceived they are!

31. They have taken their rabbis and their priests as lords instead of Allah, as well as the Messiah son of Mary. Although they were commanded to worship none but The One God. There is no god except He. Glory be to Him; High above what they associate with Him.

32. They want to extinguish Allah's light with their mouths, but Allah refuses except to complete His light, even though the disbelievers dislike it.

33. It is He who sent His Messenger with the guidance and the religion of truth, in order to make it prevail over all religions, even though the idolaters dislike it.

34. O you who believe! Many of the rabbis and priests consume people's wealth illicitly, and hinder from Allah's path. Those who hoard gold and silver, and do not spend them in Allah's cause, inform them of a painful punishment.

35. On the Day when they will be heated in the Fire of Hell, then their foreheads, and their sides, and their backs will be branded with them: "This is what you hoarded for yourselves; so taste what you used to hoard."

36. The number of months, according to Allah, is twelve months—in the decree of Allah—since the Day He created the heavens and the earth, of which four are sacred. This is the correct religion. So do not wrong yourselves during them. And fight the polytheists collectively, as they fight you collectively, and know that Allah is with the righteous.

37. Postponement is an increase in disbelief—by which those who disbelieve are led astray. They allow it one year, and forbid it another year, in order to conform to the number made sacred by Allah, thus permitting what Allah has forbidden. The evil of their deeds seems good to them. Allah does not guide the disbelieving people.

38. O you who believe! What is the matter with you, when it is said to you, "Mobilize in the cause of Allah," you cling heavily to the earth? Do you prefer the present life to the Hereafter? The enjoyment of the present life, compared to the Hereafter, is only a little.

39. Unless you mobilize, He will punish you most painfully, and will replace you with another people, and you will not harm Him at all. Allah has power over all things.

40. If you do not help him, Allah has already helped him, when those who disbelieved expelled him, and he was the second of two in the cave. He said to his friend, "Do not worry, Allah is with us." And Allah made His tranquility descend upon him, and supported him with forces you did not see, and made the word of those who disbelieved the lowest, while the Word of Allah is the Highest. Allah is Mighty and Wise.

41. Mobilize, light or heavy, and strive with your possessions and your lives in the cause of Allah. That is better for you, if you only knew.

42. Had the gain been immediate, and the journey shorter, they would have followed you; but the distance seemed too long for them. Still they swear by Allah: "Had we been able, we would have marched out with you." They damn their own souls, and Allah knows that they are lying.

43. May Allah pardon you! Why did you give them permission before it became clear to you who are the truthful ones, and who are the liars?

9. REPENTANCE (at-Tawbah)

44. Those who believe in Allah and the Last Day do not ask you for exemption from striving with their possessions and their lives. Allah is fully aware of the righteous.

45. Only those who do not believe in Allah and the Last Day ask you for exemption. Their hearts are full of doubts, so they waver in their doubts.

46. Had they wanted to mobilize, they would have made preparations for it; but Allah disliked their participation, so he held them back, and it was said, "Stay behind with those who stay behind."

47. Had they mobilized with you, they would have added only to your difficulties, and they would have spread rumors in your midst, trying to sow discord among you. Some of you are avid listeners to them. Allah is Aware of the wrongdoers.

48. They tried to cause conflict before, and they hatched plots against you, until the truth prevailed, and the command of Allah became evident—in spite of their dislike.

49. Among them is he who says, "Excuse me, and do not trouble me." In fact, they sunk into trouble. In fact, Hell will engulf the disbelievers.

50. If something good happens to you, it upsets them; and if a calamity befalls you, they say, "We took our precautions in advance," and they depart, happy.

51. Say, "Nothing will happen to us except what Allah has ordained for us; He is our Protector." In Allah let the faithful put their trust.

52. Say, "Are you expecting for us anything other than one of the two excellences? As for us: we are expecting that Allah will afflict you with a punishment from Himself, or at our hands. So wait, we are waiting with you."

53. Say, "Whether you spend willingly or unwillingly, it will not be accepted from you. You are evil people."

54. What prevents the acceptance of their contributions is nothing but the fact that they disbelieved in Allah and His Messenger, and that they do not approach the prayer except lazily, and that they do not spend except grudgingly.

55. Let neither their possessions nor their children impress you. Allah intends to torment them through them in this worldly life, and that their souls depart while they are disbelievers.

56. They swear by Allah that they are of you. But they are not of you. They are divisive people.

57. Were they to find a shelter, or a cave, or a hideout, they would go to it, rushing.

58. And among them are those who criticize you in regard to charities. If they are given some of it, they become pleased; but if they are not given any, they grow resentful.

59. If only they were content with what Allah and His Messenger have given them, and said, "Allah is sufficient for us; Allah will give us of His bounty, and so will His Messenger; to Allah we eagerly turn."

60. Charities are for the poor, and the destitute, and those who administer them, and for reconciling hearts, and for freeing slaves, and for those in debt, and in the path of Allah, and for the traveler in need—an obligation from Allah. Allah is All-Knowing, Most Wise.

61. And among them are those who insult the Prophet, and say, "He is all ears." Say, "He listens for your own good. He believes in Allah, and trusts the believers, and is mercy for those of you who believe." Those who insult the Messenger of Allah will have a painful penalty.

62. They swear to you by Allah to please you. But it is more proper for them to please Allah and His Messenger, if they are believers.

63. Do they not know that whoever opposes Allah and His Messenger, will have the Fire of Hell, abiding in it forever? That is the supreme disgrace.

64. The hypocrites worry lest a chapter may be revealed about them, informing them of what

9. REPENTANCE (at-Tawbah)

is in their hearts. Say, "Go on mocking; Allah will bring out what you fear."

65. If you ask them, they will say, "We were just joking and playing." Say, "Were you making jokes about Allah, His revelations, and His Messenger?"

66. Do not apologize. You have disbelieved after your belief. If We pardon some of you, We will punish others, because they are guilty.

67. The hypocrite men and hypocrite women are of one another. They advocate evil, and prohibit righteousness, and withhold their hands. They forgot Allah, so He forgot them. The hypocrites are the sinners.

68. Allah has promised the hypocrite men and hypocrite women, and the disbelievers, the Fire of Hell, abiding therein forever. It is their due. And Allah has cursed them. They will have a lasting punishment.

69. Like those before you. They were more powerful than you, and had more wealth and children. They enjoyed their share, and you enjoyed your share, as those before you enjoyed their share. And you indulged, as they indulged. It is they whose works will fail in this world and in the Hereafter. It is they who are the losers.

70. Have they not heard the stories of those before them? The people of Noah, and Aad, and Thamood; and the people of Abraham, and the inhabitants of Median, and the Overturned Cities? Their messengers came to them with the clear proofs. Allah never wronged them, but they used to wrong their own selves.

71. The believing men and believing women are friends of one another. They advocate virtue, forbid evil, perform the prayers, practice charity, and obey Allah and His Messenger. These—Allah will have mercy on them. Allah is Noble and Wise.

72. Allah promises the believers, men and women, gardens beneath which rivers flow, abiding therein forever, and fine homes in the Gardens of Eden. But approval from Allah is even greater. That is the supreme achievement.

73. O Prophet! Strive against the disbelievers and the hypocrites, and be stern with them. Their abode is Hell—what a miserable destination!

74. They swear by Allah that they said nothing; but they did utter the word of blasphemy, and they renounced faith after their submission. And they plotted what they could not attain. They were resentful only because Allah and His Messenger have enriched them out of His grace. If they repent, it would be best for them; but if they turn away, Allah will afflict them with a painful punishment—in this life and in the Hereafter—and they will have on earth no protector and no savior.

75. Among them are those who promised Allah: "If He gives us of His bounty, we will donate and be among the upright."

76. But when He has given them of His bounty, they became stingy with it, and turned away in aversion.

77. So He penalized them with hypocrisy in their hearts, until the Day they face Him—because they broke their promise to Allah, and because they used to lie.

78. Do they not know that Allah knows their secrets and their conspiracies? And that Allah is the Knower of the unseen?

79. Those who criticize the believers who give charity voluntarily, and ridicule those who find nothing to give except their own efforts—Allah ridicules them. They will have a painful punishment.

80. Whether you ask forgiveness for them, or do not ask forgiveness for them—even if you ask forgiveness for them seventy times, Allah will not forgive them. That is because they disbelieved in Allah and His Messenger. Allah does not guide the immoral people.

81. Those who stayed behind rejoiced at their staying behind the Messenger of Allah. And they hated to strive with their wealth and their lives in Allah's way. And they said, "Do

9. REPENTANCE (at-Tawbah)

not venture out in the heat." Say, "The Fire of Hell is much hotter, if they only understood."

82. Let them laugh a little, and weep much; in recompense for what they used to earn.

83. If Allah brings you back to a party of them, and they ask your permission to go out, say, "You will not go out with me, ever, nor will you ever fight an enemy with me. You were content to sit back the first time, so sit back with those who stay behind."

84. You are never to pray over anyone of them who dies, nor are you to stand at his graveside. They rejected Allah and His Messenger, and died while they were sinners.

85. Do not let their possessions and their children impress you. Allah desires to torment them through them in this world, and their souls expire while they are disbelievers.

86. When a chapter is revealed, stating: "Believe in Allah and strive with His Messenger," the prominent among them ask you for exemption. They say, "Allow us to stay with those who stay behind."

87. They prefer to be with those who stay behind. Their hearts were sealed, so they do not understand.

88. But the Messenger and those who believe with him struggle with their possessions and their lives. These have deserved the good things. These are the successful.

89. Allah has prepared for them gardens beneath which rivers flow, wherein they will abide forever. That is the great victory.

90. Some of the Desert-Arabs came to make excuses, asking to be granted exemption, while those who were untrue to Allah and His Messenger stayed behind. A painful punishment will afflict those among them who disbelieved.

91. There is no blame on the weak, nor on the sick, nor on those who have nothing to give, provided they are true to Allah and His Messenger. In no way can the righteous be blamed. Allah is Forgiving and Merciful.

92. Nor on those who approach you, wishing to ride with you, and you said, "I have nothing to carry you on." So they went away, with their eyes overflowing with tears, sorrowing for not finding the means to spend.

93. But blame is on those who ask you for exemption, although they are rich. They are content to be with those who stay behind. Allah has sealed their hearts, so they do not know.

94. They present excuses to you when you return to them. Say, "Do not offer excuses; we do not trust you; Allah has informed us of you. And Allah will watch your actions, and so will the Messenger; then you will be returned to the Knower of the Invisible and the Visible, and He will inform you of what you used to do."

95. They will swear to you by Allah, when you return to them, that you may leave them alone. So leave them alone. They are a disgrace, and their destiny is Hell; a reward for what they used to earn.

96. They will swear to you that you may accept them. But even if you accept them, Allah does not accept the wicked people.

97. The Desert-Arabs are the most steeped in disbelief and hypocrisy, and the most likely to ignore the limits that Allah revealed to His Messenger. Allah is Knowing and Wise.

98. And among the Desert-Arabs are those who consider their contribution to be a fine. And they wait for a reversal of your fortunes. Upon them will fall the cycle of misfortune. Allah is Hearing and Knowing.

99. Yet among the Desert-Arabs are those who believe in Allah and the Last Day, and consider their contribution to be a means towards Allah, and the prayers of the Messenger. Surely it will draw them closer, and Allah will admit them into His mercy. Allah is Forgiving and Compassionate.

100. The Pioneers—The first of the Migrants and the Supporters, and those who followed them in righteousness. Allah is pleased with them, and they are pleased with Him. He has

9. REPENTANCE (at-Tawbah)

prepared for them Gardens beneath which rivers flow, where they will abide forever. That is the sublime triumph.

101. Among the Desert-Arabs around you there are some hypocrites, and among the inhabitants of Medina too. They have become adamant in hypocrisy. You do not know them, but We know them. We will punish them twice; then they will be returned to a severe torment.

102. Others have confessed their sins, having mixed good deeds with bad deeds. Perhaps Allah will redeem them. Allah is Forgiving and Merciful.

103. Receive contributions from their wealth, to purify them and sanctify them with it; and pray for them. Your prayer is comfort for them. Allah is Hearing and Knowing.

104. Do they not know that Allah accepts the repentance of His servants, and that He receives the contributions, and that Allah is the Acceptor of Repentance, the Merciful?

105. Say, "Work. Allah will see your work, and so will His Messenger, and the believers. Then you will be returned to the Knower of secrets and declarations, and He will inform you of what you used to do."

106. Others are held in suspense, awaiting Allah's decree, as to whether He will punish them, or accept their repentance. Allah is Aware and Wise.

107. Then there are those who establish a mosque to cause harm, and disbelief, and disunity among the believers, and as an outpost for those who fight Allah and His Messenger. They will swear: "Our intentions are nothing but good." But Allah bears witness that they are liars.

108. Do not stand in it, ever. A mosque founded upon piety from the first day is worthier of your standing in it. In it are men who love to be purified. Allah loves those who purify themselves.

109. Is he who founds his structure upon piety and acceptance from Allah better, or he who founds his structure on the brink of a cliff that is about to tumble, so it tumbles with him into the Fire of Hell? Allah does not guide the unjust people.

110. The structure which they built will remain questionable in their hearts, until their hearts are stopped. Allah is Knowing and Wise.

111. Allah has purchased from the believers their lives and their properties in exchange for Paradise. They fight in Allah's way, and they kill and get killed. It is a promise binding on Him in the Torah, and the Gospel, and the Quran. And who is more true to his promise than Allah? So rejoice in making such an exchange—that is the supreme triumph.

112. Those who repent, those who worship, those who praise, those who journey, those who kneel, those who bow down, those who advocate righteousness and forbid evil, and those who keep Allah's limits—give good news to the believers.

113. It is not for the Prophet and those who believe to ask forgiveness for the polytheists, even if they are near relatives, after it has become clear to them that they are people of Hellfire.

114. Abraham asked forgiveness for his father only because of a promise he had made to him. But when it became clear to him that he was an enemy of Allah, he disowned him. Abraham was kind and clement.

115. Allah would never lead a people astray, after He had guided them, until He makes clear to them what they should guard against. Allah has knowledge of all things.

116. To Allah belongs the dominion of the heavens and the earth. He gives life, and He causes death. And besides Allah, you have neither protector, nor supporter.

117. Allah has redeemed the Prophet, and the Emigrants, and the Supporters—those who followed him in the hour of difficulty—after the hearts of some of them almost swerved. Then He pardoned them. He is Kind towards them, Compassionate.

118. Also towards the three who were left behind. Then, when the earth, as vast as it is,

closed in on them, and their very souls closed in on them, and they realized that there was no refuge from Allah, except in Him, He redeemed them, so that they may repent. Allah is the Redeemer, the Merciful.

119. O you who believe! Be conscious of Allah, and be with the sincere.

120. It is not for the inhabitants of Medina and the Desert-Arabs around them to stay behind the Messenger of Allah, nor to prefer themselves to him. That is because they never suffer any thirst, nor fatigue, nor hunger in the cause of Allah, nor do they take one step that enrages the disbelievers, nor do they gain anything from an enemy, but it is recorded to their credit as a righteous deed. Allah does not waste the reward of the righteous.

121. Nor do they spend any expenditure, small or large, nor do they cross any valley, but it is recorded to their credit. That Allah may reward them in accordance with the best of their deeds.

122. It is not advisable for the believers to march out altogether. Of every division that marches out, let a group remain behind, to gain understanding of the religion, and to notify their people when they have returned to them, that they may beware.

123. O you who believe! Fight those of the disbelievers who attack you, and let them find severity in you, and know that Allah is with the righteous.

124. Whenever a chapter is revealed, some of them say, "Which of you has this increased in faith?" As for those who believe: it increases them in faith, and they rejoice.

125. But as for those in whose hearts is sickness: it adds disgrace to their disgrace, and they die as unbelievers.

126. Do they not see that they are tested once or twice every year? Yet they do not repent, and they do not learn.

127. And whenever a chapter is revealed, they look at one another, "Does anyone see you?" Then they slip away. Allah has diverted their hearts, because they are a people who do not understand.

128. There has come to you a messenger from among yourselves, concerned over your suffering, anxious over you. Towards the believers, he is compassionate and merciful.

129. If they turn away, say, "Allah is enough for me; there is no god except He; in Him I have put my trust; He is the Lord of the Sublime Throne."

10. JONAH
(Yunus)

*In the name of Allah,
the Gracious, the Merciful*

1. Alif, Lam, Ra. These are the Verses of the Wise Book.

2. Is it a wonder to the people that We inspired a man from among them: "Warn mankind, and give good news to those who believe that they are on a sound footing with their Lord"? The disbelievers said, "This is a manifest sorcerer."

3. Your Lord is Allah, who created the heavens and the earth in six days, then settled over the Throne, governing all things. There is no intercessor except after His permission. Such is Allah, your Lord—so serve Him. Will you not reflect?

4. To Him is your return, altogether. The promise of Allah is true. He originates creation, and then He repeats it, to reward those who believe and do good deeds with equity. As for those who disbelieve, for them is a drink of boiling water, and agonizing torment, on account of their disbelief.

5. It is He who made the sun radiant, and the moon a light, and determined phases for it—that you may know the number of years and the calculation. Allah did not create all this except with truth. He details the revelations for a people who know.

10. JONAH (Yunus)

6. In the alternation of night and day, and in what Allah created in the heavens and the earth, are signs for people who are aware.

7. Those who do not hope to meet Us, and are content with the worldly life, and are at ease in it, and those who pay no heed to Our signs.

8. These—their dwelling is the Fire—on account of what they used to do.

9. As for those who believe and do good deeds, their Lord guides them in their faith. Rivers will flow beneath them in the Gardens of Bliss.

10. Their call therein is, "Glory be to You, our God." And their greeting therein is, "Peace." And the last of their call is, "Praise be to Allah, Lord of the Worlds."

11. If Allah were to accelerate the ill for the people, as they wish to accelerate the good, their term would have been fulfilled. But We leave those who do not expect Our encounter to blunder in their excesses.

12. Whenever adversity touches the human being, he prays to Us—reclining on his side, or sitting, or standing. But when We have relieved his adversity from him, he goes away, as though he had never called on Us for trouble that had afflicted him. Thus the deeds of the transgressors appear good to them.

13. We destroyed generations before you when they did wrong. Their messengers came to them with clear signs, but they would not believe. Thus We requite the sinful people.

14. Then We made you successors on earth after them, to see how you would behave.

15. And when Our clear revelations are recited to them, those who do not hope to meet Us say, "Bring a Quran other than this, or change it." Say, "It is not for me to change it of my own accord. I only follow what is revealed to me. I fear, if I disobeyed my Lord, the torment of a terrible Day."

16. Say, "Had Allah willed, I would not have recited it to you, and He would not have made it known to you. I have lived among you for a lifetime before it. Do you not understand?"

17. Who does greater wrong than someone who fabricates lies about Allah, or denies His revelations? The guilty will never prosper.

18. And they worship, besides Allah, what neither harms them nor benefits them. And they say, "These are our intercessors with Allah." Say, "Are you informing Allah about what He does not know in the heavens or on earth?" Glorified be He, High above the associations they make.

19. Mankind was a single community; then they differed. Were it not for a prior decree from your Lord, the matters over which they had disputed would have been settled.

20. And they say, "If only a miracle was sent down to him from his Lord." Say, "The realm of the unseen belongs to Allah; so wait, I am waiting with you."

21. When We make the people taste mercy after some adversity has touched them, they begin to scheme against Our revelations. Say, "Allah is swifter in scheming." Our envoys are writing down what you scheme.

22. It is He who transports you across land and sea. Until, when you are on ships, sailing in a favorable wind, and rejoicing in it, a raging wind arrives. The waves surge over them from every side, and they realize that they are besieged. Thereupon they pray to Allah, professing sincere devotion to Him: "If You save us from this, we will be among the appreciative."

23. But then, when He has saved them, they commit violations on earth, and oppose justice. O people! Your violations are against your own souls. It is the enjoyment of the present life. Then to Us is your return, and We will inform you of what you used to do.

24. The likeness of the present life is this: water that We send down from the sky is absorbed by the plants of the earth, from which the people and the animals eat. Until, when the earth puts on its fine appearance, and is beautified, and its inhabitants think that they have

10. JONAH (Yunus)

mastered it, Our command descends upon it by night or by day, and We turn it into stubble, as if it had not flourished the day before. We thus clarify the revelations for people who reflect.

25. Allah invites to the Home of Peace, and guides whomever He wills to a straight path.

26. For those who have done good is goodness, and more. Neither gloom nor shame will come over their faces. These are the inhabitants of Paradise, abiding therein forever.

27. As for those who have earned evil deeds: a reward of similar evil, and shame will cover them. They will have no defense against Allah—as if their faces are covered with dark patches of night. These are the inmates of the Fire, abiding therein forever.

28. On the Day when We will gather them altogether, then say to those who ascribed partners, "To your place, you and your partners." Then We will separate between them, and their partners will say, "It was not us you were worshiping."

29. "Allah is sufficient witness between us and you. We were unaware of your worshiping us."

30. There, every soul will experience what it had done previously; and they will be returned to Allah, their True Master; and what they used to invent will fail them.

31. Say, "Who provides for you from the heaven and the earth? And who controls the hearing and the sight? And who produces the living from the dead, and produces the dead from the living? And who governs the Order?" They will say, "Allah." Say, "Will you not be careful?"

32. Such is Allah, your Lord—the True. What is there, beyond the truth, except falsehood? How are you turned away?

33. Thus your Lord's Word proved true against those who disobeyed, for they do not believe.

34. Say, "Can any of your partners initiate creation, and then repeat it?" Say, "Allah initiates creation, and then repeats it. How are you so deluded?"

35. Say, "Can any of your partners guide to the truth?" Say, "Allah guides to the truth. Is He who guides to the truth more worthy of being followed, or he who does not guide, unless he himself is guided? What is the matter with you? How do you judge?"

36. Most of them follow nothing but assumptions; and assumptions avail nothing against the truth. Allah is fully aware of what they do.

37. This Quran could not have been produced by anyone other than Allah. In fact, it is a confirmation of what preceded it, and an elaboration of the Book. There is no doubt about it—it is from the Lord of the Universe.

38. Or do they say, "He has forged it"? Say, "Then produce a single chapter like it, and call upon whomever you can, apart from Allah, if you are truthful."

39. In fact, they deny what is beyond the limits of their knowledge, and whose explanation has not yet reached them. Thus those before them refused to believe. So note the consequences for the wrongdoers.

40. Among them are those who believe in it, and among them are those who do not believe in it. Your Lord is fully aware of the mischief-makers.

41. If they accuse you of lying, say, "I have my deeds, and you have your deeds. You are quit of what I do, and I am quit of what you do."

42. And among them are those who listen to you. But can you make the deaf hear, even though they do not understand?

43. And among them are those who look at you. But can you guide the blind, even though they do not see?

44. Allah does not wrong the people in the least, but the people wrong their own selves.

45. On the Day when He rounds them up—as if they had tarried only one hour of a day—they will recognize one another. Those who

10. JONAH (Yunus)

denied the meeting with Allah will be the losers. They were not guided.

46. Whether We show you some of what We promise them, or take you, to Us is their return. Allah is witness to everything they do.

47. Every community has a messenger. When their messenger has come, judgment will be passed between them with fairness, and they will not be wronged.

48. And they say, "When will this promise be fulfilled, if you are truthful?"

49. Say, "I have no power to harm or benefit myself, except as Allah wills. To every nation is an appointed time. Then, when their time arrives, they can neither postpone it by one hour, nor advance it.

50. Say, "Have you considered? If His punishment overtakes you by night or by day, what part of it will the guilty seek to hasten?"

51. "Then, when it falls, will you believe in it? Now? When before you tried to hasten it?"

52. Then it will be said to those who did wrong, "Taste the torment of eternity. Will you be rewarded except for what you used to do?"

53. And they inquire of you, "Is it true?" Say, "Yes, by my Lord, it is true, and you cannot evade it."

54. Had every soul which had done wrong possessed everything on earth, it would offer it as a ransom. They will hide the remorse when they witness the suffering, and it will be judged between them equitably, and they will not be wronged.

55. Assuredly, to Allah belongs everything in the heavens and the earth. Assuredly, the promise of Allah is true. But most of them do not know.

56. He gives life and causes death, and to Him you will be returned.

57. O people! There has come to you advice from your Lord, and healing for what is in the hearts, and guidance and mercy for the believers.

58. Say, "In Allah's grace and mercy let them rejoice. That is better than what they hoard."

59. Say, "Have you considered the sustenance Allah has sent down for you, some of which you made unlawful, and some lawful?" Say, "Did Allah give you permission, or do you fabricate lies and attribute them to Allah?"

60. What will they think—those who fabricate lies and attribute them to Allah—on the Day of Resurrection? Allah is bountiful towards the people, but most of them do not give thanks.

61. You do not get into any situation, nor do you recite any Quran, nor do you do anything, but We are watching over you as you undertake it. Not even the weight of an atom, on earth or in the sky, escapes your Lord, nor is there anything smaller or larger, but is in a clear record.

62. Unquestionably, Allah's friends have nothing to fear, nor shall they grieve.

63. Those who believe and are aware.

64. For them is good news in this life, and in the Hereafter. There is no alteration to the words of Allah. That is the supreme triumph.

65. And let not their sayings dishearten you. All power is Allah's. He is the Hearer, the Knower.

66. Certainly, to Allah belongs everyone in the heavens and everyone on earth. Those who invoke other than Allah do not follow partners; they follow only assumptions, and they only guess.

67. It is He who made the night for your rest, and the daylight for visibility. Surely in that are signs for people who listen.

68. And they said, "Allah has taken a son." Be He glorified. He is the Self-Sufficient. His is everything in the heavens and everything on earth. Do you have any proof for this? Or are you saying about Allah what you do not know?

69. Say, "Those who fabricate lies about Allah will not succeed."

10. JONAH (Yunus)

70. Some enjoyment in this world; then to Us is their return; then We will make them taste the severe punishment on account of their disbelief.

71. And relate to them the story of Noah, when he said to his people, "O my people, if my presence among you and my reminding you of Allah's signs is too much for you, then in Allah I have put my trust. So come to a decision, you and your partners, and do not let the matter perplex you; then carry out your decision on me, and do not hold back."

72. "But if you turn away, I have not asked you for any wage. My wage falls only on Allah, and I was commanded to be of those who submit."

73. But they denounced him, so We saved him and those with him in the Ark, and We made them successors, and We drowned those who rejected Our signs. So consider the fate of those who were warned.

74. Then, after him, We sent messengers to their people. They came to them with the clear proofs, but they would not believe in anything they had already rejected. Thus We set a seal on the hearts of the hostile.

75. Then, after them, We sent Moses and Aaron with Our proofs to Pharaoh and his dignitaries. But they acted arrogantly. They were sinful people.

76. And when the truth came to them from Us, they said, "This is clearly sorcery."

77. Moses said, "Is this what you say of the truth when it has come to you? Is this sorcery? Sorcerers do not succeed."

78. They said, "Did you come to us to divert us from what we found our ancestors following, and so that you become prominent in the land? We will never believe in you."

79. Pharaoh said, "Bring me every experienced sorcerer."

80. And when the sorcerers came, Moses said to them, "Throw whatever you have to throw."

81. And when they threw, Moses said, "What you produced is sorcery, and Allah will make it fail. Allah does not foster the efforts of the corrupt."

82. "And Allah upholds the truth with His words, even though the sinners detest it."

83. But none believed in Moses except some children of his people, for fear that Pharaoh and his chiefs would persecute them. Pharaoh was high and mighty in the land. He was a tyrant.

84. Moses said, "O my people, if you have believed in Allah, then put your trust in Him, if you have submitted."

85. They said, "In Allah we have put our trust. Our Lord, do not make us victims of the oppressive people."

86. "And deliver us, by Your mercy, from the disbelieving people."

87. And We inspired Moses and his brother, "Settle your people in Egypt, and make your homes places of worship, and perform the prayer, and give good news to the believers."

88. Moses said, "Our Lord, you have given Pharaoh and his chiefs splendor and wealth in the worldly life. Our Lord, for them to lead away from Your path. Our Lord, obliterate their wealth, and harden their hearts, they will not believe until they see the painful torment."

89. He said, "Your prayer has been answered, so go straight, and do not follow the path of those who do not know."

90. And We delivered the Children of Israel across the sea. Pharaoh and his troops pursued them, defiantly and aggressively. Until, when he was about to drown, he said, "I believe that there is no god except the One the Children of Israel believe in, and I am of those who submit."

91. Now? When you have rebelled before, and been of the mischief-makers?

92. Today We will preserve your body, so that you become a sign for those after you. But most people are heedless of Our signs.

11. HUD (Hud)

⁹³· And We settled the Children of Israel in a position of honor, and provided them with good things. They did not differ until knowledge came to them. Your Lord will judge between them on the Day of Resurrection regarding their differences.

⁹⁴· If you are in doubt about what We revealed to you, ask those who read the Scripture before you. The truth has come to you from your Lord, so do not be of those who doubt.

⁹⁵· And do not be of those who deny Allah's revelations, lest you become one of the losers.

⁹⁶· Those against whom your Lord's Word is justified will not believe.

⁹⁷· Even if every sign comes to them—until they see the painful punishment.

⁹⁸· If only there was one town that believed and benefited by its belief. Except for the people of Jonah. When they believed, We removed from them the suffering of disgrace in the worldly life, and We gave them comfort for a while.

⁹⁹· Had your Lord willed, everyone on earth would have believed. Will you compel people to become believers?

¹⁰⁰· No soul can believe except by Allah's leave; and He lays disgrace upon those who refuse to understand.

¹⁰¹· Say, "Look at what is in the heavens and the earth." But signs and warnings are of no avail for people who do not believe.

¹⁰²· Do they expect anything but the likes of the days of those who passed away before them? Say, "Then wait, I will be waiting with you."

¹⁰³· Then We save Our messengers and those who believe. It is binding on Us to save the believers.

¹⁰⁴· Say, "O people, if you are in doubt about my religion—I do not serve those you serve apart from Allah. But I serve Allah, the one who will terminate your lives. And I was commanded to be of the believers."

¹⁰⁵· And dedicate yourself to the true religion—a monotheist—and never be of the polytheists.

¹⁰⁶· And do not call, apart from Allah, on what neither benefits you nor harms you. If you do, you are then one of the wrongdoers.

¹⁰⁷· If Allah afflicts you with harm, none can remove it except He. And if He wants good for you, none can repel His grace. He makes it reach whomever He wills of His servants. He is the Forgiver, the Merciful.

¹⁰⁸· Say, "O people, the truth has come to you from your Lord. Whoever accepts guidance is guided for his own soul; and whoever strays only strays to its detriment. I am not a guardian over you."

¹⁰⁹· And follow what is revealed to you, and be patient until Allah issues His judgment, for He is the Best of judges.

11. HUD
(Hud)

In the name of Allah,
the Gracious, the Merciful

¹· Alif, Lam, Ra. A Scripture whose Verses were perfected, then elaborated, from One who is Wise and Informed.

²· That you shall worship none but Allah. "I am a warner to you from Him, and a bearer of good news."

³· "And ask your Lord for forgiveness, and repent to Him. He will provide you with good sustenance until a stated term, and will bestow His grace on every possessor of virtue. But if you turn away, then I fear for you the punishment of a grievous Day."

⁴· "To Allah is your return, and He is Capable of all things."

⁵· They wrap their chests to hide from Him. But even as they cover themselves with their clothes, He knows what they conceal and what they reveal. He knows what lies within the hearts.

11. HUD (Hud)

6. There is no moving creature on earth but its sustenance depends on Allah. And He knows where it lives and where it rests. Everything is in a Clear Book.

7. It is He who created the heavens and the earth in six days—and His Throne was upon the waters—in order to test you—which of you is best in conduct. And if you were to say, "You will be resurrected after death," those who disbelieve would say, "This is nothing but plain witchcraft."

8. And if We postponed their punishment until a stated time, they would say, "What holds it back?" On the Day when it reaches them, it will not be averted from them, and what they used to ridicule will besiege them.

9. If We give the human being a taste of mercy from Us, and then withdraw it from him, he becomes despairing and ungrateful.

10. And if We give him a taste of prosperity, after some adversity has afflicted him, he will say, "Troubles have gone away from me." He becomes excited and proud.

11. Except those who are patient and do good deeds—these will have forgiveness and a great reward.

12. Perhaps you wish to disregard some of what is revealed to you, and you may be stressed because of it, since they say, "If only a treasure was sent down to him, or an angel came with him." You are only a warner, and Allah is Responsible for all things.

13. Or do they say, "He invented it?" Say, "Then produce ten chapters like it, invented, and call upon whomever you can, besides Allah, if you are truthful."

14. But if they fail to answer you, know that it was revealed with Allah's knowledge, and that there is no god but He. Will you then submit?

15. Whoever desires the worldly life and its glitter—We will fully recompense them for their deeds therein, and therein they will not be defrauded.

16. These—they will have nothing but the Fire in the Hereafter. Their deeds are in vain therein, and their works are null.

17. Is he who possesses a clear proof from his Lord, recited by a witness from Him, and before it the Book of Moses, a guide and a mercy? These believe in it. But whoever defies it from among the various factions, the Fire is his promise. So have no doubt about it. It is the truth from your Lord, but most people do not believe.

18. Who does greater wrong than he who fabricates lies about Allah? These will be presented before their Lord, and the witnesses will say, "These are they who lied about their Lord." Indeed, the curse of Allah is upon the wrongdoers.

19. Those who hinder others from the path of Allah, and seek to make it crooked; and regarding the Hereafter, they are in denial.

20. These will not escape on earth, and they have no protectors besides Allah. The punishment will be doubled for them. They have failed to hear, and they have failed to see.

21. Those are the ones who lost their souls, and what they had invented has strayed away from them.

22. Without a doubt, in the Hereafter, they will be the biggest losers.

23. As for those who believe and do good deeds, and humble themselves before their Lord—these are the inhabitants of Paradise, where they will abide forever.

24. The parable of the two groups is that of the blind and the deaf, and the seeing and the hearing. Are they equal in comparison? Will you not reflect?

25. We sent Noah to his people, "I am to you a clear warner."

26. "That you shall worship none but Allah. I fear for you the agony of a painful Day."

27. The notables who disbelieved among his people said, "We see in you nothing but a man like us, and we see that only the worst

among us have followed you, those of immature judgment. And we see that you have no advantage over us. In fact, we think you are liars."

28. He said, "O my people, Have you considered? If I stand on clear evidence from my Lord, and He has given me a mercy from Himself, but you were blind to it, can we compel you to accept it, even though you dislike it?"

29. "O my people! I ask of you no money for it. My reward lies only with Allah. And I am not about to dismiss those who believed; they will surely meet their Lord. And I see that you are ignorant people."

30. "O my people! Who will support me against Allah, if I dismiss them? Will you not give a thought?"

31. "I do not say to you that I possess the treasures of Allah, nor do I know the future, nor do I say that I am an angel. Nor do I say of those who are despicable in your eyes that Allah will never give them any good. Allah is Aware of what lies in their souls. If I did, I would be one of the wrongdoers."

32. They said, "O Noah, you have argued with us, and argued a great deal. Now bring upon us what you threaten us with, if you are truthful."

33. He said, "It is Allah who will bring it upon you, if He wills, and you will not be able to escape."

34. "My advice will not benefit you, much as I may want to advise you, if Allah desires to confound you. He is your Lord, and to Him you will be returned."

35. Or do they say, "He made it up?" Say, "If I made it up, upon me falls my crime, and I am innocent of the crimes you commit."

36. And it was revealed to Noah: "None of your people will believe, except those who have already believed, so do not grieve over what they do."

37. "And build the Ark, under Our eyes, and with Our inspiration, and do not address Me regarding those who did wrong; they are to be drowned."

38. As he was building the ark, whenever some of his people passed by him, they ridiculed him. He said, "If you ridicule us, we will ridicule you, just as you ridicule."

39. "You will surely know upon whom will come a torment that will abase him, and upon whom will fall a lasting torment."

40. Until, when Our command came, and the volcano erupted, We said, "Board into it a pair of every kind, and your family—except those against whom the sentence has already been passed—and those who have believed." But those who believed with him were only a few.

41. He said, "Embark in it. In the name of Allah shall be its sailing and its anchorage. My Lord is indeed Forgiving and Merciful."

42. And so it sailed with them amidst waves like hills. And Noah called to his son, who had kept away, "O my son! Embark with us, and do not be with the disbelievers."

43. He said, "I will take refuge on a mountain—it will protect me from the water." He said, "There is no protection from Allah's decree today, except for him on whom He has mercy." And the waves surged between them, and he was among the drowned.

44. And it was said, "O earth, swallow your waters," and "O heaven, clear up." And the waters receded, and the event was concluded, and it settled on Judi, and it was proclaimed: "Away with the wicked people."

45. And Noah called to his Lord. He said, "O My Lord, my son is of my family, and Your promise is true, and You are the Wisest of the wise."

46. He said, "O Noah, he is not of your family. It is an unrighteous deed. So do not ask Me about something you know nothing about. I admonish you, lest you be one of the ignorant."

47. He said, "O My Lord, I seek refuge with You, from asking You about what I have no

11. HUD (Hud)

knowledge of. Unless You forgive me, and have mercy on me, I will be one of the losers."

48. It was said, "O Noah, disembark with peace from Us; and with blessings upon you, and upon communities from those with you. And other communities We will grant prosperity, and then a painful torment from Us will befall them."

49. These are some stories from the past that we reveal to you. Neither you, nor your people knew them before this. So be patient. The future belongs to the pious.

50. And to Aad, their brother Hud. He said, "O my people, worship Allah, you have no other god besides Him. You do nothing but invent lies."

51. "O my people, I ask you no wage for it; my wage lies with Him who originated me. Do you not understand?"

52. "O my people, ask forgiveness from your Lord, and repent to Him. He will release the sky pouring down upon you, and will add strength to your strength. And do not turn away and be wicked."

53. They said, "O Hud, you did not bring us any evidence, and we are not about to abandon our gods at your word, and we are not believers in you."

54. "We only say that some of our gods have possessed you with evil." He said, "I call Allah to witness, and you to witness, that I am innocent of what you associate.

55. Besides Him. So scheme against me, all of you, and do not hesitate.

56. I have placed my trust in Allah, my Lord and your Lord. There is not a creature but He holds it by the forelock. My Lord is on a straight path.

57. If you turn away, I have conveyed to you what I was sent to you with; and my Lord will replace you with another people, and you will not cause Him any harm. My Lord is Guardian over all things."

58. And when Our decree came, We saved Hud and those who believed with him, by a mercy from Us, and We delivered them from a harsh punishment.

59. That was Aad; they denied the signs of their Lord, and defied His messengers, and followed the lead of every stubborn tyrant.

60. And they were pursued by a curse in this world, and on the Day of Resurrection. Indeed, Aad blasphemed against their Lord—so away with Aad, the people of Hud.

61. And to Thamood, their brother Saleh. He said, "O my people, worship Allah, you have no god other than Him. He initiated you from the earth, and settled you in it. So seek His forgiveness, and repent to Him. My Lord is Near and Responsive."

62. They said, "O Saleh, we had hopes in you before this. Are you trying to prevent us from worshiping what our parents worship? We are in serious doubt regarding what you are calling us to."

63. He said, "O my people, have you considered? If I stand upon clear evidence from my Lord, and He has given me mercy from Him, who would protect me from Allah, if I disobeyed Him? You add nothing for me except loss."

64. "O my people, this is the she-camel of Allah, a sign for you. Let her graze on Allah's land, and do not harm her, lest an imminent punishment overtakes you."

65. But they hamstrung her, and so He said, "Enjoy yourselves in your homes for three days. This is a prophecy that is infallible."

66. Then, when Our command came, We saved Saleh and those who believed with him, by a mercy from Us, from the disgrace of that day. Your Lord is the Strong, the Mighty.

67. And the Scream struck those who transgressed, and they became motionless bodies in their homes.

68. As if they had never prospered therein. Indeed, Thamood rejected their Lord, so away with Thamood.

69. Our messengers came to Abraham with good news. They said, "Peace." He said,

"Peace." Soon after, he came with a roasted calf.

70. But when he saw their hands not reaching towards it, he became suspicious of them, and conceived a fear of them. They said, "Do not fear, we were sent to the people of Lot."

71. His wife was standing by, so she laughed. And We gave her good news of Isaac; and after Isaac, Jacob.

72. She said, "Alas for me. Shall I give birth, when I am an old woman, and this, my husband, is an old man? This is truly a strange thing."

73. They said, "Do you marvel at the decree of Allah? The mercy and blessings of Allah are upon you, O people of the house. He is Praiseworthy and Glorious."

74. When Abraham's fear subsided, and the good news had reached him, he started pleading with Us concerning the people of Lot.

75. Abraham was gentle, kind, penitent.

76. "O Abraham, refrain from this. The command of your Lord has come; they have incurred an irreversible punishment."

77. And when Our envoys came to Lot, he was anxious for them, and concerned for them. He said, "This is a dreadful day."

78. And his people came rushing towards him—they were in the habit of committing sins. He said, "O my people, these are my daughters; they are purer for you. So fear Allah, and do not embarrass me before my guests. Is there not one reasonable man among you?"

79. They said, "You know well that we have no right to your daughters, and you know well what we want."

80. He said, "If only I had the strength to stop you, or could rely on some strong support."

81. They said, "O Lot, we are the envoys of your Lord; they will not reach you. So set out with your family during the cover of the night, and let none of you look back, except for your wife. She will be struck by what will strike them. Their appointed time is the morning. Is not the morning near?"

82. And when Our command came about, We turned it upside down, and We rained down on it stones of baked clay.

83. Marked from your Lord, and never far from the wrongdoers.

84. And to Median, their brother Shuaib. He said, "O my people, worship Allah; you have no god other than Him. And do not short measure or short weight. I see you in good circumstances, but I fear for you the agony of an encompassing Day."

85. "O my people! Give full measure and full weight, in all fairness, and do not cheat the people out of their rights, and do not spread corruption in the land.

86. What is left by Allah is best for you, if you are believers. And I am not a guardian over you."

87. They said, "O Shuaib, does your prayer command you that we abandon what our ancestors worshiped, or doing with our wealth what we want? You are the one who is intelligent and wise."

88. He said, "O my people, have you considered? What if I have clear evidence from my Lord, and He has given me good livelihood from Himself? I have no desire to do what I forbid you from doing. I desire nothing but reform, as far as I can. My success lies only with Allah. In Him I trust, and to Him I turn."

89. "O my people, let not your hostility towards me cause you to suffer what was suffered by the people of Noah, or the people of Hud, or the people of Saleh. The people of Lot are not far away from you."

90. "And ask your Lord for forgiveness, and repent to Him. My Lord is Merciful and Loving."

91. They said, "O Shuaib, we do not understand much of what you say, and we see that you are weak among us. Were it not for your

11. HUD (Hud)

tribe, we would have stoned you. You are of no value to us."

⁹². He said, "O my people, is my tribe more important to you than Allah? And you have turned your backs on Him? My Lord comprehends everything you do."

⁹³. "O my people, do as you may, and so will I. You will know to whom will come a punishment that will shame him, and who is a liar. So look out; I am on the lookout with you."

⁹⁴. And when Our command came, We saved Shuaib and those who believed with him, by mercy from Us, and the Blast struck the wrongdoers, and they became motionless bodies in their homes.

⁹⁵. As though they never flourished therein. Away with Median, as was done away with Thamood.

⁹⁶. And We sent Moses with Our signs and a clear mandate.

⁹⁷. To Pharaoh and his nobles, but they followed the command of Pharaoh, and the command of Pharaoh was not wise.

⁹⁸. He will precede his people on the Day of Resurrection, and will lead them into the Fire. Miserable is the place he placed them in.

⁹⁹. They were followed by a curse in this, and on the Day of Resurrection. Miserable is the path they followed.

¹⁰⁰. These are of the reports of the towns—We relate them to you. Some are still standing, and some have withered away.

¹⁰¹. We did not wrong them, but they wronged themselves. Their gods, whom they invoked besides Allah, availed them nothing when the command of your Lord arrived. In fact, they added only to their ruin.

¹⁰². Such is the grip of your Lord when He seizes the towns in the midst of their sins. His grip is most painful, most severe.

¹⁰³. In that is a sign for whoever fears the punishment of the Hereafter. That is a Day for which humanity will be gathered together—that is a Day to be witnessed.

¹⁰⁴. We only postpone it until a predetermined time.

¹⁰⁵. On the Day when it arrives, no soul will speak without His permission. Some will be miserable, and some will be happy.

¹⁰⁶. As for those who are miserable, they will be in the Fire. They will have therein sighing and wailing.

¹⁰⁷. Remaining therein for as long as the heavens and the earth endure, except as your Lord wills. Your Lord is Doer of whatever He wills.

¹⁰⁸. And as for those who are happy, they will be in Paradise, remaining therein for as long as the heavens and the earth endure, except as your Lord wills—a reward without end.

¹⁰⁹. So be not in doubt regarding what these people worship. They worship only as their ancestors worshiped before. We will pay them their due in full, without any reduction.

¹¹⁰. We gave Moses the Scripture, but it was disputed. Were it not for a prior word from your Lord, it would have been settled between them. They are in serious doubt concerning it.

¹¹¹. Your Lord will repay each one of them in full for their deeds. He is Aware of everything they do.

¹¹². So be upright, as you are commanded, along with those who repented with you, and do not transgress. He is Seeing of everything you do.

¹¹³. And do not incline towards those who do wrong, or the Fire may touch you; and you will have no protectors besides Allah, and you will not be saved.

¹¹⁴. Perform the prayer at the borders of the day, and during the approaches of the night. The good deeds take away the bad deeds. This is a reminder for those who remember.

¹¹⁵. And be patient. Allah will not waste the reward of the virtuous.

¹¹⁶. If only there were, among the generations before you, people with wisdom, who spoke against corruption on earth—except for the few whom We saved. But the wrongdoers

pursued the luxuries they were indulged in, and thus became guilty.

117. Your Lord would never destroy the towns wrongfully, while their inhabitants are righteous.

118. Had your Lord willed, He could have made humanity one community, but they continue to differ.

119. Except those on whom your Lord has mercy—for that reason He created them. The Word of your Lord is final: "I will fill Hell with jinn and humans, altogether."

120. Everything We narrate to you of the history of the messengers is to strengthen your heart therewith. The truth has come to you in this, and a lesson, and a reminder for the believers.

121. And say to those who do not believe, "Act according to your ability; and so will we."

122. "And wait; we too are waiting."

123. To Allah belongs the future of the heavens and the earth, and to Him all authority goes back. So worship Him, and rely on Him. Your Lord is never unaware of what you do.

12. JOSEPH
(Yusuf)

*In the name of Allah,
the Gracious, the Merciful*

1. Alif, Lam, Ra. These are the Verses of the Clear Book.

2. We have revealed it an Arabic Quran, so that you may understand.

3. We narrate to you the most accurate history, by revealing to you this Quran. Although, prior to it, you were of the unaware.

4. When Joseph said to his father, "O my father, I saw eleven planets, and the sun, and the moon; I saw them bowing down to me."

5. He said, "O my son, do not relate your vision to your brothers, lest they plot and scheme against you. Satan is man's sworn enemy.

6. And thus your Lord will choose you, and will teach you the interpretation of events, and will complete His blessing upon you and upon the family of Jacob, as He has completed it before upon your forefathers Abraham and Isaac. Your Lord is Knowing and Wise.

7. In Joseph and his brothers are lessons for the seekers.

8. When they said, "Joseph and his brother are dearer to our father than we are, although we are a whole group. Our father is obviously in the wrong.

9. "Kill Joseph, or throw him somewhere in the land, and your father's attention will be yours. Afterwards, you will be decent people."

10. One of them said, "Do not kill Joseph, but throw him into the bottom of the well; some caravan may pick him up—if you must do something."

11. They said, "Father, why do you not trust us with Joseph, although we care for him?"

12. "Send him with us tomorrow, that he may roam and play; we will take care of him."

13. He said, "It worries me that you would take him away. And I fear the wolf may eat him while you are careless of him."

14. They said, "If the wolf ate him, and we are many, we would be good for nothing."

15. So they went away with him, and agreed to put him at the bottom of the well. And We inspired him, "You will inform them of this deed of theirs when they are unaware."

16. And they came to their father in the evening weeping.

17. They said, "O father, we went off racing one another, and left Joseph by our belongings; and the wolf ate him. But you will not believe us, even though we are being truthful."

18. And they brought his shirt, with fake blood on it. He said, "Your souls enticed you to do something. But patience is beautiful, and Allah is my Help against what you describe."

12. JOSEPH (Yusuf)

19. A caravan passed by, and they sent their water-carrier. He lowered his bucket, and said, "Good news. Here is a boy." And they hid him as merchandise. But Allah was aware of what they did.

20. And they sold him for a cheap price—a few coins—they considered him to be of little value.

21. The Egyptian who bought him said to his wife, "Take good care of him; he may be useful to us, or we may adopt him as a son." We thus established Joseph in the land, to teach him the interpretation of events. Allah has control over His affairs, but most people do not know.

22. When he reached his maturity, We gave him wisdom and knowledge. We thus reward the righteous.

23. She in whose house he was living tried to seduce him. She shut the doors, and said, "I am yours." He said, "Allah forbid! He is my Lord. He has given me a good home. Sinners never succeed."

24. She desired him, and he desired her, had he not seen the proof of his Lord. It was thus that We diverted evil and indecency away from him. He was one of Our loyal servants.

25. As they raced towards the door, she tore his shirt from behind. At the door, they ran into her husband. She said, "What is the penalty for him who desired to dishonor your wife, except imprisonment or a painful punishment?"

26. He said, "It was she who tried to seduce me." A witness from her household suggested: "If his shirt is torn from the front: then she has told the truth, and he is the liar.

27. But if his shirt is torn from the back: then she has lied, and he is the truthful."

28. And when he saw that his shirt was torn from the back, he said, "This is a woman's scheme. Your scheming is serious indeed."

29. "Joseph, turn away from this. And you, woman, ask forgiveness for your sin; you are indeed in the wrong."

30. Some ladies in the city said, "The governor's wife is trying to seduce her servant. She is deeply in love with him. We see she has gone astray."

31. And when she heard of their gossip, she invited them, and prepared for them a banquet, and she gave each one of them a knife. She said, "Come out before them." And when they saw him, they marveled at him, and cut their hands. They said, "Good Allah, this is not a human, this must be a precious angel."

32. She said, "Here he is, the one you blamed me for. I did try to seduce him, but he resisted. But if he does not do what I tell him to do, he will be imprisoned, and will be one of the despised."

33. He said, "My Lord, prison is more desirable to me than what they call me to. Unless You turn their scheming away from me, I may yield to them, and become one of the ignorant."

34. Thereupon his Lord answered him, and diverted their scheming away from him. He is the Hearer, the Knower.

35. Then it occurred to them, after they had seen the signs, to imprison him for a while.

36. Two youth entered the prison with him. One of them said, "I see myself pressing wine." The other said, "I see myself carrying bread on my head, from which the birds are eating. Tell us their interpretation—we see that you are one of the righteous."

37. He said, "No food is served to you, but I have informed you about it before you have received it. That is some of what my Lord has taught me. I have forsaken the tradition of people who do not believe in Allah; and regarding the Hereafter, they are deniers."

38. "And I have followed the faith of my forefathers, Abraham, and Isaac, and Jacob. It is not for us to associate anything with Allah. This is by virtue of Allah's grace upon us and upon the people, but most people do not give thanks.

39. "O My fellow inmates, are diverse lords better, or Allah, the One, the Supreme?"

12. JOSEPH (Yusuf)

⁴⁰· "You do not worship, besides Him, except names you have named, you and your ancestors, for which Allah has sent down no authority. Judgment belongs to none but Allah. He has commanded that you worship none but Him. This is the right religion, but most people do not know.

⁴¹· "O my fellow inmates! One of you will serve his master wine; while the other will be crucified, and the birds will eat from his head. Thus the matter you are inquiring about is settled."

⁴²· And he said to the one he thought would be released, "Mention me to your master." But Satan caused him to forget mentioning him to his master, so he remained in prison for several years.

⁴³· The king said, "I see seven fat cows being eaten by seven lean ones, and seven green spikes, and others dried up. O elders, explain to me my vision, if you are able to interpret visions."

⁴⁴· They said, "Jumbles of dreams, and we know nothing of the interpretation of dreams."

⁴⁵· The one who was released said, having remembered after a time, "I will inform you of its interpretation, so send me out."

⁴⁶· "Joseph, O man of truth, inform us concerning seven fat cows being eaten by seven lean ones, and seven green spikes, and others dried up, so that I may return to the people, so that they may know."

⁴⁷· He said, "You will farm for seven consecutive years. But whatever you harvest, leave it in its spikes, except for the little that you eat.

⁴⁸· Then after that will come seven difficult ones, which will consume what you have stored for them, except for the little that you have preserved.

⁴⁹· Then after that will come a year that brings relief to the people, and during which they will press.

⁵⁰· The king said, "Bring him to me." And when the envoy came to him, he said, "Go back to your master, and ask him about the intentions of the women who cut their hands; my Lord is well aware of their schemes."

⁵¹· He said, "What was the matter with you, women, when you tried to seduce Joseph?" They said, "Allah forbid! We knew of no evil committed by him." The governor's wife then said, "Now the truth is out. It was I who tried to seduce him, and he is telling the truth."

⁵²· "This is that he may know that I did not betray him in secret, and that Allah does not guide the scheming of the betrayers."

⁵³· "Yet I do not claim to be innocent. The soul commands evil, except those on whom my Lord has mercy. Truly my Lord is Forgiving and Merciful."

⁵⁴· The king said, "Bring him to me, and I will reserve him for myself." And when he spoke to him, he said, "This day you are with us established and secure."

⁵⁵· He said, "Put me in charge of the storehouses of the land; I am honest and knowledgeable."

⁵⁶· And thus We established Joseph in the land, to live therein wherever he wished. We touch with Our mercy whomever We will, and We never waste the reward of the righteous.

⁵⁷· But the reward of the Hereafter is better for those who believe and observed piety.

⁵⁸· And Joseph's brothers came, and entered into his presence. He recognized them, but they did not recognize him.

⁵⁹· When he provided them with their provisions, he said, "Bring me a brother of yours from your father. Do you not see that I fill up the measure, and I am the best of hosts?"

⁶⁰· "But if you do not bring him to me, you will have no measure from me, and you will not come near me."

⁶¹· They said, "We will solicit him from his father. We will surely do."

⁶²· He said to his servants, "Put their goods in their saddlebags; perhaps they will recognize

12. JOSEPH (Yusuf)

them when they return to their families, and maybe they will come back."

63. When they returned to their father, they said, "O father, we were denied measure, but send our brother with us, and we will obtain measure. We will take care of him."

64. He said, "Shall I trust you with him, as I trusted you with his brother before? Allah is the Best Guardian, and He is the Most Merciful of the merciful."

65. And when they opened their baggage, they found that their goods were returned to them. They said, "Father, what more do we want? Here are our goods, returned to us. We will provide for our family, and protect our brother, and have an additional camel-load. This is easy commerce."

66. He said, "I will not send him with you, unless you give me a pledge before Allah that you will bring him back to me, unless you get trapped." And when they gave him their pledge, he said, "Allah is witness to what we say."

67. And he said, "O my sons, do not enter by one gate, but enter by different gates. I cannot avail you anything against Allah. The decision rests only with Allah. On Him I rely, and on Him let the reliant rely."

68. And when they entered as their father had instructed them, it did not avail them anything against Allah; it was just a need in the soul of Jacob, which he carried out. He was a person of knowledge inasmuch as We had taught him, but most people do not know.

69. And when they entered into the presence of Joseph, he embraced his brother, and said, "I am your brother; do not be saddened by what they used to do."

70. Then, when he provided them with their provisions, he placed the drinking-cup in his brother's saddlebag. Then an announcer called out, "O people of the caravan, you are thieves."

71. They said, as they came towards them, "What are you missing?"

72. They said, "We are missing the king's goblet. Whoever brings it will have a camel-load; and I personally guarantee it."

73. They said, "By Allah, you know we did not come to cause trouble in the land, and we are not thieves."

74. They said, "What shall be his punishment, if you are lying?"

75. They said, "His punishment, if it is found in his bag: he will belong to you. Thus we penalize the guilty."

76. So he began with their bags, before his brother's bag. Then he pulled it out of his brother's bag. Thus We devised a plan for Joseph; he could not have detained his brother under the king's law, unless Allah so willed. We elevate by degrees whomever We will; and above every person of knowledge, there is one more learned.

77. They said, "If he has stolen, a brother of his has stolen before." But Joseph kept it to himself, and did not reveal it to them. He said, "You are in a worse situation, and Allah is Aware of what you allege."

78. They said, "O noble prince, he has a father, a very old man, so take one of us in his place. We see that you are a good person."

79. He said, "Allah forbid that we should arrest anyone except him in whose possession we found our property; for then we would be unjust."

80. And when they despaired of him, they conferred privately. Their eldest said, "Don't you know that your father received a pledge from you before Allah, and in the past you failed with regard to Joseph? I will not leave this land until my father permits me, or Allah decides for me; for He is the Best of Deciders."

81. "Go back to your father, and say, 'Our father, your son has stolen. We testify only to what we know, and we could not have prevented the unforeseen.'"

82. "Ask the town where we were, and the caravan in which we came. We are being truthful."

12. JOSEPH (Yusuf)

83. He said, "Rather, your souls have contrived something for you. Patience is a virtue. Perhaps Allah will bring them all back to me. He is the Knowing, the Wise."

84. Then he turned away from them, and said, "O my bitterness for Joseph." And his eyes turned white from sorrow, and he became depressed.

85. They said, "By Allah, you will not stop remembering Joseph, until you have ruined your health, or you have passed away."

86. He said, "I only complain of my grief and sorrow to Allah, and I know from Allah what you do not know."

87. "O my sons, go and inquire about Joseph and his brother, and do not despair of Allah's comfort. None despairs of Allah's comfort except the disbelieving people."

88. Then, when they entered into his presence, they said, "Mighty governor, adversity has befallen us, and our family. We have brought scant merchandise. But give us full measure, and be charitable towards us—Allah rewards the charitable."

89. He said, "Do you realize what you did with Joseph and his brother, in your ignorance?"

90. They said, "Is that you, Joseph?" He said, "I am Joseph, and this is my brother. Allah has been gracious to us. He who practices piety and patience—Allah never fails to reward the righteous."

91. They said, "By Allah, Allah has preferred you over us. We were definitely in the wrong."

92. He said, "There is no blame upon you today. Allah will forgive you. He is the Most Merciful of the merciful."

93. "Take this shirt of mine, and lay it over my father's face, and he will recover his sight. And bring your whole family to me."

94. As the caravan set out, their father said, "I sense the presence of Joseph, though you may think I am senile."

95. They said, "By Allah, you are still in your old confusion."

96. Then, when the bearer of good news arrived, he laid it over his face, and he regained his sight. He said, "Did I not say to you that I know from Allah what you do not know?"

97. They said, "Father, pray for the forgiveness of our sins; we were indeed at fault."

98. He said, "I will ask my Lord to forgive you. He is the Forgiver, the Most Merciful."

99. Then, when they entered into the presence of Joseph, he embraced his parents, and said, "Enter Egypt, Allah willing, safe and secure."

100. And he elevated his parents on the throne, and they fell prostrate before him. He said, "Father, this is the fulfillment of my vision of long ago. My Lord has made it come true. He has blessed me, when he released me from prison, and brought you out of the wilderness, after the devil had sown conflict between me and my brothers. My Lord is Most Kind towards whomever He wills. He is the All-knowing, the Most Wise."

101. "My Lord, You have given me some authority, and taught me some interpretation of events. Initiator of the heavens and the earth; You are my Protector in this life and in the Hereafter. Receive my soul in submission, and unite me with the righteous."

102. This is news from the past that We reveal to you. You were not present with them when they plotted and agreed on a plan.

103. But most people, for all your eagerness, are not believers.

104. You ask them no wage for it. It is only a reminder for all mankind.

105. How many a sign in the heavens and the earth do they pass by, paying no attention to them?

106. And most of them do not believe in Allah unless they associate others.

107. Do they feel secure that a covering of Allah's punishment will not come upon them, or that the Hour will not come upon them suddenly, while they are unaware?

108. Say, "This is my way; I invite to Allah, based on clear knowledge—I and whoever

follows me. Glory be to Allah; and I am not of the polytheists."

109. We did not send before you except men, whom We inspired, from the people of the towns. Have they not roamed the earth and seen the consequences for those before them? The Home of the Hereafter is better for those who are righteous. Do you not understand?

110. Until, when the messengers have despaired, and thought that they were rejected, Our help came to them. We save whomever We will, and Our severity is not averted from the guilty people.

111. In their stories is a lesson for those who possess intelligence. This is not a fabricated tale, but a confirmation of what came before it, and a detailed explanation of all things, and guidance, and mercy for people who believe.

13. THUNDER
(ar-Ra'd)

*In the name of Allah,
the Gracious, the Merciful*

1. Alif, Lam, Meem, Ra. These are the signs of the Scripture. What is revealed to you from your Lord is the truth, but most people do not believe.

2. Allah is He who raised the heavens without pillars that you can see, and then settled on the Throne. And He regulated the sun and the moon, each running for a specified period. He manages all affairs, and He explains the signs, that you may be certain of the meeting with your Lord.

3. And it is He who spread the earth, and placed in it mountains and rivers. And He placed in it two kinds of every fruit. He causes the night to overlap the day. In that are signs for people who reflect.

4. On earth are adjacent terrains, and gardens of vines, and crops, and date-palms, from the same root or from distinct roots, irrigated with the same water. We make some taste better than others. In that are proofs for people who reason.

5. Should you wonder—the real wonder is their saying: "When we have become dust, will we be in a new creation?" Those are they who defied their Lord. Those are they who will have yokes around their necks. Those are the inhabitants of the Fire, where they will remain forever.

6. And they urge you to hasten evil before good, though examples have passed away before them. Your Lord is full of forgiveness towards the people for their wrongdoings, yet your Lord is severe in retribution.

7. Those who disbelieve say, "Why was a miracle not sent down to him from his Lord?" You are only a warner, and to every community is a guide.

8. Allah knows what every female bears, and every increase and decrease of the wombs. With Him, everything is by measure.

9. The Knower of the Invisible and the Visible; the Grand, the Supreme.

10. It is the same; whether one of you conceals his speech, or declares it; whether he goes into hiding by night, or goes out by day.

11. He has a succession; before him and behind him, protecting him by Allah's command. Allah does not change the condition of a people until they change what is within themselves. And if Allah wills any hardship for a people, there is no turning it back; and apart from Him they have no protector.

12. It is He who shows you the lightening, causing fear and hope. And He produces the heavy clouds.

13. The thunder praises His glory, and so do the angels, in awe of Him. And He sends the thunderbolts, striking with them whomever He wills. Yet they argue about Allah, while He is Tremendous in might.

14. To Him belongs the call to truth. Those they call upon besides Him do not respond to them with anything—except as someone who stretches his hands towards water, so that it

13. THUNDER (ar-Ra'd)

may reach his mouth, but it does not reach it. The prayers of the unbelievers are only in vain.

15. To Allah prostrates everyone in the heavens and the earth, willingly or unwillingly, as do their shadows, in the morning and in the evening.

16. Say, "Who is the Lord of the heavens and the earth?" Say, "Allah." Say, "Have you taken besides Him protectors, who have no power to profit or harm even themselves?" Say, "Are the blind and the seeing equal? Or are darkness and light equal? Or have they assigned to Allah associates, who created the likes of His creation, so that the creations seemed to them alike? Say, "Allah is the Creator of all things, and He is The One, the Irresistible."

17. He sends down water from the sky, and riverbeds flow according to their capacity. The current carries swelling froth. And from what they heat in fire of ornaments or utensils comes a similar froth. Thus Allah exemplifies truth and falsehood. As for the froth, it is swept away, but what benefits the people remains in the ground. Thus Allah presents the analogies.

18. For those who respond to their Lord is the best. But as for those who do not respond to Him, even if they possessed everything on earth, and twice as much, they could not redeem themselves with it. Those will have the worst reckoning; and their home is Hell—a miserable destination.

19. Is he who knows that what was revealed to your from your Lord is the truth, like him who is blind? Only those who reason will remember.

20. Those who fulfill the promise to Allah, and do not violate the agreement.

21. And those who join what Allah has commanded to be joined, and fear their Lord, and dread the dire reckoning.

22. And those who patiently seek the presence of their Lord, and pray regularly, and spend from Our provisions to them, secretly and openly, and repel evil with good. These will have the Ultimate Home.

23. Everlasting Gardens, which they will enter, along with the righteous among their parents, and their spouses, and their descendants. And the angels will enter upon them from every gate.

24. "Peace be upon you, because you endured patiently. How excellent is the Final Home."

25. As for those who violate the promise to Allah, after pledging to keep it, and sever what Allah has commanded to be joined, and spread corruption on earth—these, the curse will be upon them, and they will have the Worst Home.

26. Allah dispenses the provisions to whomever He wills, and restricts. And they delight in the worldly life; yet the worldly life, compared to the Hereafter, is only enjoyment.

27. Those who disbelieve say, "If only a miracle was sent down to him from his Lord." Say, "Allah leads astray whomever He wills, and He guides to Himself whoever repents."

28. Those who believe, and whose hearts find comfort in the remembrance of Allah. Surely, it is in the remembrance of Allah that hearts find comfort."

29. For those who believe and do righteous deeds—for them is happiness and a beautiful return.

30. Thus We sent you among a community before which other communities have passed away, that you may recite to them what We revealed to you. Yet they deny the Benevolent One. Say, "He is my Lord; there is no god but He; in Him I trust, and to Him is my repentance."

31. Even if there were a Quran, by which mountains could be set in motion, or by which the earth could be shattered, or by which the dead could be made to speak. In fact, every decision rests with Allah. Did the believers not give up and realize that had Allah willed, He would have guided all humanity? Disasters will continue to strike those who disbelieve, because of their deeds, or

they fall near their homes, until Allah's promise comes true. Allah never breaks a promise.

32. Messengers before you were ridiculed, but I granted the disbelievers respite, and then I seized them. What a punishment it was!

33. Is He who is watchful over the deeds of every soul? Yet they ascribe associates to Allah. Say, "Name them! Or are you informing Him of something on earth He does not know, or is it a show of words?" In fact, the scheming of those who disbelieve is made to appear good to them, and they are averted from the path. Whomever Allah misguides has no guide.

34. There is for them torment in the worldly life, but the torment of the Hereafter is harsher. And they have no defender against Allah.

35. The likeness of the Garden promised to the righteous: rivers flowing beneath it; its food is perpetual, and so is its shade. Such is the sequel for those who guard against evil, but the sequel of the disbelievers is the Fire.

36. Those to whom We gave the Scripture rejoice in what was revealed to you, while some factions reject parts of it. Say, "I am commanded to worship Allah, and to never associate anything with Him. To Him I invite, and to Him is my return."

37. Thus We revealed it an Arabic code of law. Were you to follow their desires, after the knowledge that has come to you, you would have neither ally nor defender against Allah.

38. We sent messengers before you, and We assigned for them wives and offspring. No messenger could bring a sign except with the permission of Allah. For every era is a scripture.

39. Allah abolishes whatever He wills, and He affirms. With Him is the source of the Scripture.

40. Whether We show you some of what We have promised them, or We cause you to die—your duty is to inform, and Ours is the reckoning.

41. Do they not see how We deal with the earth, diminishing it at its edges? Allah judges; and nothing can hold back His judgment. And He is quick to settle accounts.

42. Those before them planned, but the entire plan is up to Allah. He knows what every soul earns. Those who disbelieve will know to whom the Ultimate Home is.

43. Those who disbelieve say, "You are not a messenger." Say, "Allah is a sufficient witness between me and you, and whoever has knowledge of the Scripture."

14. ABRAHAM
(Ibrahim)

*In the name of Allah,
the Gracious, the Merciful*

1. Alif, Lam, Ra. A Scripture that We revealed to you, that you may bring humanity from darkness to light—with the permission of their Lord—to the path of the Almighty, the Praiseworthy.

2. Allah—to whom belongs what is in the heavens and the earth. And woe to the disbelievers from a severe torment.

3. Those who prefer the present life to the Hereafter, and repel from the path of Allah, and seek to make it crooked—these are far astray.

4. We never sent any messenger except in the language of his people, to make things clear for them. Allah leads astray whom He wills, and guides whom He wills. He is the Mighty, the Wise.

5. We sent Moses with Our signs: "Bring your people out of darkness into light, and remind them of the Days of Allah." In that are signs for every patient and thankful person."

6. Moses said to his people, "Remember Allah's blessings upon you, as He delivered you from the people of Pharaoh, who inflicted on you terrible suffering, slaughtering your sons while sparing your daughters. In that was a serious trial from your Lord."

14. ABRAHAM (Ibrahim)

7. And when your Lord proclaimed: "If you give thanks, I will grant you increase; but if you are ungrateful, My punishment is severe."

8. And Moses said, "Even if you are ungrateful, together with everyone on earth—Allah is in no need, Worthy of Praise."

9. Has not the story reached you, of those before you, the people of Noah, and Aad, and Thamood—and those after them? None knows them except Allah. Their messengers came to them with the clear proofs, but they tried to silence them, and said, "We reject what you are sent with, and we are in serious doubt regarding what you are calling us to."

10. Their messengers said, "Is there any doubt about Allah, Maker of the heavens and the earth? He calls you to forgive you your sins, and to defer you until a stated term." They said, "You are only humans like us; you want to turn us away from what our ancestors worshiped; so bring us a clear proof."

11. Their messengers said to them, "We are only humans like you, but Allah favors whomever He wills from among His servants. We cannot possibly show you any proof, except by leave of Allah. In Allah let the faithful put their trust."

12. "And why should we not trust in Allah, when He has guided us in our ways? We will persevere in the face of your persecution. And upon Allah the reliant should rely."

13. Those who disbelieved said to their messengers, "We will expel you from our land, unless you return to our religion." And their Lord inspired them: "We will destroy the wrongdoers."

14. "And We will settle you in the land after them. That is for him who fears My Majesty, and fears My threats."

15. And they prayed for victory, and every stubborn tyrant came to disappointment.

16. Beyond him lies Hell, and he will be given to drink putrid water.

17. He will guzzle it, but he will not swallow it. Death will come at him from every direction, but he will not die. And beyond this is relentless suffering.

18. The likeness of those who disbelieve in their Lord: their works are like ashes, in a fierce wind, on a stormy day. They have no control over anything they have earned. That is the utmost misguidance.

19. Do you not see that Allah created the heavens and the earth with truth? If He wills, He can do away with you, and bring a new creation.

20. And that is not difficult for Allah.

21. They will emerge before Allah, altogether. The weak will say to those who were proud, "We were your followers, can you protect us at all against Allah's punishment?" They will say, "Had Allah guided us, we would have guided you. It is the same for us; whether we mourn, or are patient; there is no asylum for us."

22. And Satan will say, when the issue is settled, "Allah has promised you the promise of truth, and I promised you, but I failed you. I had no authority over you, except that I called you, and you answered me. So do not blame me, but blame yourselves. I cannot come to your aid, nor can you come to my aid. I reject your associating with me in the past. The wrongdoers will have a torment most painful."

23. But those who believed and did good deeds will be admitted into gardens beneath which rivers flow, to remain therein forever, by leave of their Lord. Their greeting therein will be: "Peace."

24. Do you not see how Allah presents a parable? A good word is like a good tree—its root is firm, and its branches are in the sky.

25. It yields its fruits every season by the will of its Lord. Allah presents the parables to the people, so that they may reflect.

26. And the parable of a bad word is that of a bad tree—it is uprooted from the ground; it has no stability.

14. ABRAHAM (Ibrahim)

27. Allah gives firmness to those who believe, with the firm word, in this life, and in the Hereafter. And Allah leads the wicked astray. Allah does whatever He wills.

28. Have you not seen those who exchanged the blessing of Allah with blasphemy, and landed their people into the house of perdition?

29. Hell—they will roast in it. What a miserable settlement.

30. And they set up rivals to Allah, in order to lead away from His path. Say, "Enjoy yourselves; your destination is the Fire."

31. Tell My servants who have believed to perform the prayers, and to give from what We have given them, secretly and publicly, before a Day comes in which there is neither trading nor friendship.

32. Allah is He Who created the heavens and the earth, and sends down water from the sky, and with it produces fruits for your sustenance. And He committed the ships to your service, sailing through the sea by His command, and He committed the rivers to your service.

33. And He committed the sun and the moon to your service, both continuously pursuing their courses, and He committed the night and the day to your service.

34. And He has given you something of all what you asked. And if you were to count Allah's blessings, you would not be able to enumerate them. The human being is unfair and ungrateful.

35. Recall that Abraham said, "O my Lord, make this land peaceful, and keep me and my sons from worshiping idols."

36. "My Lord, they have led many people astray. Whoever follows me belongs with me; and whoever disobeys me—You are Forgiving and Merciful."

37. "Our Lord, I have settled some of my offspring in a valley of no vegetation, by Your Sacred House, our Lord, so that they may perform the prayers. So make the hearts of some people incline towards them, and provide them with fruits, that they may be thankful."

38. "Our Lord, You know what we conceal and what we reveal. And nothing is hidden from Allah, on earth or in the heaven."

39. "Praise be to Allah, Who has given me, in my old age, Ishmael and Isaac. My Lord is the Hearer of Prayers."

40. "My Lord, make me one who performs the prayer, and from my offspring. Our Lord, accept my supplication."

41. "Our Lord, forgive me, and my parents, and the believers, on the Day the Reckoning takes place."

42. Do not ever think that Allah is unaware of what the wrongdoers do. He only defers them until a Day when the sights stare.

43. Their necks outstretched, their heads upraised, their gaze unblinking, their hearts void.

44. And warn mankind of the Day when the punishment will come upon them, and the wicked will say, "Our Lord, defer us for a little while, and we will answer Your call and follow the messengers." Did you not swear before that there will be no passing away for you?

45. And you inhabited the homes of those who wronged themselves, and it became clear to you how We dealt with them, and We cited for you the examples.

46. They planned their plans, but their plans are known to Allah, even if their plans can eliminate mountains.

47. Do not ever think that Allah will break His promise to His messengers. Allah is Strong, Able to Avenge.

48. On the Day when the earth is changed into another earth, and the heavens, and they will emerge before Allah, the One, the Irresistible.

49. On that Day, you will see the sinners bound together in chains.

50. Their garments made of tar, and the Fire covering their faces.

51. That Allah may repay each soul according to what it has earned. Allah is Quick in reckoning.

52. This is a proclamation for mankind, that they may be warned thereby, and know that He is One God, and that people of understanding may remember.

15. THE ROCK
(al-Hijr)

*In the name of Allah,
the Gracious, the Merciful*

1. Alif, Lam, Ra. These are the Verses of the Book; a Quran that makes things clear.

2. Perhaps those who disbelieve would like to become Muslims.

3. Leave them to eat, and enjoy, and be lulled by hope. They will find out.

4. We have never destroyed a town unless it had a set time.

5. No nation can bring its time forward, nor can they delay it.

6. And they said, "O you who received the message, you are insane."

7. Why do you not bring us the angels, if you are truthful?"

8. We do not send the angels down except with reason, and they will not be held back.

9. Surely We revealed the Message, and We will surely preserve it.

10. We sent others before you, to the former communities.

11. But no messenger came to them, but they ridiculed him.

12. Thus We slip it into the hearts of the guilty.

13. They do not believe in it, though the ways of the ancients have passed away.

14. Even if We opened for them a gateway into the sky, and they began to ascend through it.

15. They would still say, "Our eyes are hallucinating; in fact, we are people bewitched."

16. We placed constellations in the sky, and made them beautiful to the beholders.

17. And We guarded them from every outcast devil.

18. Except one who steals a hearing, and is followed by a visible projectile.

19. We spread the earth, and placed stabilizers in it, and in it We grew all things in proper measure.

20. And in it We created livelihoods for you, and for those for whom you are not the providers.

21. There is not a thing but with Us are its stores, and We send it down only in precise measure.

22. We send the fertilizing winds; and send down water from the sky, and give it to you to drink, and you are not the ones who store it.

23. It is We who give life and cause death, and We are the Inheritors.

24. And We know those of you who go forward, and We know those who lag behind.

25. It is your Lord who will gather them together. He is the Wise, the Knowing.

26. We created the human being from clay, from molded mud.

27. And the jinn We created before, from piercing fire.

28. Your Lord said to the angels, "I am creating a human being from clay, from molded mud."

29. "When I have formed him, and breathed into him of My spirit, fall down prostrating before him."

30. So the angels prostrated themselves, all together.

31. Except for Satan. He refused to be among those who prostrated themselves.

15. THE ROCK (al-Hijr)

32. He said, "O Satan, what kept you from being among those who prostrated themselves?"

33. He said, "I am not about to prostrate myself before a human being, whom You created from clay, from molded mud."

34. He said, "Then get out of here, for you are an outcast".

35. "And the curse will be upon you until the Day of Judgment."

36. He said, "My Lord, reprieve me until the Day they are resurrected."

37. He said, "You are of those reprieved."

38. "Until the Day of the time appointed."

39. He said, "My Lord, since You have lured me away, I will glamorize for them on earth, and I will lure them all away."

40. "Except for Your sincere servants among them."

41. He said, "This is a right way with Me."

42. "Over My servants you have no authority, except for the sinners who follow you."

43. And Hell is the meeting-place for them all.

44. "It has seven doors; for each door is an assigned class."

45. But the righteous will be in gardens with springs.

46. "Enter it in peace and security."

47. And We will remove all ill-feelings from their hearts—brothers and sisters, on couches facing one another.

48. No fatigue will ever touch them therein, nor will they be asked to leave it.

49. Inform My servants that I am the Forgiver, the Merciful.

50. And that My punishment is the painful punishment.

51. And inform them of the guests of Abraham.

52. When they entered upon him, and said, "Peace." He said, "We are wary of you."

53. They said, "Do not fear; we bring you good news of a boy endowed with knowledge."

54. He said, "Do you bring me good news, when old age has overtaken me? What good news do you bring?"

55. They said, "We bring you good news in truth, so do not despair."

56. He said, "And who despairs of his Lord's mercy but the lost?"

57. He said, "So what is your business, O envoys?"

58. They said, "We were sent to a sinful people."

59. "Except for the family of Lot; we will save them all."

60. "Except for his wife." We have determined that she will be of those who lag behind.

61. And when the envoys came to the family of Lot.

62. He said, "You are a people unknown to me."

63. They said, "We bring you what they have doubts about."

64. "We bring you the truth, and we are truthful."

65. "Travel with your family at the dead of the night, and follow up behind them, and let none of you look back, and proceed as commanded."

66. And We informed him of Our decree: the last remnant of these will be uprooted by early morning.

67. And the people of the town came joyfully.

68. He said, "These are my guests, so do not embarrass me."

69. "And fear Allah, and do not disgrace me."

70. They said, "Did we not forbid you from strangers?"

71. He said, "These are my daughters, if you must."

72. By your life, they were blundering in their drunkenness.

16. THE BEE (an-Nahl)

73. So the Blast struck them at sunrise.

74. And We turned it upside down, and rained down upon them stones of baked clay.

75. Surely in that are lessons for those who read signs.

76. And it is on an existing road.

77. Surely in that is a sign for the believers.

78. The people of the Woods were also wrong-doers.

79. So We took revenge upon them. Both are clearly documented.

80. The people of the Rock also rejected the messengers.

81. We gave them Our revelations, but they turned away from them.

82. They used to carve homes in the mountains, feeling secure.

83. But the Blast struck them in the morning.

84. All they had acquired was of no avail to them.

85. We did not create the heavens and the earth, and what lies between them, except with truth. The Hour is coming, so forgive with gracious forgiveness.

86. Your Lord is the All-Knowing Creator.

87. We have given you seven of the pairs, and the Grand Quran.

88. Do not extend your eyes towards what We have bestowed on some couples of them to enjoy, and do not grieve over them, and lower your wing to the believers.

89. And say, "I am the clear warner."

90. Just as We sent down to the separatists.

91. Those who made the Quran obsolete.

92. By your Lord, we will question them all.

93. About what they used to do.

94. So proclaim openly what you are commanded, and turn away from the polytheists.

95. We are enough for you against the mockers.

96. Those who set up another god with Allah. They will come to know.

97. We are aware that your heart is strained by what they say.

98. So glorify the praise of your Lord, and be among those who bow down.

99. And worship your Lord in order to attain certainty.

16. THE BEE (an-Nahl)

In the name of Allah, the Gracious, the Merciful

1. The command of Allah has come, so do not rush it. Glory be to Him; exalted above what they associate.

2. He sends down the angels with the Spirit by His command, upon whom He wills of His servants: "Give warning that there is no god but Me, and fear Me."

3. He created the heavens and the earth with justice. He is exalted above the associations they attribute.

4. He created the human being from a drop of fluid, yet he becomes an open adversary.

5. And the livestock—He created them for you. In them are warmth and benefits for you, and of them you eat.

6. And there is beauty in them for you, when you bring them home, and when you drive them to pasture.

7. And they carry your loads to territory you could not have reached without great hardship. Your Lord is Clement and Merciful.

8. And the horses, and the mules, and the donkeys—for you to ride, and for luxury. And He creates what you do not know.

9. It is for Allah to point out the paths, but some of them are flawed. Had He willed, He could have guided you all.

16. THE BEE (an-Nahl)

10. It is He Who sends down for you from the sky water. From it is drink, and with it grows vegetation for grazing.

11. And He produces for you grains with it, and olives, and date-palms, and grapes, and all kinds of fruits. Surely in that is a sign for people who think.

12. And He regulated for you the night and the day; and the sun, and the moon, and the stars are disposed by His command. Surely in that are signs for people who ponder.

13. And whatsoever He created for you on earth is of diverse colors. Surely in that is a sign for people who are mindful.

14. And it is He who made the sea to serve you, that you may eat from it tender meat, and extract from it ornaments that you wear. And you see the ships plowing through it, as you seek His bounties, so that you may give thanks.

15. And he cast mountains on the earth, lest it shifts with you; and rivers, and roads, so that you may be guided.

16. And landmarks. And by the stars they guide themselves.

17. Is He who creates like him who does not create? Will you not take a lesson?

18. And if you tried to enumerate the favors of Allah, you will not be able to count them. Allah is Forgiving and Merciful.

19. And Allah knows what you hide and what you disclose.

20. Those they invoke besides Allah create nothing, but are themselves created.

21. They are dead, not alive; and they do not know when they will be resurrected.

22. Your God is one God. As for those who do not believe in the Hereafter, their hearts are in denial, and they are arrogant.

23. Without a doubt, Allah knows what they conceal and what they reveal. He does not like the arrogant.

24. And when it is said to them, "What has your Lord sent down?" They say, "Legends of the ancients."

25. So let them carry their loads complete on the Day of Resurrection, and some of the loads of those they misguided without knowledge. Evil is what they carry.

26. Those before them also schemed, but Allah took their structures from the foundations, and the roof caved in on them. The punishment came at them from where they did not perceive.

27. Then, on the Day of Resurrection, He will disgrace them, and say, "Where are My associates for whose sake you used to dispute?" Those who were given knowledge will say, "Today shame and misery are upon the disbelievers."

28. Those wronging their souls while the angels are taking them away—they will propose peace: "We did no wrong." Yes you did. Allah is aware of what you used to do."

29. Enter the gates of Hell, to dwell therein forever. Miserable is the residence of the arrogant.

30. And it will be said to those who maintained piety, "What has your Lord revealed?" They will say, "Goodness." To those who do good in this world is goodness, and the Home of the Hereafter is even better. How wonderful is the residence of the pious.

31. The Gardens of Perpetuity, which they will enter, beneath which rivers flow, where they will have whatever they desire. Thus Allah rewards the pious.

32. Those who are in a wholesome state when the angels take them—will say, "Peace be upon you; enter Paradise, for what you used to do."

33. Are they but waiting for the angels to come to them, or for the command of your Lord to arrive? Those before them did likewise. Allah did not wrong them, but they used to wrong their own souls.

16. THE BEE (an-Nahl)

34. So the evils of their deeds assailed them, and what they used to ridicule engulfed them.

35. The idolaters say, "Had Allah willed, we would not have worshiped anything besides Him, neither us, nor our ancestors, nor would we have prohibited anything besides His prohibitions." Those before them did likewise. Are the messengers responsible for anything but clear communication?

36. To every community We sent a messenger: "Worship Allah, and avoid idolatry." Some of them Allah guided, while others deserved misguidance. So travel through the earth, and see what the fate of the deniers was.

37. Even though you may be concerned about their guidance, Allah does not guide those who misguide. And they will have no saviors.

38. And they swear by Allah with their most solemn oaths, "Allah will not resurrect anyone who dies." Yes indeed, it is a promise binding on Him, but most people do not know.

39. To clarify for them what they differed about, and for the faithless to know that they were liars.

40. When We intend for something to happen, We say to it, "Be," and it becomes.

41. Those who emigrate for Allah's sake after being persecuted, We will settle them in a good place in this world; but the reward of the Hereafter is greater, if they only knew.

42. Those who endure patiently, and in their Lord they put their trust.

43. We did not send before you except men whom We inspired. So ask the people of knowledge, if you do not know.

44. With the clarifications and the scriptures. And We revealed to you the Reminder, that you may clarify to the people what was revealed to them, and that they may reflect.

45. Do those who scheme evils feel secure that Allah will not cause the earth to cave in with them, or that the punishment will not come upon them from where they do not perceive?

46. Or that He will not seize them during their activities? And they will not be able to prevent it.

47. Or that He will not seize them while in dread? Your Lord is Gentle and Merciful.

48. Have they not observed what Allah has created? Their shadows revolve from the right and the left, bowing to Allah as they shrink away.

49. To Allah bows down everything in the heavens and everything on earth—every living creature, and the angels, and without being proud.

50. They fear their Lord above them, and they do what they are commanded.

51. Allah has said: "Do not take two gods; He is only One God; so fear only Me."

52. To Him belongs everything in the heavens and the earth; and to Him obedience is due always. Do you, then, fear anyone other than Allah?

53. Whatever blessing you have is from Allah. And when harm touches you, it is to Him that you groan.

54. But when He lifts the harm from you, some of you associate others with their Lord.

55. To show ingratitude for what We have given them. Enjoy yourselves. You will soon know.

56. And they allocate, to something they do not know, a share of what We have provided for them. By Allah, you will be questioned about what you have been inventing.

57. And they attribute to Allah daughters—exalted is He—and for themselves what they desire.

58. And when one of them is given news of a female infant, his face darkens, and he chokes with grief.

59. He hides from the people because of the bad news given to him. Shall he keep it in humiliation, or bury it in the dust? Evil is the decision they make.

16. THE BEE (an-Nahl)

60. Those who do not believe in the Hereafter set a bad example, while Allah sets the Highest Example. He is the Mighty, the Wise.

61. If Allah were to hold mankind for their injustices, He would not leave upon it a single creature, but He postpones them until an appointed time. Then, when their time arrives, they will not delay it by one hour, nor will they advance it.

62. And they attribute to Allah what they themselves dislike, while their tongues utter the lie that theirs is the goodness. Without a doubt, for them is the Fire, and they will be neglected.

63. By Allah, We sent messengers to communities before you, but Satan made their deeds appear alluring to them. He is their master today, and they will have a painful punishment.

64. We revealed to you the Scripture only to clarify for them what they differ about, and guidance and mercy for people who believe.

65. Allah sends down water from the sky, with which He revives the earth after its death. In this is a sign for people who listen.

66. And there is a lesson for you in cattle: We give you a drink from their bellies, from between waste and blood, pure milk, refreshing to the drinkers.

67. And from the fruits of date-palms and grapevines, you derive sugar and wholesome food. In this is a sign for people who understand.

68. And your Lord inspired the bee: "Set up hives in the mountains, and in the trees, and in what they construct."

69. Then eat of all the fruits, and go along the pathways of your Lord, with precision. From their bellies emerges a fluid of diverse colors, containing healing for the people. Surely in this is a sign for people who reflect.

70. Allah created you; then He takes you away. Some of you will be brought back to the worst age, so that he will no longer know anything, after having acquired knowledge. Allah is Omniscient and Omnipotent.

71. Allah has favored some of you over others in livelihood. Those who are favored would not give their properties to their servants, to the extent of making them partners in it. Will they then renounce Allah's blessings?

72. Allah has given you mates from among yourselves; and has produced for you, from your mates, children and grandchildren; and has provided you with good things. Will they then believe in falsehood, and refuse Allah's favors?

73. And yet they serve besides Allah what possesses no provisions for them in the heavens, nor on earth, nor are they capable.

74. So do not cite the examples for Allah. Allah knows, and you do not know.

75. Allah cites the example of a bonded slave, who has no power over anything; and someone to whom We have given plentiful provision, from which he gives secretly and openly. Are they equal in comparison? All praise belongs to Allah, but most of them do not know.

76. And Allah cites the example of two men: one of them dumb, unable to do anything, and is a burden on his master; whichever way he directs him, he achieves nothing good. Is he equal to him who commands justice, and is on a straight path?

77. To Allah belongs the unseen of the heavens and the earth. The coming of the Hour is only as the twinkling of the eye, or even nearer. Allah has power over everything.

78. Allah brought you out of your mothers' wombs, not knowing anything; and He gave you the hearing, and the eyesight, and the brains; that you may give thanks.

79. Have they not seen the birds, flying in the midst of the sky? None sustains them except Allah. In this are signs for people who believe.

80. And Allah has given you in your homes habitats for you, and has provided for you out of the hides of livestock portable homes for

16. THE BEE (an-Nahl)

you, so you can use them when you travel, and when you camp; and from their wool, and fur, and hair, furnishings and comfort for a while.

81. And Allah has made for you shade out of what He has created, and has given you resorts in the mountains, and has given you garments to protect you from the heat, and garments to protect you from your violence. Thus He completes His blessings upon you, so that you may submit.

82. But if they turn away, your only duty is clear communication.

83. They recognize Allah's blessing, but then deny it, as most of them are ungrateful.

84. On the Day when We raise up a witness from every community—those who disbelieved will not be permitted, nor will they be excused.

85. When those who did wrong see the punishment, it will not be lightened for them, nor will they be reprieved.

86. And when the idolaters see their associates, they will say, "Our Lord, these are our associates whom we used to invoke besides You." They will strike back at them with the saying, "Surely you are liars."

87. On that Day they will offer their submission to Allah, and what they had invented will abandon them.

88. Those who disbelieve and obstruct from Allah's path—We will add punishment to their punishment, on account of the mischief they used to make.

89. On the Day when We raise in every community a witness against them, from among them, and bring you as a witness against these. We have revealed to you the Book, as an explanation of all things, and guidance, and mercy and good news for those who submit.

90. Allah commands justice, and goodness, and generosity towards relatives. And He forbids immorality, and injustice, and oppression. He advises you, so that you may take heed.

91. Fulfill Allah's covenant when you make a covenant, and do not break your oaths after ratifying them. You have made Allah your guarantor, and Allah knows what you do.

92. And do not be like her who unravels her yarn, breaking it into pieces, after she has spun it strongly. Nor use your oaths as means of deception among you, because one community is more prosperous than another. Allah is testing you thereby. On the Day of Resurrection, He will make clear to you everything you had disputed about.

93. Had Allah willed, He would have made you one congregation, but He leaves astray whom He wills, and He guides whom He wills. And you will surely be questioned about what you used to do.

94. And do not use your oaths to deceive one another, so that a foot may not slip after being firm, and you taste misery because you hindered from Allah's path, and incur a terrible torment.

95. And do not exchange Allah's covenant for a small price. What is with Allah is better for you, if you only knew.

96. What you have runs out, but what is with Allah remains. We will reward those who are patient according to the best of their deeds.

97. Whoever works righteousness, whether male or female, while being a believer, We will grant him a good life—and We will reward them according to the best of what they used to do.

98. When you read the Quran, seek refuge with Allah from Satan the outcast.

99. He has no authority over those who believe and trust in their Lord.

100. His authority is only over those who follow him, and those who associate others with Him.

101. When We substitute a verse in place of another verse—and Allah knows best what He

16. THE BEE (an-Nahl)

reveals—they say, "You are an impostor." But most of them do not know.

102. Say, "The Holy Spirit has brought it down from your Lord, truthfully, in order to stabilize those who believe, and as guidance and good news for those who submit."

103. We are well aware that they say, "It is a human being who is teaching him." But the tongue of him they allude to is foreign, while this is a clear Arabic tongue.

104. Those who do not believe in Allah's revelations—Allah will not guide them, and for them is a painful punishment.

105. It is those who do not believe in Allah's revelations who fabricate falsehood. These are the liars.

106. Whoever renounces faith in Allah after having believed—except for someone who is compelled, while his heart rests securely in faith—but whoever willingly opens up his heart to disbelief—upon them falls wrath from Allah, and for them is a tremendous torment.

107. That is because they have preferred the worldly life to the Hereafter, and because Allah does not guide the people who refuse.

108. It is they whom Allah has sealed their hearts, and their hearing, and their sight. It is they who are the heedless.

109. There is no doubt that in the Hereafter they will be the losers.

110. But then your Lord—for those who emigrated after being persecuted, then struggled and persevered—your Lord thereafter is Forgiving and Merciful.

111. On the Day when every soul will come pleading for itself, and every soul will be paid in full for what it has done, and they will not be wronged.

112. And Allah cites the example of a town that was secure and peaceful, with its livelihood coming to it abundantly from every direction. But then it turned unappreciative of Allah's blessings, so Allah made it taste the robe of hunger and fear, because of what they used to craft.

113. A messenger from among them had come to them, but they denounced him, so the punishment seized them in the midst of their wrongdoing.

114. Eat of the lawful and good things Allah has provided for you, and be thankful for Allah's blessings, if it is Him that you serve.

115. He has forbidden you carrion, and blood, and the flesh of swine, and anything consecrated to other than Allah. But if anyone is compelled by necessity, without being deliberate or malicious, then Allah is Forgiving and Merciful.

116. And do not say of falsehood asserted by your tongues, "This is lawful, and this is unlawful," in order to invent lies and attribute them to Allah. Those who invent lies and attribute them to Allah will not succeed.

117. A brief enjoyment—then they will have a painful punishment.

118. For those who are Jews, We have prohibited what We related to you before. We did not wrong them, but they used to wrong their own selves.

119. But towards those who do wrongs in ignorance, and then repent afterwards and reform, your Lord thereafter is Forgiving and Merciful.

120. Abraham was an exemplary leader, devoted to Allah, a monotheist, and was not of the polytheists.

121. Thankful for His blessings. He chose him, and guided him to a straight path.

122. And We gave him goodness in this world, and in the Hereafter he will be among the righteous.

123. Then We inspired you: "Follow the religion of Abraham, the Monotheist. He was not an idol-worshiper."

124. The Sabbath was decreed only for those who differed about it. Your Lord will judge between them on the Day of Resurrection regarding their differences.

125. Invite to the way of your Lord with wisdom and good advice, and debate with them in the most dignified manner. Your Lord is aware of those who stray from His path, and He is aware of those who are guided.

126. If you were to retaliate, retaliate to the same degree as the injury done to you. But if you resort to patience—it is better for the patient.

127. So be patient. Your patience is solely from Allah. And do not grieve over them, and do not be stressed by their schemes.

128. Allah is with those who are righteous and those who are virtuous.

17. THE NIGHT JOURNEY (al-Isra')

*In the name of Allah,
the Gracious, the Merciful*

1. Glory to Him who journeyed His servant by night, from the Sacred Mosque, to the Farthest Mosque, whose precincts We have blessed, in order to show him of Our wonders. He is the Listener, the Beholder.

2. And We gave Moses the Scripture, and made it a guide for the Children of Israel: Take none for protector other than Me.

3. The descendants of those We carried with Noah. He was an appreciative servant.

4. And We conveyed to the Children of Israel in the Scripture: You will commit evil on earth twice, and you will rise to a great height.

5. When the first of the two promises came true, We sent against you servants of Ours, possessing great might, and they ransacked your homes. It was a promise fulfilled.

6. Then We gave you back your turn against them, and supplied you with wealth and children, and made you more numerous.

7. If you work righteousness, you work righteousness for yourselves; and if you commit evil, you do so against yourselves. Then, when the second promise comes true, they will make your faces filled with sorrow, and enter the Temple as they entered it the first time, and utterly destroy all that falls into their power.

8. Perhaps your Lord will have mercy on you. But if you revert, We will revert. We have made Hell a prison for the disbelievers.

9. This Quran guides to what is most upright; and it gives good news to the believers who do good deeds, that they will have a great reward.

10. And those who do not believe in the Hereafter—We have prepared for them a painful punishment.

11. The human being prays for evil as he prays for good. The human being is very hasty.

12. We have made the night and the day two wonders. We erased the wonder of the night, and made the wonder of the day revealing, that you may seek bounty from your Lord, and know the number of years, and the calculation. We have explained all things in detail.

13. For every person We have attached his fate to his neck. And on the Day of Resurrection, We will bring out for him a book which he will find spread open.

14. "Read your book; today there will be none but yourself to call you to account."

15. Whoever is guided—is guided for his own good. And whoever goes astray—goes astray to his detriment. No burdened soul carries the burdens of another, nor do We ever punish until We have sent a messenger.

16. When We decide to destroy a town, We command its affluent ones, they transgress in it, so the word becomes justified against it, and We destroy it completely.

17. How many generations have We destroyed after Noah? Your Lord is sufficient as Knower and Beholder of the sins of his servants.

18. Whoever desires the fleeting life, We expedite for him what We decide to give him, to whomever We desire. Then We consign him

17. THE NIGHT JOURNEY (al-Isra')

to Hell, where he will roast, condemned and defeated.

19. But whoever desires the Hereafter, and pursues it as it should be pursued, while he is a believer; these—their effort will be appreciated.

20. To all—these and those—We extend from the gifts of your Lord. The gifts of your Lord are not restricted.

21. See how We have favored some of them over others; yet the Hereafter is greater in ranks, and greater in favors.

22. Do not set up another god with Allah, lest you become condemned and damned.

23. Your Lord has commanded that you worship none but Him, and that you be good to your parents. If either of them or both of them reach old age with you, do not say to them a word of disrespect, nor scold them, but say to them kind words.

24. And lower to them the wing of humility, out of mercy, and say, "My Lord, have mercy on them, as they raised me when I was a child."

25. Your Lord knows best what is in your minds. If you are righteous—He is Forgiving to the obedient.

26. And give the relative his rights, and the poor, and the wayfarer, and do not squander wastefully.

27. The extravagant are brethren of the devils, and the devil is ever ungrateful to his Lord.

28. But if you turn away from them, seeking mercy from your Lord which you hope for, then say to them words of comfort.

29. And do not keep your hand tied to your neck, nor spread it out fully, lest you end up liable and regretful.

30. Your Lord expands the provision for whomever He wills, and restricts it. He is fully Informed, Observant of His servants.

31. And do not kill your children for fear of poverty. We provide for them, and for you. Killing them is a grave sin.

32. And do not come near adultery. It is immoral, and an evil way.

33. And do not kill the soul which Allah has made sacred, except in the course of justice. If someone is killed unjustly, We have given his next of kin certain authority. But he should not be excessive in killing, for he will be supported.

34. And do not go near the orphan's property, except with the best of intentions, until he has reached his maturity. And honor your pledge, because the pledge involves responsibility.

35. And give full measure when you measure, and weigh with accurate scales. That is fair, and the best determination.

36. And do not occupy yourself with what you have no knowledge of. The hearing, and the sight, and the brains—all these will be questioned.

37. And do not walk proudly on earth. You can neither pierce the earth, nor can you match the mountains in height.

38. The evil of all these is disliked by your Lord.

39. That is some of the wisdom your Lord has revealed to you. Do not set up with Allah another god, or else you will be thrown in Hell, rebuked and banished.

40. Has your Lord favored you with sons, while choosing for Himself daughters from among the angels? You are indeed saying a terrible thing.

41. We have explained in this Quran in various ways, that they may remember, but it only adds to their rebellion.

42. Say, "If there were other gods with Him, as they say, they would have sought a way to the Lord of the Throne."

43. Be He glorified. He is exalted, far above what they say.

44. Praising Him are the seven heavens, and the earth, and everyone in them. There is not a thing that does not glorify Him with praise,

17. THE NIGHT JOURNEY (al-Isra')

but you do not understand their praises. He is indeed Forbearing and Forgiving.

45. When you read the Quran, We place between you and those who do not believe in the Hereafter an invisible barrier.

46. And We drape veils over their hearts, preventing them from understanding it, and heaviness in their ears. And when you mention your Lord alone in the Quran, they turn their backs in aversion.

47. We know well what they listen to, when they listen to you, as they conspire, when the wrongdoers say, "You only follow a man bewitched."

48. Note what they compared you to. They are lost, and unable to find a way.

49. And they say, "When we have become bones and fragments, shall we really be resurrected as a new creation?"

50. Say, "Even if you become rocks or iron.

51. Or some substance, which, in your minds, is even harder." Then they will say, "Who will restore us?" Say, "The One who originated you the first time." Then they will nod their heads at you, and say, "When will it be?" Say, "Perhaps it will be soon."

52. On the Day when He calls you, you will respond with His praise, and you will realize that you stayed only a little.

53. Tell My servants to say what is best. Satan sows discord among them. Satan is to man an open enemy.

54. Your Lord knows you best. If He wills, He will have mercy on you; and if He wills, He will punish you. We did not send you as their advocate.

55. Your Lord knows well everyone in the heavens and the earth. We have given some prophets advantage over others; and to David We gave the Psalms.

56. Say, "Call upon those you claim besides Him. They have no power to relieve your adversity, nor can they change it."

57. Those they call upon are themselves seeking means of access to their Lord, vying to be nearer, and hoping for His mercy, and fearing His punishment. The punishment of your Lord is to be dreaded.

58. There is no city but We will destroy before the Day of Resurrection, or punish it with a severe punishment. This is inscribed in the Book.

59. Nothing prevents Us from sending miraculous signs, except that the ancients called them lies. We gave Thamood the she-camel, a visible sign, but they mistreated her. We do not send the signs except to instill reverence.

60. We said to you that your Lord encompasses humanity. We did not make the vision We showed you, except as a test for the people, and the tree cursed in the Quran. We frighten them, but that only increases their defiance.

61. When We said to the angels, "Bow down before Adam," they bowed down, except for Satan. He said, "Shall I bow down before someone You created from mud?"

62. He said, "Do You see this one whom You have honored more than me? If You reprieve me until the Day of Resurrection, I will bring his descendants under my sway, except for a few."

63. He said, "Begone! Whoever of them follows you—Hell is your reward, an ample reward."

64. "And entice whomever of them you can with your voice, and rally against them your cavalry and your infantry, and share with them in wealth and children, and make promises to them." But Satan promises them nothing but delusion.

65. "As for My devotees, you have no authority over them." Your Lord is an adequate Guardian.

66. Your Lord is He who propels for you the ships at sea, that you may seek of His bounty. He is towards you Most Merciful.

17. THE NIGHT JOURNEY (al-Isra')

67. When harm afflicts you at sea, those you pray to vanish, except for Him. But when He saves you to land, you turn away. The human being is ever thankless.

68. Are you confident that He will not cause a track of land to cave in beneath you, or unleash a tornado against you, and then you find no protector?

69. Or are you confident that He will not return you to it once again, and unleash a hurricane against you, and drown you for your ingratitude? Then you will find no helper against Us.

70. We have honored the Children of Adam, and carried them on land and sea, and provided them with good things, and greatly favored them over many of those We created.

71. On the Day when We call every people with their leader. Whoever is given his record in his right hand—these will read their record, and they will not be wronged one bit.

72. But whoever is blind in this, he will be blind in the Hereafter, and further astray from the way.

73. They almost lured you away from what We have revealed to you, so that you would invent something else in Our name. In that case, they would have taken you for a friend.

74. Had We not given you stability, you might have inclined towards them a little.

75. Then We would have made you taste double in life, and double at death; then you would have found for yourself no helper against Us.

76. They almost provoked you, to expel you from the land. In that case, they would not have lasted after you, except briefly.

77. The tradition of the messengers We sent before you—you will find no change in Our rules.

78. Perform the prayer at the decline of the sun, until the darkness of the night; and the Quran at dawn. The Quran at dawn is witnessed.

79. And keep vigil with it during parts of the night, as an extra prayer. Perhaps your Lord will raise you to a laudable position.

80. And say, "My Lord, lead me in through an entry of truth, and lead me out through an exit of truth, and grant me from You a supporting power."

81. And say, "The truth has come, and falsehood has withered away; for falsehood is bound to wither away."

82. We send down in the Quran healing and mercy for the believers, but it increases the wrongdoers only in loss.

83. When We bless the human being, he turns away and distances himself. But when adversity touches him, he is in despair.

84. Say, "Each does according to his disposition. Your Lord knows best who is better guided in the way."

85. And they ask you about the Spirit. Say, "The Spirit belongs to the domain of my Lord; and you were given only little knowledge."

86. If We willed, We could take away what We revealed to you. Then you will find for yourself no protecting guardian against Us.

87. Except through a mercy from your Lord. His favors upon you have been great.

88. Say, "If mankind and jinn came together to produce the like of this Quran, they could never produce the like of it, even if they backed up one another."

89. We have displayed for mankind in this Quran every kind of similitude, but most people insist on denying the truth.

90. And they said, "We will not believe in you unless you make a spring burst from the ground for us.

91. Or you have a garden of palms and vines; then cause rivers to gush pouring through them.

92. Or make the sky fall on us in pieces, as you claim, or bring Allah and the angels before us.

18. THE CAVE (al-Kahf)

93. Or you possess a house of gold. Or you ascend into the sky. Even then, we will not believe in your ascension, unless you bring down for us a book that we can read." Say, "Glory be to my Lord. Am I anything but a human messenger?"

94. Nothing prevented the people from believing, when guidance has come to them, except that they said, "Did Allah send a human messenger?"

95. Say, "If there were angels on earth, walking around in peace, We would have sent down to them from heaven an angel messenger."

96. Say, "Allah is enough witness between you and me. He is fully aware of His servants, and He sees them well."

97. Whomever Allah guides is the guided one. And whomever He leaves astray—for them you will find no protectors apart from Him. And We will gather them on the Day of Resurrection, on their faces, blind, dumb, and deaf. Their abode is Hell; whenever it abates, We intensify the blaze for them.

98. This is their repayment for having blasphemed against Our revelations, and having said, "Shall we, when we have become bones and fragments, be resurrected as a new creation?"

99. Do they not consider that Allah, Who created the heavens and the earth, is Able to create the likes of them? He has assigned for them a term, in which there is no doubt. But the wrongdoers persist in denying the truth.

100. Say, "If you possessed the treasuries of my Lord's mercy, you would have withheld them for fear of spending." The human being has always been stingy.

101. We gave Moses nine clear signs—ask the Children of Israel. When he went to them, Pharaoh said to him, "I think that you, Moses, are bewitched."

102. He said, "You know that none sent these down except the Lord of the heavens and the earth—eye openers; and I think that you, Pharaoh, are doomed."

103. He resolved to scare them off the land, but We drowned him, and those with him, altogether.

104. After him, We said to the Children of Israel, "Inhabit the land, and when the promise of the Hereafter arrives, We will bring you all together."

105. With the truth We sent it down, and with the truth it descended. We sent you only as a bearer of good news and a warner.

106. A Quran which We unfolded gradually, that you may recite to the people over time. And We revealed it in stages.

107. Say, "Believe in it, or do not believe." Those who were given knowledge before it, when it is recited to them, they fall to their chins, prostrating.

108. And they say, "Glory to our Lord. The promise of our Lord is fulfilled."

109. And they fall to their chins, weeping, and it adds to their humility.

110. Say, "Call Him Allah, or call Him the Most Merciful. Whichever name you use, to Him belong the Best Names." And be neither loud in your prayer, nor silent in it, but follow a course in between.

111. And say, "Praise be to Allah, who has not begotten a son, nor has He a partner in sovereignty, nor has He an ally out of weakness, and glorify Him constantly."

18. THE CAVE (al-Kahf)

*In the name of Allah,
the Gracious, the Merciful*

1. Praise be to Allah, who revealed the Book to His servant, and allowed in it no distortion.

2. Valuable—to warn of severe punishment from Himself; and to deliver good news to the believers who do righteous deeds, that they will have an excellent reward.

3. In which they will abide forever.

18. THE CAVE (al-Kahf)

4. And to warn those who say, "Allah has begotten a son."

5. They have no knowledge of this, nor did their forefathers. Grave is the word that comes out of their mouths. They say nothing but a lie.

6. Perhaps you may destroy yourself with grief, chasing after them, if they do not believe in this information.

7. We made what is upon the earth an ornament for it, to test them as to which of them is best in conduct.

8. And We will turn what is on it into barren waste.

9. Did you know that the People of the Cave and the Inscription were of Our wondrous signs?

10. When the youths took shelter in the cave, they said, "Our Lord, give us mercy from Yourself, and bless our affair with guidance."

11. Then We sealed their ears in the cave for a number of years.

12. Then We awakened them to know which of the two groups could better calculate the length of their stay.

13. We relate to you their story in truth. They were youths who believed in their Lord, and We increased them in guidance.

14. And We strengthened their hearts, when they stood up and said, "Our Lord is the Lord of the heavens and the earth; we will not call on any god besides Him, for then we would have spoken an outrage."

15. "These people, our people, have taken to themselves gods other than Him. Why do they not bring a clear proof concerning them? Who, then, does greater wrong than he who invents lies and attributes them to Allah?"

16. "Now that you have withdrawn from them, and from what they worship besides Allah, take shelter in the cave. And your Lord will unfold His mercy for you, and will set your affair towards ease."

17. You would have seen the sun, when it rose, veering away from their cave towards the right, and when it sets, moving away from them to the left, as they lay in the midst of the cave. That was one of Allah's wonders. He whom Allah guides is truly guided; but he whom He misguides, for him you will find no directing friend.

18. You would think them awake, although they were asleep. And We turned them over to the right, and to the left, with their dog stretching its paws across the threshold. Had you looked at them, you would have turned away from them in flight, and been filled with fear of them.

19. Even so, We awakened them, so that they may ask one another. A speaker among them said, "How long have you stayed?" They said, "We have stayed a day, or part of a day." They said, "Your Lord knows best how long you have stayed." "Send one of you to the city, with this money of yours, and let him see which food is most suitable, and let him bring you some provision thereof. And let him be gentle, and let no one become aware of you."

20. "If they discover you, they will stone you, or force you back into their religion; then you will never be saved."

21. So it was, that We caused them to be discovered, that they would know that the promise of Allah is true, and that of the Hour there is no doubt. As they were disputing their case among themselves, they said, "Build over them a building." Their Lord knows best about them. Those who prevailed over their case said, "We will set up over them a place of worship."

22. They will say, "Three, and their fourth being their dog." And they will say, "Five, and their sixth being their dog," guessing at the unknown. And they will say, "Seven, and their eighth being their dog." Say, "My Lord knows best their number." None knows them except a few. So do not argue concerning them except with an obvious argument, and do not consult any of them about them.

18. THE CAVE (al-Kahf)

23. And never say about anything, "I will do that tomorrow."

24. Without saying, "If Allah wills." And remember your Lord if you forget, and say, "Perhaps my Lord will guide me to nearer than this in integrity."

25. And they stayed in their cave for three hundred years, adding nine.

26. Say, "Allah knows best how long they stayed." His is the mystery of the heavens and the earth. By Him you see and hear. They have no guardian apart from Him, and He shares His Sovereignty with no one.

27. And recite what was revealed to you from the Book of your Lord. There is no changing His words, and you will find no refuge except in Him.

28. And content yourself with those who pray to their Lord morning and evening, desiring His Presence. And do not turn your eyes away from them, desiring the glitter of this world. And do not obey him whose heart We have made heedless of Our remembrance—so he follows his own desires—and his priorities are confused.

29. And say, "The truth is from your Lord. Whoever wills—let him believe. And whoever wills—let him disbelieve". We have prepared for the unjust a Fire, whose curtains will hem them in. And when they cry for relief, they will be relieved with water like molten brass, which scalds the faces. What a miserable drink, and what a terrible place.

30. As for those who believe and lead a righteous life—We will not waste the reward of those who work righteousness.

31. These will have the Gardens of Eden, beneath which rivers flow. Reclining on comfortable furnishings, they will be adorned with bracelets of gold, and will wear green garments of silk and brocade. What a wonderful reward, and what an excellent resting-place.

32. And cite for them the parable of two men. To one of them We gave two gardens of vine, and We surrounded them with palm-trees, and We placed between them crops.

33. Both gardens produced their harvest in full, and suffered no loss. And We made a river flow through them.

34. And thus he had abundant fruits. He said to his friend, as he conversed with him, "I am wealthier than you, and greater in manpower."

35. And he entered his garden, wronging himself. He said, "I do not think this will ever perish."

36. "And I do not think the Hour is coming. And even if I am returned to my Lord, I will find something better than this in return."

37. His friend said to him, as he conversed with him, "Are you being ungrateful to Him who created you from dust, then from a sperm-drop, then evolved you into a man?

38. But as for me, He is Allah, my Lord, and I never associate with my Lord anyone.

39. When you entered your garden, why did you not say, "As Allah wills; there is no power except through Allah"? Although you see me inferior to you in wealth and children.

40. Perhaps my Lord will give me something better than your garden, and release upon it thunderbolts from the sky, so it becomes barren waste.

41. Or its water will sink into the ground, and you will be unable to draw it."

42. And ruin closed in on his crops, and so he began wringing his hands over what he had invested in it, as it lays fallen upon its trellises. And he was saying, "I wish I never associated anyone with my Lord."

43. He had no faction to help him besides Allah, and he was helpless.

44. That is because authority belongs to Allah, the True. He is Best in rewarding, and Best in requiting.

45. And cite for them the parable of the present life: it is like water that We send down from the sky; the plants of the earth absorb it;

18. THE CAVE (al-Kahf)

but then it becomes debris, scattered by the wind. Allah has absolute power over everything.

46. Wealth and children are the adornments of the present life. But the things that last, the virtuous deeds, are better with your Lord for reward, and better for hope.

47. On the Day when We set the mountains in motion; and you see the earth emerging; and We gather them together, and leave none of them behind.

48. They will be presented before your Lord in a row. "You have come to Us as We created you the first time. Although you claimed We would not set a meeting for you."

49. And the book will be placed, and you will see the sinners fearful of its contents. And they will say, "Woe to us! What is with this book that leaves nothing, small or big, but it has enumerated it?" They will find everything they had done present. Your Lord does not wrong anyone.

50. We said to the angels, "Bow down to Adam." So they bowed down, except for Satan. He was of the jinn, and he defied the command of his Lord. Will you take him and his offspring as lords instead of Me, when they are an enemy to you? Evil is the exchange for the wrongdoers.

51. I did not call them to witness the creation of the heavens and the earth, nor their own creation; and I do not take the misleaders for assistants.

52. On the Day when He will say, "Call on My partners whom you have claimed." They will call on them, but they will not answer them. And We will place between them a barrier.

53. And the sinners will see the Fire, and will realize that they will tumble into it. They will find no deliverance from it.

54. We have elaborated in this Quran for the people every kind of example, but the human being is a most argumentative being.

55. What prevented people from accepting faith, when guidance has come to them, and from seeking their Lord's forgiveness? Unless they are waiting for the precedent of the ancients to befall them, or to have the punishment come upon them face to face.

56. We send the messengers only as deliverers of good news and warners. Those who disbelieve argue with false argument, in order to defeat the truth thereby. They take My Verses, and the warnings, for a joke.

57. Who does greater wrong than he, who, when reminded of his Lord's revelations, turns away from them, and forgets what his hands have put forward? We have placed coverings over their hearts, lest they understand it, and heaviness in their ears. And if you call them to guidance, they will not be guided, ever.

58. Your Lord is the Forgiver, Possessor of Mercy. Were He to call them to account for what they have earned, He would have hastened the punishment for them. But they have an appointment from which they will find no escape.

59. And these towns—We destroyed them when they committed injustices, and We set for their destruction an appointed time.

60. Recall when Moses said to his servant, "I will not give up until I reach the junction of the two rivers, even if it takes me years."

61. Then, when they reached the junction between them, they forgot about their fish. It found its way into the river, slipping away.

62. When they went further, he said to his servant, "Bring us our lunch; we were exposed in our travel to much fatigue."

63. He said, "Do you remember when we rested by the rock? I forgot about the fish. It was only the devil who made me forget it. And so it found its way to the river, amazingly."

64. He said, "This is what we were seeking." And so they turned back retracing their steps.

65. Then they came upon a servant of Ours, whom We had blessed with mercy from Us,

18. THE CAVE (al-Kahf)

and had taught him knowledge from Our Own.

66. Moses said to him, "May I follow you, so that you may teach me some of the guidance you were taught?"

67. He said, "You will not be able to endure with me.

68. And how will you endure what you have no knowledge of?"

69. He said, "You will find me, Allah willing, patient; and I will not disobey you in any order of yours."

70. He said, "If you follow me, do not ask me about anything, until I myself make mention of it to you."

71. So they set out. Until, when they had boarded the boat, he holed it. He said, "Did you hole it, to drown its passengers? You have done something awful."

72. He said, "Did I not tell you that you will not be able to endure with me?"

73. He said, "Do not rebuke me for forgetting, and do not make my course difficult for me."

74. Then they set out. Until, when they encountered a boy, he killed him. He said, "Did you kill a pure soul, who killed no one? You have done something terrible."

75. He said, "Did I not tell you that you will not be able to endure with me?"

76. He said, "If I ask you about anything after this, then do not keep company with me. You have received excuses from me."

77. So they set out. Until, when they reached the people of a town, they asked them for food, but they refused to offer them hospitality. There they found a wall about to collapse, and he repaired it. He said, "If you wanted, you could have obtained a payment for it."

78. He said, "This is the parting between you and me. I will tell you the interpretation of what you were unable to endure.

79. As for the boat, it belonged to paupers working at sea. I wanted to damage it because there was a king coming after them seizing every boat by force.

80. As for the boy, his parents were believers, and we feared he would overwhelm them with oppression and disbelief.

81. So we wanted their Lord to replace him with someone better in purity, and closer to mercy.

82. And as for the wall, it belonged to two orphaned boys in the town. Beneath it was a treasure that belonged to them. Their father was a righteous man. Your Lord wanted them to reach their maturity, and then extract their treasure—as a mercy from your Lord. I did not do it of my own accord. This is the interpretation of what you were unable to endure."

83. And they ask you about Zul-Qarnain. Say, "I will tell you something about him."

84. We established him on earth, and gave him all kinds of means.

85. He pursued a certain course.

86. Until, when he reached the setting of the sun, he found it setting in a murky spring, and found a people in its vicinity. We said, "O Zul-Qarnain, you may either inflict a penalty, or else treat them kindly."

87. He said, "As for him who does wrong, we will penalize him, then he will be returned to his Lord, and He will punish him with an unheard-of torment.

88. "But as for him who believes and acts righteously, he will have the finest reward, and We will speak to him of Our command with ease."

89. Then he pursued a course.

90. Until, when he reached the rising of the sun, he found it rising on a people for whom We had provided no shelter from it.

91. And so it was. We had full knowledge of what he had.

92. Then he pursued a course.

93. Until, when he reached the point separating the two barriers, he found beside them a

people who could barely understand what is said.

94. They said, "O Zul-Qarnain, the Gog and Magog are spreading chaos in the land. Can we pay you, to build between us and them a wall?"

95. He said, "What my Lord has empowered me with is better. But assist me with strength, and I will build between you and them a dam."

96. "Bring me blocks of iron." So that, when he had leveled up between the two cliffs, he said, "Blow." And having turned it into a fire, he said, "Bring me tar to pour over it."

97. So they were unable to climb it, and they could not penetrate it.

98. He said, "This is a mercy from my Lord. But when the promise of my Lord comes true, He will turn it into rubble, and the promise of my Lord is always true."

99. On that Day, We will leave them surging upon one another. And the Trumpet will be blown, and We will gather them together.

100. On that Day, We will present the disbelievers to Hell, all displayed.

101. Those whose eyes were screened to My message, and were unable to hear.

102. Do those who disbelieve think that they can take My servants for masters instead of Me? We have prepared Hell for the hospitality of the faithless.

103. Say, "Shall We inform you of the greatest losers in their works?"

104. "Those whose efforts in this world are misguided, while they assume that they are doing well."

105. It is they who rejected the communications of their Lord, and the encounter with Him. So their works are in vain. And on the Day of Resurrection, We will consider them of no weight.

106. That is their requital—Hell—on account of their disbelief, and their taking My revelations and My messengers in mockery.

107. As for those who believe and do righteous deeds, they will have the Gardens of Paradise for hospitality.

108. Abiding therein forever, without desiring any change therefrom.

109. Say, "If the ocean were ink for the words of my Lord, the ocean would run out, before the words of my Lord run out," even if We were to bring the like of it in addition to it.

110. Say, "I am only a human being like you, being inspired that your god is One God. Whoever hopes to meet his Lord, let him work righteousness, and never associate anyone with the service of his Lord."

19. MARY
(Maryam)

*In the name of Allah,
the Gracious, the Merciful*

1. Kaf, Ha, Ya, Ayn, Saad.

2. A mention of the mercy of your Lord towards His servant Zechariah.

3. When he called on his Lord, a call in seclusion.

4. He said, "My Lord, my bones have become feeble, and my hair is aflame with gray, and never, Lord, have I been disappointed in my prayer to you.

5. "And I fear for my dependents after me, and my wife is barren. So grant me, from Yourself, an heir.

6. To inherit me, and inherit from the House of Jacob, and make him, my Lord, pleasing."

7. "O Zechariah, We give you good news of a son, whose name is John, a name We have never given before."

8. He said, "My Lord, how can I have a son, when my wife is barren, and I have become decrepit with old age?"

9. He said, "It will be so, your Lord says, 'it is easy for me, and I created you before, when you were nothing.'"

19. MARY (Maryam)

10. He said, "My Lord, give me a sign." He said, "Your sign is that you will not speak to the people for three nights straight."

11. And he came out to his people, from the sanctuary, and signaled to them to praise morning and evening.

12. "O John, hold on to the Scripture firmly," and We gave him wisdom in his youth.

13. And tenderness from Us, and innocence. He was devout.

14. And kind to his parents; and he was not a disobedient tyrant.

15. And peace be upon him the day he was born, and the day he dies, and the Day he is raised alive.

16. And mention in the Scripture Mary, when she withdrew from her people to an eastern location.

17. She screened herself away from them, and We sent to her Our spirit, and He appeared to her as an immaculate human.

18. She said, "I take refuge from you in the Most Merciful, should you be righteous."

19. He said, "I am only the messenger of your Lord, to give you the gift of a pure son."

20. She said, "How can I have a son, when no man has touched me, and I was never unchaste?"

21. He said, "Thus said your Lord, 'It is easy for Me, and We will make him a sign for humanity, and a mercy from Us. It is a matter already decided.'"

22. So she carried him, and secluded herself with him in a remote place.

23. The labor-pains came upon her, by the trunk of a palm-tree. She said, "I wish I had died before this, and been completely forgotten."

24. Whereupon he called her from beneath her: "Do not worry; your Lord has placed a stream beneath you.

25. And shake the trunk of the palm-tree towards you, and it will drop ripe dates by you."

26. "So eat, and drink, and be consoled. And if you see any human, say, 'I have vowed a fast to the Most Gracious, so I will not speak to any human today.'"

27. Then she came to her people, carrying him. They said, "O Mary, you have done something terrible.

28. O sister of Aaron, your father was not an evil man, and your mother was not a whore."

29. So she pointed to him. They said, "How can we speak to an infant in the crib?"

30. He said, "I am the servant of Allah. He has given me the Scripture, and made me a prophet.

31. And has made me blessed wherever I may be; and has enjoined on me prayer and charity, so long as I live.

32. And kind to my mother, and He did not make me a disobedient rebel.

33. So Peace is upon me the day I was born, and the day I die, and the Day I get resurrected alive."

34. That is Jesus son of Mary—the Word of truth about which they doubt.

35. It is not for Allah to have a child—glory be to Him. To have anything done, He says to it, "Be," and it becomes.

36. "Allah is my Lord and your Lord, so worship Him. That is a straight path."

37. But the various factions differed among themselves. So woe to those who disbelieve from the scene of a tremendous Day.

38. Listen to them and watch for them the Day they come to Us. But the wrongdoers today are completely lost.

39. And warn them of the Day of Regret, when the matter will be concluded. Yet they are heedless, and they do not believe.

40. It is We who will inherit the earth and everyone on it, and to Us they will be returned.

41. And mention in the Scripture Abraham. He was a man of truth, a prophet.

19. MARY (Maryam)

42. He said to his father, "O my father, why do you worship what can neither hear, nor see, nor benefit you in any way?

43. O my father, there has come to me knowledge that never came to you. So follow me, and I will guide you along a straight way.

44. O my father, do not worship the devil. The devil is disobedient to the Most Gracious.

45. O my father, I fear that a punishment from the Most Gracious will afflict you, and you become an ally of the devil."

46. He said, "Are you renouncing my gods, O Abraham? If you do not desist, I will stone you. So leave me alone for a while."

47. He said, "Peace be upon you. I will ask my Lord to forgive you; He has been Kind to me.

48. And I will withdraw from you, and from what you pray to instead of Allah. And I will pray to my Lord, and I hope I will not be disappointed in my prayer to my Lord."

49. When he withdrew from them, and from what they worship besides Allah, We granted him Isaac and Jacob. And each We made a prophet.

50. And We gave them freely of Our mercy, and gave them a noble reputation of truth.

51. And mention in the Scripture Moses. He was dedicated. He was a messenger and a prophet.

52. And We called him from the right side of the Mount, and brought him near in communion.

53. And We granted him, out of Our mercy, his brother Aaron, a prophet.

54. And mention in the Scripture Ishmael. He was true to his promise, and was a messenger, a prophet.

55. And he used to enjoin on his people prayer and charity, and he was pleasing to his Lord.

56. And mention in the Scripture Enoch. He was a man of truth, a prophet.

57. And We raised him to a high position.

58. These are some of the prophets Allah has blessed, from the descendants of Adam, and from those We carried with Noah, and from the descendants of Abraham and Israel, and from those We guided and selected. Whenever the revelations of the Most Gracious are recited to them, they would fall down, prostrating and weeping.

59. But they were succeeded by generations who lost the prayers and followed their appetites. They will meet perdition.

60. Except for those who repent, and believe, and act righteously. These will enter Paradise, and will not be wronged in the least.

61. The Gardens of Eden, promised by the Most Merciful to His servants in the Unseen. His promise will certainly come true.

62. They will hear no nonsense therein, but only peace. And they will have their provision therein, morning and evening.

63. Such is Paradise which We will give as inheritance to those of Our servants who are devout.

64. "We do not descend except by the command of your Lord. His is what is before us, and what is behind us, and what is between them. Your Lord is never forgetful."

65. Lord of the heavens and the earth and what is between them. So worship Him, and persevere in His service. Do you know of anyone equal to Him?

66. And the human being says, "When I am dead, will I be brought back alive?"

67. Does the human being not remember that We created him before, when he was nothing?

68. By your Lord, We will round them up, and the devils, then We will bring them around Hell, on their knees.

69. Then, out of every sect, We will snatch those most defiant to the Most Merciful.

70. We are fully aware of those most deserving to scorch in it.

71. There is not one of you but will go down to it. This has been an unavoidable decree of your Lord.

72. Then We will rescue those who were devout, and leave the wrongdoers in it, on their knees.

73. When Our clear revelations are recited to them, those who disbelieve say to those who believe, "Which of the two parties is better in position, and superior in influence?"

74. How many a generation have We destroyed before them, who surpassed them in riches and splendor?

75. Say, "Whoever is in error, the Most Merciful will lead him on." Until, when they see what they were promised—either the punishment, or the Hour. Then they will know who was in worse position and weaker in forces.

76. Allah increases in guidance those who accept guidance. And the things that endure—the righteous deeds—have the best reward with your Lord, and the best outcome.

77. Have you seen him who denied Our revelations, and said, "I will be given wealth and children"?

78. Did he look into the future, or did he receive a promise from the Most Merciful?

79. No indeed! We will write what he says, and will keep extending the agony for him.

80. Then We will inherit from him what he speaks of, and he will come to Us alone.

81. And they took, besides Allah, other gods, to be for them a source of strength.

82. By no means! They will reject their worship of them, and become opponents to them.

83. Have you not considered how We dispatch the devils against the disbelievers, exciting them with incitement?

84. So do not hurry against them. We are counting for them a countdown.

85. On the Day when We will gather the righteous to the Most Merciful, as guests.

86. And herd the sinners into hell, like animals to water.

87. They will have no power of intercession, except for someone who has an agreement with the Most Merciful.

88. And they say, "The Most Merciful has begotten a son."

89. You have come up with something monstrous.

90. At which the heavens almost rupture, and the earth splits, and the mountains fall and crumble.

91. Because they attribute a son to the Most Merciful.

92. It is not fitting for the Most Merciful to have a son.

93. There is none in the heavens and the earth but will come to the Most Merciful as a servant.

94. He has enumerated them, and counted them one by one.

95. And each one of them will come to Him on the Day of Resurrection alone.

96. Those who believe and do righteous deeds, the Most Merciful will give them love.

97. We made it easy in your tongue, in order to deliver good news to the righteous, and to warn with it a hostile people.

98. How many a generation have We destroyed before them? Can you feel a single one of them, or hear from them the slightest whisper?

20. TA-HA
(Ta-Ha)

*In the name of Allah,
the Gracious, the Merciful*

1. Ta, Ha.

2. We did not reveal the Quran to you to make you suffer.

3. But only as a reminder for him who fears.

4. A revelation from He who created the earth and the high heavens.

20. TA-HA (Ta-Ha)

5. The Most Merciful; on the Throne He settled.

6. To Him belongs everything in the heavens and the earth, and everything between them, and everything beneath the soil.

7. If you speak aloud—He knows the secret, and the most hidden.

8. Allah, there is no god but He, His are the Most Beautiful Names.

9. Has the story of Moses reached you?

10. When he saw a fire, he said to his family, "Stay; I have noticed a fire; Perhaps I can bring you a torch therefrom, or find some guidance by the fire."

11. Then, when he reached it, he was called, "O Moses.

12. I—I am your Lord. Take off your shoes. You are in the sacred valley of Tuwa.

13. I have chosen you, so listen to what is revealed.

14. I—I am Allah. There is no God but I. So serve Me, and practice the prayer for My remembrance.

15. The Hour is coming—but I keep it almost hidden—so that each soul will be paid for what it endeavors.

16. And do not let him who denies it and follows his desire turn you away from it, lest you fall.

17. And what is that in your right-hand, O Moses?"

18. He said, "This is my staff. I lean on it, and herd my sheep with it, and I have other uses for it."

19. He said, "Throw it, O Moses."

20. So he threw it—thereupon it became a moving serpent.

21. He said, "Take hold of it, and do not fear. We will restore it to its original condition.

22. And press your hand to your side; it will come out white, without a blemish—another sign.

23. That We may show you some of Our greatest signs.

24. Go to Pharaoh; He has transgressed."

25. He said, "My Lord, put my heart at peace for me.

26. And ease my task for me.

27. And untie the knot from my tongue.

28. So they can understand my speech.

29. And appoint an assistant for me, from my family.

30. Aaron, my brother.

31. Strengthen me with him.

32. And have him share in my mission.

33. That we may glorify You much.

34. And remember You much.

35. You are always watching over us."

36. He said, "You are granted your request, O Moses.

37. We had favored you another time.

38. When We inspired your mother with the inspiration.

39. 'Put him in the chest; then cast him into the river. The river will wash him to shore, where an enemy of Mine and an enemy of his will pick him up. And I have bestowed upon you love from Me, so that you may be reared before My eye.

40. When your sister walked along, and said, 'Shall I tell you about someone who will take care of him?' So We returned you to your mother, that she may be comforted, and not sorrow. And you killed a person, but We saved you from stress; and We tested you thoroughly. And you stayed years among the people of Median. Then you came back, as ordained, O Moses.

41. And I made you for Myself.

42. Go, you and your brother, with My signs, and do not neglect My remembrance.

43. Go to Pharaoh. He has tyrannized.

44. But speak to him nicely. Perhaps he will remember, or have some fear."

45. They said, "Lord, we fear he may persecute us, or become violent."

46. He said, "Do not fear, I am with you, I hear and I see.

47. Approach him and say, 'We are the messengers of your Lord; so let the Children of Israel go with us, and do not torment them. We bring you a sign from your Lord, and peace be upon him who follows guidance.

48. It was revealed to us that the punishment falls upon him who disbelieves and turns away.'"

49. He said, "Who is your Lord, O Moses."

50. He said, "Our Lord is He who gave everything its existence, then guided it."

51. He said, "What about the first generations?"

52. He said, "Knowledge thereof is with my Lord, in a Book. My Lord never errs, nor does He forget."

53. He who made the earth a habitat for you; and traced in it routes for you; and sent down water from the sky, with which We produce pairs of diverse plants.

54. Eat and pasture your livestock. In that are signs for those with understanding.

55. From it We created you, and into it We will return you, and from it We will bring you out another time.

56. We showed him Our signs, all of them, but he denied and refused.

57. He said, "Did you come to us to drive us out of our land with your magic, O Moses?

58. We will produce for you magic like it; so make an appointment between us and you, which we will not miss—neither us, nor you—in a central place."

59. He said, "Your appointment is the day of the festival, so let the people be gathered together at mid-morning."

60. Pharaoh turned away, put together his plan, and then came back.

61. Moses said to them, "Woe to you. Do not fabricate lies against Allah, or He will destroy you with a punishment. He who invents lies will fail."

62. They disagreed among themselves over their affair, and conferred secretly.

63. They said, "These two are magicians who want to drive you out of your land with their magic, and to abolish your exemplary way of life.

64. So settle your plan, and come as one front. Today, whoever gains the upper hand will succeed."

65. They said, "O Moses, either you throw, or we will be the first to throw."

66. He said, "You throw." And suddenly, their ropes and sticks appeared to him, because of their magic, to be crawling swiftly.

67. So Moses felt apprehensive within himself.

68. We said, "Do not be afraid, you are the uppermost.

69. Now throw down what is in your right hand—it will swallow what they have crafted. What they have crafted is only a magician's trickery. But the magician will not succeed, no matter what he does."

70. And the magicians fell down prostrate. They said, "We have believed in the Lord of Aaron and Moses."

71. He said, "Did you believe in him before I have given you permission? He must be your chief, who has taught you magic. I will cut off your hands and your feet on alternate sides, and I will crucify you on the trunks of the palm-trees. Then you will know which of us is more severe in punishment, and more lasting."

72. They said, "We will not prefer you to the proofs that have come to us, and Him who created us. So issue whatever judgment you wish to issue. You can only rule in this lowly life.

20. TA-HA (Ta-Ha)

73. We have believed in our Lord, so that He may forgive us our sins, and the magic you have compelled us to practice. Allah is Better, and more Lasting."

74. Whoever comes to his Lord guilty, for him is Hell, where he neither dies nor lives.

75. But whoever comes to Him a believer, having worked righteousness—these will have the highest ranks.

76. The Gardens of Perpetuity, beneath which rivers flow, dwelling therein forever. That is the reward for him who purifies himself.

77. And We inspired Moses: "Travel by night with My servants, and strike for them a dry path across the sea, not fearing being overtaken, nor worrying."

78. Pharaoh pursued them with his troops, but the sea overwhelmed them, and completely engulfed them.

79. Pharaoh misled his people, and did not guide them.

80. O Children of Israel! We have delivered you from your enemy, and promised you by the right side of the Mount, and sent down to you manna and quails.

81. Eat of the good things We have provided for you, but do not be excessive therein, lest My wrath descends upon you. He upon whom My wrath descends has fallen.

82. And I am Forgiving towards him who repents, believes, acts righteously, and then remains guided.

83. "And what made you rush ahead of your people, O Moses?"

84. He said, "They are following in my footsteps; and I hurried on to You, my Lord, that you may be pleased."

85. He said, "We have tested your people in your absence, and the Samarian misled them."

86. So Moses returned to his people, angry and disappointed. He said, "O my people, did your Lord not promise you a good promise? Was the time too long for you? Or did you want wrath from your Lord to descend upon you, so you broke your promise to me?"

87. They said, "We did not break our promise to you by our choice, but we were made to carry loads of the people's ornaments, and we cast them in. That was what the Samarian suggested."

88. So he produced for them a calf—a mere body which lowed. And they said, "This is your god, and the god of Moses, but he has forgotten."

89. Did they not see that it cannot return a word to them, and has no power to harm them or benefit them?

90. Aaron had said to them before, "O my people, you are being tested by this. And your Lord is the Merciful, so follow me, and obey my command."

91. They said, "We will not give up our devotion to it, until Moses returns to us."

92. He said, "O Aaron, what prevented you, when you saw them going astray.

93. From following me? Did you disobey my command?"

94. He said, "Son of my mother, do not seize me by my beard or my head. I feared you would say, 'You have caused division among the Children of Israel, and did not regard my word.'"

95. He said, "What do you have to say, O Samarian?"

96. He said, "I saw what they did not see, so I grasped a handful from the Messenger's traces, and I flung it away. Thus my soul prompted me."

97. He said, "Begone! Your lot in this life is to say, 'No contact.' And you have an appointment that you will not miss. Now look at your god that you remained devoted to—we will burn it up, and then blow it away into the sea, as powder."

98. Surely your god is Allah, the One besides whom there is no other god. He comprehends everything in knowledge.

20. TA-HA (Ta-Ha)

99. Thus We narrate to you reports of times gone by; and We have given you a message from Our Presence.

100. Whoever turns away from it will carry on the Day of Resurrection a burden.

101. Abiding therein forever. And wretched is their burden on the Day of Resurrection.

102. On the Day when the Trumpet is blown—We will gather the sinners on that Day, blue.

103. Murmuring among themselves: "You have lingered only for ten."

104. We are fully aware of what they say, when the most exemplary of them in conduct will say, "You have lingered only a day."

105. And they ask you about the mountains. Say, "My Lord will crumble them utterly."

106. And leave them desolate waste.

107. You will see in them neither crookedness, nor deviation."

108. On that Day, they will follow the caller, without any deviation. Voices will be hushed before the Merciful, and you will hear nothing but murmur.

109. On that Day, intercession will not avail, except for him permitted by the Merciful, and whose words He has approved.

110. He knows what is before them and what is behind them, and they cannot comprehend Him in their knowledge.

111. Faces will be humbled before the Living, the Eternal. Whoever carries injustice will despair.

112. But whoever has done righteous deeds, while being a believer—will fear neither injustice, nor grievance.

113. Thus We have revealed it an Arabic Quran, and We have diversified the warnings in it, that perhaps they would become righteous, or it may produce a lesson for them.

114. Exalted is Allah, the True King. Do not be hasty with the Quran before its inspiration to you is concluded, and say, "My Lord, increase me in knowledge."

115. And We covenanted with Adam before, but he forgot, and We found in him no resolve.

116. And when We said to the angels, "Bow down to Adam." They bowed down, except for Satan; he refused.

117. We said, "O Adam, this is an enemy to you and to your wife. So do not let him make you leave the Garden, for then you will suffer.

118. In it you will never go hungry, nor be naked.

119. Nor will you be thirsty in it, nor will you swelter."

120. But Satan whispered to him. He said, "O Adam, shall I show you the Tree of Immortality, and a kingdom that never decays?"

121. And so they ate from it; whereupon their bodies became visible to them, and they started covering themselves with the leaves of the Garden. Thus Adam disobeyed his Lord, and fell.

122. But then his Lord recalled him, and pardoned him, and guided him.

123. He said, "Go down from it, altogether; some of you enemies of some others. But whenever guidance comes to you from Me, whoever follows My guidance, will not go astray, nor suffer.

124. But whoever turns away from My Reminder, for him is a confined life. And We will raise him on the Day of Resurrection blind."

125. He will say, "My Lord, why did You raise me blind, though I was seeing?"

126. He will say, "Just as Our revelations came to you, and you forgot them, today you will be forgotten."

127. Thus We recompense him who transgresses and does not believe in the revelations of his Lord. The punishment of the Hereafter is more severe, and more lasting.

128. Is it not instructive to them, how many generations before them We destroyed, in

whose settlements they walk? Surely in that are signs for people of understanding.

129. Were it not for a word that issued from your Lord, the inevitable would have happened, but there is an appointed term.

130. So bear patiently what they say, and celebrate the praises of your Lord before the rising of the sun, and before its setting. And during the hours of the night glorify Him, and at the borders of the day, that you may be satisfied.

131. And do not extend your glance towards what We have given some classes of them to enjoy—the splendor of the life of this world—that We may test them thereby. Your Lord's provision is better, and more lasting.

132. And exhort your people to pray, and patiently adhere to it. We ask of you no sustenance, but it is We who sustain you. The good ending is that for righteousness.

133. And they say, "Why does he not bring us a miracle from his Lord?" Were they not given enough miracles in the former scriptures?

134. Had We destroyed them with a punishment before him, they would have said, "Our Lord, if only You had sent us a messenger, we would have followed Your revelations before we were humiliated and disgraced."

135. Say, "Everybody is waiting, so wait. You will know who the people of the straight path are, and who is rightly-guided.

21. THE PROPHETS
(al-Anbiya)

*In the name of Allah,
the Gracious, the Merciful*

1. Mankind's reckoning has drawn near, but they turn away heedlessly.

2. No fresh reminder comes to them from their Lord, but they listen to it playfully.

3. Their hearts distracted, the wrongdoers confer secretly, "Is this anything but a mortal like you? Will you take to sorcery, with open eyes?"

4. He said, "My Lord knows what is said in the heaven and the earth; and He is the Hearer, the Knower."

5. And they said, "A jumble of dreams," and, "He made it up," and, "He is a poet," "let him bring us a sign, like those sent to the ancients."

6. None of the towns We destroyed before them had believed. Will they, then, believe?

7. We did not send before you except men, whom We inspired. Ask the people of knowledge, if you do not know.

8. We did not make them mere bodies that ate no food, nor were they immortal.

9. Then We fulfilled Our promise to them, and We saved them together with whomever We willed, and We destroyed the extravagant.

10. We have sent down to you a Book, containing your message. Do you not understand?

11. How many a guilty town have We crushed, and established thereafter another people?

12. Then, when they sensed Our might, they started running away from it.

13. Do not run, but come back to your luxuries, and to your homes, that you may be questioned.

14. They said, "Woe to us; we were unfair."

15. This continued to be their cry, until We made them silent ashes.

16. We did not create the sky and the earth and what is between them for amusement.

17. If We wanted amusement, We could have found it within Us, were We to do so.

18. In fact, We hurl the truth against falsehood, and it crushes it, so it vanishes. Woe unto you, for what you describe.

19. To Him belongs everyone in the heavens and the earth. Those near Him are not too proud to worship Him, nor do they waver.

21. THE PROPHETS (al-Anbiya)

20. They praise night and day, without ever tiring.

21. Or have they taken to themselves gods from the earth who resurrect?

22. If there were in them gods other than Allah, they would have gone to ruin. So glory be to Allah, Lord of the Throne, beyond what they allege.

23. He will not be questioned about what He does, but they will be questioned.

24. Or have they taken, besides Him, other gods? Say, "Bring your proof. This is a message for those with me, and a message of those before me." But most of them do not know the truth, so they turn away.

25. We never sent a messenger before you without inspiring him that: "There is no god but I, so worship Me."

26. And they say, "The Most Merciful has taken to himself a son." Be He glorified; they are but honored servants.

27. They never speak before He has spoken, and they only act on His command.

28. He knows what is before them, and what is behind them; and they do not intercede except for him whom He approves; and they tremble in awe of Him.

29. And whoever of them says, "I am a god besides Him," We will reward him with Hell. Thus We reward the wrongdoers.

30. Do the disbelievers not see that the heavens and the earth were one mass, and We tore them apart? And We made from water every living thing. Will they not believe?

31. And We placed on earth stabilizers, lest it sways with them, and We placed therein signposts and passages, that they may be guided.

32. And We made the sky a protected ceiling; yet they turn away from its wonders.

33. It is He who created the night and the day, and the sun and the moon; each floating in an orbit.

34. We did not grant immortality to any human being before you. Should you die, are they then the immortal?

35. Every soul will taste death. We burden you with adversity and prosperity—a test. And to Us you will be returned.

36. When those who disbelieve see you, they treat you only with ridicule: "Is this the one who mentions your gods?" And they reject the mention of the Merciful.

37. The human being was created of haste. I will show you My signs, so do not seek to rush Me.

38. And they say, "When will this promise come true, if you are truthful?"

39. If those who disbelieve only knew, when they cannot keep the fire off their faces and off their backs, and they will not be helped.

40. In fact, it will come upon them suddenly, and bewilder them. They will not be able to repel it, and they will not be reprieved.

41. Messengers before you were also ridiculed, but those who jeered were surrounded by what they had ridiculed.

42. Say, "Who guards you against the Merciful by night and by day?" But they turn away from the mention of their Lord.

43. Or do they have gods who can defend them against Us? They cannot help themselves, nor will they be protected from Us.

44. We have given these enjoyments, and their ancestors, until time grew long upon them. Do they not see how We gradually reduce the land from its extremities? Are they then the victors?

45. Say, "I am warning you through inspiration." But the deaf cannot hear the call when they are being warned.

46. And when a breath of your Lord's punishment touches them, they say, "Woe to us, we were truly wicked."

47. We will set up the scales of justice for the Day of Resurrection, so that no soul will suffer the least injustice. And even if it be the

21. THE PROPHETS (al-Anbiya)

weight of a mustard-seed, We will bring it up. Sufficient are We as Reckoners.

48. We gave Moses and Aaron the Criterion, and illumination, and a reminder for the righteous.

49. Those who fear their Lord in private, and are apprehensive of the Hour.

50. This too is a blessed message that We revealed. Are you going to deny it?

51. We gave Abraham his integrity formerly, and We knew him well.

52. When he said to his father and his people, "What are these statues to which you are devoted?"

53. They said, "We found our parents worshiping them."

54. He said, "You and your parents are in evident error."

55. They said, "Are you telling us the truth, or are you just playing?"

56. He said, "Your Lord is the Lord of the heavens and the earth, the One who created them, and I bear witness to that.

57. "By Allah, I will have a plan for your statues after you have gone away."

58. So he reduced them into pieces, except for their biggest, that they may return to it.

59. They said, "Who did this to our gods? He is certainly one of the wrongdoers."

60. They said, "We heard a youth mentioning them. He is called Abraham."

61. They said, "Bring him before the eyes of the people, so that they may witness."

62. They said, "Are you the one who did this to our gods, O Abraham?"

63. He said, "But it was this biggest of them that did it. Ask them, if they can speak."

64. Then they turned to one another, and said, "You yourselves are the wrongdoers."

65. But they reverted to their old ideas: "You certainly know that these do not speak."

66. He said, "Do you worship, instead of Allah, what can neither benefit you in anything, nor harm you?

67. Fie on you, and on what you worship instead of Allah. Do you not understand?"

68. They said, "Burn him and support your gods, if you are going to act."

69. We said, "O fire, be coolness and safety upon Abraham."

70. They planned to harm him, but We made them the worst losers.

71. And We delivered him, and Lot, to the land that We blessed for all people.

72. And We granted him Isaac and Jacob as a gift; and each We made righteous.

73. And We made them leaders, guiding by Our command; and We inspired them to do good works, and to observe the prayer, and to give out charity. They were devoted servants to Us.

74. And Lot—We gave him judgment and knowledge, and We delivered him from the town that practiced the abominations. They were wicked and perverted people.

75. And We admitted him into Our mercy; for He was one of the righteous.

76. And Noah, when he called before. So We answered him, and delivered him and his family from the great disaster.

77. And We supported him against the people who rejected Our signs. They were an evil people, so We drowned them all.

78. And David and Solomon, when they gave judgment in the case of the field, when some people's sheep wandered therein by night; and We were witnesses to their judgment.

79. And so We made Solomon understand it, and to each We gave wisdom and knowledge. And We subjected the mountains along with David to sing Our praises, and the birds as well—surely We did.

80. And We taught him the making of shields for you, to protect you from your violence. Are you, then, appreciative?

21. THE PROPHETS (al-Anbiya)

⁸¹· And to Solomon the stormy wind, blowing at His command towards the land that We have blessed. We are aware of everything.

⁸²· And of the devils were some that dived for him, and performed other, lesser tasks. But We kept them restrained.

⁸³· And Job, when he cried out to his Lord: "Great harm has afflicted me, and you are the Most Merciful of the merciful."

⁸⁴· So We answered him, lifted his suffering, and restored his family to him, and their like with them—a mercy from Us, and a reminder for the worshipers.

⁸⁵· And Ishmael, and Enoch, and Ezekiel; each was one of the steadfast.

⁸⁶· And We admitted them into Our mercy. They were among the righteous.

⁸⁷· And Jonah, when he stormed out in fury, thinking We had no power over him. But then He cried out in the darkness, "There is no god but You! Glory to You! I was one of the wrongdoers!"

⁸⁸· So We answered him, and saved him from the affliction. Thus We save the faithful.

⁸⁹· And Zechariah, when he called out to his Lord, "My Lord, do not leave me alone, even though you are the Best of heirs."

⁹⁰· So We answered him, and gave him John. And We cured his wife for him. They used to vie in doing righteous deeds, and used to call on Us in love and awe, and they used to humble themselves to Us.

⁹¹· And she who guarded her virginity. We breathed into her of Our spirit, and made her and her son a sign to the world.

⁹²· This community of yours is one community, and I am your Lord, so worship Me.

⁹³· But they splintered themselves into factions. They will all return to Us.

⁹⁴· Whoever does righteous deeds, and is a believer, his effort will not be denied. We are writing it down for him.

⁹⁵· There is a ban on the town that We had destroyed—that they will not return.

⁹⁶· Until, when Gog and Magog are let loose, and they swarm down from every mound.

⁹⁷· The promise of truth has drawn near. The eyes of those who disbelieved will stare in horror: "Woe to us. We were oblivious to this. In fact, we were wrongdoers."

⁹⁸· You and what you worship besides Allah are fuel for Hell. You will descend into it.

⁹⁹· Had these been gods, they would not have descended into it. All will abide in it.

¹⁰⁰· In it they will wail. In it they will not hear.

¹⁰¹· As for those who deserved goodness from Us—these will be kept away from it.

¹⁰²· They will not hear its hissing, and they will forever abide in what their hearts desire.

¹⁰³· The Supreme Fear will not worry them, and the angels will receive them: "This is your Day which you were promised."

¹⁰⁴· On the Day when We fold the heaven, like the folding of a book. Just as We began the first creation, We will repeat it—a promise binding on Us. We will act.

¹⁰⁵· We have written in the Psalms, after the Reminder, that the earth will be inherited by My righteous servants.

¹⁰⁶· Indeed, in this is a message for people who worship.

¹⁰⁷· We did not send you except as mercy to mankind.

¹⁰⁸· Say, "It is revealed to me that your God is One God. Are you going to submit?"

¹⁰⁹· But if they turn away, say, "I have informed you sufficiently. Although I do not know whether what you are promised is near or far."

¹¹⁰· He knows what is said openly, and He knows what you conceal.

¹¹¹· "And I do not know whether it is perhaps a trial for you, and an enjoyment for a while."

¹¹²· He said, "My Lord, judge with justice." And, "Our Lord is the Gracious, Whose help is sought against what you allege."

22. THE PILGRIMAGE (al-Hajj)

In the name of Allah, the Gracious, the Merciful

1. O people, be conscious of your Lord. The quaking of the Hour is a tremendous thing.

2. On the Day when you will see it: every nursing mother will discard her infant, and every pregnant woman will abort her load, and you will see the people drunk, even though they are not drunk—but the punishment of Allah is severe.

3. Among the people is he who argues about Allah without knowledge, and follows every defiant devil.

4. It was decreed for him, that whoever follows him—he will misguide him, and lead him to the torment of the Blaze.

5. O people! If you are in doubt about the Resurrection—We created you from dust, then from a small drop, then from a clinging clot, then from a lump of flesh, partly developed and partly undeveloped. In order to clarify things for you. And We settle in the wombs whatever We will for a designated term, and then We bring you out as infants, until you reach your full strength. And some of you will pass away, and some of you will be returned to the vilest age, so that he may not know, after having known. And you see the earth still; but when We send down water on it, it vibrates, and swells, and grows all kinds of lovely pairs.

6. That is because Allah is the truth, and because He gives life to the dead, and because He is Capable of everything.

7. And because the Hour is coming—there is no doubt about it—and because Allah will resurrect those in the graves.

8. And among the people is he who argues about Allah without knowledge, or guidance, or an enlightening scripture.

9. Turning aside in contempt, to lead away from the path of Allah. He will have humiliation in this world, and on the Day of Resurrection We will make him taste the agony of burning.

10. That is for what your hands have advanced, and because Allah is not unjust to the servants.

11. And among the people is he who worships Allah on edge. When something good comes his way, he is content with it. But when an ordeal strikes him, he makes a turnaround. He loses this world and the next. That is the obvious loss.

12. He invokes, instead of Allah, what can neither harm him nor benefit him. That is the far straying.

13. He invokes one whose harm is closer than his benefit. What a miserable master. What a miserable companion.

14. Allah will admit those who believe and do righteous deeds into Gardens beneath which rivers flow. Allah does whatever He wills.

15. Whoever thinks that Allah will not help him in this life and in the Hereafter—let him turn to heaven, then sever, and see if his cunning eliminates what enrages him.

16. Thus We revealed it as clarifying signs, and Allah guides whomever He wills.

17. Those who believe, and those who are Jewish, and the Sabeans, and the Christians, and the Zoroastrians, and the Polytheists—Allah will judge between them on the Day of Resurrection. Allah is witness to all things.

18. Do you not realize that to Allah prostrates everyone in the heavens and everyone on earth, and the sun, and the moon, and the stars, and the mountains, and the trees, and the animals, and many of the people? But many are justly deserving of punishment. Whomever Allah shames, there is none to honor him. Allah does whatever He wills.

19. Here are two adversaries feuding regarding their Lord. As for those who disbelieve, garments of fire will be tailored for them, and

22. THE PILGRIMAGE (al-Hajj)

scalding water will be poured over their heads.

20. Melting their insides and their skins.

21. And they will have maces of iron.

22. Whenever they try to escape the gloom, they will be driven back to it: "Taste the suffering of burning."

23. But Allah will admit those who believe and do good deeds into Gardens beneath which rivers flow. They will be decorated therein with bracelets of gold and pearls, and their garments therein will be of silk.

24. They were guided to purity of speech. They were guided to the path of the Most Praised.

25. As for those who disbelieve and repel from Allah's path and from the Sacred Mosque—which We have designated for all mankind equally, whether residing therein or passing through—and seek to commit sacrilege therein—We will make him taste of a painful punishment.

26. We showed Abraham the location of the House: "Do not associate anything with Me; and purify My House for those who circle around, and those who stand to pray, and those who kneel and prostrate."

27. And announce the pilgrimage to humanity. They will come to you on foot, and on every transport. They will come from every distant point.

28. That they may witness the benefits for themselves, and celebrate the name of Allah during the appointed days, for providing them with the animal livestock. So eat from it, and feed the unfortunate poor.

29. Then let them perform their acts of cleansing, and fulfill their vows, and circle around the Ancient House.

30. All that. Whoever venerates the sanctities of Allah—it is good for him with his Lord. All livestock are permitted to you, except what is recited to you. So stay away from the abomination of idols, and stay away from perjury.

31. Being true to Allah, without associating anything with Him. Whoever associates anything with Allah—it is as though he has fallen from the sky, and is snatched by the birds, or is swept away by the wind to a distant abyss.

32. So it is. Whoever venerates the sacraments of Allah—it is from the piety of the hearts.

33. In them are benefits for you until a certain time. Then their place is by the Ancient House.

34. We have appointed a rite for every nation, that they may commemorate Allah's name over the livestock He has provided for them. Your God is One God, so to Him submit, and announce good news to the humble.

35. Those whose hearts tremble when Allah is mentioned, and those who endure what has befallen them, and those who perform the prayer and spend from what We have provided for them.

36. We have made the animal offerings emblems of Allah for you. In them is goodness for you. So pronounce Allah's name upon them as they line up. Then, when they have fallen on their sides, eat of them and feed the contented and the beggar. Thus We have subjected them to you, that you may be thankful.

37. Neither their flesh, nor their blood, ever reaches Allah. What reaches Him is the righteousness from you. Thus He subdued them to you, that you may glorify Allah for guiding you. And give good news to the charitable.

38. Allah defends those who believe. Allah does not love any ungrateful traitor.

39. Permission is given to those who are fought against, and Allah is Able to give them victory.

40. Those who were unjustly evicted from their homes, merely for saying, "Our Lord is Allah." Were it not that Allah repels people by means of others: monasteries, churches, synagogues, and mosques—where the name of Allah is mentioned much—would have been demolished. Allah supports whoever supports Him. Allah is Strong and Mighty.

22. THE PILGRIMAGE (al-Hajj)

41. Those who, when We empower them in the land, observe the prayer, and give regular charity, and command what is right, and forbid what is wrong. To Allah belongs the outcome of events.

42. If they deny you—before them the people of Noah, and Aad, and Thamood also denied.

43. And the people of Abraham, and the people of Lot.

44. And the inhabitants of Median. And Moses was denied. Then I reprieved those who disbelieved, but then I seized them. So how was My rejection?

45. How many a town have We destroyed while it was doing wrong? They lie in ruins; with stilled wells, and lofty mansions.

46. Have they not journeyed in the land, and had minds to reason with, or ears to listen with? It is not the eyes that go blind, but it is the hearts, within the chests, that go blind.

47. And they ask you to hasten the punishment. But Allah never breaks His promise. A day with your Lord is like a thousand years of your count.

48. How many a town have I reprieved, although it was unjust? Then I seized it. To Me is the destination.

49. Say, "O people, I am only a plain warner to you."

50. Those who believe and work righteousness—for them is forgiveness and a generous provision.

51. But those who strive against Our revelations—these are the inmates of Hell.

52. We never sent a messenger before you, or a prophet, but when he had a desire Satan interfered in his wishes. But Allah nullifies what Satan interjects, and Allah affirms His revelations. Allah is Omniscient and Wise.

53. In order to make Satan's suggestions a trial for those whose hearts are diseased, and those whose hearts are hardened. The wrongdoers are in profound discord.

54. And so that those endowed with knowledge may know that it is the truth from your Lord, and so believe in it, and their hearts soften to it. Allah guides those who believe to a straight path.

55. Those who disbelieve will continue to be hesitant about it, until the Hour comes upon them suddenly, or there comes to them the torment of a desolate Day.

56. Sovereignty on that Day belongs to Allah; He will judge between them. Those who believe and do good deeds will be in the Gardens of Bliss.

57. But those who disbelieve and reject Our revelations—these will have a humiliating punishment.

58. Those who emigrate in Allah's cause, then get killed, or die, Allah will provide them with fine provisions. Allah is the Best of Providers.

59. He will admit them an admittance that will please them. Allah is Knowing and Clement.

60. That is so! Whoever retaliates similarly to the affliction he was made to suffer, and then he is wronged again, Allah will definitely assist him. Allah is Pardoning and Forgiving.

61. That is because Allah merges the night into the day, and He merges the day into the night, and because Allah is Hearing and Seeing.

62. That is because Allah is the Reality, and what they invoke besides Him is vanity, and because Allah is the Sublime, the Grand.

63. Do you not see that Allah sends down water from the sky, and the land becomes green? Allah is Kind and Aware.

64. To Him belongs everything in the heavens and everything on earth. Allah is the Rich, the Praised.

65. Do you not see that Allah made everything on earth subservient to you? How the ships sail at sea by His command? That He holds up the sky lest it falls on earth—except by His permission? Allah is Gracious towards the people, Most Merciful.

23. THE BELIEVERS (al-Mu'minun)

66. And it is He who gives you life, then makes you die, then revives you. The human being is unappreciative.

67. For every congregation We have appointed acts of devotion, which they observe. So do not let them dispute with you in this matter. And invite to your Lord; you are upon a straight guidance.

68. But if they dispute with you, say, "Allah is fully aware of what you do."

69. Allah will judge between you on the Day of Resurrection regarding what you disagree about.

70. Do you not know that Allah knows everything in the heavens and the earth? This is in a book. That is easy for Allah.

71. Yet they worship, besides Allah, things for which He sent down no warrant, and what they have no knowledge of. There is no savior for the transgressors.

72. And when Our Clear Verses are recited to them, you will recognize disgust on the faces of those who disbelieve. They nearly assault those who recite to them Our Verses. Say, "Shall I inform you of something worse than that? The Fire! Allah has promised it to those who disbelieve. And what a wretched outcome!"

73. O people! A parable is presented, so listen to it: Those you invoke besides Allah will never create a fly, even if they banded together for that purpose. And if the fly steals anything from them, they cannot recover it from it. Weak are the pursuer and the pursued.

74. They do not value Allah as He should be valued. Allah is Strong and Powerful.

75. Allah chooses messengers from among the angels, and from among the people. Allah is Hearing and Seeing.

76. He knows what is before them, and what is behind them. To Allah all matters are referred.

77. O you who believe! Kneel, and prostrate, and worship your Lord, and do good deeds, so that you may succeed.

78. And strive for Allah, with the striving due to Him. He has chosen you, and has not burdened you in religion—the faith of your father Abraham. It is he who named you Muslims before, and in this. So that the Messenger may be a witness over you, and you may be witnesses over the people. So pray regularly, and give regular charity, and cleave to Allah. He is your Protector. What an excellent Protector, and what an excellent Helper.

23. THE BELIEVERS (al-Mu'minun)

In the name of Allah, the Gracious, the Merciful

1. Successful are the believers.

2. Those who are humble in their prayers.

3. Those who avoid nonsense.

4. Those who work for charity.

5. Those who safeguard their chastity.

6. Except from their spouses, or their dependents—for then they are free from blame.

7. But whoever seeks anything beyond that—these are the transgressors.

8. Those who are faithful to their trusts and pledges.

9. Those who safeguard their prayers.

10. These are the inheritors.

11. Who will inherit Paradise, wherein they will dwell forever.

12. We created man from an extract of clay.

13. Then We made him a seed, in a secure repository.

14. Then We developed the seed into a clot. Then We developed the clot into a lump. Then We developed the lump into bones. Then We clothed the bones with flesh. Then We produced it into another creature. Most Blessed is Allah, the Best of Creators.

23. THE BELIEVERS (al-Mu'minun)

15. Then, after that, you will die.

16. Then, on the Day of Resurrection, you will be resurrected.

17. We created above you seven pathways, and We are never heedless of the creation.

18. And We sent down water from the sky in proper quantity, and settled it in the ground, and We are Able to take it away.

19. With it We produce for you gardens of palms and vines, yielding abundant fruit for you to eat.

20. And a tree springing out of Mount Sinai, producing oil, and seasoning for those who eat.

21. And there is a lesson for you in livestock: We give you to drink from what is in their bellies, and you have many benefits in them, and from them you eat.

22. And on them, and on the ships, you are transported.

23. We sent Noah to his people. He said, "O my people, worship Allah, you have no deity other than Him. Will you not take heed?"

24. But the notables of his people, who disbelieved, said, "This is nothing but a human like you, who wants to gain superiority over you. Had Allah willed, He would have sent down angels. We never heard of this from our forefathers of old.

25. He is nothing but a man possessed. Just ignore him for a while."

26. He said, "My Lord, help me, for they have rejected me."

27. So We inspired him: "Build the Ark under Our observation and by Our inspiration. And when Our decree comes to pass, and the oven boils over, load into it two pairs of every kind, together with your family, except those of them against whom the word has already been pronounced. And do not speak to me concerning those who did wrong; for they are to be drowned."

28. Then, when you and those with you are settled in the Ark, say, "Praise be to Allah, who has saved us from the wrongdoing people."

29. And say, "My Lord, land me with a blessed landing, as you are the best of transporters."

30. Surely in that are signs. We are always testing.

31. Then, after them, We established another generation.

32. And We sent among them a messenger from themselves: "Serve Allah. You have no god other than Him. Will you not be cautious?"

33. But the dignitaries of his people, those who disbelieved and denied the meeting of the Hereafter, and We had indulged them in the present life, said, "This is nothing but a human like you; he eats what you eat, and he drinks what you drink.

34. If you obey a human being like yourselves, then you will be losers.

35. Does he promise you that when you have died and become dust and bones, you will be brought out?

36. Farfetched, farfetched is what you are promised.

37. There is nothing but our life in this world. We die, and we live, and we are not resurrected.

38. He is nothing but a man, making up lies about Allah. We have no faith in him."

39. He said, "My Lord, help me, for they have rejected me."

40. He said, "Soon they will be filled with regret."

41. Then the Blast struck them, justifiably, and We turned them into scum. So away with the wicked people.

42. Then, after them, We raised other generations.

43. No nation can advance its time, nor can they postpone it.

23. THE BELIEVERS (al-Mu'minun)

44. Then We sent Our messengers in succession. Every time a messenger came to his community, they called him a liar. So We made them follow one another, and made them history. So away with a people who do not believe.

45. Then We sent Moses and his brother Aaron, with Our signs and a clear authority.

46. To Pharaoh and his nobles, but they turned arrogant. They were oppressive people.

47. They said, "Are we to believe in two mortals like us, and their people are our slaves?"

48. So they called them liars, and thus were among those destroyed.

49. And We gave Moses the Scripture, that they may be guided.

50. And We made Mary's son and his mother a sign, and We sheltered them on high ground with security and flowing springs.

51. O messengers, eat of the good things, and act with integrity. I am aware of what you do.

52. This nation of yours is one nation, and I am your Lord, so fear Me.

53. But they tore themselves into sects; each party happy with what they have.

54. So leave them in their bewilderment until a time.

55. Do they assume that, in furnishing them with wealth and children.

56. We race to give them the good things? In fact, they have no idea.

57. Those who, from awe of their Lord, are fearful.

58. And those who believe in their Lord's Verses.

59. And those who associate no partners with their Lord.

60. And those who give what they give, while their hearts quake, knowing that to their Lord they will return.

61. It is they who race towards goodness. It is they who will reach it first.

62. We never burden any soul beyond its capacity. And with Us is a record that tells the truth, and they will not be wronged.

63. But their hearts are puzzled because of this; and they have deeds that do not conform to this, which they continue to perpetrate.

64. Until, when We seize the decadent among them with torment, they begin to groan.

65. Do not groan today. You will receive no help from Us.

66. My Verses were recited to you, but you turned back on your heels.

67. Arrogant towards it—talked nonsense about it—disregarded it.

68. Have they not pondered the Word? Or has there come to them what came not to their forefathers of old?

69. Or is it that they did not recognize their messenger, so they are denying him?

70. Or do they say, "He is possessed?" In fact, he brought them the truth, but most of them hate the truth.

71. If the truth conformed to their desires, the heavens, the earth, and everyone in them would have gone to ruin. In fact, We have given them their message, but they keep avoiding their message.

72. Or are you asking them for a payment? The revenue from your Lord is better, and He is the Best of providers.

73. You are inviting them to a straight path.

74. But those who do not believe in the Hereafter are swerving from the path.

75. Even if We had mercy on them, and relieved their problems, they would still blindly persist in their defiance.

76. We have already gripped them with suffering, but they did not surrender to their Lord, nor did they humble themselves.

77. Until, when We have opened before them a gate of intense agony, at once they will despair.

23. THE BELIEVERS (al-Mu'minun)

78. It is He who produced for you the hearing, and the eyesight, and the feelings. But little gratitude you show.

79. And it is He who multiplied you on earth, and to Him you will be gathered.

80. And it is He who gives life and brings death, and to Him is the alternation of night and day. Do you not understand?

81. But they say the like of what the ancients said.

82. They say, "After we have died, and become dust and bones, will we be resurrected?

83. We were promised this before—we and our ancestors—these are nothing but legends of the ancients."

84. Say, "To whom does the earth belong, and everyone in it, if you happen to know?"

85. They will say, "To Allah." Say, "Will you not reflect?"

86. Say, "Who is the Lord of the seven heavens, and Lord of the Splendid Throne?"

87. They will say, "To Allah." Say, "Will you not become righteous?"

88. Say, "In whose hand is the dominion of all things, and He protects and cannot be protected from, if you happen to know?"

89. They will say, "To Allah." Say, "Then are you bewitched?"

90. In fact, We have given them the truth, and they are liars.

91. Allah has never begotten a son, nor is there any god besides Him. Otherwise, each god would have taken away what it has created, and some of them would have gained supremacy over others. Glory be to Allah, far beyond what they describe.

92. The Knower of the hidden and the manifest. He is exalted, far above what they associate.

93. Say, "My Lord, if You would show me what they are promised.

94. My Lord, do not place me among the wicked people."

95. We are surely Able to show you what We promise them.

96. Repel evil by what is better. We are aware of what they describe.

97. And say, "My Lord, I seek refuge with You from the urgings of the devils.

98. And I seek refuge with You, my Lord, lest they become present."

99. Until, when death comes to one of them, he says, "My Lord, send me back.

100. That I may do right in what I have neglected." By no means! It is just a word that he utters. And behind them is a barrier, until the Day they are resurrected.

101. When the Horn is blown, no relations between them will exist on that Day, and they will not ask after one another.

102. Those whose scales are heavy—those are the successful.

103. But those whose scales are light—those are they who have lost their souls; in Hell they will dwell forever.

104. The Fire lashes their faces, and therein they grimace.

105. "Were not My revelations recited to you, and you kept on rejecting them?"

106. They will say, "Our Lord, our wretchedness prevailed over us, and we were a people astray.

107. Our Lord! Bring us out of this. If we ever returned, we would truly be evil."

108. He will say, "Be despised therein, and do not speak to Me.

109. There was a group of My servants who would say, 'Our Lord, we have believed, so forgive us, and have mercy on us; You are the Best of the merciful.'

110. But you made them a target of ridicule, until they made you forget My remembrance; and you used to laugh at them.

111. Today, I have rewarded them for their endurance. They are the ones who are the triumphant."

24. THE LIGHT (an-Nur)

112. He will say, "How many years did you remain on earth?"

113. They will say, "We remained a day, or part of a day; but ask those who keep count."

114. He will say, "You remained only for a little while, if you only knew."

115. Did you think that We created you in vain, and that to Us you will not be returned?"

116. So Exalted is Allah, the Ruler, the Real. There is no god except He, the Lord of the Noble Throne.

117. Whoever invokes another god besides Allah—he has no proof thereof—his reckoning rests with his Lord. The disbelievers will not succeed.

118. And say, "My Lord, forgive and have mercy, for You are the Best of the merciful."

24. THE LIGHT
(an-Nur)

*In the name of Allah,
the Gracious, the Merciful*

1. A chapter that We have revealed, and made obligatory, and revealed in it clear Verses, that you may take heed.

2. The adulteress and the adulterer—whip each one of them a hundred lashes, and let no pity towards them overcome you regarding Allah's Law, if you believe in Allah and the Last Day. And let a group of believers witness their punishment.

3. The adulterer shall marry none but an adulteress or an idolatress; and the adulteress shall marry none but an adulterer or an idolater. That has been prohibited for the believers.

4. Those who accuse chaste women, then cannot bring four witnesses, whip them eighty lashes, and do not ever accept their testimony. For these are the immoral.

5. Except for those who repent afterwards, and reform; for Allah is Forgiving and Merciful.

6. As for those who accuse their own spouses, but have no witnesses except themselves, the testimony of one of them is equivalent to four testimonies, if he swears by Allah that he is truthful.

7. And the fifth time, that Allah's curse be upon him, if he is a liar.

8. But punishment shall be averted from her, if she swears four times by Allah, that he is a liar.

9. And the fifth time, that Allah's wrath be upon her, if he is truthful.

10. Were it not for Allah's grace upon you, and His mercy, and that Allah is Conciliatory and Wise.

11. Those who perpetrated the slander are a band of you. Do not consider it bad for you, but it is good for you. Each person among them bears his share in the sin. As for him who played the major role—for him is a terrible punishment.

12. Why, when you heard about it, the believing men and women did not think well of one another, and say, "This is an obvious lie"?

13. Why did they not bring four witnesses to testify to it? If they fail to bring the witnesses, then in Allah's sight, they are liars.

14. Were it not for Allah's favor upon you, and His mercy, in this world and the Hereafter, you would have suffered a great punishment for what you have ventured into.

15. When you rumored it with your tongues, and spoke with your mouths what you had no knowledge of, and you considered it trivial; but according to Allah, it is serious.

16. When you heard it, you should have said, "It is not for us to repeat this. By Your glory, this is a serious slander."

17. Allah cautions you never to return to the like of it, if you are believers.

18. Allah explains the Verses to you. Allah is Knowing and Wise.

19. Those who love to see immorality spread among the believers—for them is a painful

24. THE LIGHT (an-Nur)

punishment, in this life and in the Hereafter. Allah knows, and you do not know.

20. Were it not for Allah's grace upon you, and His mercy, and that Allah is Clement and Merciful.

21. O you who believe! Do not follow Satan's footsteps. Whoever follows Satan's footsteps—he advocates obscenity and immorality. Were it not for Allah's grace towards you, and His mercy, not one of you would have been pure, ever. But Allah purifies whomever He wills. Allah is All-Hearing, All-Knowing.

22. Those of you who have affluence and means should not refuse to give to the relatives, and the needy, and the emigrants for the sake of Allah. And let them pardon, and let them overlook. Do you not love for Allah to pardon you? Allah is All-Forgiving, Most Merciful.

23. Those who slander honorable, innocent, believing women are cursed in this life and in the Hereafter. They will have a terrible punishment.

24. On the Day when their tongues, and their hands, and their feet will testify against them regarding what they used to do.

25. On that Day, Allah will pay them their account in full, and they will know that Allah is the Evident Reality.

26. Bad women are for bad men, and bad men are for bad women, and good women are for good men, and good men are for good women. Those are acquitted of what they say. There is forgiveness for them, and a generous provision.

27. O you who believe! Do not enter homes other than your own, until you have asked permission and greeted their occupants. That is better for you, that you may be aware.

28. And if you find no one in them, do not enter them until you are given permission. And if it is said to you, "Turn back," then turn back. That is more proper for you. Allah is aware of what you do.

29. There is no blame on you for entering uninhabited houses, in which are belongings of yours. Allah knows what you reveal and what you conceal.

30. Tell the believing men to restrain their looks, and to guard their privates. That is purer for them. Allah is cognizant of what they do.

31. And tell the believing women to restrain their looks, and to guard their privates, and not display their beauty except what is apparent thereof, and to draw their coverings over their breasts, and not expose their beauty except to their husbands, their fathers, their husbands' fathers, their sons, their husbands' sons, their brothers, their brothers' sons, their sisters' sons, their women, what their right hands possess, their male attendants who have no sexual desires, or children who are not yet aware of the nakedness of women. And they should not strike their feet to draw attention to their hidden beauty. And repent to Allah, all of you believers, so that you may succeed.

32. And wed the singles among you, and those who are fit among your servants and maids. If they are poor, Allah will enrich them from His bounty. Allah is All-Encompassing, All-Knowing.

33. And let those who do not find the means to marry abstain, until Allah enriches them from His bounty. If any of your servants wish to be freed, grant them their wish, if you recognize some good in them. And give them of Allah's wealth which he has given you. And do not compel your girls to prostitution, seeking the materials of this life, if they desire to remain chaste. Should anyone compel them—after their compulsion, Allah is Forgiving and Merciful.

34. We have sent down to you clarifying revelations, and examples of those who passed on before you, and advice for the righteous.

35. Allah is the Light of the heavens and the earth. The allegory of His light is that of a pillar on which is a lamp. The lamp is within a glass. The glass is like a brilliant planet, fueled

24. THE LIGHT (an-Nur)

by a blessed tree, an olive tree, neither eastern nor western. Its oil would almost illuminate, even if no fire has touched it. Light upon Light. Allah guides to His light whomever He wills. Allah thus cites the parables for the people. Allah is cognizant of everything.

36. In houses which Allah has permitted to be raised, and His name is celebrated therein. He is glorified therein, morning and evening.

37. By men who neither trading nor commerce distracts them from Allah's remembrance, and from performing the prayers, and from giving alms. They fear a Day when hearts and sights are overturned.

38. Allah will reward them according to the best of what they did, and He will increase them from His bounty. Allah provides for whomever He wills without reckoning.

39. As for those who disbelieve, their works are like a mirage in a desert. The thirsty assumes it is to be water. Until, when he has reached it, he finds it to be nothing, but there he finds Allah, Who settles his account in full. Allah is swift in reckoning.

40. Or like utter darkness in a vast ocean, covered by waves, above which are waves, above which is fog. Darkness upon darkness. If he brings out his hand, he will hardly see it. He to whom Allah has not granted a light has no light.

41. Do you not realize that Allah is glorified by whatever is in the heavens and the earth, and even by the birds in formation? Each knows its prayer and its manner of praise. Allah knows well what they do.

42. To Allah belongs the dominion of the heavens and the earth, and to Allah is the ultimate return.

43. Have you not seen how Allah propels the clouds, then brings them together, then piles them into a heap, and you see rain drops emerging from its midst? How He brings down loads of hail from the sky, striking with it whomever He wills, and diverting it from whomever He wills? The flash of its lightening almost snatches the sight away.

44. Allah alternates the night and the day. In that is a lesson for those who have insight.

45. Allah created every living creature from water. Some of them crawl on their bellies, and some walk on two feet, and others walk on four. Allah creates whatever He wills. Allah is Capable of everything.

46. We sent down enlightening revelations, and Allah guides whomever He wills to a straight path.

47. And they say, "We have believed in Allah and the Messenger, and we obey," but some of them turn away afterwards. These are not believers.

48. And when they are called to Allah and His Messenger, in order to judge between them, some of them refuse.

49. But if justice is on their side, they accept it willingly.

50. Is there sickness in their hearts? Or are they suspicious? Or do they fear that Allah may do them injustice? Or His Messenger? In fact, they themselves are the unjust.

51. The response of the believers, when they are called to Allah and His Messenger in order to judge between them, is to say, "We hear and we obey." These are the successful.

52. Whoever obeys Allah and His Messenger, and fears Allah, and is conscious of Him—these are the winners.

53. And they swear by Allah with their solemn oaths, that if you commanded them, they would mobilize. Say, "Do not swear. Obedience will be recognized. Allah is experienced with what you do."

54. Say, "Obey Allah and obey the Messenger." But if they turn away, then he is responsible for his obligations, and you are responsible for your obligations. And if you obey him, you will be guided. It is only incumbent on the Messenger to deliver the Clarifying Message.

55. Allah has promised those of you who believe and do righteous deeds, that He will make them successors on earth, as He made

those before them successors, and He will establish for them their religion—which He has approved for them—and He will substitute security in place of their fear. They worship Me, never associating anything with Me. But whoever disbelieves after that—these are the sinners.

56. Pray regularly, and give regular charity, and obey the Messenger, so that you may receive mercy.

57. Never think that those who disbelieve can escape on earth. Their place is the Fire; a miserable destination.

58. O you who believe! Permission must be requested by your servants and those of you who have not reached puberty. On three occasions: before the Dawn Prayer, and at noon when you change your clothes, and after the Evening Prayer. These are three occasions of privacy for you. At other times, it is not wrong for you or them to intermingle with one another. Allah thus clarifies the revelations for you. Allah is Knowledgeable and Wise.

59. When the children among you reach puberty, they must ask permission, as those before them asked permission. Allah thus clarifies His revelations for you. Allah is Knowledgeable and Wise.

60. Women past the age of childbearing, who have no desire for marriage, commit no wrong by taking off their outer clothing, provided they do not flaunt their finery. But to maintain modesty is better for them. Allah is Hearing and Knowing.

61. There is no blame on the blind, nor any blame on the lame, nor any blame on the sick, nor on yourselves for eating at your homes, or your fathers' homes, or your mothers' homes, or your brothers' homes, or your sisters' homes, or the homes of your paternal uncles, or the homes of your paternal aunts, or the homes of your maternal uncles, or the homes of your maternal aunts, or those whose keys you own, or the homes of your friends. You commit no wrong by eating together or separately. But when you enter any home, greet one another with a greeting from Allah, blessed and good. Allah thus explains the revelations for you, so that you may understand.

62. The believers are those who believe in Allah and His Messenger, and when they are with him for a matter of common interest, they do not leave until they have asked him for permission. Those who ask your permission are those who believe in Allah and His Messenger. So when they ask your permission to attend to some affair of theirs, give permission to any of them you wish, and ask Allah's forgiveness for them. Allah is Forgiving and Merciful.

63. Do not address the Messenger in the same manner you address one another. Allah knows those of you who slip away using flimsy excuses. So let those who oppose his orders beware, lest an ordeal strikes them, or a painful punishment befalls them.

64. Surely, to Allah belongs everything in the heavens and the earth. He knows what you are about. And on the Day they are returned to Him, He will inform them of what they did. Allah has full knowledge of all things.

25. THE CRITERION
(al-Furqan)

*In the name of Allah,
the Gracious, the Merciful*

1. Blessed is He who sent down the Criterion upon His servant, to be a warning to humanity.

2. He to whom belongs the kingdom of the heavens and the earth, who took to Himself no son, who never had a partner in His kingship; who created everything and determined its measure.

3. And yet, instead of Him, they produce for themselves gods that create nothing, but are themselves created; that have no power to harm or benefit themselves; and no power over life, death, or resurrection.

25. THE CRITERION (al-Furqan)

4. Those who disbelieve say, "This is nothing but a lie that he made up, and others have helped him at it." They have committed an injustice and a perjury.

5. And they say, "Tales of the ancients; he wrote them down; they are dictated to him morning and evening."

6. Say, "It was revealed by He who knows the Secret in the heavens and the earth. He is always Forgiving and Merciful."

7. And they say, "What sort of messenger is this, who eats food, and walks in the marketplaces? If only an angel was sent down with him, to be alongside him a warner."

8. Or, "If only a treasure was dropped on him." Or, "If only he had a garden from which he eats." The evildoers also say, "You are following but a man under spell."

9. Look how they invent examples for you. They have gone astray, and cannot find a way.

10. Blessed is He who, if He wills, can provide you with better than that—gardens beneath which rivers flow—and He will give you palaces.

11. In fact, they have denied the Hour, and We have prepared for those who deny the Hour a Blaze.

12. When it sees them from a distant place, they will hear it raging and roaring.

13. And when they are thrown into it, into a tight place, shackled, they will plead there for death.

14. "Do not plead for one death today, but plead for a great many deaths."

15. Say, "Is this better, or the Garden of Eternity promised to the righteous? It is for them a reward and a destination.

16. They will have therein whatever they desire, forever. That is upon your Lord a binding promise.

17. On the Day when He gathers them, and what they worshiped besides Allah, He will say, "Was it you who misled these servants of Mine, or was it they who lost the way?"

18. They will say, "Glory be to You. It was not for us to take any lords besides You. But you gave them enjoyments, and their ancestors, until they forgot the Message, and became ruined people."

19. They have denied you because of what you say; so you can neither avert, nor help. Whoever among you commits injustice, We will make him taste a grievous punishment.

20. We never sent any messengers before you, but they ate food and walked in the marketplaces. And We made some of you tempters for one another—will you be patient? Your Lord is always Observing.

21. Those who do not expect to meet Us say, "If only the angels were sent down to us, or we could see our Lord." They have grown arrogant within themselves, and have become excessively defiant.

22. On the Day when they see the angels—there will be no good news for sinners on that Day; and they will say, "A protective refuge."

23. We will proceed to the works they did, and will turn them into scattered dust.

24. The companions of Paradise on that Day will be better lodged, and more fairly accommodated.

25. The Day when the sky is cleft with clouds, and the angels are sent down in streams.

26. On that Day, true sovereignty will belong to the Merciful, and it will be a difficult Day for the disbelievers.

27. On that Day, the wrongdoer will bite his hands, and say, "If only I had followed the way with the Messenger.

28. Oh, woe to me; I wish I never took so-and-so for a friend.

29. He led me away from the Message after it had come to me; for Satan has always been a betrayer of man."

30. And the Messenger will say, "My Lord, my people have abandoned this Quran."

25. THE CRITERION (al-Furqan)

31. Likewise, to every prophet We assign enemies from among the wicked. But your Lord suffices as a Guide and Savior.

32. Those who disbelieve say, "Why was the Quran not revealed to him at once?" Thus in order to strengthen your heart thereby, and We revealed it in stages.

33. Whatever argument they come to you with, We provide you with the truth, and a better exposition.

34. Those who are herded into Hell on their faces—those are in a worse position, and further astray from the way.

35. We gave Moses the Scripture, and appointed his brother Aaron as his assistant.

36. We said, "Go to the people who rejected Our signs," and We destroyed them completely.

37. And the people of Noah: when they rejected the messengers, We drowned them, and made them a lesson for mankind. We have prepared for the wrongdoers a painful retribution.

38. And Aad, and Thamood, and the inhabitants of Arras, and many generations in between.

39. To each We presented the parables; and each We devastated utterly.

40. And they came upon the city that was drenched by the terrible rain. Did they not see it? But they do not expect resurrection.

41. And when they see you, they take you for nothing but mockery: "Is this the one Allah sent as a messenger?"

42. "He nearly led us away from our gods, had we not patiently adhered to them." But they will know, when they witness the torment, who is further away from the way.

43. Have you seen him who chose his desire as his god? Would you be an agent for him?

44. Or do you assume that most of them hear or understand? They are just like cattle, but even more errant in their way.

45. Do you not see how your Lord extends the shadow? Had He willed, He could have made it still. And We made the sun a pointer to it.

46. Then We withdraw it towards Us gradually.

47. And it is He who made the night a covering for you, and sleep for rest; and He made the day a revival.

48. And it is He who sends the winds, bringing advance news of His mercy; and We send down from the sky pure water.

49. To revive dead lands thereby, and to provide drink for the multitude of animals and humans We created.

50. We have circulated it among them, that they may reflect, but most people persist in thanklessness.

51. Had We willed, We could have sent to every town a warner.

52. So do not obey the disbelievers, but strive against them with it, a mighty struggle.

53. And it is He who merged the two seas; this one fresh and sweet, and that one salty and bitter; and He placed between them a barrier, and an impassable boundary.

54. And it is He who, from fluid, created the human being. Then He made relationships through marriage and mating. Your Lord is Omnipotent.

55. And yet, instead of Allah, they serve what neither profits them nor harms them. The disbeliever has always turned his back on his Lord.

56. We sent you only as a herald of good news and a warner.

57. Say, "I ask of you no payment for this—only that whoever wills may take a path to his Lord."

58. And put your trust in the Living, the One who never dies; and celebrate His praise. He suffices as the All-Informed Knower of the faults of His creatures.

59. He who created the heavens and the earth and everything between them in six days,

then settled on the Throne. The Most Merciful. Ask about Him a well-informed.

60. And when it is said to them, "Bow down to the Merciful," they say, "And what is the Merciful? Are we to bow down to whatever you command us?" And it increases their aversion.

61. Blessed is He who placed constellations in the sky, and placed in it a lamp, and an illuminating moon.

62. And it is He who made the night and the day alternate—for whoever desires to reflect, or desires to show gratitude.

63. The servants of the Merciful are those who walk the earth in humility, and when the ignorant address them, they say, "Peace."

64. And those who pass the night prostrating themselves to their Lord and standing up.

65. And those who say, "Our Lord, avert from us the suffering of Hell, for its suffering is continuous.

66. It is indeed a miserable residence and destination."

67. And those who, when they spend, are neither wasteful nor stingy, but choose a middle course between that.

68. And those who do not implore besides Allah any other god, and do not kill the soul which Allah has made sacred—except in the pursuit of justice—and do not commit adultery. Whoever does that will face penalties.

69. The punishment will be doubled for him on the Day of Resurrection, and he will dwell therein in humiliation forever.

70. Except for those who repent, and believe, and do good deeds. These—Allah will replace their bad deeds with good deeds. Allah is ever Forgiving and Merciful.

71. Whoever repents and acts righteously—has inclined towards Allah with repentance.

72. And those who do not bear false witness; and when they come across indecencies, they pass by with dignity.

73. And those who, when reminded of the revelations of their Lord, do not fall before them deaf and blind.

74. And those who say, "Our Lord, grant us delight in our spouses and our children, and make us a good example for the righteous."

75. Those will be awarded the Chamber for their patience, and will be greeted therein with greetings and peace.

76. Abiding therein forever—it is an excellent residence and destination.

77. Say, "What are you to my Lord without your prayers? You have denied the truth, and the inevitable will happen."

26. THE POETS (ash-Shu'ara')

In the name of Allah, the Gracious, the Merciful

1. Ta, Seen, Meem.

2. These are the Verses of the Clarifying Book.

3. Perhaps you will destroy yourself with grief, because they do not become believers.

4. If We will, We can send down upon them a sign from heaven, at which their necks will stay bent in humility.

5. No fresh reminder comes to them from the Most Merciful, but they turn their backs at it.

6. They have denied the truth, but soon will come to them the news of what they ridiculed.

7. Have they not seen the earth, and how many beautiful pairs We produced therein?

8. Surely in this is a sign, but most of them are not believers.

9. Most surely, your Lord is the Almighty, the Merciful.

10. Your Lord called to Moses, "Go to the tyrannical people.

11. The people of Pharaoh. Will they not fear?"

26. THE POETS (ash-Shu'ara')

12. He said, "My Lord, I fear they will reject me.

13. And I become stressed, and my tongue is not fluent, so send Aaron too.

14. And they have a charge against me, so I fear they will kill me."

15. He said, "No. Go, both of you, with Our proofs. We will be with you, listening.

16. Go to Pharaoh, and say, 'We are the Messengers of the Lord of the Worlds.

17. Let the Children of Israel go with us.'"

18. He said, "Did we not raise you among us as a child, and you stayed among us for many of your years?

19. And you committed that deed you committed, and you were ungrateful."

20. He said, "I did it then, when I was of those astray.

21. And I fled from you when I feared you; but my Lord gave me wisdom, and made me one of the messengers.

22. Is that the favor you taunt me with, although you have enslaved the Children of Israel?"

23. Pharaoh said, "And what is the Lord of the Worlds?"

24. He said, "The Lord of the heavens and the earth, and everything between them, if you are aware."

25. He said to those around him, "Do you not hear?"

26. He said, "Your Lord and the Lord of your ancestors of old."

27. He said, "This messenger of yours, who is sent to you, is crazy."

28. He said, "Lord of the East and the West, and everything between them, if you understand."

29. He said, "If you accept any god other than me, I will make you a prisoner."

30. He said, "What if I bring you something convincing?"

31. He said, "Bring it, if you are being truthful."

32. So he cast his staff; and it was a serpent, plain to see.

33. And he pulled his hand; and it was white, for all to see.

34. He said to the dignitaries around him, "This is a skilled magician.

35. He intends to drive you out of your land with his magic, so what do you recommend?"

36. They said, "Delay him and his brother, and send recruiters to the cities.

37. To bring you every experienced magician."

38. So the magicians were gathered for the appointment on a specified day.

39. And it was said to the people, "Are you all gathered?

40. That we may follow the magicians, if they are the winners."

41. When the magicians arrived, they said to Pharaoh, "Is there a reward for us, if we are the winners?"

42. He said, "Yes, and you will be among those favored."

43. Moses said to them, "Present what you intend to present."

44. So they threw their ropes and their sticks, and said, "By the majesty of Pharaoh, we will be the winners."

45. Then Moses threw his staff, and behold, it began swallowing their trickery.

46. And the magicians fell down prostrating.

47. They said, "We have believed in the Lord of the Worlds.

48. The Lord of Moses and Aaron."

49. He said, "Did you believe in Him before I have given you permission? He must be your chief, who taught you magic. You will soon know. I will cut off your hands and feet on opposite sides, and I will crucify you all."

50. They said, "No problem. To our Lord we will return.

26. THE POETS (ash-Shu'ara')

51. We are eager for our Lord to forgive us our sins, since we are the first of the believers."

52. And We inspired Moses: "Travel with My servants by night. You will be followed."

53. Pharaoh sent heralds to the cities.

54. "These are a small gang.

55. And they are enraging us.

56. But we are a vigilant multitude."

57. So We drove them out of gardens and springs.

58. And treasures and noble dwellings.

59. So it was. And We made the Children of Israel inherit them.

60. And they pursued them at sunrise.

61. When the two groups sighted each other, the followers of Moses said, "We are being overtaken."

62. He said, "No; my Lord is with me, He will guide me."

63. We inspired Moses: "Strike the sea with your staff." Whereupon it parted, and each part was like a huge hill.

64. And there We brought the others near.

65. And We saved Moses and those with him, all together.

66. Then We drowned the others.

67. In that there is a sign, but most of them are not believers.

68. Surely, your Lord is the Almighty, the Merciful.

69. And relate to them the story of Abraham.

70. When he said to his father and his people, "What do you worship?"

71. They said, "We worship idols, and we remain devoted to them."

72. He said, "Do they hear you when you pray?

73. Or do they benefit you, or harm you?"

74. They said, "But we found our ancestors doing so."

75. He said, "Have you considered what you worship.

76. You and your ancient ancestors?

77. They are enemies to me, but not so the Lord of the Worlds.

78. He who created me, and guides me.

79. He who feeds me, and waters me.

80. And when I get sick, He heals me.

81. He who makes me die, and then revives me.

82. He who, I hope, will forgive my sins on the Day of the Reckoning."

83. "My Lord! Grant me wisdom, and include me with the righteous.

84. And give me a reputation of truth among the others.

85. And make me of the inheritors of the Garden of Bliss.

86. And forgive my father—he was one of the misguided.

87. And do not disgrace me on the Day they are resurrected.

88. The Day when neither wealth nor children will help.

89. Except for him who comes to Allah with a sound heart."

90. And Paradise will be brought near for the righteous.

91. And the Blaze will be displayed to the deviators.

92. And it will be said to them, "Where are those you used to worship?"

93. Besides Allah? Can they help you, or help themselves?"

94. Then they will be toppled into it, together with the seducers.

95. And the soldiers of Satan, all of them.

96. They will say, as they feud in it.

97. "By Allah, We were in evident error.

98. For equating you with the Lord of the Worlds.

26. THE POETS (ash-Shu'ara')

99. No one misled us except the sinners.

100. Now we have no intercessors.

101. And no sincere friend.

102. If only we could have another chance, we would be among the faithful."

103. Surely in this is a sign, but most of them are not believers.

104. Your Lord is the Almighty, the Merciful.

105. The people of Noah disbelieved the messengers.

106. Their brother Noah said to them, "Do you not fear?

107. I am to you a faithful messenger.

108. So fear Allah, and obey me.

109. I ask of you no payment for this. My payment is only from the Lord of the Worlds.

110. So fear Allah, and obey me."

111. They said, "Shall we believe in you, when it is the lowliest who follow you?"

112. He said, "What do I know about what they do?

113. Their account rests only with my Lord, if you have sense.

114. And I am not about to drive away the believers.

115. I am only a clear warner."

116. They said, "If you do not refrain, O Noah, you will be stoned."

117. He said, "My Lord, my people have denied me.

118. So judge between me and them decisively, and deliver me and the believers who are with me.

119. So We delivered him and those with him in the laden Ark.

120. Then We drowned the rest.

121. In that is a sign, but most of them are not believers.

122. Your Lord is the Almighty, the Merciful.

123. Aad disbelieved the messengers.

124. When their brother Hud said to them, "Do you not fear?

125. I am to you a faithful messenger.

126. So fear Allah, and obey me.

127. I ask of you no payment for this. My payment is only from the Lord of the Worlds.

128. Do you build a monument on every height for vanity's sake?

129. And you set up fortresses, hoping to live forever?

130. And when you strike, you strike mercilessly?

131. So fear Allah, and obey me.

132. And reverence Him, who supplied you with everything you know.

133. He supplied you with livestock and children.

134. And gardens and springs.

135. I fear for you the punishment of an awesome Day."

136. They said, "It is the same for us, whether you lecture us, or do not lecture.

137. This is nothing but morals of the ancients.

138. And we will not be punished."

139. So they denied him, and We destroyed them. Surely in this is a sign, but most of them are not believers.

140. Your Lord is the Almighty, the Merciful.

141. Thamood disbelieved the messengers.

142. When their brother Saleh said to them, "Do you not fear?

143. I am to you a faithful messenger.

144. So fear Allah, and obey me.

145. I ask of you no payment for it. My payment is only from the Lord of the Worlds.

146. Will you be left secure in what is here?

147. In gardens and springs?

148. And fields, and palm-trees whose fruits are delicious?

26. THE POETS (ash-Shu'ara')

149. And you skillfully carve houses in the mountains?

150. So fear Allah, and obey me.

151. And do not obey the command of the extravagant.

152. Who spread turmoil on earth, and do not reform."

153. They said, "You are surely one of the bewitched.

154. You are nothing but a man like us. So bring us a sign, if you are truthful.

155. He said, "This is a she-camel; she has her turn of drinking, and you have your turn of drinking—on a specified day.

156. And do not touch her with harm, lest the punishment of a great day seizes you."

157. But they slaughtered her, and became full of remorse.

158. So the punishment overtook them. Surely in this is a sign, but most of them are not believers.

159. Your Lord is the Almighty, the Merciful.

160. The people of Lot disbelieved the messengers.

161. When their brother Lot said to them, "Do you not fear?

162. I am to you a faithful messenger.

163. So fear Allah, and obey me.

164. I ask of you no payment for it. My payment is only from the Lord of the Worlds.

165. Do you approach the males of the world?

166. And forsake the wives your Lord created for you? Indeed, you are intrusive people."

167. They said, "Unless you refrain, O Lot, you will be expelled."

168. He said, "I certainly deplore your conduct."

169. "My Lord, save me and my family from what they do."

170. So We saved him and his family, altogether.

171. Except for an old woman among those who tarried.

172. Then We destroyed the others.

173. And We rained down on them a rain. Dreadful is the rain of those forewarned.

174. Surely in this is a sign, but most of them are not believers.

175. Your Lord is the Almighty, the Merciful.

176. The People of the Woods disbelieved the messengers.

177. When Shuaib said to them, "Do you not fear?

178. I am to you a trustworthy messenger.

179. So fear Allah, and obey me.

180. I ask of you no payment for it. My payment is only from the Lord of the Worlds.

181. Give full measure, and do not cheat.

182. And weigh with accurate scales.

183. And do not defraud people of their belongings, and do not work corruption in the land.

184. And fear Him who created you and the masses of old."

185. They said, "You are one of those bewitched.

186. And you are nothing but a man like us; and we think that you are a liar.

187. So bring down on us pieces from the sky, if you are truthful."

188. He said, "My Lord is Well Aware of what you do."

189. But they denied him. So the punishment of the day of gloom gripped them. It was the punishment of a great day.

190. Surely in this is a sign, but most of them are not believers.

191. Your Lord is the Almighty, the Merciful.

192. It is a revelation from the Lord of the Worlds.

193. The Honest Spirit came down with it.

27. THE ANT (an-Naml)

194. Upon your heart, that you may be one of the warners.

195. In a clear Arabic tongue.

196. And it is in the scriptures of the ancients.

197. Is it not a sign for them that the scholars of the Children of Israel recognized it?

198. Had We revealed it to one of the foreigners.

199. And he had recited it to them, they still would not have believed in it.

200. Thus We make it pass through the hearts of the guilty.

201. They will not believe in it until they witness the painful punishment.

202. It will come to them suddenly, while they are unaware.

203. Then they will say, "Are we given any respite?"

204. Do they seek to hasten Our punishment?

205. Have you considered: if We let them enjoy themselves for some years.

206. Then there comes to them what they were promised.

207. Of what avail to them will be their past enjoyments?

208. Never did We destroy a town, but it had warners.

209. As a reminder—We are never unjust.

210. It was not the devils that revealed it.

211. It is not in their interests, nor in their power.

212. They are barred from hearing.

213. So do not pray to another god with Allah, else you will be of those tormented.

214. And warn your close relatives.

215. And lower your wing to those of the believers who follow you.

216. And if they disobey you, say, "I am innocent of what you do."

217. And put your trust in the Almighty, the Merciful.

218. He Who sees you when you rise.

219. And your devotions amidst the worshipers.

220. He is indeed the Hearer, the Aware.

221. Shall I inform you upon whom the devils descend?

222. They descend upon every sinful liar.

223. They give ear, and most of them are liars.

224. And as for the poets—the deviators follow them.

225. Do you not see how they ramble in every style?

226. And how they say what they do not do?

227. Except for those who believe, and do good deeds, and remember Allah frequently, and defend themselves after they are wronged. As for those who do wrong, they will know by what overturning they will be overturned.

27. THE ANT
(an-Naml)

In the name of Allah,
the Gracious, the Merciful

1. Ta, Seen. These are the Signs of the Quran—a book that makes things clear.

2. Guidance and good news for the believers.

3. Those who observe the prayers, and give charity regularly, and are certain of the Hereafter.

4. As for those who do not believe in the Hereafter: We made their deeds appear good to them, so they wander aimlessly.

5. It is they who will receive the grievous punishment—and in the Hereafter they will be the greatest losers.

6. You are receiving the Quran from an All-Wise, All-Knowing.

7. When Moses said to his family, "I have glimpsed a fire. I will bring you some news from it; or bring you a firebrand, that you may warm yourselves."

27. THE ANT (an-Naml)

8. Then, when he reached it, he was called: "Blessed is He who is within the fire, and He who is around it, and glorified be Allah, Lord of the Worlds.

9. O Moses, it is I, Allah, the Almighty, the Wise.

10. Throw down your staff." But when he saw it quivering, as though it were a demon, he turned around not looking back. "O Moses, do not fear; the messengers do not fear in My presence.

11. But whoever has done wrong, and then substituted goodness in place of evil. I am Forgiving and Merciful.

12. Put your hand inside your pocket, and it will come out white, without blemish—among nine miracles to Pharaoh and his people, for they are immoral people."

13. Yet when Our enlightening signs came to them, they said, "This is obvious witchcraft."

14. And they rejected them, although their souls were certain of them, out of wickedness and pride. So see how the outcome was for the mischief-makers.

15. And We gave David and Solomon knowledge. They said, "Praise Allah, who has favored us over many of His believing servants."

16. And Solomon succeeded David. He said, "O people, we were taught the language of birds, and we were given from everything. This is indeed a real blessing."

17. To the service of Solomon were mobilized his troops of sprites, and men, and birds—all held in strict order.

18. Until, when they came upon the Valley of Ants, an ant said, "O ants! Go into your nests, lest Solomon and his troops crush you without noticing."

19. He smiled and laughed at her words, and said, "My Lord, direct me to be thankful for the blessings you have bestowed upon me and upon my parents, and to do good works that please You. And admit me, by Your grace, into the company of Your virtuous servants."

20. Then he inspected the birds, and said, "Why do I not see the hoopoe? Or is he among the absentees?

21. I will punish him most severely, or slay him, unless he gives me a valid excuse."

22. But he did not stay for long. He said, "I have learnt something you did not know. I have come to you from Sheba, with reliable information.

23. I found a woman ruling over them, and she was given of everything, and she has a magnificent throne.

24. I found her and her people worshiping the sun, instead of Allah. Satan made their conduct appear good to them, and diverted them from the path, so they are not guided.

25. If only they would worship Allah, who brings to light the mysteries of the heavens and the earth, and knows what you conceal and what you reveal.

26. Allah—There is no god but He, the Lord of the Sublime Throne."

27. He said, "We will see, whether you have spoken the truth, or whether you are a liar.

28. Go with this letter of mine, and deliver it to them; then withdraw from them, and see how they respond."

29. She said, "O Counselors, a gracious letter was delivered to me.

30. It is from Solomon, and it is, 'In the Name of Allah, the Gracious, the Merciful.

31. Do not defy me, and come to me submissively.'"

32. She said, "O counselors, advise me in this matter of mine. I never make a decision unless you are present."

33. They said, "We are a people of might and great courage, but the decision is yours, so consider what you wish to command."

34. She said, "When kings enter a city, they devastate it, and subjugate its dignified people. Thus they always do.

27. THE ANT (an-Naml)

35. I am sending them a gift, and will see what the envoys bring back."

36. When he came to Solomon, he said, "Are you supplying me with money? What Allah has given me is better than what He has given you. It is you who delight in your gift.

37. Go back to them. We will come upon them with troops they cannot resist; and we will expel them from there, disgraced and humiliated."

38. He said, "O notables, which one of you will bring me her throne before they come to me in submission?"

39. An imp of the sprites said, "I will bring it to you before you rise from your seat. I am strong and reliable enough to do it."

40. He who had knowledge from the Book said, "I will bring it to you before your glance returns to you." And when he saw it settled before him, he said, "This is from the grace of my Lord, to test me, whether I am grateful or ungrateful. He who is grateful, his gratitude is to his own credit; but he who is ungrateful—my Lord is Independent and Generous."

41. He said, "Disguise her throne for her, and we shall see whether she will be guided, or remains one of the misguided."

42. When she arrived, it was said, "Is your throne like this?" She said, "As if this is it." "We were given knowledge before her, and we were submissive."

43. But she was prevented by what she worshiped besides Allah; she belonged to a disbelieving people.

44. It was said to her, "Go inside the palace." And when she saw it, she thought it was a deep pond, and she bared her legs. He said, "It is a palace paved with glass." She said, "My Lord, I have done wrong to myself, and I have submitted with Solomon, to Allah, Lord of the Worlds."

45. And We sent to Thamood their brother Saleh: "Worship Allah." But they became two disputing factions.

46. He said, "O my people, why are you quick to do evil rather than good? If only you would seek Allah's forgiveness, so that you may be shown mercy."

47. They said, "We consider you an ill omen, and those with you." He said, "Your omen is with Allah. In fact, you are a people being tested."

48. In the city was a gang of nine who made mischief in the land and did no good.

49. They said, "Swear by Allah to one another that we will attack him and his family by night, and then tell his guardian, 'We did not witness the murder of his family, and we are being truthful.'"

50. They planned a plan, and We planned a plan, but they did not notice.

51. So note the outcome of their planning; We destroyed them and their people, altogether.

52. Here are their homes, in ruins, on account of their iniquities. Surely in this is a sign for people who know.

53. And We saved those who believed and were pious.

54. And Lot, when he said to his people, "Do you commit lewdness with open eyes?

55. Do you lust after men instead of women? You are truly ignorant people."

56. But the only response of his people was to say, "Expel the family of Lot from your town. They are purist people."

57. So We saved him and his family, except for his wife, whom We destined to be among the laggards.

58. And We rained upon them a rain. Miserable was the rain of those forewarned.

59. Say, "Praise Allah, and peace be upon His servants whom He has selected. Is Allah better, or what they associate?"

60. Or, who created the heavens and the earth, and rains down water from the sky for you? With it We produce gardens full of beauty, whose trees you could not have produced. Is

27. THE ANT (an-Naml)

there another god with Allah? But they are a people who equate.

61. Or, who made the earth habitable, and made rivers flow through it, and set mountains on it, and placed a partition between the two seas? Is there another god with Allah? But most of them do not know.

62. Or, who answers the one in need when he prays to Him, and relieves adversity, and makes you successors on earth? Is there another god with Allah? How hardly you pay attention.

63. Or, who guides you through the darkness of land and sea, and who sends the winds as heralds of His mercy? Is there another god with Allah? Most exalted is Allah, above what they associate.

64. Or, who originates the creation and then repeats it, and who gives you livelihood from the sky and the earth? Is there another god with Allah? Say, "Produce your evidence, if you are truthful."

65. Say, "No one in the heavens or on earth knows the future except Allah; and they do not perceive when they will be resurrected."

66. In fact, their knowledge of the Hereafter is confused. In fact, they are in doubt about it. In fact, they are blind to it.

67. Those who disbelieve say, "When we have become dust, and our ancestors, shall we be brought out?

68. We were promised that before, we and our ancestors—these are nothing but legends of the ancients."

69. Say, travel through the earth, and observe the fate of the guilty."

70. But do not grieve over them, and do not be troubled by what they plot.

71. And they say, "When is this promise, if you are truthful?"

72. Say, "Perhaps some of what you are impatient for has drawn near."

73. Your Lord is gracious towards humanity, but most of them are not thankful.

74. And your Lord knows what their hearts conceal, and what they reveal.

75. There is no mystery in the heaven and the earth, but it is in a Clear Book.

76. This Quran relates to the Children of Israel most of what they differ about.

77. And it is guidance and mercy for the believers.

78. Your Lord will judge between them by His wisdom. He is the Almighty, the All-Knowing.

79. So rely on Allah. You are upon the clear truth.

80. You cannot make the dead hear, nor can you make the deaf hear the call if they turn their backs and flee.

81. Nor can you guide the blind out of their straying. You can make no one listen, except those who believe in Our verses; for they are Muslims.

82. And when the Word has fallen on them, We will bring out for them from the earth a creature which will say to them that the people are uncertain of Our revelations.

83. On the Day when We gather from every community a group of those who rejected Our revelations; and they will be restrained.

84. Until, when they arrive, He will say, "Did you reject My revelations without comprehending them? Or what is it you were doing?"

85. The Word will come down upon them for their wrongdoing, and they will not speak.

86. Do they not see that We made the night for them to rest therein, and the day for visibility? Surely in that are signs for people who believe.

87. On the Day when the Trumpet is blown, everyone in the heavens and the earth will be horrified, except whomever Allah wills; and everyone will come before Him in humility.

88. And you see the mountains, and imagine them fixed, yet they pass, as the passing of the

clouds—the making of Allah, who has perfected everything. He is fully Informed of what you do.

89. Whoever brings a virtue will receive better than it—and they will be safe from the horrors of that Day.

90. But whoever brings evil—their faces will be tumbled into the Fire. Will you be rewarded except for what you used to do?

91. "I was commanded to worship the Lord of this town, who has sanctified it, and to Whom everything belongs; and I was commanded to be of those who submit.

92. And to recite the Quran." Whoever is guided—is guided to his own advantage. And whoever goes astray, then say, "I am one of the warners."

93. And say, "Praise belongs to Allah; He will show you His signs, and you will recognize them. Your Lord is not heedless of what you do."

28. HISTORY
(al-Qasas)

In the name of Allah,
the Gracious, the Merciful

1. Ta, Seen, Meem.

2. These are the Verses of the Clear Book.

3. We narrate to you from the history of Moses and Pharaoh—in truth—for people who believe.

4. Pharaoh exalted himself in the land, and divided its people into factions. He persecuted a group of them, slaughtering their sons, while sparing their daughters. He was truly a corrupter.

5. But We desired to favor those who were oppressed in the land, and to make them leaders, and to make them the inheritors.

6. And to establish them in the land; and to show Pharaoh, Hamaan, and their troops, the very thing they feared.

7. We inspired the mother of Moses: "Nurse him; then, when you fear for him, cast him into the river, and do not fear, nor grieve; We will return him to you, and make him one of the messengers."

8. Pharaoh's household picked him up, to be an opponent and a sorrow for them. Pharaoh, Hamaan, and their troops were sinners.

9. Pharaoh's wife said, "An eye's delight for me and for you. Do not kill him; perhaps he will be useful to us, or we may adopt him as a son." But they did not foresee.

10. The heart of Moses' mother became vacant. She was about to disclose him, had We not steadied her heart, that she may remain a believer.

11. She said to his sister, "Trail him." So she watched him from afar, and they were unaware.

12. We forbade him breastfeeding at first. So she said, "Shall I tell you about a family that can raise him for you, and will look after him?"

13. Thus We returned him to his mother, that she may be comforted, and not grieve, and know that Allah's promise is true. But most of them do not know.

14. And when he reached his maturity, and became established, We gave him wisdom and knowledge. Thus do We reward the virtuous.

15. Once he entered the city, unnoticed by its people. He found in it two men fighting—one of his own sect, and one from his enemies. The one of his sect solicited his assistance against the one from his enemies; so Moses punched him, and put an end to him. He said, "This is of Satan's doing; he is an enemy that openly misleads."

16. He said, "My Lord, I have wronged myself, so forgive me." So He forgave him. He is the Forgiver, the Merciful.

17. He said, "My Lord, in as much as you have favored me, I will never be a supporter of the criminals."

28. HISTORY (al-Qasas)

18. The next morning, he went about in the city, fearful and vigilant, when the man who had sought his assistance the day before was shouting out to him. Moses said to him, "You are clearly a troublemaker."

19. As he was about to strike the one who was their enemy, he said, "O Moses, do you intend to kill me, as you killed someone yesterday? You only want to be a bully in the land, and do not want to be a peacemaker."

20. And a man came from the farthest part of the city running. He said, "O Moses, the authorities are considering killing you, so leave; I am giving you good advice."

21. So he left, fearful and vigilant. He said, "My Lord, deliver me from the wrongdoing people."

22. As he headed towards Median, he said, "Perhaps my Lord will guide me to the right way."

23. And when he arrived at the waters of Median, he found there a crowd of people drawing water, and he noticed two women waiting on the side. He said, "What is the matter with you?" They said, "We cannot draw water until the shepherds depart, and our father is a very old man."

24. So he drew water for them, and then withdrew to the shade, and said, "My Lord, I am in dire need of whatever good you might send down to me."

25. Then, one of the two women approached him, walking bashfully. She said, "My father is calling you, to reward you for drawing water for us." And when he came to him, and told him the story, he said, "Do not fear, you have escaped from the wrongdoing people."

26. One of the two women said, "Father, hire him; the best employee for you is the strong and trustworthy."

27. He said, "I want to marry you to one of these two daughters of mine, provided you work for me for eight years. But if you complete ten, that is up to you. I do not intend to impose any hardship on you. You will find me, Allah willing, one of the righteous."

28. He said, "Let this be an agreement between you and me. Whichever of the two terms I fulfill, there shall be no reprisal against me; and Allah is witness over what we say."

29. When Moses had completed the term, and departed with his family, he noticed a fire by the side of the Mount. He said to his family, "Stay here, I have glimpsed a fire. Perhaps I can bring you some information from there, or an ember from the fire, that you may warm yourselves."

30. When he reached it, he was called from the right side of the valley, at the Blessed Spot, from the bush: "O Moses, it is I, Allah, the Lord of the Worlds.

31. Throw down your staff." And when he saw it wiggling, as if it were possessed, he turned his back to flee, and did not look back. "O Moses, come forward, and do not fear, you are perfectly safe.

32. Put your hand inside your pocket, and it will come out white, without blemish. And press your arm to your side, against fear. These are two proofs from your Lord, to Pharaoh and his dignitaries. They are truly sinful people."

33. He said, "My Lord, I have killed one of them, and I fear they will kill me.

34. And my brother Aaron, he is more eloquent than me, so send him with me, to help me, and to confirm my words, for I fear they will reject me."

35. He said, "We will strengthen your arm with your brother, and We will give you authority, so they will not touch you. By virtue of Our signs, you and those who follow you will be the triumphant."

36. But when Moses came to them with Our signs, clear and manifest, they said, "This is nothing but fabricated magic, and We never heard of this from our ancestors of old."

37. Moses said, "My Lord is well aware of him who brings guidance from Him, and him who will have the sequel of the abode. The wrongdoers will not succeed."

28. HISTORY (al-Qasas)

38. Pharaoh said, "O nobles, I know of no god for you other than me. So fire-up the bricks for me O Hamaan, and build me a tower, that I may ascend to the God of Moses, though I think he is a liar."

39. He and his troops acted arrogantly in the land, with no justification. They thought they would not be returned to Us.

40. So We seized him, and his troops, and We threw them into the sea. Observe, therefore, what was the end of the oppressors.

41. And We made them leaders calling to the Fire. And on Resurrection Day, they will not be saved.

42. And We pursued them in this world with a curse. And on Resurrection Day, they will be among the despised.

43. We gave Moses the Scripture after We had annihilated the previous generations; as an illumination for mankind, and guidance, and mercy, so that they may remember.

44. You were not on the Western Side when We decreed the command to Moses, nor were you among the witnesses.

45. But We established many generations, and time took its toll on them. Nor were you among the people of Median, reciting Our revelations to them. But We kept sending messengers.

46. Nor were you by the side of the Mount when We proclaimed. Rather, it was a mercy from your Lord, that you may warn people who received no warner before you, so that they may take heed.

47. Otherwise, if a calamity befell them as a result of what their hands have perpetrated, they would say, "Our Lord, if only You had sent us a messenger, we would have followed Your revelations, and been among the believers."

48. But when the truth came to them from Us, they said, "If only he was given the like of what was given to Moses." Did they not disbelieve in what was given to Moses in the past? They said, "Two works of magic backing one another." And they said, "We are disbelieving in both."

49. Say, "Then bring a scripture from Allah, more conductive to guidance than both, and I will follow it, if you are truthful."

50. But if they fail to respond to you, know that they follow their fancies. And who is more lost than him who follows his fancy without guidance from Allah? Allah does not guide the unjust people.

51. We have delivered the Word to them, that they may remember.

52. Those to whom We gave the Scripture before it believe in it.

53. When it is recited to them, they say, "We have believed in it; it is the truth from our Lord; we were Muslims prior to it."

54. These will be given their reward twice, because they persevered; and they counter evil with good; and from Our provisions to them, they give.

55. And when they hear vain talk, they avoid it, and say, "We have our deeds, and you have your deeds; peace be upon you; we do not desire the ignorant."

56. You cannot guide whom you love, but Allah guides whom He wills, and He knows best those who are guided.

57. And they say, "If we follow the guidance with you, we will be snatched from our land." Did We not establish for them a Safe Sanctuary, to which are brought all kinds of fruits, as provision from Ourselves? But most of them do not know.

58. And how many a city did We destroy for turning unappreciative of its livelihood? Here are their homes, uninhabited after them, except for a few. And We became the Inheritors.

59. Your Lord never destroys cities without first sending a messenger in their midst, reciting to them Our revelations. And We never destroy the cities, unless their people are wrongdoers.

28. HISTORY (al-Qasas)

60. Whatever thing you are given is but the material of this world, and its glitter. But what is with Allah is better, and longer lasting. Do you not comprehend?

61. Can someone to whom We have made a fine promise—which he will attain—be equal to someone to whom We have given enjoyments in this world, but who will be, on Resurrection Day, among the arraigned?

62. On the Day when He will call to them, and say, "Where are My associates whom you used to claim?"

63. Those against whom the sentence is justified will say, "Our Lord, these are they whom we misled. We misled them, as we were misled. We beg Your forgiveness; it was not us they used to worship."

64. And it will be said, "Call on your partners." And they will call on them, but they will not respond to them. And they will see the suffering. If only they were guided.

65. On the Day when He will call to them, and say, "What did you answer the Messengers?"

66. They will be blinded by the facts on that Day, and they will not question each other.

67. But he who repents, and believes, and does righteous deeds, may well be among the winners.

68. Your Lord creates whatever He wills, and He chooses. The choice is not theirs. Glory be to Allah, and exalted be He above the associations they make.

69. And your Lord knows what their hearts conceal, and what they reveal.

70. And He is Allah. There is no god but He. To Him belongs all praise in this life, and in the next. And His is the decision, and to Him you will be returned.

71. Say, "Have you considered? Had Allah made the night perpetual over you until the Day of Resurrection, which god other than Allah will bring you illumination? Do you not hear?"

72. Say, "Have you considered? Had Allah made the day perpetual over you until the Day of Resurrection, which god other than Allah will bring you night to rest in? Do you not see?"

73. It is out of His mercy that He made for you the night and the day, that you may rest in it, and seek some of His bounty; and that you may give thanks.

74. On the Day when He will call to them, and say, "Where are My associates whom you used to claim?"

75. And We will draw out from every community a witness, and say, "Produce your evidence." Then they will realize that the truth is Allah's, and those they used to invent have forsaken them.

76. Quaroon belonged to the clan of Moses, but he oppressed them. We had given him treasures, the keys of which would weigh down a group of strong men. His people said to him, "Do not exult; Allah does not love the exultant.

77. But seek, with what Allah has given you, the Home of the Hereafter, and do not neglect your share of this world. And be charitable, as Allah has been charitable to you. And do not seek corruption in the land. Allah does not like the seekers of corruption."

78. He said, "I was given all this on account of knowledge I possess." Did he not know that Allah destroyed many generations before him, who were stronger than he, and possessed greater riches? But the guilty will not be asked about their sins.

79. And he went out before his people in his splendor. Those who desired the worldly life said, "If only we possessed the likes of what Quaroon was given. He is indeed very fortunate."

80. But those who were given knowledge said, "Woe to you! The reward of Allah is better for those who believe and do righteous deeds." Yet none attains it except the steadfast.

81. So We caused the earth to cave in on him and his mansion. He had no company to save him from Allah, and he could not defend himself.

29. THE SPIDER (al-'Ankabut)

82. Those who had wished they were in his position the day before were saying, "Indeed, it is Allah who spreads the bounty to whomever He wills of His servants, and restricts it. Had Allah not been gracious to us, He would have caved in on us. No wonder the ungrateful never prosper."

83. That Home of the Hereafter—We assign it for those who seek no superiority on earth, nor corruption. And the outcome is for the cautious.

84. Whoever brings a virtue will receive better than it. But whoever brings evil—the evildoers will be rewarded only according to what they used to do.

85. He Who ordained the Quran for you will return you Home. Say, "My Lord knows best who comes with guidance, and who is in manifest error."

86. You did not expect the Scripture to be transmitted to you, except as mercy from your Lord. Therefore, do not be a supporter of the disbelievers.

87. And do not let them divert you from Allah's revelations after they have been revealed to you. And pray to your Lord, and never be of the polytheists.

88. And do not invoke with Allah any other god. There is no god but He. All things perish, except His presence. His is the judgment, and to Him you will be returned.

29. THE SPIDER
(al-'Ankabut)

*In the name of Allah,
the Gracious, the Merciful*

1. Alif, Lam, Meem.

2. Have the people supposed that they will be left alone to say, "We believe," without being put to the test?

3. We have tested those before them. Allah will surely know the truthful, and He will surely know the liars.

4. Or do those who commit sins think they can fool Us? Terrible is their opinion!

5. Whoever looks forward to the meeting with Allah—the appointed time of Allah is coming. He is the All-Hearing, the All-Knowing.

6. Whoever strives, strives only for himself. Allah is Independent of the beings.

7. Those who believe and do righteous deeds—We will remit their sins, and We will reward them according to the best of what they used to do.

8. We have advised the human being to be good to his parents. But if they urge you to associate with Me something you have no knowledge of, do not obey them. To Me is your return; and I will inform you of what you used to do.

9. Those who believe and do good works—We will admit them into the company of the righteous.

10. Among the people is he who says, "We have believed in Allah." Yet when he is harmed on Allah's account, he equates the people's persecution with Allah's retribution. And if help comes from your Lord, he says, "We were actually with you." Is not Allah aware of what is inside the hearts of the people?

11. Allah certainly knows those who believe, and He certainly knows the hypocrites.

12. Those who disbelieve say to those who believe, "Follow our way, and we will carry your sins." In no way can they carry any of their sins. They are liars.

13. They will carry their own loads, and other loads with their own. And they will be questioned on the Day of Resurrection concerning what they used to fabricate.

14. We sent Noah to his people, and He stayed among them for a thousand years minus fifty years. Then the Deluge swept them; for they were wrongdoers.

15. But We saved him, together with the company of the Ark, and We made it a sign for all peoples.

29. THE SPIDER (al-'Ankabut)

16. And Abraham, when he said to his people, "Worship Allah, and fear Him. That is better for you, if you only knew.

17. You worship idols besides Allah, and you fabricate falsehoods. Those you worship, instead of Allah, cannot provide you with livelihood. So seek your livelihood from Allah, and worship Him, and thank Him. To Him you will be returned."

18. If you disbelieve, communities before you have also disbelieved. The Messenger is only responsible for clear transmission.

19. Have they not seen how Allah originates the creation, and then reproduces it? This is easy for Allah.

20. Say, "Roam the earth, and observe how He originated the creation." Then Allah will bring about the next existence. Allah has power over all things."

21. He punishes whom He wills, and He grants mercy to whom He wills, and to Him you will be restored.

22. You cannot escape, on earth or in the heaven; and you have no protector and no savior besides Allah.

23. Those who disbelieved in Allah's signs and His encounter—these have despaired of My mercy. For them is a painful torment.

24. But the only response from his people was their saying, "Kill him, or burn him." But Allah saved him from the fire. Surely in that are signs for people who believe.

25. And he said, "You have chosen idols instead of Allah, out of affection for one another in the worldly life. But then, on the Day of Resurrection, you will disown one another, and curse one another. Your destiny is Hell, and you will have no saviors."

26. Then Lot believed in him, and said, "I am emigrating to my Lord. He is the Noble, the Wise."

27. And We granted him Isaac and Jacob, and conferred on his descendants the Prophethood and the Book, and gave him his reward in this life; and in the Hereafter he will be among the upright.

28. And Lot, when he said to his people, "You are committing an obscenity not perpetrated before you by anyone in the whole world.

29. You approach men, and cut off the way, and commit lewdness in your gatherings." But the only response from his people was to say, "Bring upon us Allah's punishment, if you are truthful."

30. He said, "My Lord, help me against the people of corruption."

31. And when Our envoys brought Abraham the good news, they said, "We are going to destroy the people of this town; its people are wrongdoers."

32. He said, "Yet Lot is in it." They said, "We are well aware of who is in it. We will save him, and his family, except for his wife, who will remain behind."

33. Then, when Our envoys came to Lot, they were mistreated, and he was troubled and distressed on their account. They said, "Do not fear, nor grieve. We will save you and your family, except for your wife, who will remain behind."

34. "We will bring down upon the people of this town a scourge from heaven, because of their wickedness."

35. And We left behind a clear trace of it, for people who understand.

36. And to Median, their brother Shuaib. He said, "O my people, worship Allah and anticipate the Last Day, and do not spread corruption in the land."

37. But they rejected him, so the tremor overtook them, and they were left motionless in their homes.

38. And Aad and Thamood. It has become clear to you from their dwellings. Satan embellished for them their deeds, barring them from the path, even though they could see.

29. THE SPIDER (al-'Ankabut)

39. And Quaroon, and Pharaoh, and Hamaan—Moses went to them with clear arguments, but they acted arrogantly in the land. And they could not get ahead.

40. Each We seized by his sin. Against some We sent a sandstorm. Some were struck by the Blast. Some We caused the ground to cave in beneath them. And some We drowned. It was not Allah who wronged them, but it was they who wronged their own selves.

41. The likeness of those who take to themselves protectors other than Allah is that of the spider. It builds a house. But the most fragile of houses is the spider's house. If they only knew.

42. Allah knows what they invoke besides Him. He is the Almighty, the Wise.

43. These examples—We put them forward to the people; but none grasps them except the learned.

44. Allah created the heavens and the earth with truth. Surely in that is a sign for the believers.

45. Recite what is revealed to you of the Scripture, and perform the prayer. The prayer prevents indecencies and evils. And the remembrance of Allah is greater. And Allah knows what you do.

46. And do not argue with the People of the Scripture except in the best manner possible, except those who do wrong among them. And say, "We believe in what was revealed to us, and in what was revealed to you; and our God and your God is One; and to Him we are submissive."

47. Likewise, We revealed to you the Scripture. Those to whom We gave the Scripture believe in it, and some of these believe in it. None renounce Our communications except the disbelievers.

48. You did not read any scripture before this, nor did you write it down with your right hand; otherwise the falsifiers would have doubted.

49. In fact, it is clear signs in the hearts of those given knowledge. No one renounce Our signs except the unjust.

50. And they said, "If only a miracle from his Lord was sent down to him." Say, "Miracles are only with Allah, and I am only a clear warner."

51. Does it not suffice them that We revealed to you the Scripture, which is recited to them? In that is mercy and a reminder for people who believe.

52. Say, "Allah suffices as witness between you and me. He knows everything in the heavens and the Earth. Those who believe in vanity and reject Allah—it is they who are the losers."

53. And they urge you to hasten the punishment. Were it not for a specified time, the punishment would have come to them. But it will come upon them suddenly, while they are unaware.

54. They urge you to hasten the punishment. But Hell will engulf the disbelievers.

55. On the Day when the punishment will envelop them, from above them, and from beneath their feet, He will say, "Taste what you used to do!"

56. O My servants who have believed: My earth is vast, so worship Me alone.

57. Every soul will taste death. Then to Us you will be returned.

58. Those who believe and work righteousness—We will settle them in Paradise, in mansions under which rivers flow, dwelling therein forever. Excellent is the compensation for the workers.

59. Those who endure patiently, and in their Lord they trust.

60. How many a creature there is that does not carry its provision? Allah provides for them, and for you. He is the Hearer, the Knowledgeable.

61. And if you asked them, "Who created the heavens and the earth and regulated the sun and the moon?" They would say, "Allah." Why then do they deviate?

62. Allah expands the provision for whomever He wills of His servants, and restricts it. Allah is Cognizant of all things.

63. And if you asked them, "Who sends water down from the sky, with which He revives the earth after it had died?" They would say, "Allah." Say, "Praise be to Allah." But most of them do not understand.

64. The life of this world is nothing but diversion and play, and the Home of the Hereafter is the Life, if they only knew.

65. When they embark on a vessel, they pray to Allah, devoting their faith to Him; but once He has delivered them safely to land, they attribute partners to Him.

66. To be ungrateful for what We have given them, and to enjoy themselves. They will surely come to know.

67. Do they not see that We established a Secure Sanctuary, while all around them the people are being carried away? Do they believe in falsehood, and reject the blessings of Allah?

68. And who does greater wrong than he who fabricates lies and attributes them to Allah, or calls the truth a lie when it has come to him? Is there not in Hell a dwelling for the blasphemers?

69. As for those who strive for Us—We will guide them in Our ways. Allah is with the doers of good.

30. THE ROMANS
(ar-Rum)

*In the name of Allah,
the Gracious, the Merciful*

1. Alif, Lam, Meem.

2. The Romans have been defeated.

3. In a nearby territory. But following their defeat, they will be victorious.

4. In a few years. The matter is up to Allah, in the past, and in the future. On that day, the believers will rejoice.

5. In Allah's support. He supports whomever He wills. He is the Almighty, the Merciful.

6. The promise of Allah—Allah never breaks His promise, but most people do not know.

7. They know an outer aspect of the worldly life, but they are heedless of the Hereafter.

8. Do they not reflect within themselves? Allah did not create the heavens and the earth, and what is between them, except with reason, and for a specific duration. But most people, regarding meeting their Lord, are disbelievers.

9. Have they not travelled the earth and seen how those before them ended up? They were more powerful than them, and they cultivated the land and developed it more than they developed it, and their messengers came to them with clear signs. Allah would never wrong them, but they used to wrong themselves.

10. Then, evil was the end of those who committed evil. That is because they rejected Allah's revelations, and used to ridicule them.

11. Allah originates creation, and then repeats it. Then to Him you will be returned.

12. On the Day when the Hour takes place, the guilty will despair.

13. They will have no intercessors from among their idols, and they will disown their partners.

14. On the Day when the Hour takes place—on that Day they will separate.

15. As for those who believed and did good deeds—they will be delighted in meadows.

16. But as for those who disbelieved, and rejected Our signs and the encounter of the Hereafter—those will be hauled into the torment.

17. So glorify Allah when you retire at night, and when you rise in the morning.

30. THE ROMANS (ar-Rum)

18. His is the praise in the heavens and on earth, and in the evening, and when you reach midday.

19. He brings the living out of the dead, and He brings the dead out of the living, and He revives the land after it had died. Likewise you will be resurrected.

20. And of His signs is that He created you from dust; and behold, you become humans spreading out.

21. And of His signs is that He created for you mates from among yourselves, so that you may find tranquility in them; and He planted love and compassion between you. In this are signs for people who reflect.

22. And of His signs is the creation of the heavens and the earth, and the diversity of your languages and colors. In this are signs for those who know.

23. And of His signs are your sleep by night and day, and your pursuit of His bounty. In this are signs for people who listen.

24. And of His signs is that He shows you the lightning, causing fear and hope. And He brings down water from the sky, and with it He revives the earth after it was dead. In this are signs for people who understand.

25. And of His signs is that the heaven and the earth stand at His disposal. And then, when He calls you out of the earth, you will emerge at once.

26. To Him belongs everyone in the heavens and the earth. All are submissive to Him.

27. It is He who initiates creation, and then repeats it, something easy for Him. His is the highest attribute, in the heavens and the earth. He is the Almighty, the Wise.

28. He illustrates an example for you, from your own selves: do you make your servants full partners in the wealth We have given you? Do you revere them as you revere one another? We thus explain the revelations for a people who understand.

29. Yet the wrongdoers follow their desires without knowledge. But who can guide whom Allah leaves astray? They will have no helpers.

30. So devote yourself to the religion of monotheism—the natural instinct Allah has instilled in mankind. There is no altering Allah's creation. This is the true religion, but most people do not know.

31. Turning towards Him—and be conscious of Him, and perform the prayer, and do not be of the idolaters.

32. Of those who divided their religion, and became sects; each faction pleased with what they have.

33. When affliction touches the people, they call on their Lord, turning to Him in repentance. But then, when He gives them a taste of His mercy, some of them attribute partners to their Lord.

34. To show ingratitude for what We have given them. Indulge yourselves—you will surely know.

35. Have We sent down to them any authority, which speaks in support of their idols?

36. When We give people a taste of mercy, they rejoice in it. But when adversity befalls them, because of what their hands have perpetrated, they begin to despair.

37. Do they not see that Allah expands the provision for whomever He wills, or restricts it? Surely in this are signs for people who believe.

38. So give the relative his rights, and the destitute, and the wayfarer. That is best for those who seek Allah's presence. Those are the prosperous.

39. The usury you practice, seeking thereby to multiply people's wealth, will not multiply with Allah. But what you give in charity, desiring Allah's approval—these are the multipliers.

40. Allah is He who created you, then provides for you, then makes you die, then brings you back to life. Can any of your idols do any of that? Glorified is He, and Exalted above what they associate.

41. Corruption has appeared on land and sea, because of what people's hands have earned, in order to make them taste some of what they have done, so that they might return.

42. Say, "Roam the earth, and observe the fate of those who came before. Most of them were idolaters."

43. So devote yourself to the upright religion, before there comes from Allah a Day that cannot be averted. On that Day, they will be shocked.

44. Whoever disbelieves, upon him falls his disbelief. And whoever acts righteously—they are preparing for themselves.

45. So that He may reward those who have believed and done the righteous deeds out of His bounty. Indeed, He does not love the ungrateful.

46. And of His signs is that He sends the winds bearing good news, to give you a taste of His mercy, and so that the ships may sail by His command, and so that you may seek of His bounty, and so that you may give thanks.

47. Before you, We sent messengers to their people. They came to them with clear proofs. Then We took revenge on those who sinned. It is incumbent on Us to help the believers.

48. Allah is He who sends the winds. They stir up clouds. Then He spreads them in the sky as He wills. And He breaks them apart. Then you see rain drops issuing from their midst. Then, when He makes it fall upon whom He wills of His servants, behold, they rejoice.

49. Although they were before this—before it was sent down upon them—in despair.

50. So observe the effects of Allah's mercy—how He revives the earth after it was dead. Indeed, He is the Reviver of the dead. He is Capable of everything.

51. But if We send a wind, and they see it turning things yellow, they would continue thereafter to disbelieve.

52. You cannot make the dead hear, nor can you make the deaf hear the call when they turn away.

53. Nor can you guide the blind out of their error. You can make hear only those who believe in Our signs, and so have submitted.

54. Allah is He Who created you weak, then after weakness gave you strength, then after strength gave you weakness and gray hair. He creates whatever He wills. He is the Omniscient, the Omnipotent.

55. On the Day when the Hour takes place, the sinners will swear they had stayed but an hour. Thus they were deluded.

56. But those endowed with knowledge and faith will say, "You remained in Allah's Book until the Day of Resurrection. This is the Day of Resurrection, but you did not know."

57. On that Day, the sinners' excuses will not benefit them, nor will they be excused.

58. We have cited in this Quran for the people every sort of parable. But even if you bring them a miracle, those who disbelieve will say, "You are nothing but fakers."

59. Allah thus seals the hearts of those who do not know.

60. So be patient. The promise of Allah is true. And do not let those who lack certainty belittle you.

31. LUQMAN
(Luqman)

*In the name of Allah,
the Gracious, the Merciful*

1. Alif, Lam, Meem.

2. These are the Verses of the Wise Book.

3. A guide and a mercy for the righteous.

4. Those who observe the prayer, and pay the obligatory charity, and are certain of the Hereafter.

5. These are upon guidance from their Lord. These are the successful.

6. Among the people is he who trades in distracting tales; intending, without knowledge, to lead away from Allah's way, and to make a

31. LUQMAN (Luqman)

mockery of it. These will have a humiliating punishment.

7. And when Our Verses are recited to him, he turns away in pride, as though he did not hear them, as though there is deafness in his ears. So inform him of a painful punishment.

8. As for those who believe and do good deeds—for them are the Gardens of Bliss.

9. Dwelling therein forever. The promise of Allah is true. He is the Mighty, the Wise.

10. He created the heavens without pillars that you can see, and placed stabilizers on earth lest it shifts with you, and scattered throughout it all kinds of creatures. And from the sky We sent down water, and caused to grow therein of every noble pair.

11. Such is Allah's creation. Now show me what those besides Him have created. In fact, the wicked are in obvious error.

12. We endowed Luqman with wisdom: "Give thanks to Allah." Whoever is appreciative—is appreciative for the benefit of his own soul. And whoever is unappreciative—Allah is Sufficient and Praiseworthy.

13. When Luqman said to his son, as he advised him, "O my son, do not associate anything with Allah, for idolatry is a terrible wrong."

14. We have entrusted the human being with the care of his parents. His mother carried him through hardship upon hardship, weaning him in two years. So give thanks to Me, and to your parents. To Me is the destination.

15. But if they strive to have you associate with Me something of which you have no knowledge, do not obey them. But keep them company in this life, in kindness, and follow the path of him who turns to Me. Then to Me is your return; and I will inform you of what you used to do.

16. "O my son, even if it were the weight of a mustard-seed, in a rock, or in the heavens, or on earth, Allah will bring it to light. Allah is Kind and Expert.

17. O my son, observe the prayer, advocate righteousness, forbid evil, and be patient over what has befallen you. These are of the most honorable traits.

18. And do not treat people with arrogance, nor walk proudly on earth. Allah does not love the arrogant showoffs.

19. And moderate your stride, and lower your voice. The most repulsive of voices is the donkey's voice."

20. Do you not see how Allah placed at your service everything in the heavens and the earth? How He showered you with His blessings, both outward and inward? Yet among the people is he who argues about Allah without knowledge, without guidance, and without an enlightening Scripture.

21. And when it is said to them, "Follow what Allah has revealed," they say, "Rather, we follow what we found our parents devoted to." Even if Satan is calling them to the suffering of the Blaze?

22. Whoever submits himself wholly to Allah, and is a doer of good, has grasped the most trustworthy handle. With Allah rests the outcome of all events.

23. Whoever disbelieves—let not his disbelief sadden you. To Us is their return. Then We will inform them of what they did. Allah knows what lies within the hearts.

24. We give them a little comfort; then We compel them to a harsh torment.

25. And if you ask them, "Who created the heavens and the earth?" They will say, "Allah." Say, "Praise be to Allah." But most of them do not know.

26. To Allah belongs everything in the heavens and the earth. Allah is the Rich, the Praised.

27. If all the trees on earth were pens, filled by the ocean, with seven more oceans besides, the Words of Allah would not run out. Allah is Majestic and Wise.

28. Your creation and your resurrection are only as a single soul. Allah is Hearing and Seeing.

32. PROSTRATION (as-Sajdah)

29. Have you not seen how Allah merges the night into the day, and merges the day into the night? That He subjected the sun and the moon, each running for a stated term? And that Allah is Cognizant of everything you do?

30. That is because Allah is the Reality, and what they worship besides Him is falsehood, and because Allah is the Exalted, the Supreme.

31. Have you not seen how the ships sail through the sea, by the grace of Allah, to show you of His wonders? In that are signs for every persevering, thankful person.

32. When waves, like canopies, cover them, they call upon Allah, devoting their religion to Him. But when He has delivered them to dry land, some of them waver. No one renounces Our revelations except the treacherous blasphemer.

33. O people! Be conscious of your Lord, and dread a Day when no parent can avail his child, nor can a child avail his parent, in anything. The promise of Allah is true. Therefore, do not let this life deceive you, nor let illusions deceive you regarding Allah.

34. With Allah rests the knowledge of the Hour. He sends down the rain, and He knows what the wombs contain. No soul knows what it will reap tomorrow, and no soul knows in what land it will die. Allah is All-Knowing, Well-Informed.

32. PROSTRATION
(as-Sajdah)

*In the name of Allah,
the Gracious, the Merciful*

1. Alif, Lam, Meem.

2. The revelation of the Book, without a doubt, is from the Lord of the Universe.

3. Yet they say, "He made it up." In fact, it is the Truth from your Lord, to warn a people who received no warner before you, that they may be guided.

4. Allah is He who created the heavens and the earth and everything between them in six days, and then established Himself on the Throne. Apart from Him, you have no master and no intercessor. Will you not reflect?

5. He regulates all affairs, from the heavens, to the earth. Then it ascends to Him on a Day the length of which is a thousand years by your count.

6. That is the Knower of the Invisible and the Visible, the Powerful, the Merciful.

7. He who perfected everything He created, and originated the creation of man from clay.

8. Then made his reproduction from an extract of an insignificant fluid.

9. Then He proportioned him, and breathed into him of His Spirit. Then He gave you the hearing, and the eyesight, and the brains—but rarely do you give thanks.

10. And they say, "When we are lost into the earth, shall we be in a new creation?" In fact, they deny the meeting with their Lord.

11. Say, "The angel of death put in charge of you will reclaim you. Then to your Lord you will be returned."

12. If only you could see the guilty, bowing their heads before their Lord: "Our Lord, we have seen and we have heard, so send us back, and we will act righteously; we are now convinced."

13. Had We willed, We could have given every soul its guidance, but the declaration from Me will come true: "I will fill Hell with jinn and humans, altogether."

14. So taste, because you forgot the meeting of this Day of yours; We have forgotten you; so taste the eternal torment for what you used to do.

15. They believe in Our communications, those who, when reminded of them, fall down prostrate, and glorify their Lord with praise, and are not proud.

16. Their sides shun their beds, as they pray to their Lord, out of reverence and hope; and from Our provisions to them, they give.

17. No soul knows what eye's delight awaits them—a reward for what they used to do.

18. Is someone who is faithful like someone who is a sinner? They are not equal.

19. As for those who believe and do righteous deeds, for them are the Gardens of Shelter—hospitality for what they used to do.

20. But as for those who transgressed, their shelter is the Fire. Every time they try to get out of it, they will be brought back into it, and it will be said to them, "Taste the suffering of the Fire which you used to deny."

21. We will make them taste the lesser torment, prior to the greater torment, so that they may return.

22. Who is more wrong than he, who, when reminded of his Lord's revelations, turns away from them? We will certainly wreak vengeance upon the criminals.

23. We gave Moses the Book; so do not be in doubt regarding His encounter; and We made it a guidance for the Children of Israel.

24. And We appointed leaders from among them, guiding by Our command, as long as they persevered and were certain of Our communications.

25. Your Lord will judge between them on the Day of Resurrection regarding everything they had disputed.

26. Is it not a lesson for them, how many generations We have destroyed before them, in whose habitations they walk? Surely in that are signs. Do they not hear?

27. Do they not see how We conduct the water to a dry land, and with it We produce vegetation, from which their livestock eat, and themselves? Do they not see?

28. And they say, "When is this victory, if you are truthful?"

29. Say, "On the day of victory, the faith of those who disbelieved will be of no avail to them, and they will not be granted respite."

30. So turn away from them, and wait. They too are waiting.

33. THE CONFEDERATES
(al-Ahzab)

In the name of Allah,
the Gracious, the Merciful

1. O Prophet! Fear Allah, and do not obey the unbelievers and the hypocrites. Allah is Knowledgeable and Wise.

2. And follow what is revealed to you from your Lord. Allah is fully aware of what you do.

3. And put your trust in Allah. Allah is enough as a trustee.

4. Allah did not place two hearts inside any man's body. Nor did He make your wives whom you equate with your mothers, your actual mothers. Nor did He make your adopted sons, your actual sons. These are your words coming out of your mouths. Allah speaks the truth, and guides to the path.

5. Call them after their fathers; that is more equitable with Allah. But if you do not know their fathers, then your brethren in faith and your friends. There is no blame on you if you err therein, barring what your hearts premeditates. Allah is Forgiving and Merciful.

6. The Prophet is more caring of the believers than they are of themselves, and his wives are mothers to them. And blood-relatives are closer to one another in Allah's Book than the believers or the emigrants, though you should do good to your friends. That is inscribed in the Book.

7. Recall that We received a pledge from the prophets, and from you, and from Noah, and Abraham, and Moses, and Jesus son of Mary. We received from them a solemn pledge.

8. That He may ask the sincere about their sincerity. He has prepared for the disbelievers a painful punishment.

9. O you who believe! Remember Allah's blessings upon you, when forces came against you, and We sent against them a wind, and

33. THE CONFEDERATES (al-Ahzab)

forces you did not see. Allah is Observant of what you do.

10. When they came upon you, from above you, and from beneath you; and the eyes became dazed, and the hearts reached the throats, and you harbored doubts about Allah.

11. There and then the believers were tested, and were shaken most severely.

12. When the hypocrites and those in whose hearts is sickness said, "Allah and His Messenger promised us nothing but illusion."

13. And when a group of them said, "O people of Yathrib, you cannot make a stand, so retreat." And a faction of them asked the Prophet to excuse them, saying, "Our homes are exposed," although they were not exposed. They only wanted to flee.

14. Had it been invaded from its sides, and they were asked to dissent, they would have done so with little hesitation.

15. Although they had made a pledged to Allah, in the past, that they will not turn their backs. A pledge to Allah is a responsibility.

16. Say, "Flight will not benefit you, if you flee from death or killing, even then you will be given only brief enjoyment."

17. Say, "Who is it who will shield you from Allah, if He intends adversity for you, or intends mercy for you?" Besides Allah, they will find for themselves neither friend nor helper.

18. Allah already knows the hinderers among you, and those who say to their brethren, "Come and join us." Rarely do they mobilize for battle.

19. Being stingy towards you. And when fear approaches, you see them staring at you—their eyes rolling—like someone fainting at death. Then, when panic is over, they whip you with sharp tongues. They resent you any good. These have never believed, so Allah has nullified their works; a matter easy for Allah.

20. They assumed that the confederates had not withdrawn. But were the confederates to advance, they would wish they were in the desert with the Bedouins, inquiring about your news. And if they were among you, they would have done little fighting.

21. You have an excellent example in the Messenger of Allah; for anyone who seeks Allah and the Last Day, and remembers Allah frequently.

22. And when the believers saw the confederates, they said, "This is what Allah and His messenger have promised us; and Allah and His messenger have told the truth." And it only increased them in faith and submission.

23. Of the believers are men who are true to what they pledged to Allah. Some of them have fulfilled their vows; and some are still waiting, and never wavering.

24. That Allah may reward the truthful for their truthfulness; and punish the hypocrites, if He wills, or pardon them. Allah is Forgiving and Merciful.

25. Allah repelled the disbelievers in their rage; they gained no advantage. Allah thus spared the believers combat. Allah is Strong and Mighty.

26. And He brought down from their strongholds those of the People of the Book who backed them, and He threw terror into their hearts. Some of them you killed, and others you took captive.

27. And He made you inherit their land, and their homes, and their possessions, and a region you have never stepped on. Allah has power over all things.

28. O Prophet! Say to your wives, "If you desire the life of this world and its finery, then let me compensate you, and release you kindly.

29. But if you desire Allah, His Messenger, and the Home of the Hereafter, then Allah has prepared for the righteous among you a magnificent compensation."

30. O wives of the Prophet! Whoever of you commits a proven indecency, the punishment for her will be doubled. And that would be easy for Allah.

33. THE CONFEDERATES (al-Ahzab)

31. But whoever of you remains obedient to Allah and His Messenger, and acts righteously, We will give her a double reward; and We have prepared for her a generous provision.

32. O wives of the Prophet! You are not like any other women, if you observe piety. So do not speak too softly, lest the sick at heart lusts after you, but speak in an appropriate manner.

33. And settle in your homes; and do not display yourselves, as in the former days of ignorance. And perform the prayer, and give regular charity, and obey Allah and His Messenger. Allah desires to remove all impurity from you, O People of the Household, and to purify you thoroughly.

34. And remember what is recited in your homes of Allah's revelations and wisdom. Allah is Kind and Informed.

35. Muslim men and Muslim women, believing men and believing women, obedient men and obedient women, truthful men and truthful women, patient men and patient women, humble men and humble women, charitable men and charitable women, fasting men and fasting women, men who guard their chastity and women who guard, men who remember Allah frequently and women who remember—Allah has prepared for them a pardon, and an immense reward.

36. It is not for any believer, man or woman, when Allah and His Messenger have decided a matter, to have liberty of choice in their decision. Whoever disobeys Allah and His Messenger has gone far astray.

37. When you said to him whom Allah had blessed, and you had favored, "Keep your wife to yourself, and fear Allah." But you hid within yourself what Allah was to reveal. And you feared the people, but it was Allah you were supposed to fear. Then, when Zaid ended his relationship with her, We gave her to you in marriage, that there may be no restriction for believers regarding the wives of their adopted sons, when their relationship has ended. The command of Allah was fulfilled.

38. There is no blame on the Prophet regarding what Allah has ordained for him. Such is the pattern of Allah among those who passed before. The command of Allah is an absolute decree.

39. Those who deliver the messages of Allah, and fear Him, and never fear anyone except Allah. Allah is sufficient as a reckoner.

40. Muhammad is not the father of any of your men; but he is the Messenger of Allah, and the seal of the prophets. Allah is Cognizant of everything.

41. O you who believe, remember Allah with frequent remembrance.

42. And glorify Him morning and evening.

43. It is He who reaches out to you, and His angels, to bring you out of darkness into the light. And He is Ever-Merciful towards the believers.

44. Their greeting on the Day they meet Him is, "Peace," and He has prepared for them a generous reward.

45. O prophet! We have sent you as a witness, and a bearer of good news, and a warner.

46. And a caller towards Allah by His leave, and an illuminating beacon.

47. And give the believers the good news that for them is a great reward.

48. And do not obey the blasphemers and the hypocrites, and ignore their insults, and rely on Allah. Allah is a sufficient protector.

49. O you who believe! When you marry believing women, but then divorce them before you have touched them, there is no waiting period for you to observe in respect to them; but compensate them, and release them in a graceful manner.

50. O Prophet! We have permitted to you your wives to whom you have given their dowries, and those you already have, as granted to you by Allah, and the daughters of your paternal uncle, and the daughters of your paternal

33. THE CONFEDERATES (al-Ahzab)

aunts, and the daughters of your maternal uncle, and the daughters of your maternal aunts who emigrated with you, and a believing woman who has offered herself to the Prophet, if the Prophet desires to marry her, exclusively for you, and not for the believers. We know what We have ordained for them regarding their wives and those their right-hands possess. This is to spare you any difficulty. Allah is Forgiving and Merciful.

51. You may defer any of them you wish, and receive any of them you wish. Should you desire any of those you had deferred, there is no blame on you. This is more proper, so that they will be comforted, and not be grieved, and be content with what you have given each one of them. Allah knows what is within your hearts. Allah is Omniscient and Clement.

52. Beyond that, no other women are permissible for you, nor can you exchange them for other wives, even if you admire their beauty, except those you already have. Allah is Watchful over all things.

53. O you who believe! Do not enter the homes of the Prophet, unless you are given permission to come for a meal; and do not wait for its preparation. And when you are invited, go in. And when you have eaten, disperse, without lingering for conversation. This irritates the Prophet, and he shies away from you, but Allah does not shy away from the truth. And when you ask his wives for something, ask them from behind a screen; that is purer for your hearts and their hearts. You must never offend the Messenger of Allah, nor must you ever marry his wives after him, for that would be an enormity with Allah.

54. Whether you declare a thing, or hide it, Allah is Aware of all things.

55. There is no blame on them concerning their fathers, or their sons, or their brothers, or their brothers' sons, or their sisters' sons, or their women, or their female servants. But they should remain conscious of Allah. Allah is Witness over all things.

56. Allah and His angels give blessings to the Prophet. O you who believe, call for blessings on him, and greet him with a prayer of peace.

57. Those who insult Allah and His Messenger, Allah has cursed them in this life and in the Hereafter, and has prepared for them a demeaning punishment.

58. Those who harm believing men and believing women, for acts they did not commit, bear the burden of perjury and a flagrant sin.

59. O Prophet! Tell your wives, and your daughters, and the women of the believers, to lengthen their garments. That is more proper, so they will be recognized and not harassed. Allah is Forgiving and Merciful.

60. If the hypocrites, and those with sickness in their hearts, and the rumormongers in the City, do not desist, We will incite you against them; then they will not be your neighbors there except for a short while.

61. They are cursed; wherever they are found, they should be captured and killed outright.

62. Such has been Allah's precedent with those who passed away before. You will find no change in Allah's system.

63. The people ask you about the Hour. Say, "The knowledge thereof rests with Allah. But what do you know? Perhaps the hour is near."

64. Allah has cursed the disbelievers, and has prepared for them a Blaze.

65. Dwelling therein forever, not finding a protector or a savior.

66. The Day when their faces are flipped into the Fire, they will say, "If only we had obeyed Allah and obeyed the Messenger."

67. And they will say, "Lord, we have obeyed our superiors and our dignitaries, but they led us away from the way.

68. Lord, give them double the punishment, and curse them with a great curse."

69. O you who believe! Do not be like those who abused Moses; but Allah cleared him of what they said. He was distinguished with Allah.

70. O you who believe! Be conscious of Allah, and speak in a straightforward manner.

71. He will rectify your conduct for you, and will forgive you your sins. Whoever obeys Allah and His Messenger has won a great victory.

72. We offered the Trust to the heavens, and the earth, and the mountains; but they refused to bear it, and were apprehensive of it; but the human being accepted it. He was unfair and ignorant.

73. Allah will punish the hypocrites, men and women, and the idolaters, men and women. And Allah will redeem the believers, men and women. Allah is Ever-Forgiving, Most Merciful.

34. SHEBA
(Saba')

*In the name of Allah,
the Gracious, the Merciful*

1. Praise be to Allah, to Whom belongs everything in the heavens and the earth; and praise be to Him in the Hereafter. He is the Wise, the Expert.

2. He knows what penetrates into the earth, and what comes out of it, and what descends from the sky, and what ascends to it. He is the Merciful, the Forgiving.

3. Those who disbelieve say, "The Hour will not come upon us." Say, "Yes indeed, by my Lord, it will come upon you. He is the Knower of the unseen." Not an atom's weight in the heavens and the earth, or anything smaller or larger, escapes His knowledge. All are in a Clear Record.

4. That He may recompense those who believe and do good works. Those will have forgiveness, and a generous provision.

5. As for those who strive against Our revelations, seeking to undermine them—for them is a punishment of a painful plague.

6. Those who received knowledge know that what is revealed to you from your Lord is the truth; and it guides to the path of the Majestic, the Praiseworthy.

7. Those who disbelieved said, "Shall we point out to you a man, who will tell you that, once torn into shreds, you will be in a new creation?

8. Did he invent a lie about Allah, or is there madness in him?" Indeed, those who do not believe in the Hereafter are in torment, and far astray.

9. Do they not reflect upon what lies before them and behind them, of the heaven and the earth? If We will, We can make the earth cave in beneath them, or make pieces of the sky fall down on them. In that is a sign for every devout servant.

10. We bestowed upon David favor from Us: "O mountains, and birds: echo with him." And We softened iron for him.

11. "Make coats of armor, and measure the links well; and work righteousness. I am Observant of everything you do."

12. And for Solomon the wind—its outward journey was one month, and its return journey was one month. And We made a spring of tar flow for him. And there were sprites that worked under him, by the leave of his Lord. But whoever of them swerved from Our command, We make him taste of the punishment of the Inferno.

13. They made for him whatever he wished: sanctuaries, statues, bowls like pools, and heavy cauldrons. "O House of David, work with appreciation," but a few of My servants are appreciative.

14. Then, when We decreed death for him, nothing indicated his death to them except an earthworm eating at his staff. Then, when he fell down, it became clear to the sprites that, had they known the unseen, they would not have remained in the demeaning torment.

15. In Sheba's homeland there used to be a wonder: two gardens, on the right, and on the left. "Eat of your Lord's provision, and give thanks to Him." A good land, and a forgiving Lord.

34. SHEBA (Saba')

16. But they turned away, so We unleashed against them the flood of the dam; and We substituted their two gardens with two gardens of bitter fruits, thorny shrubs, and meager harvest.

17. We thus penalized them for their ingratitude. Would We penalize any but the ungrateful?

18. Between them and the towns We had blessed, We placed prominent towns, and We made the travel between them easy. "Travel between them by night and day, in safety."

19. But they said, "Our Lord, lengthen the distances of our journeys." They wronged themselves; so We made them history, and We scattered them in every direction. In this are lessons for every steadfast and appreciative person.

20. Satan was correct in his assessment of them. They followed him, except for a group of believers.

21. He had no authority over them; except that We willed to distinguish him who believes in the Hereafter, from him who is doubtful about it. Your Lord is Guardian over all things.

22. Say, "Call upon those whom you claim besides Allah. They possess not an atom's weight in the heavens or the earth, and they possess no share of either, and He has no backers from among them."

23. Intercession with Him is of no value, except for someone He has permitted. Until, when fear has subsided from their hearts, they will say, "What did your Lord say?" They will say, "The truth, and He is the High, the Great."

24. Say, "Who provides for you from the heavens and the earth?" Say, "Allah. And Either you, or we, are rightly guided, or in evident error."

25. Say, "You will not be asked about our misdeeds, nor will we be asked about what you do."

26. Say, "Our Lord will bring us together; then He will judge between us equitably. He is the All-Knowing Judge."

27. Say, "Show me those you have attached to Him as associates. No indeed! But He is Allah, the Powerful, the Wise."

28. We sent you only universally to all people, a herald and warner, but most people do not know.

29. And they say, "When is this promise due, if you are truthful?"

30. Say, "You are promised a Day, which you cannot postpone by one hour, nor bring forward."

31. Those who disbelieve say, "We will never believe in this Quran, nor in what came before it." If you could only see the wrongdoers, captive before their Lord, throwing back allegations at one another. Those who were oppressed will say to those who were arrogant, "Were it not for you, we would have been believers."

32. Those who were arrogant will say to those who were oppressed, "Was it us who turned you away from guidance when it came to you? No indeed, you yourselves were sinful."

33. And those who were oppressed will say to those who were arrogant, "It was your scheming by night and day; as you instructed us to reject Allah, and to set up rivals to Him." They will hide their remorse when they see the retribution. We will put yokes around the necks of those who disbelieved. Will they be repaid for anything other than what they used to do?

34. We sent no warner to any town, without its affluent saying, "We reject what you are sent with."

35. And they say, "We have more wealth and more children, and we will not be punished."

36. Say, "My Lord spreads out His bounty to whomever He wills, or restricts it; but most people do not know."

37. It is neither your wealth nor your children that bring you closer to Us, but it is he who

believes and does good deeds. These will have a double reward for what they did; and they will reside in the Chambers, in peace and security.

38. But those who work against Our revelations, seeking to undermine them—those will be summoned to the punishment.

39. Say, "My Lord extends the provision to whomever He wills of His servants, or withholds it. Anything you spend, He will replace it. He is the Best of providers."

40. On the Day when He gathers them all together, then say to the angels, "Was it you these used to worship?"

41. They will say, "Be You glorified; You are our Master, not them. In fact, they used to worship the jinn, and most of them had faith in them."

42. "Today, none of you has the power to profit or harm the other." And We will say to those who did wrong, "Taste the agony of the Fire which you used to deny."

43. And when Our enlightening Verses are recited to them, they say, "This is nothing but a man who wants to divert you from what your ancestors used to worship." And they say, "This is nothing but a fabricated lie." And when the Truth comes to them, the blasphemers say of the Truth, "This is nothing but plain magic."

44. But We gave them no book to study, and We did not send them any warner before you.

45. Those before them also denied the Truth, yet they have not attained one-tenth of what We had given them. They rejected My messengers, so how was My disapproval?

46. Say, "I offer you a single advice: devote yourselves to Allah, in pairs, or individually; and reflect. There is no madness in your friend. He is just a warner to you, before the advent of a severe punishment."

47. Say, "Whatever compensation I have asked of you, is yours. My compensation comes only from Allah, and He is Witness over all things."

48. Say, "My Lord projects the truth. He is the Knower of the Unseen."

49. Say, "The Truth has come; while falsehood can neither originate, nor regenerate."

50. Say, "If I err, I err only to my own loss; but if I am guided, it is by what my Lord inspires me. He is Hearing and Near."

51. If you could only see when they are terrified, and there is no escape, and they are seized from a nearby place.

52. And they say, "We have believed in it." But how can they attain it from a distant place?

53. They have rejected it in the past, and made allegations from a far-off place.

54. A barrier will be placed between them and what they desire, as was done formerly with their counterparts. They were in disturbing doubt.

35. ORIGINATOR
(Fatir)

In the name of Allah,
the Gracious, the Merciful

1. Praise be to Allah, Originator of the heavens and the earth, Maker of the angels messengers with wings—double, triple, and quadruple. He adds to creation as He wills. Allah is Able to do all things.

2. Whatever mercy Allah unfolds for the people, none can withhold it. And if He withholds it, none can release it thereafter. He is the Exalted in Power, Full of Wisdom.

3. O people! Remember Allah's blessings upon you. Is there a creator other than Allah who provides for you from the heaven and the earth? There is no god but He. So how are you misled?

4. If they reject you, messengers before you were also rejected. To Allah all matters are returned.

5. O people! The promise of Allah is true; so let not the lowly life seduce you, and let not the Tempter tempt you away from Allah.

35. ORIGINATOR (Fatir)

6. Satan is an enemy to you, so treat him as an enemy. He only invites his gang to be among the inmates of the Inferno.

7. Those who disbelieve will suffer a harsh punishment, but those who believe and do righteous deeds will have forgiveness and a great reward.

8. What of him whose evil deed was made attractive to him, and so he regards it as good? Allah leads astray whomever He wills, and He guides whomever He wills. Therefore, do not waste yourself sorrowing over them. Allah knows exactly what they do.

9. Allah is He who sends the winds, which agitate clouds, which We drive to a dead land, and thereby revive the ground after it had died. Likewise is the Resurrection.

10. Whoever desires honor—all honor belongs to Allah. To Him ascends speech that is pure, and He elevates righteous conduct. As for those who plot evil, a terrible punishment awaits them, and the planning of these will fail.

11. Allah created you from dust, then from a small drop; then He made you pairs. No female conceives, or delivers, except with His knowledge. No living thing advances in years, or its life is shortened, except it be in a Record. That is surely easy for Allah.

12. The two seas are not the same. One is fresh, sweet, good to drink, while the other is salty and bitter. Yet from each you eat tender meat, and extract jewelry which you wear. And you see the ships plowing through them, so that you may seek of His bounty, so that you may give thanks.

13. He merges the night into the day, and He merges the day into the night; and He regulates the sun and the moon, each running for a stated term. Such is Allah, your Lord; His is the sovereignty. As for those you call upon besides Him, they do not possess a speck.

14. If you pray to them, they cannot hear your prayer. And even if they heard, they would not answer you. And on the Day of Resurrection, they will reject your partnership. None informs you like an Expert.

15. O people! It is you who are the poor, in need of Allah; while Allah is the Rich, the Praiseworthy.

16. If He wills, He can do away with you, and produce a new creation.

17. And that would not be difficult for Allah.

18. No burdened soul can carry the burden of another. Even if one weighted down calls for help with its burden, nothing can be lifted from it, even if they were related. You are to warn those who fear their Lord inwardly, and perform the prayer. He who purifies himself purifies himself for his own good. To Allah is the ultimate return.

19. Not equal are the blind and the seeing.

20. Nor are the darkness and the light.

21. Nor are the shade and the torrid heat.

22. Nor are equal the living and the dead. Allah causes whomever He wills to hear, but you cannot make those in the graves hear.

23. You are only a warner.

24. We sent you with the truth; a bearer of good news, and a warner. There is no community but a warner has passed through it.

25. If they disbelieve you, those before them also disbelieved. Their messengers came to them with the clear proofs, with the Psalms, and with the Enlightening Scripture.

26. Then I seized those who disbelieved—so how was My rejection?

27. Have you not seen that Allah sends down water from the sky? With it We produce fruits of various colors. And in the mountains are streaks of white and red—varying in their hue—and pitch-black.

28. Likewise, human beings, animals, and livestock come in various colors. From among His servants, the learned fear Allah. Allah is Almighty, Oft-Forgiving.

29. Those who recite the Book of Allah, and perform the prayer, and spend of what We

have provided for them, secretly and publicly, expect a trade that will not fail.

30. He will pay them their dues in full, and will increase them from His bounty. He is Forgiving and Appreciative.

31. What We inspired in you, of the Book, is the truth, confirming what preceded it. Allah is Well-Informed of His servants, All-Seeing.

32. Then We passed the Book to those of Our servants whom We chose. Some of them wrong their souls, and some follow a middle course, and some are in the foremost in good deeds by Allah's leave; that is the greatest blessing.

33. The Gardens of Eden, which they will enter. They will be adorned therein with gold bracelets and pearls, and their garments therein will be of silk.

34. And they will say, "Praise Allah, who has lifted all sorrow from us. Our Lord is Most Forgiving, Most Appreciative.

35. He Who settled us in the Home of Permanence, by His grace, where boredom will not touch us, and fatigue will not afflict us."

36. As for those who disbelieve, for them is the Fire of Hell, wherein they will never be finished off and die, nor will its punishment be lightened for them. Thus We will repay every ingrate.

37. And they will scream therein, "Our Lord, let us out, and we will act righteously, differently from the way we used to act." Did We not give you a life long enough, in which anyone who wanted to understand would have understood? And the warner did come to you. So taste. The evildoers will have no helper.

38. Allah is the Knower of the future of the heavens and the earth. He knows what the hearts contain.

39. It is He who made you successors on earth. Whoever disbelieves, his disbelief will recoil upon him. The disbelief of the disbelievers adds only to their Lord's disfavor of them. The disbelief of the disbelievers adds only to their perdition.

40. Say, "Have you considered those partners of yours that you worship instead of Allah? Show me what they have created on earth. Or do they have any share in the heavens?" Or have We given them a book whose clear teachings they follow? In fact, the wrongdoers promise one another nothing but delusions.

41. Allah holds the heavens and the earth, lest they fall apart. And were they to fall apart, there is none to hold them together except He. He is Most Clement, Most Forgiving.

42. And they swore by Allah with their solemn oaths, that if a warner came to them, they would be more guided than any other people. Yet when a warner came to them, it only increased them in aversion.

43. Priding themselves on earth, and scheming evil. But evil scheming overwhelms none but its authors. Do they expect anything but the precedent of the ancients? You will not find any change in Allah's practice, and you will not find any substitute to Allah's practice.

44. Have they not journeyed in the land and observed the fate of those who preceded them? They were superior to them in strength. But nothing can defeat Allah in the heavens or on Earth. He is indeed Omniscient and Omnipotent.

45. If Allah were to punish the people for what they have earned, He would not leave a single living creature on its surface. But He defers them until a stated time. Then, when their time has arrived—Allah is Observant of His creatures.

36. YA-SEEN
(Ya-Seen)

*In the name of Allah,
the Gracious, the Merciful*

1. Ya, Seen.

2. By the Wise Quran.

36. YA-SEEN (Ya-Seen)

3. You are one of the messengers.

4. On a straight path.

5. The revelation of the Almighty, the Merciful.

6. To warn a people whose ancestors were not warned, and so they are unaware.

7. The Word was realized against most of them, for they do not believe.

8. We placed shackles around their necks, up to their chins, so they are stiff-necked.

9. And We placed a barrier in front of them, and a barrier behind them, and We have enshrouded them, so they cannot see.

10. It is the same for them, whether you warn them, or do not warn them—they will not believe.

11. You warn only him who follows the Message, and fears the Most Gracious inwardly. So give him good news of forgiveness, and a generous reward.

12. It is We who revive the dead; and We write down what they have forwarded, and their traces. We have tallied all things in a Clear Record.

13. And cite for them the parable of the landlords of the town—when the messengers came to it.

14. We sent them two messengers, but they denied them both, so We reinforced them with a third. They said, "We are messengers to you."

15. They said, "You are nothing but humans like us, and the Gracious did not send down anything; you are only lying."

16. They said, "Our Lord knows that we are messengers to you.

17. And our only duty is clear communication."

18. They said, "We see an evil omen in you; if you do not give up, we will stone you, and a painful punishment from us will befall you."

19. They said, "Your evil omen is upon you. Is it because you were reminded? But you are an extravagant people."

20. Then a man came running from the remotest part of the city. He said, "O my people, follow the messengers.

21. Follow those who ask you of no wage, and are themselves guided.

22. "And why should I not worship Him Who created me, and to Whom you will be returned?

23. Shall I take other gods instead of Him? If the Merciful desires harm for me, their intercession will not avail me at all, nor will they save me.

24. In that case, I would be completely lost.

25. I have believed in your Lord, so listen to me."

26. It was said, "Enter Paradise." He said, "If only my people knew.

27. How my Lord has forgiven me, and made me one of the honored."

28. After him, We sent down no hosts from heaven to his people; nor would We ever send any down.

29. It was just one Cry, and they were stilled.

30. Alas for the servants. No messenger ever came to them, but they ridiculed him.

31. Have they not considered how many generations We destroyed before them; and that unto them they will not return?

32. All of them, every single one of them, will be arraigned before Us.

33. And there is a sign for them in the dead land: We give it life, and produce from it grains from which they eat.

34. And We place in it gardens of palm-trees and vines, and cause springs to gush out of it.

35. That they may eat from its fruits, although their hands did not make it. Will they not be appreciative?

36. YA-SEEN (Ya-Seen)

36. Glory be to Him who created all the pairs; of what the earth produces, and of their own selves, and of what they do not know.

37. Another sign for them is the night: We strip the day out of it—and they are in darkness.

38. And the sun runs towards its destination. Such is the design of the Almighty, the All-Knowing.

39. And the moon: We have disposed it in phases, until it returns like the old twig.

40. The sun is not to overtake the moon, nor is the night to outpace the day. Each floats in an orbit.

41. Another sign for them is that We carried their offspring in the laden Ark.

42. And We created for them the like of it, in which they ride.

43. If We will, We can drown them—with no screaming to be heard from them, nor will they be saved.

44. Except by a mercy from Us, and enjoyment for a while.

45. Yet when it is said to them, "Beware of what lies before you, and what lies behind you, that you may receive mercy."

46. Yet never came to them a sign of their Lord's signs, but they turned away from it.

47. And when it is said to them, "Spend of what Allah has provided for you," those who disbelieve say to those who believe, "Shall we feed someone whom Allah could feed, if He so willed? You must be deeply misguided."

48. And they say, "When will this promise be, if you are truthful?"

49. All they can expect is a single blast, which will seize them while they feud.

50. They will not be able to make a will, nor will they return to their families.

51. The Trumpet will be blown, then behold, they will rush from the tombs to their Lord.

52. They will say, "Woe to us! Who resurrected us from our resting-place?" This is what the Most Gracious had promised, and the messengers have spoken the truth."

53. It will be but a single scream; and behold, they will all be brought before Us.

54. On that Day, no soul will be wronged in the least, and you will be recompensed only for what you used to do.

55. The inhabitants of Paradise, on that Day, will be happily busy.

56. They and their spouses, in shades, reclining on couches.

57. They will have therein fruits. They will have whatever they call for.

58. Peace—a saying from a Most Merciful Lord.

59. But step aside today, you criminals.

60. Did I not covenant with you, O Children of Adam, that you shall not serve the devil? That he is your sworn enemy?

61. And that you shall serve Me? This is a straight path.

62. He has misled a great multitude of you. Did you not understand?

63. This is Hellfire, which you were promised.

64. Roast in it today, because you persistently disbelieved.

65. On this Day, We will seal their mouths, and their hands will speak to Us, and their feet will testify to everything they had done.

66. If We will, We can blind their eyes as they rush towards the path—but how will they see?

67. And if We will, We can cripple them in their place; so they can neither move forward, nor go back.

68. Whomever We grant old age, We reverse his development. Do they not understand?

69. We did not teach him poetry, nor is it proper for him. It is only a reminder, and a Clear Quran.

70. That he may warn whoever is alive, and prove the Word against the faithless.

71. Have they not seen that We created for them, of Our Handiwork, livestock that they own?

72. And We subdued them for them. Some they ride, and some they eat.

73. And they have in them other benefits, and drinks. Will they not give thanks?

74. Yet they have taken to themselves gods other than Allah, that perhaps they may be helped.

75. They cannot help them, although they are arrayed as troops for them.

76. So let their words not sadden you. We know what they conceal, and what they reveal.

77. Does the human being not consider that We created him from a seed? Yet he becomes a fierce adversary.

78. And he produces arguments against Us, and he forgets his own creation. He says, "Who will revive the bones when they have decayed?"

79. Say, "He who initiated them in the first instance will revive them. He has knowledge of every creation."

80. He who produced fuel for you from the green trees, with which you kindle a fire.

81. Is not He who created the heavens and the earth able to create the like of them? Certainly. He is the Supreme All-Knowing Creator.

82. His command, when He wills a thing, is to say to it, "Be," and it comes to be.

83. So glory be to Him in whose hand is the dominion of everything, and to Him you will be returned.

37. THE ALIGNERS
(as-Saffat)

*In the name of Allah,
the Gracious, the Merciful*

1. By the aligners aligning.

2. And the drivers driving.

3. And the reciters of the Reminder.

4. Your God is indeed One.

5. Lord of the heavens and the earth, and everything between them; and Lord of the Easts.

6. We have adorned the lower heaven with the beauty of the planets.

7. And guarded it against every defiant devil.

8. They cannot eavesdrop on the Supernal Elite, for they get bombarded from every side.

9. Repelled—they will have a lingering torment.

10. Except for him who snatches a fragment—he gets pursued by a piercing projectile.

11. Inquire of them, "Are they more difficult to create, or the others We created?" We created them from sticky clay.

12. But you wonder, and they ridicule.

13. And when reminded, they pay no attention.

14. And when they see a sign, they ridicule.

15. And they say, "This is nothing but plain magic.

16. When we have died and become dust and bones, shall we be resurrected?

17. And our ancestors of old?"

18. Say, "Yes indeed, and you will be totally subdued."

19. It will be a single nudge, and they will be staring.

20. They will say, "Woe to us. This is the Day of Judgment."

21. "This is the Day of Separation which you used to deny.

22. Gather those who did wrong, and their mates, and what they used to worship.

23. Besides Allah, and lead them to the way to Hell.

24. And stop them. They are to be questioned."

25. What is the matter with you? Why do you not help one another?

37. THE ALIGNERS (as-Saffat)

26. In fact, on that Day, they will be submissive.

27. They will come to one another, questioning one another.

28. They will say, "You used to come at us from the right."

29. They will say, "You yourselves were not believers.

30. We had no authority over you. You yourselves were rebellious people.

31. The Word of our Lord has been realized against us. We are tasting it.

32. We seduced you. We were seducers."

33. On that Day, they will share in the punishment.

34. Thus We deal with the sinners.

35. When it was said to them, "There is no god except Allah," they grew arrogant.

36. And said, "Are we to abandon our gods for a mad poet?"

37. In fact, he came with the truth, and he confirmed the messengers.

38. Most assuredly, you will taste the painful punishment.

39. And you will be repaid only for what you used to do.

40. Except for Allah's sincere servants.

41. For them is a known provision.

42. Fruits; and they will be honored.

43. In the Gardens of Bliss.

44. On furnishings, facing one another.

45. They will be offered a cup of pure drink.

46. White; a delight to those who drink.

47. Never polluted, and never intoxicating.

48. With them will be bashful women with lovely eyes.

49. As if they were closely guarded pearls.

50. Then they will approach one another, questioning.

51. One of them will say, "I used to have a friend.

52. Who used to say, "Are you of those who believe?

53. That after we die and become dust and bones, we will be called to account?"

54. He will say, "Will you have a look?"

55. He will look, and will see him in the pit of Hell.

56. He will say, "By Allah, you almost ruined me.

57. Were it not for the grace of my Lord, I would have been among the arraigned."

58. "We will not die.

59. Except for our first death, and we will not be punished."

60. This is the supreme triumph.

61. For the like of this let the workers work.

62. Is this a better hospitality, or the Tree of Bitterness?

63. We made it an ordeal for the unjust.

64. It is a tree that grows from the bottom of Hell.

65. Its fruits are like the devils' heads.

66. They will eat from it, and fill their bellies with it.

67. Then, on top of it, they will have a brew of boiling liquid.

68. Then their return will be to the Blaze.

69. They had found their parents astray.

70. And rushed along in their footsteps.

71. And most of the ancients before them went astray.

72. Even though We sent messengers to warn them.

73. So observe the end of those who were warned.

74. Except for the sincere servants of Allah.

75. And Noah called out to Us, and We are the Best of responders.

37. THE ALIGNERS (as-Saffat)

76. And We saved him and his family from the great calamity.

77. And We made his descendants the survivors.

78. And We left mention of him among those who succeeded.

79. Peace be upon Noah among all people.

80. We thus reward the righteous.

81. He was one of Our believing servants.

82. Then We drowned the others.

83. Of his kind was Abraham.

84. When he came to his Lord with a sound heart.

85. He said to his father and his people, "What are you worshiping?

86. Is it falsified gods, instead of Allah, that you want?

87. So what is your opinion about the Lord of the Worlds?"

88. Then he took a glance at the stars.

89. And said, "I am sick."

90. But they turned their backs on him, and went away.

91. Then he turned to their gods, and said, "will you not eat?

92. What is it with you, that you do not speak?"

93. Then he turned on them, striking with his right hand.

94. And they came running towards him.

95. He said, "Do you worship what you carve?

96. When Allah created you, and what you manufacture?"

97. They said, "Build a pyre for him, and throw him into the furnace."

98. They wished him ill, but We made them the losers.

99. He said, "I am going towards my Lord, and He will guide me."

100. "My Lord, give me one of the righteous."

101. So We gave him good news of a clement boy.

102. Then, when he was old enough to accompany him, he said, "O My son, I see in a dream that I am sacrificing you; see what you think." He said, "O my Father, do as you are commanded; you will find me, Allah willing, one of the steadfast."

103. Then, when they had submitted, and he put his forehead down.

104. We called out to him, "O Abraham!

105. You have fulfilled the vision." Thus We reward the doers of good.

106. This was certainly an evident test.

107. And We redeemed him with a great sacrifice.

108. And We left with him for later generations.

109. Peace be upon Abraham.

110. Thus We reward the doers of good.

111. He was one of Our believing servants.

112. And We gave him good news of Isaac, a prophet, one of the righteous.

113. And We blessed him, and Isaac. But among their descendants are some who are righteous, and some who are clearly unjust to themselves.

114. And We blessed Moses and Aaron.

115. And We delivered them and their people from the terrible disaster.

116. And We supported them, and so they were the victors.

117. And We gave them the Clarifying Scripture.

118. And We guided them upon the straight path.

119. And We left with them for later generations.

120. Peace be upon Moses and Aaron.

121. Thus We reward the righteous.

122. They were of Our believing servants.

37. THE ALIGNERS (as-Saffat)

123. Also Elijah was one of the messengers.

124. He said to his people, "Do you not fear?

125. Do you call on Baal, and forsake the Best of creators?

126. Allah is your Lord, and the Lord of your ancestors."

127. But they called him a liar, and thus they will be brought forward.

128. Except for Allah's sincere servants.

129. And We left with him for later generations.

130. Peace be upon the House of Elijah.

131. Thus We reward the virtuous.

132. He was one of Our believing servants.

133. And Lot was one of the messengers.

134. We saved him and his family, all of them.

135. Except for an old woman who lagged behind.

136. Then We annihilated the others.

137. You pass by them in the morning.

138. And at night. Do you not understand?

139. And Jonah was one of the messengers.

140. When he fled to the laden boat.

141. He gambled and lost.

142. Then the fish swallowed him, and he was to blame.

143. Had he not been one of those who praised.

144. He would have stayed in its belly until the Day they are raised.

145. Then We threw him into the wilderness, and he was sick.

146. And We made a gourd tree grow over him.

147. Then We sent him to a hundred thousand, or more.

148. And they believed, so We gave them enjoyment for a while.

149. Ask them, "Are the daughters for your Lord, while for them the sons?"

150. Or did We create the angels females, as they witnessed?"

151. No indeed! It is one of their lies when they say.

152. "Allah has begotten." They are indeed lying.

153. So He preferred girls over boys?

154. What is the matter with you? How do you judge?

155. Will you not reflect?

156. Or do you have some clear proof?

157. Then bring your book, if you are telling the truth.

158. And they invented a relationship between Him and the jinn. But the jinn know that they will be arraigned.

159. Allah be glorified, far above what they allege.

160. Except for Allah's sincere servants.

161. Surely, you and what you serve.

162. Cannot seduce away from Him.

163. Except for he who will be roasting in Hell.

164. "There is not one of us but has an assigned position.

165. And we are the arrangers.

166. And we are the glorifiers."

167. Even though they used to say.

168. "Had we received advice from the ancients.

169. We would have been Allah's faithful servants."

170. But they rejected it, so they will find out.

171. Our Word has already gone out to our servant messengers.

172. It is they who will be supported.

173. And Our troops will be the victors.

174. So disregard them for a while.

175. And watch them—they will soon see.

176. Are they seeking to hasten Our punishment?

177. When it descends into their yard, miserable will be the morning of those forewarned.

178. So avoid them for a while.

179. And watch—they will soon see.

180. Exalted be your Lord, the Lord of Glory, beyond their allegations.

181. And peace be upon the messengers.

182. And praise be to Allah, the Lord of the Worlds.

38. SAAD
(Saad)

*In the name of Allah,
the Gracious, the Merciful*

1. Saad. By the renowned Quran.

2. Those who disbelieve are steeped in arrogance and defiance.

3. How many generations have We destroyed before them? They cried out when it was too late to escape.

4. And they marveled that a warner has come to them from among them. The disbelievers said, "This is a lying magician."

5. "Did he turn all the gods into one God? This is something strange."

6. The notables among them announced: "Go on, and hold fast to your gods. This is something planned.

7. We never heard of this in the former faith. This is nothing but a fabrication.

8. Was the message sent down to him, out of all of us?" In fact, they are doubtful of My warning. In fact, they have not yet tasted My punishment.

9. Or do they possess the treasuries of the mercy of your Lord—the Majestic, the Giver?

10. Or do they possess the sovereignty of the heavens and the earth and what is between them? Then let them ascend the ropes.

11. An army of confederates will be defeated there.

12. Before them the people of Noah denied the truth; as did Aad, and Pharaoh of the Stakes.

13. And Thamood, and the people of Lot, and the dwellers of the Woods—these were the confederates.

14. None of them but denied the messengers, so My retribution was deserved.

15. These can expect only a single scream, from which there is no recovery.

16. And they say, "Our Lord, hasten Your writ upon us, before the Day of Account."

17. Be patient in the face of what they say, and mention Our servant David, the resourceful. He was obedient.

18. We committed the mountains to glorify with him, in the evening and at daybreak.

19. And the birds, gathered together. All obedient to him.

20. And We strengthened his kingdom, and gave him wisdom and decisive speech.

21. Has the story of the two disputants reached you? When they scaled the sanctuary?

22. When they entered upon David, and he was startled by them. They said, "Do not fear. Two disputants; one of us has wronged the other; so judge between us fairly, and do not be biased, and guide us to the straight way."

23. "This brother of mine has ninety nine ewes, and I have one ewe, and he said, 'Entrust it to me,' and he pressured me with words."

24. He said, "He has done you wrong by asking your ewe in addition to his ewes. Many partners take advantage of one another, except those who believe and do good deeds, but these are so few." David realized that We were testing him, so he sought forgiveness from his Lord, and fell down to his knees, and repented.

25. So We forgave him that. And for him is nearness to Us, and a good place of return.

26. "O David, We made you a ruler in the land, so judge between the people with justice, and do not follow desire, lest it diverts you from

38. SAAD (Saad)

Allah's path. Those who stray from Allah's path will have a painful punishment, for having ignored the Day of Account."

27. We did not create the heaven and the earth and everything between them in vain. That is the assumption of those who disbelieve—so woe to those who disbelieve because of the Fire.

28. Or are We to treat those who believe and do righteous deeds like those who make trouble on earth? Or are We to treat the pious like the shameless?

29. A blessed Book that We sent down to you, that they may ponder its Verses, and for those with intelligence to take heed.

30. And We granted David, Solomon, an excellent servant. He was penitent.

31. When the beautiful horses were paraded before him in the evening.

32. He said, "I have preferred the love of niceties to the remembrance of my Lord—until it disappeared behind the veil.

33. Bring them back to me." And he began caressing their legs and necks.

34. We tested Solomon, and placed a body on his throne; then he repented.

35. He said, "My Lord, forgive me, and grant me a kingdom never to be attained by anyone after me. You are the Giver."

36. So We placed the wind at his service, blowing gently by his command, wherever he directed.

37. And the demons—every builder and diver.

38. And others fettered in chains.

39. "This is Our gift; so give generously, or withhold; without account."

40. For him is nearness to Us, and a beautiful resort.

41. And mention Our servant Job, when he called out to his Lord, "Satan has afflicted me with hardship and pain."

42. "Stamp with your foot—here is cool water to wash with, and to drink."

43. And We restored his family for him, and their like with them; as a mercy from Us, and a lesson for those who possess insight.

44. "Take with your hand a bundle, and strike with it, and do not break your oath." We found him patient. What an excellent servant! He was obedient.

45. And mention Our servants Abraham, Isaac, and Jacob—endowed with ability and vision.

46. We distinguished them with a distinct quality: the remembrance of the Home.

47. To Us they are among the chosen, the outstanding.

48. And mention Ishmael, Elisha, and Ezekiel; all are among the outstanding.

49. This is a reminder. The devout will have a good place of return.

50. The Gardens of Eden, with their doors wide-open for them.

51. Relaxing therein, and calling for abundant fruit and beverage.

52. With them will be attendants with modest gaze, of same age.

53. This is what you are promised for the Day of Account.

54. Such is Our bounty, inexhaustible.

55. All This. But the transgressors will have a miserable return.

56. Hell; in which they will roast; what a miserable abode!

57. All this. Let them taste it—boiling and bitter cold.

58. And similar torments of diverse kinds.

59. "This is a crowd rushing headlong with you." There is no welcome for them. They will be scorched by the Fire.

60. They will say, "But it is you! There is no welcome for you! It is you who brought it upon us! What a miserable end!"

61. They will say, "Our Lord, whoever brought this upon us, give him double torment in the Fire."

62. And they will say, "What is it with us that we do not see men we used to count among the wicked?

63. Did we take them for mockery, or have our eyes swerved from them?

64. This is certainly true—the feuding of the people of the Fire.

65. Say, "I am only a warner, and there is no god except Allah—the One, the Conqueror.

66. The Lord of the heavens and the earth, and everything between them; the Mighty, the Forgiver."

67. Say, "It is a message of great importance.

68. From which you are turning away.

69. I have no knowledge of the Highest Assembly as they dispute.

70. It is only revealed to me that I am a clear warner."

71. Your Lord said to the angels, "I am creating a human being from clay.

72. When I have formed him, and breathed into him of My spirit, fall prostrate before him.

73. So the angels fell prostrate, all of them.

74. Except for Satan. He was too proud, and one of the faithless.

75. He said, "O Satan, what prevented you from prostrating before what I created with My Own hands? Are you too proud, or were you one of the exalted?"

76. He said, "I am better than he; You created me from fire, and You created him from clay."

77. He said, "Then get out of here! You are an outcast!

78. And My curse will be upon you until the Day of Judgment."

79. He said, "Lord, defer me until the Day they are resurrected."

80. He said, "You are one of those deferred.

81. Until the Day of the Time Appointed."

82. He said, "By Your majesty, I will seduce them all.

83. Except for your loyal servants among them."

84. He said, "The truth is, and I say the truth.

85. I will fill Hell with you, and with every one of them who follows you."

86. Say, "I ask of you no wage for this, and I am not a pretender.

87. It is but a reminder to mankind.

88. And you will know its message after a while."

39. THRONGS
(az-Zumar)

In the name of Allah,
the Gracious, the Merciful

1. The revelation of the Book is from Allah, the Mighty and Wise.

2. We sent down to you the Book with the truth, so serve Allah, devoting your religion to Him.

3. Is not to Allah that sincere faith is due? As for those who take guardians besides Him, "We only worship them that they may bring us nearer to Allah." Allah will judge between them regarding their differences. Allah does not guide the lying blasphemer.

4. If Allah wanted to have a son, He could have selected from His creation at will. Glory be to Him. He is Allah, the One, the Prevailing.

5. He created the heavens and the earth with reason. He wraps the night around the day, and He wraps the day around the night. And He regulates the sun and the moon, each running along a specific course. He is indeed the Almighty, the Forgiver.

6. He created you from one person, then made from it its mate, and brought down livestock for you—eight kinds in pairs. He creates you in the wombs of your mothers, in successive

39. THRONGS (az-Zumar)

formations, in a triple darkness. Such is Allah, your Lord. His is the kingdom. There is no god but He. So what made you deviate?

7. If you disbelieve, Allah is Independent of you, yet He does not approve ingratitude on the part of His servants. And if you are thankful, He will approve that in you. No bearer of burden can bear the burden of another. Then to your Lord is your return; and He will inform you of what you used to do. He is aware of what the hearts contain.

8. When some adversity touches the human being, he prays to his Lord, repenting to Him. But then, when He confers on him a grace of His, he forgets what he was praying for before, and he attributes rivals to Allah, in order to lead astray from His way. Say, "Enjoy your disbelief for a little while; you will be among the inmates of the Fire."

9. Is he who worships devoutly during the watches of the night, prostrating himself and standing up, mindful of the Hereafter, and placing his hope in the mercy of his Lord? Say, "Are those who know and those who do not know equal?" Only those possessed of reason will remember.

10. Say, "O My devotees who have believed, keep your duty to your Lord. For those who do good in this world, is goodness. And Allah's earth is vast. The steadfast will be paid their wages in full, without reckoning."

11. Say, "I was commanded to serve Allah, devoting my religion exclusively to Him.

12. And I was commanded to be the first of those who submit."

13. Say, "I fear, if I disobeyed my Lord, the punishment of a horrendous Day."

14. Say, "It is Allah I worship, sincere in my faith in Him."

15. "But you can worship whatever you wish besides Him." Say, "The losers are those who lose their souls and their people on the Day of Resurrection." That is indeed the obvious loss.

16. They will have layers of Fire above them, and layers beneath them. That is how Allah strikes fear into His servants—"O My servants! Beware of Me!"

17. As for those who avoid the worship of idols, and devote themselves to Allah—theirs is the good news. So give good news to My servants.

18. Those who listen to the Word, and follow the best of it. These are they whom Allah has guided. These are they who possess intellect.

19. What about someone who has deserved the sentence of punishment? Is it you who can save those in the Fire?

20. But those who fear their Lord will have mansions upon mansions, built high, with streams flowing beneath them. The promise of Allah; and Allah never breaks a promise.

21. Have you not considered how Allah sends down water from the sky, then He makes it flow into underground wells, then He produces with it plants of various colors, then they wither and you see them yellowing, then He turns them into debris? Surely in this is a reminder for those with understanding.

22. What about someone whose heart Allah has opened to Islam, so that he follows a light from His Lord? Woe to those whose hearts are hardened against the mention of Allah. Those are in manifest error.

23. Allah has sent down the best of narrations: a Scripture consistent and paired. The skins of those who reverence their Lord shiver from it, then their skins and their hearts soften up to the remembrance of Allah. Such is Allah's guidance; He guides with it whomever He wills. But whomever Allah leaves astray, for him there is no guide.

24. What about someone who covers his face against the terrible misery of the Day of Resurrection? To the evildoers it will be said, "Taste what you used to earn."

25. Those before them also denied the truth, so the penalty came upon them from where they did not perceive.

39. THRONGS (az-Zumar)

26. Allah made them taste disgrace in the present life, but the punishment of the Hereafter is worse, if they only knew.

27. We have cited in this Quran for mankind every ideal, that they may take heed.

28. An Arabic Quran, without any defect, so they may become righteous.

29. Allah cites the example of a man shared by partners at odds, and a man belonging exclusively to one man. Are they equal in status? Praise be to Allah, but most of them do not know.

30. You will die, and they will die.

31. Then, on the Day of Resurrection, you will be quarrelling before your Lord.

32. Who is more evil than he who lies about Allah, and denies the truth when it has come to him? Is there not in Hell room for the ungrateful?

33. But he who promotes the truth, and testifies to it—these are the righteous.

34. They will have whatever they please with their Lord. Such is the reward for the virtuous.

35. Allah will acquit them of the worst of their deeds, and will reward them according to the best of what they used to do.

36. Is Allah not enough for His servant? And they frighten you with those besides Him. Whomever Allah sends astray, for him there is no guide.

37. And whomever Allah guides, for him there is no misleader. Is Allah not Powerful and Vengeful?

38. And if you asked them, "Who created the heavens and the earth?" they would say, "Allah." Say, "Have you seen those you pray to instead of Allah? If Allah willed any harm for me, can they lift His harm? And if He willed a blessing for me, can they hold back His mercy?" Say, "Allah suffices for me. On Him the reliant rely."

39. Say: "O my people, work according to your ability; and so will I. Then you will know.

40. Who will receive a humiliating punishment, and on whom will fall a lasting torment."

41. We sent down upon you the Book for mankind in truth. He who follows guidance does so for the good of his soul. And he who strays in error does so to its detriment. You are not their overseer.

42. Allah takes the souls at the time of their death, and those that have not died during their sleep. He retains those for which He has decreed death, and He releases the others until a predetermined time. In that are signs for people who reflect.

43. Or have they chosen intercessors other than Allah? Say, "Even though they have no power over anything, and are devoid of reason?"

44. Say, "All intercession is up to Allah. To Him belongs the kingdom of the heavens and the earth. Then to Him you will be returned."

45. When Allah alone is mentioned, the hearts of those who do not believe in the Hereafter shrink with resentment. But when those other than Him are mentioned, they become filled with joy.

46. Say, "Our God, Initiator of the heavens and the earth, Knower of all secrets and declarations. You will judge between your servants regarding what they had differed about."

47. If those who did wrong owned everything on earth, and the like of it with it, they would redeem themselves with it from the terrible suffering on the Day of Resurrection. But there will appear to them from Allah what they never anticipated.

48. There will appear to them the evils of their deeds, and they will be surrounded by what they used to ridicule.

49. When adversity touches the human being, he calls on Us. But then, when We favor him with a blessing from Us, he says, "I have attained this by virtue of my knowledge." However, it is a test, but most of them do not know.

39. THRONGS (az-Zumar)

50. Those before them said it, but what they had earned did not avail them.

51. The evils of their deeds caught up with them. And the wrongdoers among these will also be afflicted by the evils of what they earned, and they cannot prevent it.

52. Do they not know that Allah extends the provision to whomever He wills, and constricts it? In that are signs for people who believe.

53. Say, "O My servants who have transgressed against themselves: do not despair of Allah's mercy, for Allah forgives all sins. He is indeed the Forgiver, the Clement."

54. And turn to your Lord, and submit to Him, before the retribution comes upon you. Then you will not be helped.

55. And follow the best of what was revealed to you from your Lord, before the punishment comes upon you suddenly, while you are unaware.

56. So that a soul may not say, "How sorry I am, for having neglected my duty to Allah, and for having been of the scoffers."

57. Or say, "Had Allah guided me; I would have been of the pious."

58. Or say, when it sees the penalty, "If only I had another chance, I would be of the virtuous."

59. Yes indeed! My Verses did come to you, but you called them lies, turned arrogant, and were of the faithless.

60. On the Day of Resurrection, you will see those who told lies about Allah with their faces blackened. Is there not a place in Hell for the arrogant?

61. And Allah will save those who maintained righteousness to their place of salvation. No harm will touch them, nor will they grieve.

62. Allah is the Creator of all things, and He is in Charge of all things.

63. To Him belong the reins of the heavens and the earth. But those who blaspheme against the revelations of Allah—it is they who are the losers.

64. Say, "Is it other than Allah you instruct me to worship, you ignorant ones?"

65. It was revealed to you, and to those before you, that if you idolize, your works will be in vain, and you will be of the losers.

66. Rather, worship Allah, and be of the appreciative.

67. They have not esteemed Allah as He ought to be esteemed. The entire earth will be in His grip on the Day of Resurrection, and the heavens will be folded in His right. Immaculate is He, and Transcendent He is beyond the associations they make.

68. And the Trumpet will be sounded, whereupon everyone in the heavens and the earth will be stunned, except whomever Allah wills. Then it will be sounded another time, whereupon they will rise up, looking on.

69. And the earth will shine with the Light of its Lord; and the Book will be put in place; and the prophets and the witnesses will be brought in; and Judgment will be passed among them equitably, and they will not be wronged.

70. And every soul will be fully compensated for what it had done. He is well aware of what they do.

71. Those who disbelieved will be driven to Hell in throngs. Until, when they have reached it, and its gates are opened, its keepers will say to them, "Did not messengers from among you come to you, reciting to you the revelations of your Lord, and warning you of the meeting of this Day of yours?" They will say, "Yes, but the verdict of punishment is justified against the disbelievers."

72. It will be said, "Enter the gates of Hell, to abide therein eternally." How wretched is the destination of the arrogant.

73. And those who feared their Lord will be led to Paradise in throngs. Until, when they have reached it, and its gates are opened, its keepers will say to them, "Peace be upon you, you

have been good, so enter it, to abide therein eternally."

74. And they will say, "Praise be to Allah, who has fulfilled His promise to us, and made us inherit the land, enjoying Paradise as we please." How excellent is the reward of the workers.

75. And you will see the angels hovering around the Throne, glorifying their Lord with praise. And it will be judged between them equitably, and it will be said, "Praise be to Allah, Lord of the Worlds."

40. FORGIVER
(Ghafir)

In the name of Allah, the Gracious, the Merciful

1. Ha, Meem.

2. The sending down of the Scripture is from Allah the Almighty, the Omniscient.

3. Forgiver of sins, Accepter of repentance, Severe in punishment, Bountiful in bounty. There is no god but He. To Him is the ultimate return.

4. None argues against Allah's revelations except those who disbelieve. So do not be impressed by their activities in the land.

5. Before them the people of Noah rejected the truth, as did the confederates after them. Every community plotted against their messenger, to capture him. And they argued with falsehood, to defeat with it the truth. But I seized them. What a punishment it was!

6. Thus the sentence of your Lord became realized against those who disbelieve, that they are to be inmates of the Fire.

7. Those who carry the Throne, and those around it, glorify their Lord with praise, and believe in Him, and ask for forgiveness for those who believe: "Our Lord, You have encompassed everything in mercy and knowledge; so forgive those who repent and follow Your path, and protect them from the agony of the Blaze.

8. And admit them, Our Lord, into the Gardens of Eternity, which You have promised them, and the righteous among their parents, and their spouses, and their offspring. You are indeed the Almighty, the Most Wise.

9. And shield them from the evil deeds. Whomever You shield from the evil deeds, on that Day, You have had mercy on him. That is the supreme achievement."

10. Those who disbelieved will be addressed, "The loathing of Allah is greater than your loathing of yourselves—for you were invited to the faith, but you refused."

11. They will say, "Our Lord, you made us die twice, and twice you gave us life. Now we acknowledge our sins. Is there any way out?"

12. That is because when Allah alone was called upon, you disbelieved; but when others were associated with Him, you believed. Judgment rests with Allah the Sublime, the Majestic.

13. It is He who shows you His wonders, and sends down sustenance from the sky for you. But none pays heed except the repentant.

14. So call upon Allah, with sincere devotion to Him, even though the disbelievers resent it.

15. Exalted in rank, Owner of the Throne. He conveys the Spirit, by His command, upon whomever He wills of His servants, to warn of the Day of Encounter.

16. The Day when they will emerge, nothing about them will be concealed from Allah. "To whom does the sovereignty belong today?" "To Allah, the One, the Irresistible."

17. On that Day, every soul will be recompensed for what it had earned. There will be no injustice on that Day. Allah is quick to settle accounts.

18. And warn them of the Day of Imminence, when the hearts are at the throats, choking them. The evildoers will have no intimate friend, and no intercessor to be obeyed.

19. He knows the deceptions of the eyes, and what the hearts conceal.

40. FORGIVER (Ghafir)

20. Allah judges with justice, while those whom they invoke besides Him cannot judge with anything. It is Allah who is the Hearing, the Seeing.

21. Have they not travelled through the earth, and seen the consequences for those before them? They were stronger than them, and they left more impact on earth. But Allah seized them for their sins, and they had no defender against Allah.

22. That is because their messengers used to come to them with clear proofs, but they disbelieved, so Allah seized them. He is Strong, Severe in retribution.

23. We sent Moses with Our signs, and a clear authority.

24. To Pharaoh, Hamaan, and Quaroon. But they said, "A lying sorcerer."

25. Then, when he came to them with the truth from Us, they said, "Kill the sons of those who have believed with him, and spare their daughters." But the scheming of the unbelievers can only go astray.

26. Pharaoh said, "Leave me to kill Moses, and let him appeal to his Lord. I fear he may change your religion, or spread disorder in the land."

27. Moses said, "I have sought the protection of my Lord and your Lord, from every tyrant who does not believe in the Day of Account."

28. A believing man from Pharaoh's family, who had concealed his faith, said, "Are you going to kill a man for saying, 'My Lord is Allah,' and he has brought you clear proofs from your Lord? If he is a liar, his lying will rebound upon him; but if he is truthful, then some of what he promises you will befall you. Allah does not guide the extravagant imposter.

29. O my people! Yours is the dominion today, supreme in the land; but who will help us against Allah's might, should it fall upon us?" Pharaoh said, "I do not show you except what I see, and I do not guide you except to the path of prudence."

30. The one who had believed said, "O my people, I fear for you the like of the day of the confederates.

31. Like the fate of the people of Noah, and Aad, and Thamood, and those after them. Allah wants no injustice for the servants.

32. O my people, I fear for you the Day of Calling Out.

33. The Day when you will turn and flee, having no defender against Allah. Whomever Allah misguides has no guide."

34. Joseph had come to you with clear revelations, but you continued to doubt what he came to you with. Until, when he perished, you said, "Allah will never send a messenger after him." Thus Allah leads astray the outrageous skeptic.

35. Those who argue against Allah's revelations, without any proof having come to them—a heinous sin in the sight of Allah, and of those who believe. Thus Allah seals the heart of every proud bully.

36. And Pharaoh said, "O Hamaan, build me a tower, that I may reach the pathways.

37. The pathways of the heavens, so that I may glance at the God of Moses; though I think he is lying." Thus Pharaoh's evil deeds were made to appear good to him, and he was averted from the path. Pharaoh's guile was only in defeat.

38. The one who had believed said, "O my people, follow me, and I will guide you to the path of rectitude."

39. "O my people, the life of this world is nothing but fleeting enjoyment, but the Hereafter is the Home of Permanence.

40. Whoever commits a sin will be repaid only with its like. But whoever works righteousness, whether male or female, and is a believer—these will enter Paradise, where they will be provided for without account.

41. O my people, how is it that I call you to salvation, and you call me to the Fire?

40. FORGIVER (Ghafir)

42. You call me to reject Allah, and to associate with Him what I have no knowledge of, while I call you to the Mighty Forgiver.

43. Without a doubt, what you call me to has no say in this world, or in the Hereafter; and our turning back is to Allah; and the transgressors are the inmates of the Fire.

44. You will remember what I am telling you, so I commit my case to Allah. Allah is Observant of the servants."

45. So Allah protected him from the evils of their scheming, while a terrible torment besieged Pharaoh's clan.

46. The Fire. They will be exposed to it morning and evening. And on the Day the Hour takes place: "Admit the clan of Pharaoh to the most intense agony."

47. As they quarrel in the Fire, the weak will say to those who were arrogant, "We were followers of yours; will you then spare us a portion of the Fire?"

48. Those who were arrogant will say, "We are all in it; Allah has judged between the servants."

49. And those in the Fire will say to the keepers of Hell, "Call to your Lord to lessen our suffering for one day."

50. They will say, "Did not your messengers come to you with clear signs?" They will say, "Yes." They will say, "Then pray, but the prayers of the disbelievers will always be in vain."

51. Most surely We will support Our messengers and those who believe, in this life, and on the Day the witnesses arise.

52. The Day when their excuses will not profit the wrongdoers, and the curse will be upon them, and they will have the Home of Misery.

53. We gave Moses guidance, and made the Children of Israel inherit the Scripture.

54. A guide and a reminder for those endowed with reason.

55. So be patient. The promise of Allah is true. And ask forgiveness for your sin, and proclaim the praise of your Lord evening and morning.

56. Those who dispute regarding Allah's revelations without any authority having come to them—there is nothing in their hearts but the feeling of greatness, which they will never attain. So seek refuge in Allah; for He is the All-Hearing, the All-Seeing.

57. Certainly the creation of the heavens and the earth is greater than the creation of humanity, but most people do not know.

58. Not equal are the blind and the seeing. Nor are those who believe and work righteousness equal to the sinners. How little you reflect.

59. Indeed, the Hour is coming; there is no doubt about it; but most people do not believe.

60. Your Lord has said, "Pray to Me, and I will respond to you. But those who are too proud to worship Me will enter Hell forcibly."

61. It is Allah Who made the night for you, that you may rest therein; and the day allowing sight. Allah is gracious towards the people, but most people do not give thanks.

62. Such is Allah, your Lord, Creator of all things. There is no god except Him; so how could you turn away?

63. Thus are turned away those who dispute the signs of Allah.

64. It is Allah who made the earth a habitat for you, and the sky a structure. And He designed you, and designed you well; and He provided you with the good things. Such is Allah, your Lord; so Blessed is Allah, Lord of the Worlds.

65. He is the Living One. There is no god except He. So pray to Him, devoting your religion to Him. Praise be to Allah, the Lord of the Worlds.

66. Say, "I was prohibited from worshiping those you invoke besides Allah, now that clear revelations have come to me from my

Lord; and I was commanded to submit to the Lord of the Worlds."

67. It is He who created you from dust, then from a seed, then from an embryo, then He brings you out as an infant, then He lets you reach your maturity, then you become elderly—although some of you die sooner—so that you may reach a predetermined age, so that you may understand.

68. It is He who gives life and death; and when He decides on a thing, He just says to it, "Be," and it comes to be.

69. Have you not observed those who dispute regarding Allah's revelations, how they have deviated?

70. Those who call the Book a lie, and what We sent Our messengers with—they will surely know.

71. When the yokes are around their necks, and they will be dragged by the chains.

72. Into the boiling water, then in the Fire they will be consumed.

73. Then it will be said to them, "Where are those you used to deify?

74. Instead of Allah?" They will say, "They have abandoned us. In fact, we were praying to nothing before." Thus Allah sends the disbelievers astray.

75. That is because you used to rejoice on earth in other than the truth, and because you used to behave with vanity.

76. Enter the gates of Hell, to remain therein forever. What a terrible dwelling for the arrogant.

77. So be patient. The promise of Allah is true. Whether We show you some of what We have promised them, or take you to Us, to Us they will be returned.

78. We sent messengers before you. Some of them We told you about, and some We did not tell you about. No messenger can bring a miracle except by leave of Allah. Then, when the command of Allah is issued, fair judgment will be passed, and there and then the seekers of vanity will lose.

79. Allah is He who created the domestic animals for you—some for you to ride, and some you eat.

80. And in them you have other benefits as well, and through them you satisfy your needs. And on them, and on the ships, you are transported.

81. And He shows you His signs. So which of Allah's signs will you deny?

82. Have they not journeyed through the land, and seen the outcome for those before them? They were more numerous than they, and had greater power and influence in the land. But what they had achieved availed them nothing.

83. When their messengers came to them with clear proofs, they rejoiced in the knowledge they had, and the very things they used to ridicule besieged them.

84. Then, when they witnessed Our might, they said, "We believe in Allah alone, and we reject what we used to associate with Him."

85. But their faith could not help them once they witnessed Our might. This has been Allah's way of dealing with His servants. And there and then the disbelievers lost.

41. DETAILED
(Fussilat)

*In the name of Allah,
the Gracious, the Merciful*

1. Ha, Meem.

2. A revelation from the Most Gracious, the Most Merciful.

3. A Scripture whose Verses are detailed, a Quran in Arabic for people who know.

4. Bringing good news, and giving warnings. But most of them turn away, so they do not listen.

5. And they say, "Our hearts are screened from what you call us to, and in our ears is deafness, and between us and you is a barrier. So do what you want, and so will we."

41. DETAILED (Fussilat)

6. Say, "I am only a human like you; it is inspired in me that your God is One God. So be upright towards Him, and seek forgiveness from Him." And woe to the idolaters.

7. Those who do not pay the alms; and regarding the Hereafter, they are disbelievers.

8. As for those who believe and do righteous deeds—for them is a reward uninterrupted.

9. Say, "Do you reject the One who created the earth in two days? And you attribute equals to Him? That is the Lord of the Universe."

10. He placed stabilizers over it; and blessed it; and planned its provisions in four days, equally to the seekers.

11. Then He turned to the sky, and it was smoke, and said to it and to the earth, "Come, willingly or unwillingly." They said, "We come willingly."

12. So He completed them as seven universes in two days, and He assigned to each universe its laws. And We decorated the lower universe with lamps, and for protection. That is the design of the Almighty, the All-Knowing.

13. But if they turn away, say, "I have warned you of a thunderbolt, like the thunderbolt of Aad and Thamood."

14. Their messengers came to them, from before them and from behind them, saying, "Do not worship anyone but Allah." They said, "Had our Lord willed, He would have sent down angels; Therefore, we reject what you are sent with."

15. As for Aad, they turned arrogant on earth, and opposed justice, and said, "Who is more powerful than us?" Have they not considered that Allah, who created them, is more powerful than they? And they went on denying Our revelations.

16. So We unleashed upon them a screaming wind, for a few miserable days, to make them taste the punishment of shame in this life; but the punishment of the Hereafter is more shameful; and they will not be saved.

17. And as for Thamood, We guided them, but they preferred blindness over guidance. So the thunderbolt of the humiliating punishment seized them, because of what they used to earn.

18. And We saved those who believed and were righteous.

19. The Day when Allah's enemies are herded into the Fire, forcibly.

20. Until, when they have reached it, their hearing, and their sight, and their skins will testify against them regarding what they used to do.

21. And they will say to their skins, "Why did you testify against us?" They will say, "Allah, Who made all things speak, made us speak. It is He who created you the first time, and to Him you are returned."

22. You were unable to hide yourselves from your hearing, and your sight, and your skins, to prevent them from testifying against you, and you imagined that Allah was unaware of much of what you do.

23. It is that thought of yours about your Lord that led you to ruin—so you became of the losers.

24. If they endure patiently, the Fire will be their residence; and if they make up excuses, they will not be pardoned.

25. We had assigned companions for them, who glamorized to them what was in front of them, and what was behind them. And the Word proved true against them in communities of jinn and humans that have passed away before them. They were losers.

26. Those who disbelieve say, "Do not listen to this Quran, and talk over it, so that you may prevail."

27. We will make those who disbelieve taste an intense agony, and We will recompense them according to the worst of what they used to do.

28. Such is the recompense of Allah's enemies—the Fire—where they will have their permanent home, in recompense for having disregarded Our revelations.

41. DETAILED (Fussilat)

29. Those who disbelieved will say, "Our Lord, show us those who led us astray—among jinn and humans—and we will trample them under our feet, so they become of the lowest."

30. Surely, those who say: "Our Lord is Allah," and then go straight, the angels will descend upon them: "Do not fear, and do not grieve, but rejoice in the news of the Garden which you were promised.

31. We are your allies in this life and in the Hereafter, wherein you will have whatever your souls desire, and you will have therein whatever you call for.

32. As Hospitality from an All-Forgiving, Merciful One."

33. And who is better in speech than someone who calls to Allah, and acts with integrity, and says, "I am of those who submit"?

34. Good and evil are not equal. Repel evil with good, and the person who was your enemy becomes like an intimate friend.

35. But none will attain it except those who persevere, and none will attain it except the very fortunate.

36. When a temptation from the Devil provokes you, seek refuge in Allah; He is the Hearer, the Knower.

37. And of His signs are the night and the day, and the sun and the moon. Do not bow down to the sun, nor to the moon, but bow down to Allah, Who created them both, if it is Him that you serve.

38. But if they are too proud—those in the presence of your Lord praise Him night and day, and without ever tiring.

39. And of His signs is that you see the land still. But when We send down water upon it, it stirs and grows. Surely, He Who revived it will revive the dead. He is Able to do all things.

40. Those who despise Our revelations are not hidden from Us. Is he who is hurled into the Fire better? Or he who arrives safely on the Day of Resurrection? Do as you please; He is Seeing of everything you do.

41. Those who reject the Reminder when it has come to them—it is an invincible Book.

42. Falsehood cannot approach it, from before it or behind it. It is a revelation from One Wise and Praiseworthy.

43. Nothing is said to you but was said to the Messengers before you: your Lord is Possessor of Forgiveness, and Possessor of Painful Repayment.

44. Had We made it a Quran in a foreign language, they would have said, "If only its verses were made clear." Non-Arabic and an Arab? Say, "For those who believe, it is guidance and healing. But as for those who do not believe: there is heaviness in their ears, and it is blindness for them. These are being called from a distant place."

45. We gave Moses the Book, but disputes arose concerning it. Were it not for a prior decree from your Lord, judgment would have been pronounced between them. But they are in perplexing doubt concerning it.

46. Whoever acts righteously does so for himself; and whoever works evil does so against himself. Your Lord is not unjust to the servants.

47. To Him is referred the knowledge of the Hour. No fruit emerges from its sheath, and no female conceives or delivers, except with His knowledge. And on the Day when He calls out to them, "Where are My associates?" They will say, "We admit to you, none of us is a witness."

48. What they used to pray to before will forsake them, and they will realize that they have no escape.

49. The human being never tires of praying for good things; but when adversity afflicts him, he despairs and loses hope.

50. And when We let him taste a mercy from Us, after the adversity that had afflicted him, he will say, "This is mine, and I do not think that the Hour is coming; and even if I am returned to my Lord, I will have the very best

with Him." We will inform those who disbelieve of what they did, and We will make them taste an awful punishment.

51. When We provide comfort for the human being, he withdraws and distances himself; but when adversity befalls him, he starts lengthy prayers.

52. Say, "Have you considered? If it is from Allah and you reject it—who is further astray than he who is cutoff and alienated?"

53. We will show them Our proofs on the horizons, and in their very souls, until it becomes clear to them that it is the truth. Is it not sufficient that your Lord is witness over everything?

54. Surely they are in doubt about the encounter with their Lord. Surely He comprehends everything.

42. CONSULTATION
(ash-Shura)

In the name of Allah,
the Gracious, the Merciful

1. Ha, Meem.

2. Ayn, Seen, Qaf.

3. Thus He inspires you, and those before you—Allah the Almighty, the Wise.

4. To him belongs everything in the heavens and everything on earth. He is the Sublime, the Magnificent.

5. The heavens above them almost burst apart, while the angels glorify the praises of their Lord, and ask forgiveness for those on earth. Allah is indeed the Forgiver, the Merciful.

6. As for those who take masters other than Him: Allah is in charge of them, and you are not responsible for them.

7. Thus We inspired you with an Arabic Quran, that you may warn the Central City and whoever is around it, and to warn of the Day of Assembly, of which there is no doubt; a group in the Garden, and a group in the Furnace.

8. Had Allah willed, He could have made them one community, but He admits into His mercy whomever He wills. As for the wrongdoers, they will have no protector and no savior.

9. Or have they adopted protectors besides him? But Allah is the Protector, and He gives life to the dead, and He has power over all things.

10. Whatever matter you differ about, its judgment rests with Allah. "Such is Allah, my Lord, in Whom I trust, and unto Him I repent."

11. Originator of the heavens and the earth. He made for you mates from among yourselves, and pairs of animals, by means of which He multiplies you. There is nothing like Him. He is the Hearing, the Seeing.

12. To Him belongs absolute control of the heavens and the earth. He spreads the bounties to whomever He wills, or reduces it. He is aware of all things.

13. He prescribed for you the same religion He enjoined upon Noah, and what We inspired to you, and what We enjoined upon Abraham, and Moses, and Jesus: "You shall uphold the religion, and be not divided therein." As for the idolaters, what you call them to is outrageous to them. Allah chooses to Himself whom He wills, and He guides to Himself whoever repents.

14. They became divided only after knowledge came to them, out of resentment among themselves. Were it not for a predetermined decision from your Lord, judgment would have been pronounced between them. Indeed, those who were made to inherit the Book after them are in grave doubt about it.

15. To this go on inviting, and be upright as you were commanded, and do not follow their inclinations, and say, "I believe in whatever Book Allah has sent down, and I was commanded to judge between you equitably. Allah is our Lord and your Lord. We have our deeds, and you have your deeds. Let there be no quarrel between us and you. Allah will

42. CONSULTATION (ash-Shura)

bring us together, and to Him is the ultimate return."

16. As for those who dispute about Allah after having answered His call, their argument is invalid with their Lord; and upon them falls wrath; and a grievous torment awaits them.

17. It is Allah who revealed the Book with the truth, and the Balance. And what will make you realize that perhaps the Hour is near?

18. Those who do not believe in it seek to hasten it; but those who believe are apprehensive of it, and they know it to be the truth. Absolutely, those who question the Hour are in distant error.

19. Allah is kind towards His worshipers. He provides for whomever He wills. He is the Powerful, the Honorable.

20. Whoever desires the harvest of the Hereafter, We increase for him his harvest; and whoever desires the harvest of this world, We give him thereof, and he has no share of the Hereafter.

21. Or is it that they have partners who litigate for them religious laws never authorized by Allah? Were it not for the conclusive decision, it would have been settled between them. The wicked will have a painful punishment.

22. You will see the unjust terrified of what they have earned, and it will befall them. As for those who believe and do good deeds, they will be in the Meadows of the Gardens; they will have whatever they please in the presence of their Lord; that is the supreme blessing.

23. That is the good news Allah gives to His servants who believe and do good deeds. Say, "I ask of you no wage for it, except affection among the near of kin." Whoever does a good deed, We will increase its goodness for him. Allah is Forgiving and Appreciative.

24. Or do they say, "He forged a lie about Allah." If Allah so willed, He could have sealed your heart. But Allah obliterates the false, and confirm the true by His Words. He knows what is in the hearts.

25. It is He who accepts the repentance of His worshipers, and remits the sins, and knows what you do.

26. And He answers those who believe and do good deeds, and He increases them of His grace. But the disbelievers will suffer a terrible punishment.

27. If Allah were to increase the provision to His servants, they would transgress on earth; but He sends down in precise measure whatever He wills. Surely, regarding His servants, He is Expert and Observant.

28. It is He who brings down the rain after they have despaired, and unfolds His mercy. He is the Guardian, the Praised.

29. And of His signs are the creation of the heavens and the earth, and the creatures He has spread throughout them; and He is Able to gather them at will.

30. Whatever misfortune befalls you, it is because of what your hands have earned; and yet He pardons much.

31. You are not the ones to interfere on earth; and besides Allah, you have no ally, and no helper.

32. And of His signs are the ships sailing the sea like flags.

33. If He willed, He could have stilled the winds, leaving them motionless on its surface. Surely in that are signs for every disciplined, grateful person.

34. Or He could wreck them, because of what they have earned. And yet He pardons much.

35. Those who dispute Our signs know that there is no asylum for them.

36. Whatever thing you are given is only the provision of this life. But what Allah possesses is better and more lasting for those who believe and rely on their Lord.

37. And those who avoid major sins and indecencies; and if they become angry, they forgive.

38. And those who respond to their Lord, and pray regularly, and conduct their affairs by

mutual consultation, and give of what We have provided them.

39. And those who, when wronged, defend themselves.

40. The repayment of a bad action is one equivalent to it. But whoever pardons and makes reconciliation, his reward lies with Allah. He does not love the unjust.

41. As for those who retaliate after being wronged, there is no blame on them.

42. Blame lies on those who wrong people, and commit aggression in the land without right. These will have a painful punishment.

43. But whoever endures patiently and forgives—that is a sign of real resolve.

44. Whoever Allah leaves astray has no protector apart from Him. And you will see the transgressors, when they see the torment, saying, "Is there a way of going back?"

45. And you will see them exposed to it, cowering from disgrace, looking with concealed eyes. Those who believed will say, "The losers are those who lost themselves and their families on the Day of Resurrection." Indeed, the evildoers are in a lasting torment.

46. They will have no allies to support them against Allah. Whomever Allah leaves astray has no way out.

47. Respond to your Lord before there comes from Allah a Day that cannot be turned back. You will have no refuge on that Day, and no possibility of denial.

48. But if they turn away—We did not send you as a guardian over them. Your only duty is communication. Whenever We let man taste mercy from Us, he rejoices in it; but when misfortune befalls them, as a consequence of what their hands have perpetrated, man turns blasphemous.

49. To Allah belongs the dominion of the heavens and the earth. He creates whatever He wills. He grants daughters to whomever He wills, and He grants sons to whomever He wills.

50. Or He combines them together, males and females; and He renders whomever He wills sterile. He is Knowledgeable and Capable.

51. It is not for any human that Allah should speak to him, except by inspiration, or from behind a veil, or by sending a messenger to reveal by His permission whatever He wills. He is All-High, All-Wise.

52. We thus inspired you spiritually, by Our command. You did not know what the Scripture is, nor what faith is, but We made it a light, with which We guide whomever We will of Our servants. You surely guide to a straight path.

53. The path of Allah, to whom belongs everything in the heavens and everything on earth. Indeed, to Allah all matters revert.

43. DECORATIONS
(az-Zukhruf)

In the name of Allah,
the Gracious, the Merciful

1. Ha, Meem.

2. By the Book that makes things clear.

3. We made it an Arabic Quran, so that you may understand.

4. And it is with Us, in the Source Book, sublime and wise.

5. Shall We hold back the Reminder from you, since you are a transgressing people?

6. How many a prophet did We send to the ancients?

7. No messenger came to them, but they ridiculed him.

8. We destroyed people more powerful than they, and so the example of the ancients has passed away.

9. And if you asked them, "Who created the heavens and the earth?" They would say, "The Mighty, the Knower created them."

43. DECORATIONS (az-Zukhruf)

10. He who made the earth a habitat for you, and traced pathways for you on it, that you may be guided.

11. He who sends down water from the sky in due proportion; and so We revive thereby a dead land. Thus you will be brought out.

12. He Who created all the pairs; and provided you with ships, and animals on which you ride.

13. That you may mount their backs, and remember the favor of your Lord as you sit firmly upon them, and say, "Glory be to Him Who placed these at our service; surely we could not have done it by ourselves.

14. And surely, to our Lord we will return."

15. Yet they turn one of His servants into a part of Him. Man is clearly ungrateful.

16. Or has He chosen for Himself daughters from what He creates, and favored you with sons?

17. Yet when one of them is given news of what he attributes to the Most Gracious, his face darkens, and he suppresses grief.

18. "Someone brought up to be beautiful, and unable to help in a fight?"

19. And they appoint the angels, who are servants to the Most Gracious, as females. Have they witnessed their creation? Their claim will be recorded, and they will be questioned.

20. And they say, "Had the Most Gracious willed, we would not have worshiped them." But they have no knowledge of that; they are merely guessing.

21. Or have We given them a book prior to this one, to which they adhere?

22. But they say, "We found our parents on a course, and we are guided in their footsteps."

23. Likewise, We sent no warner before you to any town, but the wealthy among them said, "We found our parents on a course, and we are following in their footsteps."

24. He would say, "Even if I bring you better guidance than what you found your parents following?" They would say, "We reject what you are sent with."

25. So We wreaked vengeance upon them. Behold, then, what was the fate of those who deny.

26. When Abraham said to his father and his people, "I am innocent of what you worship.

27. Except for He who created me, for He will guide me."

28. And he made it an enduring word in his progeny, so that they may return.

29. I gave these and their forefathers some enjoyment, until the truth and a manifest messenger came to them.

30. But when the truth came to them, they said, "This is sorcery, and we refuse to believe in it."

31. They also said, "If only this Quran was sent down to a man of importance from the two cities."

32. Is it they who allocate the mercy of your Lord? It is We who have allocated their livelihood in this life, and We elevated some of them in rank above others, that some of them would take others in service. But your Lord's mercy is better than what they amass.

33. Were it not that humanity would become a single community, We would have provided those who disbelieve in the Most Gracious with roofs of silver to their houses, and stairways by which they ascend.

34. And doors to their houses, and furnishings on which they recline.

35. And decorations. Yet all that is nothing but the stuff of this life. Yet the Hereafter, with your Lord, is for the righteous.

36. Whoever shuns the remembrance of the Most Gracious, We assign for him a devil, to be his companion.

37. They hinder them from the path, though they think they are guided.

43. DECORATIONS (az-Zukhruf)

38. Until, when He comes to Us, he will say, "If only there were between me and you the distance of the two Easts." What an evil companion!

39. It will not benefit you on that Day, since you did wrong. You are partners in the suffering.

40. Can you make the deaf hear, or guide the blind, and him who is in evident error?

41. Even if We take you away, We will wreak vengeance upon them.

42. Or show you what We have promised them; for We have absolute power over them.

43. So adhere to what is revealed to you. You are upon a straight path.

44. It is a message for you, and for your people; and you will be questioned.

45. Ask those of Our messengers We sent before you: "Did We appoint gods besides the Most Gracious to be worshiped?"

46. We sent Moses with Our revelations to Pharaoh and his dignitaries. He said, "I am the Messenger of the Lord of the Worlds."

47. But when he showed them Our signs, they started laughing at them.

48. Each sign We showed them was more marvelous than its counterpart. And We afflicted them with the plagues, so that they may repent.

49. They said, "O sorcerer, pray to your Lord for us, according to His pledge to you, and then we will be guided."

50. But when We lifted the torment from them, they immediately broke their promise.

51. Pharaoh proclaimed among his people, saying, "O my people, do I not own the Kingdom of Egypt, and these rivers flow beneath me? Do you not see?

52. Am I not better than this miserable wretch, who can barely express himself?

53. Why are bracelets of gold not dropped on him, or they angels came with him in procession?"

54. Thus he fooled his people, and they obeyed him. They were wicked people.

55. And when they provoked Our wrath, We took retribution from them, and We drowned them all.

56. Thus We made them a precedent and an example for the others.

57. And when the son of Mary was cited as an example, your people opposed.

58. They said, "Are our gods better, or he?" They cited him only for argument. In fact, they are a quarrelsome people.

59. He was just a servant whom We blessed, and We made him an example for the Children of Israel.

60. Had We willed, We would have made of you angels to be successors on earth.

61. He is a portent of the Hour, so have no doubt about it, and follow Me. This is a straight way.

62. And let not Satan divert you. He is an open enemy to you.

63. When Jesus came with the clarifications, he said, "I have come to you with wisdom, and to clarify for you some of what you differ about. So fear Allah, and obey me.

64. Allah is my Lord and your Lord, so worship Him—this is a straight path."

65. But the factions differed among themselves. So woe to the wrongdoers from the suffering of a painful Day.

66. Are they only waiting for the Hour to come upon them suddenly, while they are unaware?

67. On that Day, friends will be enemies of one another, except for the righteous.

68. O My servants, you have nothing to fear on that Day, nor will you grieve.

69. Those who believed in Our revelations, and were submissive.

70. Enter the Garden, you and your spouses, Joyfully.

71. They will be served around with trays of gold, and cups. Therein is whatever the souls desire and delights the eyes. Therein you will stay forever.

72. Such is the Garden you are made to inherit, because of what you used to do.

73. Therein you will have abundant fruit, from which you eat.

74. As for the sinners, they will be in the torment of Hell forever.

75. It will never be eased for them. In it, they will be devastated.

76. We did them no injustice, but it was they who were the unjust.

77. And they will cry, "O Malek, let your Lord finish us off." He will say, "You are staying."

78. We have given you the truth, but most of you hate the truth.

79. Have they contrived some scheme? We too are contriving.

80. Or do they think that We cannot hear their secrets and their conspiracies? Yes indeed, Our messengers are by them, writing down.

81. Say, "If the Most Gracious had a son, I would be the first to worship."

82. Glorified be the Lord of the heavens and the earth, the Lord of the Throne, beyond what they describe.

83. So leave them to blunder and play, until they encounter their Day which they are promised.

84. It is He who is Allah in heaven, and Allah on earth. He is the Wise, the Knower.

85. And blessed is He Who has sovereignty over the heavens and the earth and what is between them. He alone has knowledge of the Hour, and to Him you will be returned.

86. Those they invoke besides Him are incapable of intercession; only those who testify to the truth and have knowledge.

87. And if you asked them, "Who created them?", they would say, "Allah." Why then do they deviate?

88. As for his statement: "My Lord, these are a people who do not believe."

89. Pardon them, and say, "Peace." They will come to know.

44. SMOKE
(ad-Dukhan)

*In the name of Allah,
the Gracious, the Merciful*

1. Ha, Meem.

2. By the Enlightening Scripture.

3. We have revealed it on a Blessed Night—We have warned.

4. In it is distinguished every wise command.

5. A decree from Us. We have been sending messages.

6. As mercy from your Lord. He is the Hearer, the Knower.

7. Lord of the heavens and the earth and what is between them, if you know for sure.

8. There is no god but He. He gives life and causes death—your Lord and Lord of your ancestors of old.

9. Yet they play around in doubt.

10. So watch out for the Day when the sky produces a visible smoke.

11. Enveloping mankind; this is a painful punishment.

12. "Our Lord, lift the torment from us, we are believers."

13. But how can they be reminded? An enlightening messenger has already come to them.

14. But they turned away from him, and said, "Educated, but crazy!"

15. We will ease the punishment a little, but you will revert.

16. The Day when We launch the Great Assault—We will avenge.

17. Before them We tested the people of Pharaoh; a noble messenger came to them.

45. KNEELING (al-Jathiyah)

18. Saying, "Hand over Allah's servants to me. I am an honest messenger to you."

19. And, "Do not exalt yourselves above Allah. I come to you with clear authority.

20. I have taken refuge in my Lord and your Lord, lest you stone me.

21. But if you do not believe in me, keep away from me."

22. He appealed to his Lord: "These are a sinful people."

23. "Set out with My servants by night—you will be followed.

24. And cross the sea quickly; they are an army to be drowned."

25. How many gardens and fountains did they leave behind?

26. And plantations, and splendid buildings.

27. And comforts they used to enjoy.

28. So it was; and We passed it on to another people.

29. Neither heaven nor earth wept over them, nor were they reprieved.

30. And We delivered the Children of Israel from the humiliating persecution.

31. From Pharaoh. He was a transgressing tyrant.

32. And We chose them knowingly over all other people.

33. And We gave them many signs, in which was an obvious test.

34. These people say.

35. "There is nothing but our first death, and we will not be resurrected.

36. Bring back our ancestors, if you are truthful."

37. Are they better, or the people of Tubba and those before them? We annihilated them. They were evildoers.

38. We did not create the heavens and the earth and what is between them to play.

39. We created them only for a specific purpose, but most of them do not know.

40. The Day of Sorting Out is the appointed time for them all.

41. The Day when no friend will avail a friend in any way, and they will not be helped.

42. Except for him upon whom Allah has mercy. He is the Mighty, the Merciful.

43. The Tree of Bitterness.

44. The food of the sinner.

45. Like molten lead; boiling inside the bellies.

46. Like the boiling of seething water.

47. Seize him and drag him into the midst of Hell!

48. Then pour over his head the suffering of the Inferno!

49. Taste! You who were powerful and noble.

50. This is what you used to doubt.

51. As for the righteous, they will be in a secure place.

52. Amidst gardens and springs.

53. Dressed in silk and brocade, facing one another.

54. So it is, and We will wed them to lovely companions.

55. They will call therein for every kind of fruit, in peace and security.

56. Therein they will not taste death, beyond the first death; and He will protect them from the torment of Hell.

57. A favor from your Lord. That is the supreme salvation.

58. We made it easy in your language, so that they may remember.

59. So wait and watch. They too are waiting and watching.

45. KNEELING
(al-Jathiyah)

In the name of Allah,

45. KNEELING (al-Jathiyah)

the Gracious, the Merciful

1. Ha, Meem.

2. The revelation of the Book is from Allah, the Exalted in Might, the Wise.

3. In the heavens and the earth are proofs for the believers.

4. And in your own creation, and in the creatures He scattered, are signs for people of firm faith.

5. And in the alternation of night and day, and in the sustenance Allah sends down from the sky, with which He revives the earth after its death, and in the circulation of the winds, are marvels for people who reason.

6. These are Allah's Verses which We recite to you in truth. In which message, after Allah and His revelations, will they believe?

7. Woe to every sinful liar.

8. Who hears Allah's revelations being recited to him, yet he persists arrogantly, as though he did not hear them. Announce to him a painful punishment.

9. And when he learns something of Our revelations, he takes them in mockery. For such there is a shameful punishment.

10. Beyond them lies Hell. What they have earned will not benefit them at all, nor will those they adopted as lords instead of Allah. They will have a terrible punishment.

11. This is guidance. Those who blaspheme their Lord's revelations will have a punishment of agonizing pain.

12. It is Allah who placed the sea at your service, so that ships may run through it by His command, and that you may seek of His bounty, and that you may give thanks.

13. And He placed at your service whatever is in the heavens and whatever is on earth—all is from Him. In that are signs for a people who think.

14. Tell those who believe to forgive those who do not hope for the Days of Allah. He will fully recompense people for whatever they have earned.

15. Whoever does a good deed, it is for his soul; and whoever commits evil, it is against it; then to your Lord you will be returned.

16. We gave the Children of Israel the Book, and wisdom, and prophecy; and We provided them with the good things; and We gave them advantage over all other people.

17. And We gave them precise rulings. They fell into dispute only after knowledge came to them, out of mutual rivalry. Your Lord will judge between them on the Day of Resurrection regarding the things they differed about.

18. Then We set you upon a pathway of faith, so follow it, and do not follow the inclinations of those who do not know.

19. They will not help you against Allah in any way. The wrongdoers are allies of one another, while Allah is the Protector of the righteous.

20. This is an illumination for mankind, and guidance, and mercy for people who believe with certainty.

21. Do those who perpetrate the evil deeds assume that We will regard them as equal to those who believe and do righteous deeds, whether in their life or their death? Evil is their judgment!

22. Allah created the heavens and the earth with justice, so that every soul will be repaid for what it has earned. And they will not be wronged.

23. Have you considered him who has taken his desire for his god? Allah has knowingly led him astray, and has sealed his hearing and his heart, and has placed a veil over his vision. Who will guide him after Allah? Will you not reflect?

24. And they say, "There is nothing but this our present life; we die and we live, and nothing destroys us except time." But they have no knowledge of that; they are only guessing.

46. THE DUNES (al-Ahqaf)

25. When Our clarifying Verses are recited to them, their only argument is to say, "Bring back our ancestors, if you are truthful."

26. Say, "Allah gives you life, then He makes you die; then He gathers you for the Day of Resurrection, about which there is no doubt. But most people do not know."

27. To Allah belongs the kingship of the heavens and the earth. On the Day when the Hour takes place, on that Day the falsifiers will lose.

28. You will see every community on its knees; every community will be called to its Book: "Today you are being repaid for what you used to do.

29. This Book of Ours speaks about you in truth. We have been transcribing what you have been doing."

30. As for those who believed and did righteous deeds, their Lord will admit them into His mercy. That is the clear triumph.

31. But as for those who disbelieved: "Were My revelations not recited to you? But you turned arrogant, and were guilty people."

32. And when it was said, "The promise of Allah is true, and of the Hour there is no doubt," you said, "We do not know what the Hour is; we think it is only speculation; we are not convinced."

33. The evils of what they did will become evident to them, and the very thing they ridiculed will haunt them.

34. And it will be said, "Today We forget you, as you forgot the encounter of this Day of yours. Your abode is the Fire, and there are no saviors for you.

35. That is because you took Allah's revelations for a joke, and the worldly life lured you." So today they will not be brought out of it, and they will not be allowed to repent.

36. Praise belongs to Allah; Lord of the heavens, Lord of the earth, Lord of humanity.

37. To Him belongs all supremacy in the heavens and the earth. He is the Majestic, the Wise.

46. THE DUNES
(al-Ahqaf)

*In the name of Allah,
the Gracious, the Merciful*

1. Ha, Meem.

2. The sending down of the Scripture is from Allah, the Honorable, the Wise.

3. We did not create the heavens and the earth and what lies between them except with reason, and for a finite period. But the blasphemers continue to ignore the warnings they receive.

4. Say, "Have you considered those you worship instead of Allah? Show me which portion of the earth they have created. Or do they own a share of the heavens? Bring me a scripture prior to this one, or some trace of knowledge, if you are truthful."

5. Who is more wrong than him who invokes, besides Allah, those who will not answer him until the Day of Resurrection, and are heedless of their prayers?

6. And when humanity is gathered, they will be enemies to them, and will renounce their worship of them.

7. When Our revelations are recited to them, plain and clear, those who disbelieve say of the truth when it has come to them, "This is obviously magic."

8. Or do they say, "He invented it himself"? Say, "If I invented it myself, there is nothing you can do to protect me from Allah. He knows well what you are engaged in. He is sufficient witness between me and you. He is the Forgiver, the Merciful."

9. Say, "I am not different from the other messengers; and I do not know what will be done with me, or with you. I only follow what is inspired in me, and I am only a clear warner."

10. Say, "Have you considered? What if it is from Allah and you disbelieve in it? A witness from the Children of Israel testified to its like,

46. THE DUNES (al-Ahqaf)

and has believed, while you turned arrogant. Allah does not guide the unjust people."

11. Those who disbelieve say to those who believe, "If it were anything good, they would not have preceded us to it." And since they were not guided by it, they will say, "This is an ancient lie."

12. And before it was the Book of Moses, a model and a mercy. And this is a confirming Book, in the Arabic language, to warn those who do wrong—and good news for the doers of good.

13. Those who say, "Our Lord is Allah," then lead a righteous life—they have nothing to fear, nor shall they grieve.

14. These are the inhabitants of Paradise, where they will dwell forever—a reward for what they used to do.

15. We have enjoined upon man kindness to his parents. His mother carried him with difficulty, and delivered him with difficulty. His bearing and weaning takes thirty months. Until, when he has attained his maturity, and has reached forty years, he says, "Lord, enable me to appreciate the blessings You have bestowed upon me and upon my parents, and to act with righteousness, pleasing You. And improve my children for me. I have sincerely repented to You, and I am of those who have surrendered."

16. Those are they from whom We accept the best of their deeds, and We overlook their misdeeds, among the dwellers of Paradise—the promise of truth which they are promised.

17. As for him who says to his parents, "Enough of you! Are you promising me that I will be raised up, when generations have passed away before me?" While they cry for Allah's help, "Woe to you! Believe! The promise of Allah is true!" But he says, "These are nothing but tales of the ancients."

18. Those are they upon whom the sentence is justified, among the communities that have passed away before them, of jinn and humans. They are truly losers.

19. There are degrees for everyone, according to what they have done, and He will repay them for their works in full, and they will not be wronged.

20. On the Day when the faithless will be paraded before the Fire: "You have squandered your good in your worldly life, and you took pleasure in them. So today you are being repaid with the torment of shame, because of your unjust arrogance on earth, and because you used to sin."

21. And mention the brother of Aad, as he warned his people at the dunes. Warnings have passed away before him, and after him: "Worship none but Allah; I fear for you the punishment of a tremendous Day."

22. They said, "Did you come to us to divert us from our gods? Then bring us what you threaten us with, if you are being truthful."

23. He said, "The knowledge is only with Allah, and I inform you of what I was sent with; but I see you are an ignorant people."

24. Then, when they saw a cloud approaching their valley, they said, "This is a cloud that will bring us rain." "In fact, it is what you were impatient for: a wind in which is grievous suffering."

25. It will destroy everything by the command of its Lord. And when the morning came upon them, there was nothing to be seen except their dwellings. Thus We requite the guilty people.

26. We had empowered them in the same way as We empowered you; and We gave them the hearing, and the sight, and the minds. But neither their hearing, nor their sight, nor their minds availed them in any way. That is because they disregarded the revelations of Allah; and so they became surrounded by what they used to ridicule.

27. We have destroyed many townships around you, and diversified the signs, so that they may return.

28. Why then did the idols, whom they worshiped as means of nearness to Allah, not help them? In fact, they abandoned them. It

was their lie, a fabrication of their own making.

29. Recall when We dispatched towards you a number of jinn, to listen to the Quran. When they came in its presence, they said, "Pay attention!" Then, when it was concluded, they rushed to their people, warning them.

30. They said, "O our people, we have heard a Scripture, sent down after Moses, confirming what came before it. It guides to the truth, and to a straight path.

31. O our people! Answer the caller to Allah, and believe in Him; and He will forgive you your sins, and will save you from a painful punishment."

32. He who does not answer the caller to Allah will not escape on earth, and has no protectors besides Him. Those are in obvious error.

33. Do they not realize that Allah, who created the heavens and the earth, and was never tired by creating them, is Able to revive the dead? Yes indeed; He is Capable of everything.

34. On the Day when those who disbelieved are presented to the Fire: "Is this not real?" They will say, "Yes, indeed, by our Lord." He will say, "Then taste the suffering for having disbelieved."

35. So be patient, as the messengers with resolve were patient, and do not be hasty regarding them. On the Day when they witness what they are promised, it will seem as if they had lasted only for an hour of a day. A proclamation: Will any be destroyed except the sinful people?

47. MUHAMMAD
(Muhammad)

*In the name of Allah,
the Gracious, the Merciful*

1. Those who disbelieve and repel from the path of Allah—He nullifies their works.

2. While those who believe, and work righteousness, and believe in what was sent down to Muhammad—and it is the truth from their Lord—He remits their sins, and relieves their concerns.

3. That is because those who disbelieve follow falsehoods, while those who believe follow the truth from their Lord. Allah thus cites for the people their examples.

4. When you encounter those who disbelieve, strike at their necks. Then, when you have routed them, bind them firmly. Then, either release them by grace, or by ransom, until war lays down its burdens. Had Allah willed, He could have defeated them Himself, but He thus tests some of you by means of others. As for those who are killed in the way of Allah, He will not let their deeds go to waste.

5. He will guide them, and will improve their state of mind.

6. And will admit them into Paradise, which He has identified for them.

7. O you who believe! If you support Allah, He will support you, and will strengthen your foothold.

8. But as for those who disbelieve, for them is perdition, and He will waste their deeds.

9. That is because they hated what Allah revealed, so He nullified their deeds.

10. Have they not journeyed through the earth and seen the consequences for those before them? Allah poured destruction upon them, and for the unbelievers is something comparable.

11. That is because Allah is the Master of those who believe, while the disbelievers have no master.

12. Allah will admit those who believe and do good deeds into gardens beneath which rivers flow. As for those who disbelieve, they enjoy themselves, and eat as cattle eat, and the Fire will be their dwelling.

13. How many a town was more powerful than your town which evicted you? We destroyed them, and there was no helper for them.

14. Is he who stands upon evidence from his Lord, like someone whose evil deed is made

47. MUHAMMAD (Muhammad)

to appear good to him? And they follow their own desires?

15. The likeness of the Garden promised to the righteous: in it are rivers of pure water, and rivers of milk forever fresh, and rivers of wine delightful to the drinkers, and rivers of strained honey. And therein they will have of every fruit, and forgiveness from their Lord. Like one abiding in the Fire forever, and are given to drink boiling water, that cuts-up their bowels?

16. Among them are those who listen to you, but when they leave your presence, they say to those given knowledge, "What did he say just now?" Those are they whose hearts Allah has sealed, and they follow their own desires.

17. As for those who are guided, He increases them in guidance, and He has granted them their righteousness.

18. Are they just waiting until the Hour comes to them suddenly? Its tokens have already come. But how will they be reminded when it has come to them?

19. Know that there is no god but Allah, and ask forgiveness for your sin, and for the believing men and believing women. Allah knows your movements, and your resting-place.

20. Those who believe say, "If only a chapter is sent down." Yet when a decisive chapter is sent down, and fighting is mentioned in it, you see those in whose hearts is sickness looking at you with the look of someone fainting at death. So woe to them!

21. Obedience and upright speech. Then, when the matter is settled, being true to Allah would have been better for them.

22. If you turn away, you are likely to make mischief on earth, and sever your family ties.

23. Those are they whom Allah has cursed. He made them deaf, and blinded their sight.

24. Will they not ponder the Quran? Or are there locks upon their hearts?

25. Those who reverted after the guidance became clear to them—Satan has enticed them, and has given them latitude.

26. That is because they said to those who hated what Allah has revealed, "We will obey you in certain matters." But Allah knows their secret thoughts.

27. How about when the angels take them at death, beating their faces and their backs?

28. That is because they pursued what displeases Allah, and they disliked His approval, so He nullified their works.

29. Do those in whose hearts is sickness think that Allah will not expose their malice?

30. Had We willed, We could have shown them to you, and you would have recognized them by their marks. Yet you will recognize them by their tone of speech. And Allah knows your actions.

31. We will certainly test you, until We know those among you who strive, and those who are steadfast, and We will test your reactions.

32. Those who disbelieve, and hinder from the path of Allah, and oppose the Messenger after guidance has become clear to them—they will not hurt Allah in the least, but He will nullify their deeds.

33. O you who believe! Obey Allah, and obey the Messenger, and do not let your deeds go to waste.

34. Those who disbelieve, and hinder from Allah's path, and then die as disbelievers—Allah will not forgive them.

35. So do not waver and call for peace while you have the upper hand. Allah is with you, and He will not waste your efforts.

36. The life of this world is nothing but play and pastime. But if you have faith and lead a righteous life, He will grant you your rewards, and He will not ask you for your possessions.

37. Were He to ask you for it, and press you, you would become tightfisted, and He would expose your unwillingness.

38. Here you are, being called to spend in the cause of Allah. Among you are those who withhold; but whoever withholds is withholding against his own soul. Allah is the Rich, while you are the needy. And if you turn away, He will replace you with another people, and they will not be like you.

48. VICTORY
(al-Fath)

*In the name of Allah,
the Gracious, the Merciful*

1. We have granted you a conspicuous victory.

2. That Allah may forgive you your sin, past and to come, and complete His favors upon you, and guide you in a straight path.

3. And help you with an unwavering support.

4. It is He who sent down tranquility into the hearts of the believers, to add faith to their faith. To Allah belong the forces of the heavens and the earth. Allah is Knowing and Wise.

5. He will admit the believers, male and female, into Gardens beneath which rivers flow, to abide therein forever, and He will remit their sins. That, with Allah, is a great triumph.

6. And He will punish the hypocrites, male and female, and the idolaters, male and female, those who harbor evil thoughts about Allah. They are surrounded by evil; and Allah is angry with them, and has cursed them, and has prepared for them Hell—a miserable destination.

7. To Allah belong the troops of the heavens and the earth. Allah is Mighty and Wise.

8. We sent you as a witness, and a bearer of good news, and a warner.

9. That you may believe in Allah and His Messenger, and support Him, and honor Him, and praise Him morning and evening.

10. Those who pledge allegiance to you are pledging allegiance to Allah. The hand of Allah is over their hands. Whoever breaks his pledge breaks it to his own loss. And whoever fulfills his covenant with Allah, He will grant him a great reward.

11. The Desert-Arabs who remained behind will say to you, "Our belongings and our families have preoccupied us, so ask forgiveness for us." They say with their tongues what is not in their hearts. Say, "Who can avail you anything against Allah, if He desires loss for you, or desires gain for you?" In fact, Allah is Informed of what you do.

12. But you thought that the Messenger and the believers will never return to their families, and this seemed fine to your hearts; and you harbored evil thoughts, and were uncivilized people.

13. He who does not believe in Allah and His Messenger—We have prepared for the disbelievers a Blazing Fire.

14. To Allah belongs the kingdom of the heavens and the earth. He forgives whomever He wills, and He punishes whomever He wills. Allah is Forgiving and Merciful.

15. Those who lagged behind will say when you depart to collect the gains, "Let us follow you." They want to change the Word of Allah. Say, "You will not follow us; Allah has said so before." Then they will say, "But you are jealous of us." In fact, they understand only a little.

16. Say to the Desert-Arabs who lagged behind, "You will be called against a people of great might; you will fight them, unless they submit. If you obey, Allah will give you a fine reward. But if you turn away, as you turned away before, He will punish you with a painful punishment."

17. There is no blame on the blind, nor any blame on the lame, nor any blame on the sick. Whoever obeys Allah and His Messenger—He will admit him into gardens beneath which rivers flow; but whoever turns away—He will punish him with a painful punishment.

18. Allah was pleased with the believers, when they pledged allegiance to you under the tree.

He knew what was in their hearts, and sent down serenity upon them, and rewarded them with an imminent conquest.

19. And abundant gains for them to capture. Allah is Mighty and Wise.

20. Allah has promised you abundant gains, which you will capture. He has expedited this for you, and has restrained people's hands from you; that it may be a sign to the believers, and that He may guide you on a straight path.

21. And other things, of which you were incapable, but Allah has encompassed them. Allah is Capable of everything.

22. If those who disbelieve had fought you, they would have turned back and fled, then found neither protector nor helper.

23. It is Allah's pattern, ongoing since the past. You will never find any change in Allah's pattern.

24. It is He who withheld their hands from you, and your hands from them, in the valley of Mecca, after giving you advantage over them. Allah is Observer of what you do.

25. It is they who disbelieved, and barred you from the Sacred Mosque, and prevented the offering from reaching its destination. Were it not for faithful men and faithful women, whom you did not know, you were about to hurt them, and became guilty of an unintentional crime. Thus Allah admits into His mercy whomever He wills. Had they dispersed, We would have punished those who disbelieved among them with a painful penalty.

26. Those who disbelieved filled their hearts with rage—the rage of the days of ignorance. But Allah sent His serenity down upon His Messenger, and upon the believers, and imposed on them the words of righteousness—of which they were most worthy and deserving. Allah is aware of everything.

27. Allah has fulfilled His Messenger's vision in truth: "You will enter the Sacred Mosque, Allah willing, in security, heads shaven, or hair cut short, not fearing. He knew what you did not know, and has granted besides that an imminent victory."

28. It is He who sent His Messenger with the guidance and the religion of truth, to make it prevail over all religions. Allah suffices as Witness.

29. Muhammad is the Messenger of Allah. Those with him are stern against the disbelievers, yet compassionate amongst themselves. You see them kneeling, prostrating, seeking blessings from Allah and approval. Their marks are on their faces from the effects of prostration. Such is their description in the Torah, and their description in the Gospel: like a plant that sprouts, becomes strong, grows thick, and rests on its stem, impressing the farmers. Through them He enrages the disbelievers. Allah has promised those among them who believe and do good deeds forgiveness and a great reward.

49. THE CHAMBERS
(al-Hujurat)

*In the name of Allah,
the Gracious, the Merciful*

1. O you who believe! Do not place your opinions above that of Allah and His Messenger, and fear Allah. Allah is Hearing and Knowing.

2. O you who believe! Do not raise your voices above the voice of the Prophet, and do not speak loudly to him, as you speak loudly to one another, lest your works be in vain without you realizing.

3. Those who lower their voices before Allah's Messenger—those are they whose hearts Allah has tested for piety. They will have forgiveness and a great reward.

4. Those who call you from behind the chambers—most of them do not understand.

5. Had they remained patient until you came out to them, it would have been better for them. But Allah is Forgiving and Merciful.

6. O you who believe! If a troublemaker brings you any news, investigate, lest you harm people out of ignorance, and you become regretful for what you have done.

7. And know that among you is the Messenger of Allah. Had he obeyed you in many things, you would have suffered hardship. But Allah has given you the love of faith, and adorned it in your hearts, and made disbelief, mischief, and rebellion hateful to you. These are the rightly guided.

8. A Grace and Favor from Allah. Allah is Knowing and Wise.

9. If two groups of believers fight each other, reconcile between them. But if one group aggresses against the other, fight the aggressing group until it complies with Allah's command. Once it has complied, reconcile between them with justice, and be equitable. Allah loves the equitable.

10. The believers are brothers, so reconcile between your brothers, and remain conscious of Allah, so that you may receive mercy.

11. O you who believe! No people shall ridicule other people, for they may be better than they. Nor shall any women ridicule other women, for they may be better than they. Nor shall you slander one another, nor shall you insult one another with names. Evil is the return to wickedness after having attained faith. Whoever does not repent—these are the wrongdoers.

12. O you who believe! Avoid most suspicion—some suspicion is sinful. And do not spy on one another, nor backbite one another. Would any of you like to eat the flesh of his dead brother? You would detest it. So remain mindful of Allah. Allah is Most Relenting, Most Merciful.

13. O people! We created you from a male and a female, and made you races and tribes, that you may know one another. The best among you in the sight of Allah is the most righteous. Allah is All-Knowing, Well-Experienced.

14. The Desert-Arabs say, "We have believed." Say, "You have not believed; but say, 'We have submitted,' for faith has not yet entered into your hearts. But if you obey Allah and His Messenger, He will not diminish any of your deeds. Allah is Forgiving and Merciful."

15. The believers are those who believe in Allah and His Messenger, and then have not doubted, and strive for Allah's cause with their wealth and their persons. These are the sincere.

16. Say, "Are you going to teach Allah about your religion, when Allah knows everything in the heavens and the earth, and Allah is aware of all things?"

17. They regarded it a favor to you that they have submitted. Say, "Do not consider your submission a favor to me; it is Allah who has done you a favor by guiding you to the faith, if you are sincere."

18. Allah knows the secrets of the heavens and the earth, and Allah is seeing of everything you do.

50. QAF
(Qaf)

*In the name of Allah,
the Gracious, the Merciful*

1. Qaf. By the Glorious Quran.

2. They marveled that a warner has come to them from among them. The disbelievers say, "This is something strange.

3. When we have died and become dust? This is a farfetched return."

4. We know what the earth consumes of them, and with Us is a comprehensive book.

5. But they denied the truth when it has come to them, so they are in a confused state.

6. Have they not observed the sky above them, how We constructed it, and decorated it, and it has no cracks?

7. And the earth, how We spread it out, and set on it mountains, and grew in it all kinds of delightful pairs?

50. QAF (Qaf)

8. A lesson and a reminder for every penitent worshiper.

9. And We brought down from the sky blessed water, and produced with it gardens and grain to harvest.

10. And the soaring palm trees, with clustered dates.

11. As sustenance for the servants. And We revive thereby a dead town. Likewise is the resurrection.

12. Before them the people of Noah denied the truth, and so did the dwellers of Russ, and Thamood.

13. And Aad, and Pharaoh, and the brethren of Lot.

14. And the Dwellers of the Woods, and the people of Tubba. They all rejected the messengers, so My threat came true.

15. Were We fatigued by the first creation? But they are in doubt of a new creation.

16. We created the human being, and We know what his soul whispers to him. We are nearer to him than his jugular vein.

17. As the two receivers receive, seated to the right and to the left.

18. Not a word does he utter, but there is a watcher by him, ready.

19. The daze of death has come in truth: "This is what you tried to evade."

20. And the Trumpet is blown: "This is the Promised Day."

21. And every soul will come forward, accompanied by a driver and a witness.

22. "You were in neglect of this, so We lifted your screen from you, and your vision today is keen."

23. And His escort will say, "This is what I have ready with me."

24. "Throw into Hell every stubborn disbeliever.

25. Preventer of good, aggressor, doubter.

26. Who fabricated another god with Allah; toss him into the intense agony."

27. His escort will say, "Our Lord, I did not make him rebel, but he was far astray."

28. He will say, "Do not feud in My presence—I had warned you in advance.

29. The decree from Me will not be changed, and I am not unjust to the servants."

30. On the Day when We will say to Hell, "Are you full?" And it will say, "Are there any more?"

31. And Paradise will be brought closer to the pious, not far away.

32. "This is what you were promised—for every careful penitent.

33. Who inwardly feared the Most Gracious, and came with a repentant heart.

34. Enter it in peace. This is the Day of Eternity."

35. Therein they will have whatever they desire—and We have even more.

36. How many generations before them, who were more powerful than they, did We destroy? They explored the lands—was there any escape?

37. In that is a reminder for whoever possesses a heart, or cares to listen and witness.

38. We created the heavens and the earth and what is between them in six days, and no fatigue touched Us.

39. So endure what they say, and proclaim the praises of your Lord before the rising of the sun, and before sunset.

40. And glorify Him during the night, and at the end of devotions.

41. And listen for the Day when the caller calls from a nearby place.

42. The Day when they will hear the Shout in all truth. That is the Day of Emergence.

43. It is We who control life and death, and to Us is the destination.

44. The Day when the earth will crack for them at once. That is an easy gathering for Us.

51. THE SPREADERS (adh-Dhariyat)

45. We are fully aware of what they say, and you are not a dictator over them. So remind by the Quran whoever fears My warning.

51. THE SPREADERS
(adh-Dhariyat)

*In the name of Allah,
the Gracious, the Merciful*

1. By the spreaders spreading.

2. And those carrying loads.

3. And those moving gently.

4. And those distributing as commanded.

5. What you are promised is true.

6. Judgment will take place.

7. By the sky that is woven.

8. You differ in what you say.

9. Averted from it is he who is averted.

10. Perish the imposters.

11. Those who are dazed in ignorance.

12. They ask, "When is the Day of Judgment?"

13. The Day they are presented to the Fire.

14. "Taste your ordeal. This is what you used to challenge."

15. But the pious are amidst gardens and springs.

16. Receiving what their Lord has given them. They were virtuous before that.

17. They used to sleep a little at night.

18. And at dawn, they would pray for pardon.

19. And in their wealth, there was a share for the beggar and the deprived.

20. And on earth are signs for the convinced.

21. And within yourselves. Do you not see?

22. And in the heaven is your livelihood, and what you are promised.

23. By the Lord of the heaven and the earth, it is as true as the fact that you speak.

24. Has the story of Abraham's honorable guests reached you?

25. When they entered upon him, they said, "Peace." He said, "Peace, strangers."

26. Then he slipped away to his family, and brought a fatted calf.

27. He set it before them. He said, "Will you not eat?"

28. And he harbored fear of them. They said, "Do not fear," and they announced to him the good news of a knowledgeable boy.

29. His wife came forward crying. She clasped her face, and said, "A barren old woman?"

30. They said, "Thus spoke your Lord. He is the Wise, the Knowing."

31. He said, "What is your business, O envoys?"

32. They said, "We are sent to a people guilty of sin."

33. "To unleash upon them rocks of clay."

34. "Marked by your Lord for the excessive."

35. We evacuated all the believers who were in it.

36. But found in it only one household of Muslims.

37. And We left in it a sign for those who fear the painful punishment.

38. And in Moses. We sent him to Pharaoh with a clear authority.

39. But he turned away with his warlords, and said, "A sorcerer or a madman."

40. So We seized him and his troops, and threw them into the sea, and He was to blame.

41. And in Aad. We unleashed against them the devastating wind.

42. It spared nothing it came upon, but rendered it like decayed ruins.

43. And in Thamood. They were told, "Enjoy yourselves for a while."

52. THE MOUNT (at-Tur)

44. But they defied the command of their Lord, so the lightning struck them as they looked on.

45. They could not rise up, nor could they find help.

46. And before that, the people of Noah. They were immoral people.

47. We constructed the universe with power, and We are expanding it.

48. And the earth—We spread it out—How well We prepared it!

49. We created all things in pairs, so that you may reflect and ponder.

50. "So flee towards Allah. I am to you from Him a clear warner."

51. "And do not set up any other god with Allah. I am to you from Him a clear warner."

52. Likewise, no messenger came to those before them, but they said, "A sorcerer or a madman."

53. Did they recommend it to one another? In fact, they are rebellious people.

54. So turn away from them; you are not to blame.

55. And remind, for the reminder benefits the believers.

56. I did not create the jinn and the humans except to worship Me.

57. I need no livelihood from them, nor do I need them to feed Me.

58. Allah is the Provider, the One with Power, the Strong.

59. Those who do wrong will have their turn, like the turn of their counterparts, so let them not rush Me.

60. So woe to those who disbelieve because of that Day of theirs which they are promised.

52. THE MOUNT (at-Tur)

In the name of Allah, the Gracious, the Merciful

1. By the Mount.

2. And a Book inscribed.

3. In a published scroll.

4. And the frequented House.

5. And the elevated roof.

6. And the seething sea.

7. The punishment of your Lord is coming.

8. There is nothing to avert it.

9. On the Day when the heaven sways in agitation.

10. And the mountains go into motion.

11. Woe on that Day to the deniers.

12. Those who play with speculation.

13. The Day when they are shoved into the Fire of Hell forcefully.

14. "This is the Fire which you used to deny.

15. Is this magic, or do you not see?

16. Burn in it. Whether you are patient, or impatient, it is the same for you. You are only being repaid for what you used to do."

17. But the righteous will be amid gardens and bliss.

18. Enjoying what their Lord has given them, and their Lord has spared them the suffering of Hell.

19. Eat and drink happily, for what you used to do.

20. Relaxing on luxurious furnishings; and We will couple them with gorgeous spouses.

21. Those who believed, and their offspring followed them in faith—We will unite them with their offspring, and We will not deprive them of any of their works. Every person is hostage to what he has earned.

22. And We will supply them with fruit, and meat; such as they desire.

23. They will exchange therein a cup; wherein is neither harm, nor sin.

24. Serving them will be youths like hidden pearls.

25. And they will approach one another, inquiring.

26. They will say, "Before this, we were fearful for our families.

27. But Allah blessed us, and spared us the agony of the Fiery Winds.

28. Before this, we used to pray to Him. He is the Good, the Compassionate."

29. So remind. By the grace of your Lord, you are neither a soothsayer, nor a madman.

30. Or do they say, "A poet—we await for him a calamity of time"?

31. Say, "Go on waiting; I will be waiting with you."

32. Or is it that their dreams compel them to this? Or are they aggressive people?

33. Or do they say, "He made it up"? Rather, they do not believe.

34. So let them produce a discourse like it, if they are truthful.

35. Or were they created out of nothing? Or are they the creators?

36. Or did they create the heavens and the earth? In fact, they are not certain.

37. Or do they possess the treasuries of your Lord? Or are they the controllers?

38. Or do they have a stairway by means of which they listen? Then let their listener produce a clear proof.

39. Or for Him the daughters, and for you the sons?

40. Or do you demand a payment from them, and they are burdened by debt?

41. Or do they know the future, and they are writing it down?

42. Or are they planning a conspiracy? The conspiracy will befall the disbelievers.

43. Or do they have a god besides Allah? Allah transcends what they associate.

44. Even if they were to see lumps of the sky falling down, they would say, "A mass of clouds."

45. So leave them until they meet their Day in which they will be stunned.

46. The Day when their ploys will avail them nothing; and they will not be helped.

47. For those who do wrong, there is a punishment besides that; but most of them do not know.

48. So patiently await the decision of your Lord, for you are before Our Eyes; and proclaim the praises of your Lord when you arise.

49. And glorify Him during the night, and at the receding of the stars.

53. THE STAR
(an-Najm)

In the name of Allah,
the Gracious, the Merciful

1. By the star as it goes down.

2. Your friend has not gone astray, nor has he erred.

3. Nor does he speak out of desire.

4. It is but a revelation revealed.

5. Taught to him by the Extremely Powerful.

6. The one of vigor. He settled.

7. While he was at the highest horizon.

8. Then he came near, and hovered around.

9. He was within two bows' length, or closer.

10. Then He revealed to His servant what He revealed.

11. The heart did not lie about what it saw.

12. Will you dispute with him concerning what he saw?

13. He saw him on another descent.

14. At the Lotus Tree of the Extremity.

15. Near which is the Garden of Repose.

16. As there covered the Lotus Tree what covered it.

17. The sight did not waver, nor did it exceed.

53. THE STAR (an-Najm)

18. He saw some of the Great Signs of his Lord.

19. Have you considered al-Lat and al-Uzza?

20. And Manat, the third one, the other?

21. Are you to have the males, and He the females?

22. What a bizarre distribution.

23. These are nothing but names, which you have devised, you and your ancestors, for which Allah sent down no authority. They follow nothing but assumptions, and what the ego desires, even though guidance has come to them from their Lord.

24. Or is the human being to have whatever he desires?

25. To Allah belong the Last and the First.

26. How many an angel is there in the heavens whose intercession avails nothing, except after Allah gives permission to whomever He wills, and approves?

27. Those who do not believe in the Hereafter give the angels the names of females.

28. They have no knowledge of that. They only follow assumptions, and assumptions are no substitute for the truth.

29. So avoid him who has turned away from Our remembrance, and desires nothing but the present life.

30. That is the extent of their knowledge. Your Lord knows best who has strayed from His path, and He knows best who has accepted guidance.

31. To Allah belongs whatever is in the heavens and whatever is on earth. He will repay those who do evil according to their deeds, and recompense those who do good with the best.

32. Those who avoid gross sins and indecencies—except for minor lapses—your Lord is of Vast Forgiveness. He knows you well, ever since He created you from the earth, and ever since you were embryos in your mothers' wombs. So do not acclaim your own virtue; He is fully aware of the righteous.

33. Have you considered him who turned away?

34. And gave a little, and held back?

35. Does he possess knowledge of the unseen, and can therefore foresee?

36. Or was he not informed of what is in the Scrolls of Moses?

37. And of Abraham, who fulfilled?

38. That no soul bears the burdens of another soul.

39. And that the human being attains only what he strives for.

40. And that his efforts will be witnessed.

41. Then he will be rewarded for it the fullest reward.

42. And that to your Lord is the finality.

43. And that it is He who causes laughter and weeping.

44. And that it is He who gives death and life.

45. And that it is He who created the two kinds—the male and the female.

46. From a sperm drop, when emitted.

47. And that upon Him is the next existence.

48. And that it is He who enriches and impoverishes.

49. And that it is He who is the Lord of Sirius.

50. And that it is He who destroyed the first Aad.

51. And Thamood, sparing no one.

52. And the people of Noah before that; for they were most unjust and most oppressive.

53. And He toppled the ruined cities.

54. And covered them with whatever covered them.

55. So which of your Lord's marvels can you deny?

56. This is a warning, just like the first warnings.

57. The inevitable is imminent.

58. None besides Allah can unveil it.

54. THE MOON (al-Qamar)

59. Do you marvel at this discourse?

60. And laugh, and do not weep?

61. Lost in your frivolity?

62. So bow down to Allah, and worship!

54. THE MOON (al-Qamar)

In the name of Allah, the Gracious, the Merciful

1. The Hour has drawn near, and the moon has split.

2. Yet whenever they see a miracle, they turn away, and say, "Continuous magic."

3. They lied, and followed their opinions, but everything has its time.

4. And there came to them news containing a deterrent.

5. Profound wisdom—but warnings are of no avail.

6. So turn away from them. On the Day when the Caller calls to something terrible.

7. Their eyes humiliated, they will emerge from the graves, as if they were swarming locusts.

8. Scrambling towards the Caller, the disbelievers will say, "This is a difficult Day."

9. Before them the people of Noah disbelieved. They rejected Our servant, and said, "Crazy," and he was rebuked.

10. So he appealed to his Lord, "I am overwhelmed, so help me."

11. So We opened the floodgates of heaven with water pouring down.

12. And We made the earth burst with springs, and the waters met for a purpose already destined.

13. And We carried him on a craft of planks and nails.

14. Sailing before Our eyes; a reward for him who was rejected.

15. And We left it as a sign. Is there anyone who would take heed?

16. So how were My punishment and My warnings?

17. We made the Quran easy to learn. Is there anyone who would learn?

18. Aad denied the truth. So how were My punishment and My warnings?

19. We unleashed upon them a screaming wind, on a day of unrelenting misery.

20. Plucking the people away, as though they were trunks of uprooted palm-trees.

21. So how were My punishment and My warnings?

22. We made the Quran easy to remember. Is there anyone who would remember?

23. Thamood rejected the warnings.

24. They said, "Are we to follow one of us, a human being? We would then go astray, and end up in Hell.

25. Was the message given to him, out of all of us? In fact, he is a wicked liar."

26. They will know tomorrow who the wicked liar is.

27. We are sending the she-camel as a test for them; so watch them and be patient.

28. And inform them that the water is to be shared between them; each share of drink made available.

29. But they called their friend, and he dared, and he slaughtered.

30. So how were My punishment and My warnings?

31. We sent against them a single Scream, and they became like crushed hay.

32. We made the Quran easy to understand. Is there anyone who would understand?

33. The people of Lot rejected the warnings.

34. We unleashed upon them a shower of stones, except for the family of Lot; We rescued them at dawn.

35. A blessing from Us. Thus We reward the thankful.

36. He had warned them of Our onslaught, but they dismissed the warnings.

37. They even lusted for his guest, so We obliterated their eyes. "So taste My punishment and My warnings."

38. Early morning brought upon them enduring punishment.

39. So taste My punishment and My warnings.

40. We made the Quran easy to memorize. Is there anyone who would memorize?

41. The warnings also came to the people of Pharaoh.

42. They rejected Our signs, all of them, so We seized them—the seizure of an Almighty Omnipotent.

43. Are your unbelievers better than all those? Or do you have immunity in the scriptures?

44. Or do they say, "We are united, and we will be victorious"?

45. The multitude will be defeated, and they will turn their backs.

46. The Hour is their appointed time—the Hour is more disastrous, and most bitter.

47. The wicked are in confusion and madness.

48. The Day when they are dragged upon their faces into the Fire: "Taste the touch of Saqar."

49. Everything We created is precisely measured.

50. And Our command is but once, like the twinkling of an eye.

51. We have destroyed your likes. Is there anyone who would ponder?

52. Everything they have done is in the Books.

53. Everything, small or large, is written down.

54. The righteous will be amidst gardens and rivers.

55. In an assembly of virtue, in the presence of an Omnipotent King.

55. THE COMPASSIONATE (ar-Rahman)

In the name of Allah, the Gracious, the Merciful

1. The Compassionate.

2. Has taught the Quran.

3. He created man.

4. And taught him clear expression.

5. The sun and the moon move according to plan.

6. And the stars and the trees prostrate themselves.

7. And the sky, He raised; and He set up the balance.

8. So do not transgress in the balance.

9. But maintain the weights with justice, and do not violate the balance.

10. And the earth; He set up for the creatures.

11. In it are fruits, and palms in clusters.

12. And grains in the blades, and fragrant plants.

13. So which of your Lord's marvels will you deny?

14. He created man from hard clay, like bricks.

15. And created the jinn from a fusion of fire.

16. So which of your Lord's marvels will you deny?

17. Lord of the two Easts and Lord of the two Wests.

18. So which of your Lord's marvels will you deny?

19. He merged the two seas, converging together.

20. Between them is a barrier, which they do not overrun.

21. So which of your Lord's marvels will you deny?

22. From them emerge pearls and coral.

55. THE COMPASSIONATE (ar-Rahman)

23. So which of your Lord's marvels will you deny?

24. His are the ships, raised above the sea like landmarks.

25. So which of your Lord's marvels will you deny?

26. Everyone upon it is perishing.

27. But will remain the Presence of your Lord, Full of Majesty and Splendor.

28. So which of your Lord's marvels will you deny?

29. Everyone in the heavens and the earth asks Him. Every day He is managing.

30. So which of your Lord's marvels will you deny?

31. We will attend to you, O prominent two.

32. So which of your Lord's marvels will you deny?

33. O society of jinn and humans! If you can pass through the bounds of the heavens and the earth, go ahead and pass. But you will not pass except with authorization.

34. So which of your Lord's marvels will you deny?

35. You will be bombarded with flares of fire and brass, and you will not succeed.

36. So which of your Lord's marvels will you deny?

37. When the sky splits apart, and becomes rose, like paint.

38. So which of your Lord's marvels will you deny?

39. On that Day, no human and no jinn will be asked about his sins.

40. So which of your Lord's marvels will you deny?

41. The guilty will be recognized by their marks; they will be taken by the forelocks and the feet.

42. So which of your Lord's marvels will you deny?

43. This is Hell that the guilty denied.

44. They circulate between it and between a seething bath.

45. So which of your Lord's marvels will you deny?

46. But for him who feared the standing of his Lord are two gardens.

47. So which of your Lord's marvels will you deny?

48. Full of varieties.

49. So which of your Lord's marvels will you deny?

50. In them are two flowing springs.

51. So which of your Lord's marvels will you deny?

52. In them are fruits of every kind, in pairs.

53. So which of your Lord's marvels will you deny?

54. Reclining on furnishings lined with brocade, and the fruits of the two gardens are near at hand.

55. So which of your Lord's marvels will you deny?

56. In them are maidens restraining their glances, untouched before by any man or jinn.

57. So which of your Lord's marvels will you deny?

58. As though they were rubies and corals.

59. So which of your Lord's marvels will you deny?

60. Is the reward of goodness anything but goodness?

61. So which of your Lord's marvels will you deny?

62. And beneath them are two gardens.

63. So which of your Lord's marvels will you deny?

64. Deep green.

65. So which of your Lord's marvels will you deny?

66. In them are two gushing springs.

56. THE INEVITABLE (al-Waqi'ah)

67. So which of your Lord's marvels will you deny?

68. In them are fruits, and date-palms, and pomegranates.

69. So which of your Lord's marvels will you deny?

70. In them are good and beautiful ones.

71. So which of your Lord's marvels will you deny?

72. Companions, secluded in the tents.

73. So which of your Lord's marvels will you deny?

74. Whom no human has touched before, nor jinn.

75. So which of your Lord's marvels will you deny?

76. Reclining on green cushions, and exquisite carpets.

77. So which of your Lord's marvels will you deny?

78. Blessed be the name of your Lord, Full of Majesty and Splendor.

56. THE INEVITABLE (al-Waqi'ah)

In the name of Allah, the Gracious, the Merciful

1. When the inevitable occurs.

2. Of its occurrence, there is no denial.

3. Bringing low, raising high.

4. When the earth is shaken with a shock.

5. And the mountains are crushed and crumbled.

6. And they become scattered dust.

7. And you become three classes.

8. Those on the Right—what of those on the Right?

9. And those on the Left—what of those on the Left?

10. And the forerunners, the forerunners.

11. Those are the nearest.

12. In the Gardens of Bliss.

13. A throng from the ancients.

14. And a small band from the latecomers.

15. On luxurious furnishings.

16. Reclining on them, facing one another.

17. Serving them will be immortalized youth.

18. With cups, pitchers, and sparkling drinks.

19. Causing them neither headache, nor intoxication.

20. And fruits of their choice.

21. And meat of birds that they may desire.

22. And lovely companions.

23. The likenesses of treasured pearls.

24. As a reward for what they used to do.

25. Therein they will hear no nonsense, and no accusations.

26. But only the greeting: "Peace, peace."

27. And those on the Right—what of those on the Right?

28. In lush orchards.

29. And sweet-smelling plants.

30. And extended shade.

31. And outpouring water.

32. And abundant fruit.

33. Neither withheld, nor forbidden.

34. And uplifted mattresses.

35. We have created them of special creation.

36. And made them virgins.

37. Tender and un-aging.

38. For those on the Right.

39. A throng from the ancients.

40. And a throng from the latecomers.

41. And those on the Left—what of those on the Left?

42. Amid searing wind and boiling water.

43. And a shadow of thick smoke.

56. THE INEVITABLE (al-Waqi'ah)

44. Neither cool, nor refreshing.

45. They had lived before that in luxury.

46. And they used to persist in immense wrongdoing.

47. And they used to say, "When we are dead and turned into dust and bones, are we to be resurrected?

48. And our ancient ancestors too?"

49. Say, "The first and the last.

50. Will be gathered for the appointment of a familiar Day."

51. Then you, you misguided, who deny the truth.

52. Will be eating from the Tree of Bitterness.

53. Will be filling your bellies with it.

54. Will be drinking on top of it boiling water.

55. Drinking like thirsty camels drink.

56. That is their hospitality on the Day of Retribution.

57. We created you—if only you would believe!

58. Have you seen what you ejaculate?

59. Is it you who create it, or are We the Creator?

60. We have decreed death among you, and We will not be outstripped.

61. In replacing you with your likes, and transforming you into what you do not know.

62. You have known the first formation; if only you would remember.

63. Have you seen what you cultivate?

64. Is it you who make it grow, or are We the Grower?

65. If We will, We can turn it into rubble; then you will lament.

66. "We are penalized.

67. No, we are being deprived."

68. Have you seen the water you drink?

69. Is it you who sent it down from the clouds, or are We the Sender?

70. If We will, We can make it salty. Will you not be thankful?

71. Have you seen the fire you kindle?

72. Is it you who produce its tree, or are We the Producer?

73. We have made it a reminder, and a comfort for the users.

74. So glorify the Name of your Great Lord.

75. I swear by the locations of the stars.

76. It is an oath, if you only knew, that is tremendous.

77. It is a noble Quran.

78. In a well-protected Book.

79. None can grasp it except the purified.

80. A revelation from the Lord of the Worlds.

81. Is it this discourse that you take so lightly?

82. And you make it your livelihood to deny it?

83. So when it has reached the throat.

84. As you are looking on.

85. We are nearer to it than you are, but you do not see.

86. If you are not held to account.

87. Then bring it back, if you are truthful.

88. But if he is one of those brought near.

89. Then happiness, and flowers, and Garden of Delights.

90. And if he is one of those on the Right.

91. Then, "Peace upon you," from those on the Right.

92. But if he is one of the deniers, the mistaken.

93. Then a welcome of Inferno.

94. And burning in Hell.

95. This is the certain truth.

96. So glorify the Name of your Lord, the Magnificent.

57. IRON
(al-Hadid')

*In the name of Allah,
the Gracious, the Merciful*

1. Glorifying Allah is everything in the heavens and the earth. He is the Almighty, the Wise.

2. To Him belongs the kingdom of the heavens and the earth. He gives life and causes death, and He has power over all things.

3. He is the First and the Last, and the Outer and the Inner, and He has knowledge of all things.

4. It is He who created the heavens and the earth in six days, then settled over the Throne. He knows what penetrates into the earth, and what comes out of it, and what descends from the sky, and what ascends to it. And He is with you wherever you may be. Allah is Seeing of everything you do.

5. To Him belongs the kingship of the heavens and the earth, and to Allah all matters are referred.

6. He merges the night into the day, and He merges the day into the night; and He knows what the hearts contains.

7. Believe in Allah and His Messenger, and spend from what He made you inherit. Those among you who believe and give will have a great reward.

8. What is the matter with you that you do not believe in Allah, when the Messenger calls you to believe in your Lord, and He has received a pledge from you, if you are believers?

9. It is He who sends down upon His servant clear revelations, to bring you out of darkness into the light. Allah is Gentle towards you, Most Compassionate.

10. And why is it that you do not spend in the cause of Allah, when to Allah belongs the inheritance of the heavens and the earth? Not equal among you are those who contributed before the conquest, and fought. Those are higher in rank than those who contributed afterwards, and fought. But Allah promises both a good reward. Allah is Well Experienced in what you do.

11. Who is he who will lend Allah a loan of goodness, that He may double it for him, and will have a generous reward?

12. On the Day when you see the believing men and believing women—their light radiating ahead of them, and to their right: "Good news for you today: gardens beneath which rivers flow, dwelling therein forever. That is the great triumph."

13. On the Day when the hypocritical men and hypocritical women will say to those who believed, "Wait for us; let us absorb some of your light." It will be said, "Go back behind you, and seek light." A wall will be raised between them, in which is a door; within it is mercy, and outside it is agony.

14. They will call to them, "Were we not with you?" They will say, "Yes, but you cheated your souls, and waited, and doubted, and became deluded by wishful thinking, until the command of Allah arrived; and arrogance deceived you regarding Allah."

15. "Therefore, today no ransom will be accepted from you, nor from those who disbelieved. The Fire is your refuge. It is your companion—what an evil fate!"

16. Is it not time for those who believe to surrender their hearts to the remembrance of Allah, and to the truth that has come down, and not be like those who were given the Book previously, but time became prolonged for them, so their hearts hardened, and many of them are sinners?

17. Know that Allah revives the earth after its death. We thus explain the revelations for you, so that you may understand.

18. The charitable men and charitable women, who have loaned Allah a loan of righteousness—it will be multiplied for them, and for them is a generous reward.

19. Those who believe in Allah and His messengers—these are the sincere and the wit-

nesses with their Lord; they will have their reward and their light. But as for those who disbelieve and deny Our revelations—these are the inmates of the Blaze.

20. Know that the worldly life is only play, and distraction, and glitter, and boasting among you, and rivalry in wealth and children. It is like a rainfall that produces plants, and delights the disbelievers. But then it withers, and you see it yellowing, and then it becomes debris. While in the Hereafter there is severe agony, and forgiveness from Allah, and acceptance. The life of this world is nothing but enjoyment of vanity.

21. Race towards forgiveness from your Lord; and a Garden as vast as the heavens and the earth, prepared for those who believe in Allah and His messengers. That is the grace of Allah; He bestows it on whomever He wills. Allah is the Possessor of Immense Grace.

22. No calamity occurs on earth, or in your souls, but it is in a Book, even before We make it happen. That is easy for Allah.

23. That you may not sorrow over what eludes you, nor exult over what He has given you. Allah does not love the proud snob.

24. Those who are stingy, and induce people to be stingy. Whoever turns away—Allah is the Independent, the Praiseworthy.

25. We sent Our messengers with the clear proofs, and We sent down with them the Book and the Balance, that humanity may uphold justice. And We sent down iron, in which is violent force, and benefits for humanity. That Allah may know who supports Him and His messengers invisibly. Allah is Strong and Powerful.

26. We sent Noah and Abraham, and established in their line Prophethood and the Scripture. Some of them are guided, but many of them are sinners.

27. Then We sent in their wake Our messengers, and followed up with Jesus son of Mary, and We gave him the Gospel, and instilled in the hearts of those who followed him compassion and mercy. But as for the monasticism which they invented—We did not ordain it for them—only to seek Allah's approval. But they did not observe it with its due observance. So We gave those of them who believed their reward, but many of them are sinful.

28. O you who believe! Fear Allah, and believe in His Messenger: He will give you a double portion of His mercy, and will give you a light by which you walk, and will forgive you. Allah is Forgiving and Merciful.

29. That the People of the Book may know that they have no power whatsoever over Allah's grace, and that all grace is in Allah's hand; He gives it to whomever He wills. Allah is Possessor of Great Grace.

58. THE ARGUMENT (al-Mujadilah)

*In the name of Allah,
the Gracious, the Merciful*

1. Allah has heard the statement of she who argued with you concerning her husband, as she complained to Allah. Allah heard your conversation. Allah is Hearing and Seeing.

2. Those of you who estrange their wives by equating them with their mothers—they are not their mothers. Their mothers are none else but those who gave birth to them. What they say is evil, and a blatant lie. But Allah is Pardoning and Forgiving.

3. Those who estrange their wives by equating them with their mothers, then go back on what they said, must set free a slave before they may touch one another. To this you are exhorted, and Allah is well aware of what you do.

4. But whoever cannot find the means must fast for two consecutive months before they may touch one another. And if he is unable, then the feeding of sixty needy people. This, in order that you affirm your faith in Allah and His Messenger. These are the ordinances

58. THE ARGUMENT (al-Mujadilah)

of Allah. The unbelievers will have a painful punishment.

5. Those who oppose Allah and His Messenger will be subdued, as those before them were subdued. We have revealed clear messages. The unbelievers will have a demeaning punishment.

6. On the Day when Allah resurrects them all, and informs them of what they did. Allah has kept count of it, but they have forgotten it. Allah is Witness over everything.

7. Do you not realize that Allah knows everything in the heavens and everything on earth? There is no secret counsel between three, but He is their fourth; nor between five, but He is their sixth; nor less than that, nor more, but He is with them wherever they may be. Then, on the Day of Resurrection, He will inform them of what they did. Allah has knowledge of everything.

8. Have you noted those who were prohibited from conspiring secretly, but then reverted to what they were prohibited from? They conspire to commit sin, and aggression, and defiance of the Messenger. And when they come to you, they greet you with a greeting that Allah never greeted you with. And they say within themselves, "Why does Allah not punish us for what we say?" Hell is enough for them. They will roast in it. What a miserable destiny!

9. O you who believe! When you converse secretly, do not converse in sin, and aggression, and disobedience of the Messenger; but converse in virtue and piety; And fear Allah, to Whom you will be gathered.

10. Conspiracies are from Satan, that he may dishearten those who believe; but he will not harm them in the least, except by leave of Allah. So let the believers put their trust in Allah.

11. O you who believe! When you are told to make room in your gatherings, make room; Allah will make room for you. And when you are told to disperse, disperse. Allah elevates those among you who believe, and those given knowledge, many steps. Allah is Aware of what you do.

12. O you who believe! When you converse privately with the Messenger, offer something in charity before your conversation. That is better for you, and purer. But if you do not find the means—Allah is Forgiving and Merciful.

13. Are you reluctant to offer charity before your conversation? If you do not do so, and Allah pardons you, then perform the prayer, and give alms, and obey Allah and His Messenger. Allah is Aware of what you do.

14. Have you considered those who befriended a people with whom Allah has become angry? They are not of you, nor of them. And they swear to a lie while they know.

15. Allah has prepared for them a terrible punishment. Evil is what they used to do.

16. They took their oaths as a screen, and prevented others from Allah's path. They will have a shameful punishment.

17. Neither their possessions nor their children will avail them anything against Allah. These are the inhabitants of the Fire, dwelling therein forever.

18. On the Day when Allah will resurrect them altogether—they will swear to Him, as they swear to you, thinking that they are upon something. Indeed, they themselves are the liars.

19. Satan has taken hold of them, and so has caused them to forget the remembrance of Allah. These are the partisans of Satan. Indeed, it is Satan's partisans who are the losers.

20. Those who oppose Allah and His Messenger are among the lowliest.

21. Allah has written: "I will certainly prevail, I and My messengers." Allah is Strong and Mighty.

22. You will not find a people who believe in Allah and the Last Day, loving those who oppose Allah and His Messenger, even if they were their parents, or their children, or their siblings, or their close relatives. These—He

has inscribed faith in their hearts, and has supported them with a spirit from Him. And He will admit them into Gardens beneath which rivers flow, wherein they will dwell forever. Allah is pleased with them, and they are pleased with Him. These are the partisans of Allah. Indeed, it is Allah's partisans who are the successful.

59. THE MOBILIZATION (al-Hashr)

*In the name of Allah,
the Gracious, the Merciful*

1. Glorifying Allah is all that exists in the heavens and the earth. He is the Almighty, the Most Wise.

2. It is He who evicted those who disbelieved among the People of the Book from their homes at the first mobilization. You did not think they would leave, and they thought their fortresses would protect them from Allah. But Allah came at them from where they never expected, and threw terror into their hearts. They wrecked their homes with their own hands, and by the hands of the believers. Therefore, take a lesson, O you who have insight.

3. Had Allah not decreed exile for them, He would have punished them in this life. But in the Hereafter they will have the punishment of the Fire.

4. That is because they opposed Allah and His Messenger. Whoever opposes Allah—Allah is stern in retribution.

5. Whether you cut down a tree, or leave it standing on its trunk, it is by Allah's will. He will surely disgrace the sinners.

6. Whatever Allah has bestowed upon His Messenger from them; you spurred neither horse nor camel for them, but Allah gives authority to His messengers over whomever He will. Allah is Able to do all things.

7. Whatever Allah restored to His Messenger from the inhabitants of the villages belongs to Allah, and to the Messenger, and to the relatives, and to the orphans, and to the poor, and to the wayfarer; so that it may not circulate solely between the wealthy among you. Whatever the Messenger gives you, accept it; and whatever he forbids you, abstain from it. And fear Allah. Allah is severe in punishment.

8. To the poor refugees who were driven out of their homes and their possessions, as they sought the favor of Allah and His approval, and came to the aid of Allah and His Messenger. These are the sincere.

9. And those who, before them, had settled in the homeland, and had accepted faith. They love those who emigrated to them, and find no hesitation in their hearts in helping them. They give them priority over themselves, even if they themselves are needy. Whoever is protected from his natural greed—it is they who are the successful.

10. And those who came after them, saying, "Our Lord, forgive us, and our brethren who preceded us in faith, and leave no malice in our hearts towards those who believe. Our Lord, You are Clement and Merciful."

11. Have you not considered those who act hypocritically? They say to their brethren who disbelieved among the People of the Book, "If you are evicted, we will leave with you, and will not obey anyone against you; and should anyone fight you, we will certainly support you." But Allah bears witness that they are liars.

12. If they are evicted, they will not leave with them; and if anyone fights them, they will not support them; and if they go to their aid, they will turn their backs and flee; then they will receive no support.

13. Fear of you is more intense in their hearts than fear of Allah. That is because they are a people who do not understand.

14. They will not fight you all together except from fortified strongholds, or from behind walls. Their hostility towards each other is severe. You would think they are united, but

their hearts are diverse. That is because they are a people who do not understand.

15. Like those shortly before them. They experienced the consequences of their decisions. For them is a painful punishment.

16. Like the devil, when he says to the human being, "Disbelieve." But when he has disbelieved, he says, "I am innocent of you; I fear Allah, the Lord of the Worlds."

17. The ultimate end for both of them is the Fire, where they will dwell forever. Such is the requital for the wrongdoers.

18. O you who believe! Fear Allah, and let every soul consider what it has forwarded for the morrow, and fear Allah. Allah is Aware of what you do.

19. And do not be like those who forgot Allah, so He made them forget themselves. These are the sinners.

20. Not equal are the inhabitants of the Fire and the inhabitants of Paradise. It is the inhabitants of Paradise who are the winners.

21. Had We sent this Quran down on a mountain, you would have seen it trembling, crumbling in awe of Allah. These parables We cite for the people, so that they may reflect.

22. He is Allah. There is no god but He, the Knower of secrets and declarations. He is the Compassionate, the Merciful.

23. He is Allah; besides Whom there is no god; the Sovereign, the Holy, the Peace-Giver, the Faith-Giver, the Overseer, the Almighty, the Omnipotent, the Overwhelming. Glory be to Allah, beyond what they associate.

24. He is Allah; the Creator, the Maker, the Designer. His are the Most Beautiful Names. Whatever is in the heavens and the earth glorifies Him. He is the Majestic, the Wise.

60. THE WOMAN TESTED
(al-Mumtahina)

*In the name of Allah,
the Gracious, the Merciful*

1. O you who believe! Do not take My enemies and your enemies for supporters, offering them affection, when they have disbelieved in what has come to you of the Truth. They have expelled the Messenger, and you, because you believed in Allah, your Lord. If you have mobilized to strive for My cause, seeking My approval, how can you secretly love them? I know what you conceal and what you reveal. Whoever among you does that has strayed from the right way.

2. Whenever they encounter you, they treat you as enemies, and they stretch their hands and tongues against you with malice. They wish that you would disbelieve.

3. Neither your relatives nor your children will benefit you on the Day of Resurrection. He will separate between you. Allah is Observant of what you do.

4. You have had an excellent example in Abraham and those with him; when they said to their people, "We are quit of you, and what you worship apart from Allah. We denounce you. Enmity and hatred has surfaced between us and you, forever, until you believe in Allah alone." Except for the words of Abraham to his father, "I will ask forgiveness for you, though I have no power from Allah to do anything for you." "Our Lord, in You we trust, and to You we repent, and to You is the ultimate resort.

5. Our Lord, do not make us a target for those who disbelieve, and forgive us, our Lord. You are indeed the Mighty and Wise."

6. There is an excellent example in them for you—for anyone who seeks Allah and the Last Day. But whoever turns away—Allah is the Self-Sufficient, the Most Praised.

7. Perhaps Allah will plant affection between you and those of them you consider enemies. Allah is Capable. Allah is Forgiving and Merciful.

8. As for those who have not fought against you for your religion, nor expelled you from your homes, Allah does not prohibit you from dealing with them kindly and equitably. Allah loves the equitable.

61. COLUMN (as-Saff)

9. But Allah prohibits you from befriending those who fought against you over your religion, and expelled you from your homes, and aided in your expulsion. Whoever takes them for friends—these are the wrongdoers.

10. O you who believe! When believing women come to you emigrating, test them. Allah is Aware of their faith. And if you find them to be faithful, do not send them back to the unbelievers. They are not lawful for them, nor are they lawful for them. But give them what they have spent. You are not at fault if you marry them, provided you give them their compensation. And do not hold on to ties with unbelieving women, but demand what you have spent, and let them demand what they have spent. This is the rule of Allah; He rules among you. Allah is Knowing and Wise.

11. If any of your wives desert you to the unbelievers, and you decide to penalize them, give those whose wives have gone away the equivalent of what they had spent. And fear Allah, in whom you are believers.

12. O prophet! If believing women come to you, pledging allegiance to you, on condition that they will not associate anything with Allah, nor steal, nor commit adultery, nor kill their children, nor commit perjury as to parenthood, nor disobey you in anything righteous, accept their allegiance and ask Allah's forgiveness for them. Allah is Forgiving and Merciful.

13. O you who believe! Do not befriend people with whom Allah has become angry, and have despaired of the Hereafter, as the faithless have despaired of the occupants of the graves.

61. COLUMN
(as-Saff)

*In the name of Allah,
the Gracious, the Merciful*

1. Everything in the heavens and the earth praises Allah. He is the Almighty, the Wise.

2. O you who believe! Why do you say what you do not do?

3. It is most hateful to Allah that you say what you do not do.

4. Allah loves those who fight in His cause, in ranks, as though they were a compact structure.

5. When Moses said to his people, "O my people, why do you hurt me, although you know that I am Allah's Messenger to you?" And when they swerved, Allah swerved their hearts. Allah does not guide the sinful people.

6. And when Jesus son of Mary said, "O Children of Israel, I am Allah's Messenger to you, confirming what preceded me of the Torah, and announcing good news of a messenger who will come after me, whose name is Ahmad." But when he showed them the miracles, they said, "This is obvious sorcery."

7. And who is a greater wrongdoer than he who attributes falsehoods to Allah, when he is being invited to Islam? Allah does not guide the wrongdoing people.

8. They want to extinguish Allah's Light with their mouths; but Allah will complete His Light, even though the disbelievers dislike it.

9. It is He who sent His Messenger with the guidance and the true religion, to make it prevail over all religions, even though the idolaters dislike it.

10. O you who believe! Shall I inform you of a trade that will save you from a painful torment?

11. That you believe in Allah and His Messenger, and strive in the cause of Allah with your possessions and yourselves. That is best for you, if you only knew.

12. He will forgive you your sins; and will admit you into gardens beneath which rivers flow, and into beautiful mansions in the Gardens of Eden. That is the supreme success.

13. And something else you love: support from Allah, and imminent victory. So give good news to the believers.

62. FRIDAY (al-Jumu'ah)

14. O you who believe! Be supporters of Allah, as Jesus son of Mary said to the disciples, "Who are my supporters towards Allah?" The disciples said, "We are Allah's supporters." So a group of the Children of Israel believed, while another group disbelieved. We supported those who believed against their foe, so they became dominant.

62. FRIDAY
(al-Jumu'ah)

In the name of Allah, the Gracious, the Merciful

1. Everything in the heavens and the earth glorifies Allah the Sovereign, the Holy, the Almighty, the Wise.

2. It is He who sent among the unlettered a messenger from themselves; reciting His revelations to them, and purifying them, and teaching them the Scripture and wisdom; although they were in obvious error before that.

3. And others from them, who have not yet joined them. He is the Glorious, the Wise.

4. That is Allah's grace, which He grants to whomever He wills. Allah is Possessor of limitless grace.

5. The example of those who were entrusted with the Torah, but then failed to uphold it, is like the donkey carrying works of literature. Miserable is the example of the people who denounce Allah's revelations. Allah does not guide the wrongdoing people.

6. Say, "O you who follow Judaism; if you claim to be the chosen of Allah, to the exclusion of the rest of mankind, then wish for death if you are sincere."

7. But they will not wish for it, ever, due to what their hands have advanced. Allah knows well the wrongdoers.

8. Say, "The death from which you flee will catch up with you; then you will be returned to the Knower of the Invisible and the Visible, and He will inform you of what you used to do."

9. O you who believe! When the call is made for prayer on Congregation Day, hasten to the remembrance of Allah, and drop all business. That is better for you, if you only knew.

10. Then, when the prayer is concluded, disperse through the land, and seek Allah's bounty, and remember Allah much, so that you may prosper.

11. Yet whenever they come across some business, or some entertainment, they scramble towards it, and leave you standing. Say, "What is with Allah is better than entertainment and business; and Allah is the Best of providers."

63. THE HYPOCRITES
(al-Munafiqun)

In the name of Allah, the Gracious, the Merciful

1. When the hypocrites come to you, they say, "We bear witness that you are Allah's Messenger." Allah knows that you are His Messenger, and Allah bears witness that the hypocrites are liars.

2. They treat their oaths as a cover, and so they repel others from Allah's path. Evil is what they do.

3. That is because they believed, and then disbelieved; so their hearts were sealed, and they cannot understand.

4. When you see them, their appearance impresses you. And when they speak, you listen to what they say. They are like propped-up timber. They think every shout is aimed at them. They are the enemy, so beware of them. Allah condemns them; how deluded they are!

5. And when it is said to them, "Come, the Messenger of Allah will ask forgiveness for you," they bend their heads, and you see them turning away arrogantly.

6. It is the same for them, whether you ask forgiveness for them, or do not ask forgiveness for them; Allah will not forgive them. Allah does not guide the sinful people.

64. GATHERING (at-Taghabun)

7. It is they who say: "Do not spend anything on those who side with Allah's Messenger, unless they have dispersed." To Allah belong the treasures of the heavens and the earth, but the hypocrites do not understand.

8. They say, "If we return to the City, the more powerful therein will evict the weak." But power belongs to Allah, and His Messenger, and the believers; but the hypocrites do not know.

9. O you who believe! Let neither your possessions nor your children distract you from the remembrance of Allah. Whoever does that—these are the losers.

10. And give from what We have provided for you, before death approaches one of you, and he says, "My Lord, if only You would delay me for a short while, so that I may be charitable, and be one of the righteous."

11. But Allah will not delay a soul when its time has come. Allah is Informed of what you do.

64. GATHERING
(at-Taghabun)

In the name of Allah,
the Gracious, the Merciful

1. Everything in the heavens and the earth praises Allah. To Him belongs the Kingdom, and to Him all praise is due, and He is Able to do all things.

2. It is He who created you. Some of you are unbelievers, and some of you are believers. And Allah perceives what you do.

3. He created the heavens and the earth with truth, and He designed you, and designed you well, and to Him is the final return.

4. He knows everything in the heavens and the earth, and He knows what you conceal and what you reveal. And Allah knows what is within the hearts.

5. Has the news not reached you, of those who disbelieved before? They tasted the ill consequences of their conduct, and a painful torment awaits them.

6. That is because their messengers came to them with clear explanations, but they said, "Are human beings going to guide us?" So they disbelieved and turned away. But Allah is in no need. Allah is Independent and Praiseworthy.

7. Those who disbelieve claim that they will not be resurrected. Say, "Yes indeed, by my Lord, you will be resurrected; then you will be informed of everything you did; and that is easy for Allah."

8. So believe in Allah and His Messenger, and the Light which We sent down. Allah is Aware of everything you do.

9. The Day when He gathers you for the Day of Gathering—that is the Day of Mutual Exchange. Whoever believes in Allah and acts with integrity, He will remit his misdeeds, and will admit him into gardens beneath which rivers flow, to dwell therein forever. That is the supreme achievement.

10. But as for those who disbelieve and denounce Our revelations—these are the inmates of the Fire, dwelling therein forever; and what a miserable fate!

11. No disaster occurs except by Allah's leave. Whoever believes in Allah, He guides his heart. Allah is Aware of everything.

12. So obey Allah, and obey the Messenger. But if you turn away—it is only incumbent on Our Messenger to deliver the clear message.

13. Allah, there is no god but He; and in Allah let the believers put their trust.

14. O you who believe! Among your wives and your children are enemies to you, so beware of them. But if you pardon, and overlook, and forgive—Allah is Forgiver and Merciful.

15. Your possessions and your children are a test, but with Allah is a splendid reward.

16. So be conscious of Allah as much as you can, and listen, and obey, and give for your own good. He who is protected from his stinginess—these are the prosperous.

17. If you lend Allah a good loan, He will multiply it for you, and will forgive you. Allah is Appreciative and Forbearing.

18. The Knower of the Unseen and the Seen, the Almighty, the Wise.

65. DIVORCE
(at-Talaq)

*In the name of Allah,
the Gracious, the Merciful*

1. O Prophet! If any of you divorce women, divorce them during their period of purity, and calculate their term. And be pious before Allah, your Lord. And do not evict them from their homes, nor shall they leave, unless they have committed a proven adultery. These are the limits of Allah—whoever oversteps Allah's limits has wronged his own soul. You never know; Allah may afterwards bring about a new situation.

2. Once they have reached their term, either retain them honorably, or separate from them honorably. And call to witness two just people from among you, and give upright testimony for Allah. By that is exhorted whoever believes in Allah and the Last Day. And whoever fears Allah—He will make a way out for him.

3. And will provide for him from where he never expected. Whoever relies on Allah—He will suffice him. Allah will accomplish His purpose. Allah has set a measure to all things.

4. As for those of your women who have reached menopause, if you have any doubts, their term shall be three months—and also for those who have not menstruated. As for those who are pregnant, their term shall be until they have delivered. Whoever fears Allah—He will make things easy for him.

5. This is the ordinance of Allah, which He sent down to you. Whoever fears Allah—He will remit his sins, and will amplify his reward.

6. Allow them to reside where you reside, according to your means, and do not harass them in order to make things difficult for them. If they are pregnant, spend on them until they give birth. And if they nurse your infant, give them their payment. And conduct your relation in amity. But if you disagree, then let another woman nurse him.

7. The wealthy shall spend according to his means; and he whose resources are restricted shall spend according to what Allah has given him. Allah never burdens a soul beyond what He has given it. Allah will bring ease after hardship.

8. How many a town defied the command of its Lord and His messengers? So We held it strictly accountable, and We punished it with a dreadful punishment.

9. It tasted the result of its decisions, and the outcome of its decisions was perdition.

10. Allah has prepared for them a severe retribution. So beware of Allah, O you who possess intellect and have faith. Allah has sent down to you a Reminder.

11. A messenger who recites to you Allah's Verses, clear and distinct, that he may bring those who believe and work righteousness from darkness into light. Whoever believes in Allah and acts with integrity, He will admit him into gardens beneath which rivers flow, therein to abide forever. Allah has given him an excellent provision.

12. Allah is He Who created seven heavens, and their like of earth. The command descends through them, so that you may know that Allah is Capable of everything, and that Allah Encompasses everything in knowledge.

66. PROHIBITION
(at-Tahrim)

*In the name of Allah,
the Gracious, the Merciful*

1. O prophet! Why do you prohibit what Allah has permitted for you, seeking to please your wives? Allah is Forgiving and Merciful.

2. Allah has decreed for you the dissolution of your oaths. Allah is your Master. He is the All-Knowing, the Most Wise.

3. The Prophet told something in confidence to one of his wives. But when she disclosed it, and Allah made it known to him; he communicated part of it, and he avoided another part. Then, when he informed her of it, she said, "Who informed you of this?" He said, "The All-Knowing, the All-Informed, informed me."

4. If you repent to Allah, then your hearts have listened. But if you band together against him, then Allah is his Ally, as is Gabriel, and the righteous believers. In addition, the angels will assist him.

5. Perhaps, if he divorces you, his Lord will give him in exchange wives better than you: submissive, believing, obedient, penitent, devout, fasting—previously married, or virgins.

6. O you who believe! Protect yourselves and your families from a Fire, whose fuel is people and stones. Over it are angels, fierce and powerful. They never disobey Allah in anything He commands them, and they carry out whatever they are commanded.

7. O you who disbelieved! Make no excuses today. You are being repaid for what you used to do.

8. O you who believe! Repent to Allah with sincere repentance. Perhaps your Lord will remit your sins, and admit you into gardens beneath which rivers flow, on the Day when Allah will not disappoint the Prophet and those who believed with him. Their light streaming before them, and to their right, they will say, "Our Lord, complete our light for us, and forgive us; You are capable of all things."

9. O prophet! Strive hard against the disbelievers and the hypocrites, and be stern with them. Their abode is Hell. What a miserable destination!

10. Allah illustrates an example of those who disbelieve: the wife of Noah and the wife of Lot. They were under two of Our righteous servants, but they betrayed them. They availed them nothing against Allah, and it was said, "Enter the Fire with those who are entering."

11. And Allah illustrates an example of those who believe: the wife of Pharaoh, when she said, "My Lord, build for me, with you, a house in Paradise, and save me from Pharaoh and his works, and save me from the wrongdoing people."

12. And Mary, the daughter of Imran, who guarded her womb, and so We breathed into her of Our Spirit; and she believed in the truth of her Lord's Words and His Books, and was one of the devout.

67. SOVEREIGNTY (al-Mulk)

In the name of Allah, the Gracious, the Merciful

1. Blessed is He in whose hand is the sovereignty, and Who has power over everything.

2. He who created death and life—to test you—as to which of you is better in conduct. He is the Almighty, the Forgiving.

3. He who created seven heavens in layers. You see no discrepancy in the creation of the Compassionate. Look again. Can you see any cracks?

4. Then look again, and again, and your sight will return to you dazzled and exhausted.

5. We have adorned the lower heaven with lanterns, and made them missiles against the devils; and We have prepared for them the punishment of the Blaze.

6. For those who reject their Lord, there is the torment of Hell. What an evil destination!

7. When they are thrown into it, they will hear it roaring, as it seethes.

8. It almost bursts with fury. Every time a batch is thrown into it, its keepers will ask them, "Has no warner come to you?"

68. THE PEN (al-Qalam)

9. They will say, "Yes, a warner did come to us, but we disbelieved, and said, 'Allah did not send down anything; you are very much mistaken.'"

10. And they will say, "Had we listened or reasoned, we would not have been among the inmates of the Blaze."

11. So they will acknowledge their sins. So away with the inmates of the Blaze.

12. As for those who fear their Lord in secret— for them is forgiveness and a great reward.

13. Whether you keep your words secret, or declare them—He is Aware of the inner thoughts.

14. Would He not know, He Who created? He is the Refined, the Expert.

15. It is He who made the earth manageable for you, so travel its regions, and eat of His provisions. To Him is the Resurgence.

16. Are you confident that the One in heaven will not cause the earth to collapse beneath you as it spins?

17. Or are you confident that the One in Heaven will not unleash against you a violent storm? Then you will know what My warning is like.

18. Those before them also denied the truth; and how was My disapproval?

19. Have they not seen the birds above them, spreading their wings, and folding them? None holds them except the Compassionate. He is Perceiver of everything.

20. Or who is this who is a force for you to protect you against the Compassionate? The disbelievers are in nothing but delusion.

21. Or who is this that will provide for you, if He withholds His provision? Yet they persist in defiance and aversion.

22. Is he who walks bent on his own design better guided, or he who walks upright on a straight path?

23. Say, "It is He who produced you; and made for you the hearing, and the vision, and the organs. But rarely do you give thanks."

24. Say, "It is He who scattered you on earth, and to Him you will be rounded up."

25. And they say, "When will this promise be fulfilled, if you are truthful?"

26. Say, "Knowledge is with Allah, and I am only a clear warner."

27. But when they see it approaching, the faces of those who disbelieved will turn gloomy, and it will be said, "This is what you used to call for."

28. Say, "Have you considered? Should Allah make me perish, and those with me; or else He bestows His mercy on us; who will protect the disbelievers from an agonizing torment?"

29. Say, "He is the Compassionate. We have faith in Him, and in Him we trust. Soon you will know who is in evident error."

30. Say, "Have you considered? If your water drains away, who will bring you pure running water?"

68. THE PEN
(al-Qalam)

*In the name of Allah,
the Gracious, the Merciful*

1. Noon. By the pen, and by what they inscribe.

2. By the grace of your Lord, you are not insane.

3. In fact, you will have a reward that will never end.

4. And you are of a great moral character.

5. You will see, and they will see.

6. Which of you is the afflicted.

7. Your Lord knows best who has strayed from His path, and He knows best the well-guided.

8. So do not obey the deniers.

9. They would like you to compromise, so they would compromise.

10. And do not obey any vile swearer.

11. Backbiter, spreader of slander.

68. THE PEN (al-Qalam)

12. Preventer of good, transgressor, sinner.

13. Rude and fake besides.

14. Just because he has money and children.

15. When Our Verses are recited to him, he says, "Myths of the ancients!"

16. We will brand him on the muzzle.

17. We tested them, as We tested the owners of the garden, when they vowed to harvest it in the morning.

18. Without any reservation.

19. But a calamity from your Lord went around it while they slept.

20. And in the morning it was as if picked.

21. In the morning, they called to one another.

22. "Go early to your plantation, if you are going to harvest."

23. So off they went, murmuring to one another.

24. "No poor person is to enter it upon you today."

25. And early they went, resolved in intent.

26. But when they saw it, they said, "We were wrong.

27. We are now deprived."

28. The most reasonable of them said, "Did I not say to you, 'if only you would glorify?'"

29. They said, "Glory to our Lord—We were indeed in the wrong."

30. Then they turned to one another, blaming one another.

31. They said, "Woe to us—we were indeed domineering.

32. Perhaps our Lord will give us a better substitute for it. We are turning to our Lord."

33. Such is the punishment; but the punishment of the Hereafter is greater, if they only knew.

34. For the righteous are Gardens of Delight with their Lord.

35. Shall We treat the Muslims like the villains?

36. What is the matter with you? How do you judge?

37. Or do you have a scripture in which you study?

38. Wherein there is whatever you choose?

39. Or do you have oaths from Us, binding until the Day of Resurrection, that you will have whatever you demand?

40. Ask them, which of them will guarantee that.

41. Or do they have partners? Then let them produce their partners, if they are truthful.

42. On the Day when the Shin will be exposed, and they will be called to bow down, but they will be unable.

43. Their eyes subdued, shame will cover them. They were invited to bow down when they were sound.

44. So leave Me to those who reject this discourse; We will proceed against them gradually, from where they do not know.

45. And I will give them respite. My plan is firm.

46. Or do you ask them for a fee, so they are burdened with debt?

47. Or do they know the future, and so they write it down?

48. So wait patiently for the Decision of your Lord, and do not be like the Fellow of the Fish who cried out in despair.

49. Were it not for his Lord's favor that reached him, he would have been thrown into the wilderness, fully despised.

50. But his Lord chose him, and made him one of the righteous.

51. Those who disbelieve almost stab you with their glances when they hear the message, and say, "He is crazy!"

52. But it is no less than a reminder to all the Worlds.

69. THE REALITY (al-Haqqah)

*In the name of Allah,
the Gracious, the Merciful*

1. The Reality.

2. What is the Reality?

3. What will make you understand what the Reality is?

4. Thamood and Aad denied the Catastrophe.

5. As for Thamood, they were annihilated by the Overwhelming.

6. And as for Aad; they were annihilated by a furious, roaring wind.

7. He unleashed it upon them for seven nights and eight days, in succession. You could see the people tossed around, as though they were stumps of hollow palm-trees.

8. Can you see any remnant of them?

9. Then Pharaoh came, and those before him, and the Overturned Cities steeped in sin.

10. But they disobeyed the messenger of their Lord, so He seized them with an overpowering grip.

11. When the waters overflowed, We carried you in the cruising ship.

12. To make it a lesson for you—so that retaining ears may retain it.

13. Then, when the Trumpet is sounded a single time.

14. And the earth and the mountains are lifted up, and crushed, with a single crush.

15. On that Day, the Event will come to pass.

16. And the heaven will crack; so on that Day it will be frail.

17. And the angels will be ranged around its borders, while eight will be carrying the Throne of your Lord above them that Day.

18. On that Day you will be exposed, and no secret of yours will remain hidden.

19. As for him who is given his book in his right hand, he will say, "Here, take my book and read it.

20. I knew I would be held accountable."

21. So he will be in pleasant living.

22. In a lofty Garden.

23. Its pickings are within reach.

24. "Eat and drink merrily for what you did in the days gone by."

25. But as for him who is given his book in his left hand, he will say, "I wish I was never given my book.

26. And never knew what my account was.

27. If only it was the end.

28. My money cannot avail me.

29. My power has vanished from me."

30. "Take him and shackle him.

31. Then scorch him in the Blaze.

32. Then in a chain which length is seventy cubits tie him up.

33. For he would not believe in Allah the Great.

34. Nor would he advocate the feeding of the destitute.

35. So he has no friend here today.

36. And no food except scum.

37. Which only the sinners eat."

38. Indeed, I swear by what you see.

39. And by what you do not see.

40. It is the speech of a noble messenger.

41. And it is not the speech of a poet—little do you believe.

42. Nor is it the speech of a soothsayer—little do you take heed.

43. It is a revelation from the Lord of the Worlds.

44. Had he falsely attributed some statements to Us.

45. We would have seized him by the right arm.

46. Then slashed his lifeline.

47. And none of you could have restrained Us from him.

48. Surely, it is a message for the righteous.

49. And We know that some of you will reject it.

50. And it is surely a source of grief for the unbelievers.

51. Yet it is the absolute truth.

52. So glorify the name of your Lord, the Magnificent.

70. WAYS OF ASCENT (al-Ma'arij)

*In the name of Allah,
the Gracious, the Merciful*

1. A questioner questioned the imminent torment.

2. For the disbelievers; none can repel it.

3. From Allah, Lord of the Ways of Ascent.

4. Unto Him the angels and the Spirit ascend on a Day the duration of which is fifty thousand years.

5. So be patient, with sweet patience.

6. They see it distant.

7. But We see it near.

8. On the Day when the sky will be like molten brass.

9. And the mountains will be like tufted wool.

10. No friend will care about his friend.

11. They will be shown each other. The criminal wishes he would be redeemed from the punishment of that Day by his children.

12. And his spouse, and his brother.

13. And his family that sheltered him.

14. And everyone on earth, in order to save him.

15. By no means! It is a Raging Fire.

16. It strips away the scalps.

17. It invites him who once turned his back and fled.

18. And accumulated and hoarded.

19. Man was created restless.

20. Touched by adversity, he is fretful.

21. Touched by good, he is ungenerous.

22. Except the prayerful.

23. Those who are constant at their prayers.

24. And those in whose wealth is a rightful share.

25. For the beggar and the deprived.

26. And those who affirm the Day of Judgment.

27. And those who fear the punishment of their Lord.

28. Their Lord's punishment is not to be taken for granted.

29. And those who guard their chastity.

30. Except from their spouses or those living under their control, for then they are free of blame.

31. But whoever seeks to go beyond that—these are the transgressors.

32. And those who honor their trusts and their pledges.

33. And those who stand by their testimonies.

34. And those who are dedicated to their prayers.

35. These will be honored in Gardens.

36. What is with those who disbelieve, stretching their necks towards you.

37. From the right, and from the left, banding together?

38. Is every one of them aspiring to be admitted into a Garden of Bliss?

39. No indeed! We created them from what they know.

40. I swear by the Lord of the Easts and the Wests, that We are Able.

41. To replace them with better than they, and We are not to be outdone.

42. So leave them to blunder and play, until they meet their Day which they are promised.

43. The Day when they will emerge from the tombs in a rush, as though they were hurrying towards a target.

44. Their eyes cast down; overwhelmed by humiliation. This is the Day which they were promised.

71. NOAH
(Nuh)

*In the name of Allah,
the Gracious, the Merciful*

1. We sent Noah to his people: "Warn your people before there comes upon them a painful punishment."

2. He said, "O my people, I am to you a clear warner.

3. Worship Allah and reverence Him, and obey me.

4. And He will forgive you of your sins, and reprieve you until a stated term. Allah's term cannot be deferred once it has arrived, if you only knew."

5. He said, "My Lord, I have called my people night and day.

6. But my call added only to their flight.

7. Whenever I called them to Your forgiveness, they thrust their fingers into their ears, and wrapped themselves in their garments, and insisted, and became more and more arrogant.

8. Then I called them openly.

9. Then I appealed to them publicly, and I spoke to them privately.

10. I said, 'Ask your Lord for forgiveness; He is Forgiving.

11. He will let loose the sky upon you in torrents.

12. And provide you with wealth and children, and allot for you gardens, and allot for you rivers.

13. What is the matter with you, that you do not appreciate Allah's Greatness?

14. Although He created you in stages.

15. Do you not realize that Allah created seven heavens in layers?

16. And He set the moon in their midst for light, and He made the sun a lamp.

17. And Allah germinated you from the earth like plants.

18. Then He will return you into it, and will bring you out again.

19. And Allah made the earth a spread for you.

20. That you may travel its diverse roads.'"

21. Noah said, "My Lord, they have defied me, and followed him whose wealth and children increase him only in perdition."

22. And they schemed outrageous schemes.

23. And they said, "Do not give up your gods; do not give up Wadd, nor Souwa, nor Yaghoos, and Yaooq, and Nassr.

24. They have misled many, so do not increase the wrongdoers except in confusion."

25. Because of their wrongs, they were drowned, and were hurled into a Fire. They did not find apart from Allah any helpers.

26. Noah said, "My Lord, do not leave of the unbelievers a single dweller on earth.

27. If You leave them, they will mislead your servants, and will breed only wicked unbelievers.

28. My Lord! Forgive me and my parents, and anyone who enters my home in faith, and all the believing men and believing women; and do not increase the wrongdoers except in perdition."

72. THE JINN
(al-Jinn)

In the name of Allah,

73. THE ENWRAPPED (al-Muzzammil)

the Gracious, the Merciful

1. Say, "It was revealed to me that a band of jinn listened in, and said, 'We have heard a wondrous Quran.

2. It guides to rectitude, so we have believed in it; and we will never associate anyone with our Lord.

3. And Exalted is the Grandeur of our Lord— He never had a mate, nor a child.

4. But the fools among us used to say nonsense about Allah.

5. And we thought that humans and jinn would never utter lies about Allah.

6. Some individual humans used to seek power through some individual jinn, but they only increased them in confusion.

7. They thought, as you thought, that Allah would never resurrect anyone.

8. We probed the heaven, and found it filled with stern guards and projectiles.

9. We used to take up positions to listen in; but whoever listens now finds a projectile in wait for him.

10. We do not know whether ill is intended for those on earth, or if their Lord intends goodness for them.

11. Some of us are righteous, but some of us are less than that; we follow divergent paths.

12. We realized that we cannot defeat Allah on earth, and that we cannot escape Him by fleeing.

13. And when we heard the guidance, we believed in it. Whoever believes in his Lord fears neither loss, nor burden.

14. Among us are those who are submitting, and among us are the compromisers. As for those who have submitted—it is they who pursue rectitude.

15. But as for the compromisers—they will be firewood for Hell.'"

16. Had they kept true to the Path, We would have given them plenty water to drink.

17. To test them with it. Whoever turns away from the remembrance of his Lord, He will direct him to torment ever mounting.

18. The places of worship are for Allah. So do not call, besides Allah, upon anyone else.

19. And when the servant of Allah got up calling on Him, they almost fell on him in a mass.

20. Say, "I pray only to my Lord, and I never associate anyone with Him."

21. Say, "It is not in my power to harm you, nor to bring you to right conduct."

22. Say, "No one can protect me from Allah, and I will not find any refuge except with Him.

23. Except for a proclamation from Allah and His messages. He who defies Allah and His Messenger—for him is the Fire of Hell, in which they will dwell forever."

24. Until, when they see what they were promised, they will know who is weaker in helpers, and fewer in numbers.

25. Say, "I do not know whether what you are promised is near, or whether my Lord will extend it for a period."

26. The Knower of the Invisible; He does not disclose His Invisible to anyone.

27. Except to a Messenger of His choosing. He then dispatches guards before him and behind him.

28. That He may know that they have conveyed the messages of their Lord. He encompasses what they have, and has tallied everything by number.

73. THE ENWRAPPED (al-Muzzammil)

In the name of Allah, the Gracious, the Merciful

1. O you Enwrapped one.

2. Stay up during the night, except a little.

3. For half of it, or reduce it a little.

74. THE ENROBED (al-Muddathir)

4. Or add to it; and chant the Quran rhythmically.

5. We are about to give you a heavy message.

6. The vigil of night is more effective, and better suited for recitation.

7. In the daytime, you have lengthy work to do.

8. So remember the Name of your Lord, and devote yourself to Him wholeheartedly.

9. Lord of the East and the West. There is no god but He, so take Him as a Trustee.

10. And endure patiently what they say, and withdraw from them politely.

11. And leave Me to those who deny the truth, those of luxury, and give them a brief respite.

12. With Us are shackles, and a Fierce Fire.

13. And food that chokes, and a painful punishment.

14. On the Day when the earth and the mountains tremble, and the mountains become heaps of sand.

15. We have sent to you a messenger, a witness over you, as We sent to Pharaoh a messenger.

16. But Pharaoh defied the Messenger, so We seized him with a terrible seizing.

17. So how will you, if you persist in unbelief, save yourself from a Day which will turn the children gray-haired?

18. The heaven will shatter thereby. His promise is always fulfilled.

19. This is a reminder. So whoever wills, let him take a path to his Lord.

20. Your Lord knows that you stay up nearly two-thirds of the night, or half of it, or one-third of it, along with a group of those with you. Allah designed the night and the day. He knows that you are unable to sustain it, so He has pardoned you. So read of the Quran what is possible for you. He knows that some of you may be ill; and others travelling through the land, seeking Allah's bounty; and others fighting in Allah's cause. So read of it what is possible for you, and observe the prayers, and give regular charity, and lend Allah a generous loan. Whatever good you advance for yourselves, you will find it with Allah, better and generously rewarded. And seek Allah's forgiveness, for Allah is Forgiving and Merciful.

74. THE ENROBED (al-Muddathir)

*In the name of Allah,
the Gracious, the Merciful*

1. O you Enrobed one.

2. Arise and warn.

3. And magnify your Lord.

4. And purify your clothes.

5. And abandon abominations.

6. And show no favor seeking gain.

7. And be constant for your Lord.

8. When the Trumpet is blown.

9. That Day will be a difficult day.

10. For the disbelievers—not easy.

11. Leave Me to him whom I created alone.

12. And gave him vast wealth.

13. And children as witnesses.

14. And smoothed things for him.

15. Then he wants Me to add yet more!

16. By no means! He was stubborn towards Our revelations.

17. I will exhaust him increasingly.

18. He thought and analyzed.

19. May he perish, how he analyzed.

20. Again: may he perish, how he analyzed.

21. Then he looked.

22. Then he frowned and whined.

23. Then he turned back and was proud.

24. And said, "This is nothing but magic from the past.

25. This is nothing but the word of a mortal."

26. I will roast him in Saqar.

27. But what will explain to you what Saqar is?

28. It neither leaves, nor spares.

29. It scorches the flesh.

30. Over it are Nineteen.

31. We have appointed only angels to be wardens of the Fire, and caused their number to be a stumbling block for those who disbelieve; so that those given the Scripture may attain certainty; and those who believe may increase in faith; and those given the Scripture and the believers may not doubt; and those in whose hearts is sickness and the unbelievers may say, "What did Allah intend by this parable?" Thus Allah leads astray whom He wills, and guides whom He wills. None knows the soldiers of your Lord except He. This is nothing but a reminder for the mortals.

32. Nay! By the moon.

33. And the night as it retreats.

34. And the morning as it lights up.

35. It is one of the greatest.

36. A warning to the mortals.

37. To whomever among you wishes to advance, or regress.

38. Every soul is hostage to what it has earned.

39. Except for those on the Right.

40. In Gardens, inquiring.

41. About the guilty.

42. "What drove you into Saqar?"

43. They will say, "We were not of those who prayed.

44. Nor did we feed the destitute.

45. And we used to indulge with those who indulge.

46. And we used to deny the Day of Judgment.

47. Until the Inevitable came upon us."

48. But the intercession of intercessors will not help them.

49. Why are they turning away from the Reminder?

50. As though they were panicked donkeys.

51. Fleeing from a lion?

52. Yet every one of them desires to be given scrolls unrolled.

53. No indeed! But they do not fear the Hereafter.

54. Nevertheless, it is a reminder.

55. So whoever wills, shall remember it.

56. But they will not remember, unless Allah wills. He is the Source of Righteousness, and the Source of Forgiveness.

75. RESURRECTION (al-Qiyamah)

In the name of Allah, the Gracious, the Merciful

1. I swear by the Day of Resurrection.

2. And I swear by the blaming soul.

3. Does man think that We will not reassemble his bones?

4. Yes indeed; We are Able to reconstruct his fingertips.

5. But man wants to deny what is ahead of him.

6. He asks, "When is the Day of Resurrection?"

7. When vision is dazzled.

8. And the moon is eclipsed.

9. And the sun and the moon are joined together.

10. On that Day, man will say, "Where is the escape?"

11. No indeed! There is no refuge.

12. To your Lord on that Day is the settlement.

13. On that Day man will be informed of everything he put forward, and everything he left behind.

14. And man will be evidence against himself.

76. MAN (al-Insan)

15. Even as he presents his excuses.

16. Do not wag your tongue with it, to hurry on with it.

17. Upon Us is its collection and its recitation.

18. Then, when We have recited it, follow its recitation.

19. Then upon Us is its explanation.

20. Alas, you love the fleeting life.

21. And you disregard the Hereafter.

22. Faces on that Day will be radiant.

23. Looking towards their Lord.

24. And faces on that Day will be gloomy.

25. Realizing that a back-breaker has befallen them.

26. Indeed, when it has reached the breast-bones.

27. And it is said, "Who is the healer?"

28. And He realizes that it is the parting.

29. And leg is entwined with leg.

30. To your Lord on that Day is the drive.

31. He neither believed nor prayed.

32. But he denied and turned away.

33. Then he went to his family, full of pride.

34. Woe to you; and woe.

35. Then again: Woe to you; and woe.

36. Does man think that he will be left without purpose?

37. Was he not a drop of ejaculated semen?

38. Then he became a clot. And He created and proportioned?

39. And made of him the two sexes, the male and the female?

40. Is He not Able to revive the dead?

**76. MAN
(al-Insan)**

*In the name of Allah,
the Gracious, the Merciful*

1. Has there come upon man a period of time when he was nothing to be mentioned?

2. We created man from a liquid mixture, to test him; and We made him hearing and seeing.

3. We guided him to the way, be he appreciative or unappreciative.

4. We have prepared for the faithless chains, and yokes, and a Searing Fire.

5. But the righteous will drink from a cup whose mixture is aroma.

6. A spring from which the servants of Allah will drink, making it gush abundantly.

7. They fulfill their vows, and dread a Day whose ill is widespread.

8. And they feed, for the love of Him, the poor, and the orphan, and the captive.

9. "We only feed you for the sake of Allah. We want from you neither compensation, nor gratitude.

10. We dread from our Lord a frowning grim Day."

11. So Allah will protect them from the ills of that Day, and will grant them radiance and joy.

12. And will reward them for their patience with a Garden and silk.

13. Reclining therein on the thrones; experiencing therein neither sun, nor frost.

14. Its shade hovering over them, and its fruit brought low within reach.

15. Passing around them are vessels of silver, and cups of crystal.

16. Crystal of silver—they measured them exactly.

17. They will be served therein with a cup whose flavor is Zanjabeel.

18. A spring therein named Salsabeel.

19. Passing among them are eternalized youths. If you see them, you would think them sprinkled pearls.

77. THE UNLEASHED (al-Mursalat)

20. Wherever you look, you see bliss, and a vast kingdom.

21. Upon them are garments of green silk, and satin. And they will be adorned with bracelets of silver. And their Lord will offer them a pure drink.

22. "This is a reward for you. Your efforts are well appreciated."

23. It is We who sent down the Quran upon you—a gradual revelation.

24. So be patient for the decision of your Lord, and do not obey the sinner or the blasphemer among them.

25. And mention the Name of your Lord, morning and evening.

26. And for part of the night, prostrate yourself to Him, and glorify Him long into the night.

27. As for these: they love the fleeting life, and leave behind a Heavy Day.

28. We created them, and strengthened their frame; and whenever We will, We can replace them with others like them.

29. This is a reminder; so whoever wills, let him take a path to his Lord.

30. Yet you cannot will, unless Allah wills. Allah is Knowing and Wise.

31. He admits into His mercy whomever He wills. But as for the wrongdoers, He has prepared for them a painful punishment.

77. THE UNLEASHED (al-Mursalat)

In the name of Allah, the Gracious, the Merciful

1. By those unleashed in succession.

2. Storming turbulently.

3. Scattering far and wide.

4. Separating decisively.

5. Delivering a message.

6. Excusing or warning.

7. Surely what you are promised will happen.

8. When the stars are obliterated.

9. And the sky is fractured.

10. And the mountains are blown away.

11. And the messengers are alerted.

12. Until which day is it deferred?

13. Until the Day of Decision.

14. And what will teach you what the Day of Decision is?

15. Woe on that Day to the liars.

16. Did We not destroy the ancients?

17. Then succeeded them with the others?

18. This is how We deal with the guilty.

19. Woe on that Day to the rejecters.

20. Did We not create you from an insignificant fluid?

21. Then lodged it in a secure place?

22. For a known term?

23. We measured precisely. We are the best to measure.

24. Woe on that Day to the falsifiers.

25. Did We not make the earth a homestead?

26. For the living and the dead?

27. And set on it lofty mountains, and given you pure water to drink?

28. Woe on that Day to the deniers.

29. "Proceed to what you used to deny."

30. "Proceed to a shadow of three different masses."

31. Offering no shade, and unavailing against the flames.

32. It shoots sparks as castles.

33. As if they were yellow camels.

34. Woe on that Day to the liars.

35. This is a Day when they will not speak.

36. And they will not be allowed to apologize.

37. Woe on that Day to the rejecters.

38. This is the Day of Separation; We have gathered you, together with the ancients.

78. THE EVENT (an-Naba')

39. So if you have a strategy, use it against Me.

40. Woe on that Day to the falsifiers.

41. The righteous will be amidst shades and fountains.

42. And fruits as they desire.

43. "Eat and drink pleasantly, for what you used to do."

44. This is how We reward the doers of good.

45. Woe on that Day to the deniers.

46. "Eat and enjoy yourselves a little; you are indeed criminals."

47. Woe on that Day to the liars.

48. And when it is said to them, "Kneel", they do not kneel.

49. Woe on that Day to the rejecters.

50. In what message, beyond this, will they believe?

78. THE EVENT (an-Naba')

*In the name of Allah,
the Gracious, the Merciful*

1. What are they asking one another about?

2. About the Great Event.

3. About which they disagree.

4. Surely, they will find out.

5. Most certainly, they will find out.

6. Did We not make the earth a cradle?

7. And the mountains pegs?

8. And created you in pairs?

9. And made your sleep for rest?

10. And made the night a cover?

11. And made the day for livelihood?

12. And built above you seven strong ones?

13. And placed a blazing lamp?

14. And brought down from the clouds pouring water?

15. To produce with it grains and vegetation?

16. And luxuriant gardens?

17. The Day of Sorting has been appointed.

18. The Day when the Trumpet is blown, and you will come in droves.

19. And the sky is opened up, and becomes gateways.

20. And the mountains are set in motion, and become a mirage.

21. Hell is lying in ambush.

22. For the oppressors, a destination.

23. Where they will remain for eons.

24. They will taste therein neither coolness, nor drink.

25. Except boiling water, and freezing hail.

26. A fitting requital.

27. For they were not anticipating any reckoning.

28. And they denied Our signs utterly.

29. But We have enumerated everything in writing.

30. So taste! We will increase you only in suffering.

31. But for the righteous there is triumph.

32. Gardens and vineyards.

33. And splendid spouses, well matched.

34. And delicious drinks.

35. They will hear therein neither gossip, nor lies.

36. A reward from your Lord, a fitting gift.

37. Lord of the heavens and the earth, and everything between them—The Most Merciful—none can argue with Him.

38. On the Day when the Spirit and the angels stand in row. They will not speak, unless it be one permitted by the Most Merciful, and he will say what is right.

39. That is the Day of Reality. So whoever wills, let him take a way back to his Lord.

40. We have warned you of a near punishment—the Day when a person will observe

what his hands have produced, and the faithless will say, "O, I wish I were dust."

79. THE SNATCHERS
(an-Nazi'at)

*In the name of Allah,
the Gracious, the Merciful*

1. By those who snatch violently.
2. And those who remove gently.
3. And those who glide smoothly.
4. And those who race swiftly.
5. And those who regulate events.
6. On the Day when the Quake quakes.
7. And is followed by the Successor.
8. Hearts on that Day will be pounding.
9. Their sights downcast.
10. They say, "Are we to be restored to the original condition?
11. When we have become hollow bones?"
12. They say, "This is a losing proposition."
13. But it will be only a single nudge.
14. And they will be awake.
15. Has the story of Moses reached you?
16. When His Lord called out to him in the sacred valley of Tuwa.
17. "Go to Pharaoh—he has transgressed."
18. And say, "Do you care to be cleansed?
19. And I will guide you to your Lord, and you will turn reverent."
20. He showed him the Greatest Miracle.
21. But he denied and defied.
22. Then turned his back, and tried.
23. And gathered and proclaimed.
24. He said, "I am your Lord, the most high."
25. So Allah seized him with an exemplary punishment, in the last and in the first.
26. In this is a lesson for whoever fears.
27. Are you more difficult to create, or the heaven? He constructed it.
28. He raised its masses, and proportioned it.
29. And He dimmed its night, and brought out its daylight.
30. And the earth after that He spread.
31. And from it, He produced its water and its pasture.
32. And the mountains, He anchored.
33. A source of enjoyment for you and for your animals.
34. But when the Great Cataclysm arrives.
35. A Day when man will remember what he has endeavored.
36. And Hell will be displayed to whoever sees.
37. As for him who was defiant.
38. And preferred the life of this world.
39. Then Hell is the shelter.
40. But as for him who feared the Standing of his Lord, and restrained the self from desires.
41. Then Paradise is the shelter.
42. They ask you about the Hour, "When will it take place?"
43. You have no knowledge of it.
44. To your Lord is its finality.
45. You are just a warner for whoever dreads it.
46. On the Day when they witness it—as though they only stayed an evening, or its morning.

80. HE FROWNED
('Abasa)

*In the name of Allah,
the Gracious, the Merciful*

1. He frowned and turned away.
2. When the blind man approached him.
3. But how do you know? Perhaps he was seeking to purify himself.

81. THE ROLLING (at-Takwir)

4. Or be reminded, and the message would benefit him.

5. But as for him who was indifferent.

6. You gave him your attention.

7. Though you are not liable if he does not purify himself.

8. But as for him who came to you seeking.

9. In awe.

10. To him you were inattentive.

11. Do not. This is a Lesson.

12. Whoever wills, shall remember it.

13. On honorable pages.

14. Exalted and purified.

15. By the hands of scribes.

16. Noble and devoted.

17. Perish man! How thankless he is!

18. From what did He create him?

19. From a sperm drop He created him, and enabled him.

20. Then He eased the way for him.

21. Then He puts him to death, and buries him.

22. Then, when He wills, He will resurrect him.

23. But no, he did not fulfill what He has commanded him.

24. Let man consider his food.

25. We pour down water in abundance.

26. Then crack the soil open.

27. And grow in it grains.

28. And grapes and herbs.

29. And olives and dates.

30. And luscious gardens.

31. And fruits and vegetables.

32. Enjoyment for you, and for your livestock.

33. But when the Deafening Noise comes to pass.

34. The Day when a person will flee from his brother.

35. And his mother and his father.

36. And his consort and his children.

37. Every one of them, on that Day, will have enough to preoccupy him.

38. Faces on that Day will be radiant.

39. Laughing and rejoicing.

40. And Faces on that Day will be covered with misery.

41. Overwhelmed by remorse.

42. These are the faithless, the vicious.

81. THE ROLLING
(at-Takwir)

*In the name of Allah,
the Gracious, the Merciful*

1. When the sun is rolled up.

2. When the stars are dimmed.

3. When the mountains are set in motion.

4. When the relationships are suspended.

5. When the beasts are gathered.

6. When the oceans are set aflame.

7. When the souls are paired.

8. When the girl, buried alive, is asked:

9. For what crime was she killed?

10. When the records are made public.

11. When the sky is peeled away.

12. When the Fire is set ablaze.

13. When Paradise is brought near.

14. Each soul will know what it has readied.

15. I swear by the galaxies.

16. Precisely running their courses.

17. And by the night as it recedes.

18. And by the morn as it breathes.

19. This is the speech of a noble messenger.

82. THE SHATTERING (al-Infitar)

20. Endowed with power, eminent with the Lord of the Throne.

21. Obeyed and honest.

22. Your friend is not possessed.

23. He saw him on the luminous horizon.

24. And He does not withhold knowledge of the Unseen.

25. And it is not the word of an accursed devil.

26. So where are you heading?

27. It is only a Reminder to all mankind.

28. To whoever of you wills to go straight.

29. But you cannot will, unless Allah wills— The Lord of the Worlds.

82. THE SHATTERING (al-Infitar)

*In the name of Allah,
the Gracious, the Merciful*

1. When the sky breaks apart.

2. When the planets are scattered.

3. When the oceans are exploded.

4. When the tombs are strewn around.

5. Each soul will know what it has advanced, and what it has deferred.

6. O man! What deluded you concerning your Lord, the Most Generous?

7. He Who created you, and formed you, and proportioned you?

8. In whatever shape He willed, He assembled you.

9. But you reject the religion.

10. Though over you are watchers.

11. Honest recorders.

12. They know everything you do.

13. The virtuous will be in bliss.

14. While the wicked will be in Hell.

15. They will enter it on the Day of Justice.

16. And they will not be absent from it.

17. But what will convey to you what the Day of Justice is?

18. Then again, what will convey to you what the Day of Justice is?

19. The Day when no soul will avail another soul anything; and the decision on that Day is Allah's.

83. THE DEFRAUDERS (al-Mutaffifin)

*In the name of Allah,
the Gracious, the Merciful*

1. Woe to the defrauders.

2. Those who, when they take a measure from people, they take in full.

3. But when they measure or weigh to others, they cheat.

4. Do these not know that they will be resurrected?

5. For a Great Day?

6. The Day when mankind will stand before the Lord of the Worlds?

7. Not at all. The record of the wicked is in Sijjeen.

8. But how can you know what Sijjeen is?

9. A numerical book.

10. Woe on that Day to the deniers.

11. Those who deny the Day of Reckoning.

12. But none denies it except the sinful aggressor.

13. When Our revelations are recited to him, he says, "Legends of the ancients."

14. Not at all. Their hearts have become corroded by what they used to earn.

15. Not at all. On that Day, they will be screened from their Lord.

16. Then they will roast in Hell.

17. Then it will be said, "This is what you used to deny."

18. No indeed; the record of the righteous is in Elliyyeen.

19. But how can you know what Elliyyoon is?

20. A numerical book.

21. Witnessed by those brought near.

22. Indeed, the righteous will be amid bliss.

23. On thrones, looking on.

24. You will recognize on their faces the radiance of bliss.

25. They will be given to drink a sealed wine.

26. Whose seal is musk—this is what competitors should compete for.

27. Its mixture is of Tasneem.

28. A spring from which those brought near drink.

29. Those who committed crimes used to laugh at those who believed.

30. And when they passed by them, they would wink at one another.

31. And when they went back to their families, they would go back exulting.

32. And if they saw them, they would say, "These people are lost."

33. Yet they were not sent as guardians over them.

34. But on that Day, those who believed will laugh at the unbelievers.

35. On luxurious furnishings, looking on.

36. Have the unbelievers been repaid for what they used to do?

84. THE RUPTURE
(al-Inshiqaq)

In the name of Allah, the Gracious, the Merciful

1. When the sky is ruptured.

2. And hearkens to its Lord, as it must.

3. And when the earth is leveled out.

4. And casts out what is in it, and becomes empty.

5. And hearkens to its Lord, as it must.

6. O man! You are laboring towards your Lord, and you will meet Him.

7. As for him who is given his book in his right hand.

8. He will have an easy settlement.

9. And will return to his family delighted.

10. But as for him who is given his book behind his back.

11. He will call for death.

12. And will enter the Blaze.

13. He used to be happy among his family.

14. He thought he would never return.

15. In fact, his Lord was watching him.

16. I swear by the twilight.

17. And by the night, and what it covers.

18. And by the moon, as it grows full.

19. You will mount stage by stage.

20. What is the matter with them that they do not believe?

21. And when the Quran is read to them, they do not bow down?

22. In fact, those who disbelieve are in denial.

23. But Allah knows what they hide inside.

24. So inform them of a painful punishment.

25. Except those who believe and do good deeds; they will have an undiminished reward.

85. THE CONSTELLATIONS
(al-Buruj)

In the name of Allah, the Gracious, the Merciful

1. By the sky with the constellations.

2. And by the Promised Day.

3. And by the witness and the witnessed.

86. THE NIGHTLY VISITOR (at-Tariq)

4. Destroyed were the People of the Trench.
5. The fire supplied with fuel.
6. While they sat around it.
7. And were witnessing what they did to the believers.
8. They begrudged them only because they believed in Allah the Almighty, the Praiseworthy.
9. To Whom belongs the sovereignty of the heavens and the earth. Allah is witness over everything.
10. Those who tempt the believers, men and women, then do not repent; for them is the punishment of Hell; for them is the punishment of Burning.
11. Those who believe and do righteous deeds will have Gardens beneath which rivers flow. That is the great triumph.
12. The onslaught of your Lord is severe.
13. It is He who begins and repeats.
14. And He is the Forgiving, the Loving.
15. Possessor of the Glorious Throne.
16. Doer of whatever He wills.
17. Has there come to you the story of the legions?
18. Of Pharaoh and Thamood?
19. In fact, those who disbelieve are in denial.
20. And Allah encloses them from beyond.
21. In fact, it is a Glorious Quran.
22. In a Preserved Tablet.

86. THE NIGHTLY VISITOR
(at-Tariq)

*In the name of Allah,
the Gracious, the Merciful*

1. By the sky and at-Tariq.
2. But what will let you know what at-Tariq is?
3. The Piercing Star.
4. There is no soul without a Protector over it.
5. Let man consider what he was created from.
6. He was created from gushing liquid.
7. Issuing from between the backbone and the breastbones.
8. He is certainly able to return him.
9. On the Day when the secrets are disclosed.
10. He will have no strength, and no supporter.
11. By the sky that returns.
12. And the earth that cracks open.
13. It is a Decisive Word.
14. It is no joke.
15. They plot and scheme.
16. But I plot and scheme.
17. Therefore, give the blasphemers respite, a brief respite.

87. THE MOST HIGH
(al-A'la)

*In the name of Allah,
the Gracious, the Merciful*

1. Praise the Name of your Lord, the Most High.
2. He who creates and regulates.
3. He who measures and guides.
4. He who produces the pasture.
5. And then turns it into light debris.
6. We will make you read, so do not forget.
7. Except what Allah wills. He knows what is declared, and what is hidden.
8. We will ease you into the Easy Way.
9. So remind, if reminding helps.
10. The reverent will remember.
11. But the wretched will avoid it.
12. He who will enter the Gigantic Fire.
13. Where he will neither die, nor live.
14. Successful is he who purifies himself.

88. THE OVERWHELMING (al-Ghashiyah)

15. And mentions the name of his Lord, and prays.

16. But you prefer the present life.

17. Though the Hereafter is better, and more lasting.

18. This is in the former scriptures.

19. The Scriptures of Abraham and Moses.

88. THE OVERWHELMING (al-Ghashiyah)

In the name of Allah, the Gracious, the Merciful

1. Has there come to you the news of the overwhelming?

2. Faces on that Day will be shamed.

3. Laboring and exhausted.

4. Roasting in a scorching Fire.

5. Given to drink from a flaming spring.

6. They will have no food except thorns.

7. That neither nourishes, nor satisfies hunger.

8. Faces on that Day will be joyful.

9. Satisfied with their endeavor.

10. In a lofty Garden.

11. In it you will hear no nonsense.

12. In it is a flowing spring.

13. In it are raised beds.

14. And cups set in place.

15. And cushions set in rows.

16. And carpets spread around.

17. Do they not look at the camels—how they are created?

18. And at the sky—how it is raised?

19. And at the mountains—how they are installed?

20. And at the earth—how it is spread out?

21. So remind. You are only a reminder.

22. You have no control over them.

23. But whoever turns away and disbelieves.

24. Allah will punish him with the greatest punishment.

25. To Us is their return.

26. Then upon Us rests their reckoning.

89. THE DAWN (al-Fajr)

In the name of Allah, the Gracious, the Merciful

1. By the daybreak.

2. And ten nights.

3. And the even and the odd.

4. And the night as it recedes.

5. Is there in this an oath for a rational person?

6. Have you not seen how your Lord dealt with Aad?

7. Erum of the pillars.

8. The like of which was never created in the land.

9. And Thamood—those who carved the rocks in the valley.

10. And Pharaoh of the Stakes.

11. Those who committed excesses in the lands.

12. And spread much corruption therein.

13. So your Lord poured down upon them a scourge of punishment.

14. Your Lord is on the lookout.

15. As for man, whenever his Lord tests him, and honors him, and prospers him, he says, "My Lord has honored me."

16. But whenever He tests him, and restricts his livelihood for him, he says, "My Lord has insulted me."

17. Not at all. But you do not honor the orphan.

18. And you do not urge the feeding of the poor.

90. THE LAND (al-Balad)

19. And you devour inheritance with all greed.
20. And you love wealth with immense love.
21. No—when the earth is leveled, pounded, and crushed.
22. And your Lord comes, with the angels, row after row.
23. And on that Day, Hell is brought forward. On that Day, man will remember, but how will remembrance avail him?
24. He will say, "If only I had forwarded for my life."
25. On that Day, none will punish as He punishes.
26. And none will shackle as He shackles.
27. But as for you, O tranquil soul.
28. Return to your Lord, pleased and accepted.
29. Enter among My servants.
30. Enter My Paradise.

90. THE LAND
(al-Balad)

*In the name of Allah,
the Gracious, the Merciful*

1. I swear by this land.
2. And you are a resident of this land.
3. And by a father and what he fathered.
4. We created man in distress.
5. Does he think that no one has power over him?
6. He says, "I have used up so much money."
7. Does he think that no one sees him?
8. Did We not give him two eyes?
9. And a tongue, and two lips?
10. And We showed him the two ways?
11. But he did not brave the ascent.
12. And what will explain to you what the ascent is?
13. The freeing of a slave.
14. Or the feeding on a day of hunger.
15. An orphan near of kin.
16. Or a destitute in the dust.
17. Then he becomes of those who believe, and advise one another to patience, and advise one another to kindness.
18. These are the people of happiness.
19. But as for those who defy Our revelations—these are the people of misery.
20. Upon them is a padlocked Fire.

91. THE SUN
(ash-Shams)

*In the name of Allah,
the Gracious, the Merciful*

1. By the sun and its radiance.
2. And the moon as it follows it.
3. And the day as it reveals it.
4. And the night as it conceals it.
5. And the sky and He who built it.
6. And the earth and He who spread it.
7. And the soul and He who proportioned it.
8. And inspired it with its wickedness and its righteousness.
9. Successful is he who purifies it.
10. Failing is he who corrupts it.
11. Thamood denied in its pride.
12. When it followed its most wicked.
13. The messenger of Allah said to them, "This is the she-camel of Allah, so let her drink."
14. But they called him a liar, and hamstrung her. So their Lord crushed them for their sin, and leveled it.
15. And He does not fear its sequel.

92. THE NIGHT
(al-Layl)

In the name of Allah,

93. MORNING LIGHT (adh-Duha)

the Gracious, the Merciful

1. By the night as it covers.
2. And the day as it reveals.
3. And He who created the male and the female.
4. Your endeavors are indeed diverse.
5. As for him who gives and is righteous.
6. And confirms goodness.
7. We will ease his way towards ease.
8. But as for him who is stingy and complacent.
9. And denies goodness.
10. We will ease his way towards difficulty.
11. And his money will not avail him when he plummets.
12. It is upon Us to guide.
13. And to Us belong the Last and the First.
14. I have warned you of a Fierce Blaze.
15. None will burn in it except the very wicked.
16. He who denies and turns away.
17. But the devout will avoid it.
18. He who gives his money to become pure.
19. Seeking no favor in return.
20. Only seeking the acceptance of his Lord, the Most High.
21. And he will be satisfied.

93. MORNING LIGHT (adh-Duha)

*In the name of Allah,
the Gracious, the Merciful*

1. By the morning light.
2. And the night as it settles.
3. Your Lord did not abandon you, nor did He forget.
4. The Hereafter is better for you than the First.
5. And your Lord will give you, and you will be satisfied.
6. Did He not find you orphaned, and sheltered you?
7. And found you wandering, and guided you?
8. And found you in need, and enriched you?
9. Therefore, do not mistreat the orphan.
10. Nor rebuff the seeker.
11. But proclaim the blessings of your Lord.

94. THE SOOTHING (ash-Sharh)

*In the name of Allah,
the Gracious, the Merciful*

1. Did We not soothe your heart?
2. And lift from you your burden.
3. Which weighed down your back?
4. And raised for you your reputation?
5. With hardship comes ease.
6. With hardship comes ease.
7. When your work is done, turn to devotion.
8. And to your Lord turn for everything.

95. THE FIG (at-Tin)

*In the name of Allah,
the Gracious, the Merciful*

1. By the fig and the olive.
2. And Mount Sinai.
3. And this safe land.
4. We created man in the best design.
5. Then reduced him to the lowest of the low.
6. Except those who believe and do righteous deeds; for them is a reward without end.
7. So why do you still reject the religion?
8. Is Allah not the Wisest of the wise?

96. CLOT
(al-'Alaq)

*In the name of Allah,
the Gracious, the Merciful*

1. Read: In the Name of your Lord who created.

2. Created man from a clot.

3. Read: And your Lord is the Most Generous.

4. He who taught by the pen.

5. Taught man what he never knew.

6. In fact, man oversteps all bounds.

7. When he considers himself exempt.

8. But to your Lord is the return.

9. Have you seen him who prevents?

10. A servant when he prays?

11. Do you think he is upon guidance?

12. Or advocates righteousness?

13. Do you see how he disbelieved and turned away?

14. Does he not know that Allah sees?

15. No. If he does not desist, We will drag him by the forelock.

16. A deceitful, sinful forelock.

17. Let him call on his gang.

18. We will call the Guards.

19. No, do not obey him; but kneel down, and come near.

97. DECREE
(al-Qadr)

*In the name of Allah,
the Gracious, the Merciful*

1. We sent it down on the Night of Decree.

2. But what will convey to you what the Night of Decree is?

3. The Night of Decree is better than a thousand months.

4. In it descend the angels and the Spirit, by the leave of their Lord, with every command.

5. Peace it is; until the rise of dawn.

98. CLEAR EVIDENCE
(al-Bayyinah)

*In the name of Allah,
the Gracious, the Merciful*

1. Those who disbelieved among the People of the Scripture, and the Polytheists, were not apart, until the Clear Evidence came to them.

2. A messenger from Allah reciting purified scripts.

3. In them are valuable writings.

4. Those who were given the Scripture did not splinter, except after the Clear Evidence came to them.

5. They were commanded only to worship Allah, devoting their faith to Him alone, and to practice regular prayer, and to give alms. That is the upright religion.

6. Those who disbelieve among the People of the Scripture, and the Polytheists, will be in the Fire of Hell, where they will abide forever. These are the worst of creatures.

7. As for those who believe and lead a righteous life—these are the best of creatures.

8. Their reward is with their Lord: Gardens of Eternity beneath which rivers flow, where they will abide forever. Allah is pleased with them, and they are pleased with Him. That is for whoever fears His Lord.

99. THE QUAKE
(az-Zalzalah)

*In the name of Allah,
the Gracious, the Merciful*

1. When the earth is shaken with its quake.

2. And the earth brings out its loads.

3. And man says, "What is the matter with it?"

4. On that Day, it will tell its tales.

5. For your Lord will have inspired it.

6. On that Day, the people will emerge in droves, to be shown their works.

7. Whoever has done an atom's weight of good will see it.

8. And whoever has done an atom's weight of evil will see it.

100. THE RACERS
(al-'Adiyat)

In the name of Allah, the Gracious, the Merciful

1. By the racers panting.
2. Igniting sparks.
3. Raiding at dawn.
4. Raising clouds of dust.
5. Storming into the midst.
6. Indeed, the human being is ungrateful to his Lord.
7. And he bears witness to that.
8. And he is fierce in his love of wealth.
9. Does he not know? When the contents of the graves are scattered around.
10. And the contents of the hearts are obtained.
11. Their Lord, on that Day, is fully informed of them.

101. THE SHOCKER
(al-Qari'ah)

In the name of Allah, the Gracious, the Merciful

1. The Shocker.
2. What is the Shocker?
3. What will explain to you what the Shocker is?
4. The Day when the people will be like scattered moths.
5. And the mountains will be like tufted wool.
6. As for he whose scales are heavy.
7. He will be in a pleasant life.
8. But as for he whose scales are light.
9. His home is the Abyss.
10. Do you know what it is?
11. A Raging Fire.

102. ABUNDANCE
(at-Takathur)

In the name of Allah, the Gracious, the Merciful

1. Abundance distracts you.
2. Until you visit the graveyards.
3. Indeed, you will know.
4. Certainly, you will know.
5. If you knew with knowledge of certainty.
6. You would see the Inferno.
7. Then you will see it with the eye of certainty.
8. Then, on that Day, you will be questioned about the Bliss.

103. TIME
(al-'Asr)

In the name of Allah, the Gracious, the Merciful

1. By Time.
2. The human being is in loss.
3. Except those who believe, and do good works, and encourage truth, and recommend patience.

104. THE BACKBITER
(al-Humazah)

In the name of Allah, the Gracious, the Merciful

1. Woe to every slanderer backbiter.

2. Who gathers wealth and counts it over.

3. Thinking that his wealth has made him immortal.

4. By no means. He will be thrown into the Crusher.

5. And what will make you realize what the Crusher is?

6. Allah's kindled Fire.

7. That laps to the hearts.

8. It closes in on them.

9. In extended columns.

105. THE ELEPHANT
(al-Fil)

*In the name of Allah,
the Gracious, the Merciful*

1. Have you not considered how your Lord dealt with the People of the Elephant?

2. Did He not make their plan go wrong?

3. He sent against them swarms of birds.

4. Throwing at them rocks of baked clay.

5. Leaving them like chewed-up leaves.

106. QURAISH
(Quraysh)

*In the name of Allah,
the Gracious, the Merciful*

1. For the security of Quraish.

2. Their security during winter and summer journeys.

3. Let them worship the Lord of this House.

4. Who has fed them against hunger, and has secured them against fear.

107. ASSISTANCE
(al-Ma'un)

*In the name of Allah,
the Gracious, the Merciful*

1. Have you considered him who denies the religion?

2. It is he who mistreats the orphan.

3. And does not encourage the feeding of the poor.

4. So woe to those who pray.

5. Those who are heedless of their prayers.

6. Those who put on the appearance.

7. And withhold the assistance.

108. PLENTY
(al-Kawthar)

*In the name of Allah,
the Gracious, the Merciful*

1. We have given you plenty.

2. So pray to your Lord and sacrifice.

3. He who hates you is the loser.

109. THE DISBELIEVERS
(al-Kafirun)

*In the name of Allah,
the Gracious, the Merciful*

1. Say, "O disbelievers.

2. I do not worship what you worship.

3. Nor do you worship what I worship.

4. Nor do I serve what you serve.

5. Nor do you serve what I serve.

6. You have your way, and I have my way."

110. VICTORY
(an-Nasr)

*In the name of Allah,
the Gracious, the Merciful*

1. When there comes Allah's victory, and conquest.

2. And you see the people entering Allah's religion in multitudes.

3. Then celebrate the praise of your Lord, and seek His forgiveness. He is the Accepter of Repentance.

111. THORNS
(al-Masad)

In the name of Allah, the Gracious, the Merciful

1. Condemned are the hands of Abee Lahab, and he is condemned.

2. His wealth did not avail him, nor did what he acquired.

3. He will burn in a Flaming Fire.

4. And his wife—the firewood carrier.

5. Around her neck is a rope of thorns.

112. MONOTHEISM
(al-Ikhlas)

In the name of Allah, the Gracious, the Merciful

1. Say, "He is Allah, the One.

2. Allah, the Absolute.

3. He begets not, nor was He begotten.

4. And there is nothing comparable to Him."

113. DAYBREAK
(al-Falaq)

In the name of Allah, the Gracious, the Merciful

1. Say, "I take refuge with the Lord of Daybreak.

2. From the evil of what He created.

3. And from the evil of the darkness as it gathers.

4. And from the evil of those who practice sorcery.

5. And from the evil of an envious when he envies."

114. MANKIND
(an-Nas)

In the name of Allah, the Gracious, the Merciful

1. Say, "I seek refuge in the Lord of mankind.

2. The King of mankind.

3. The God of mankind.

4. From the evil of the sneaky whisperer.

5. Who whispers into the hearts of people.

6. From among jinn and among people."

www.ingramcontent.com/pod-product-compliance
Lightning Source LLC
Chambersburg PA
CBHW072152070526
44585CB00015B/1110